STUDIES IN BAPTIST HISTORY AND THOUGHT
VOLUME 6

'At the Pure Fountain of Thy Word'

Andrew Fuller as an Apologist

STUDIES IN BAPTIST HISTORY AND THOUGHT

A full listing of all titles in this series
appears at the close of this book

Andrew Fuller (1754–1815)
Picture courtesy of Regent's Park College, Oxford

STUDIES IN BAPTIST HISTORY AND THOUGHT
VOLUME 6

'At the Pure Fountain of Thy Word'

Andrew Fuller as an Apologist

Edited by

Michael A.G. Haykin

Foreword by Tom Ascol

Wipf & Stock
PUBLISHERS
Eugene, Oregon

Wipf and Stock Publishers
199 W 8th Ave, Suite 3
Eugene, OR 97401

"At the Pure Fountain of Thy Word"
Andrew Fuller as an Aplogist
Edited by Haykin, Michael A. G.
Copyright©2004 Paternoster
ISBN: 1-59752-797-1
Publication date 6/22/2006
Previously published by Paternoster, 2004

This Edition Published by Wipf and Stock Publishers
by arrangement with Paternoster

Paternoster
9 Holdom Avenue
Bletchley
Milton Keyes, MK1 1QR
Great Britain

STUDIES IN BAPTIST HISTORY AND THOUGHT

Series Preface

Baptists form one of the largest Christian communities in the world, and while they hold the historic faith in common with other mainstream Christian traditions, they nevertheless have important insights which they can offer to the worldwide church. *Studies in Baptist History and Thought* will be one means towards this end. It is an international series of academic studies which includes original monographs, revised dissertations, collections of essays and conference papers, and aims to cover any aspect of Baptist history and thought. While not all the authors are themselves Baptists, they nevertheless share an interest in relating Baptist history and thought to the other branches of the Christian church and to the wider life of the world.

The series includes studies in various aspects of Baptist history from the seventeenth century down to the present day, including biographical works, and Baptist thought is understood as covering the subject-matter of theology (including interdisciplinary studies embracing biblical studies, philosophy, sociology, practical theology, liturgy and women's studies). The diverse streams of Baptist life throughout the world are all within the scope of these volumes.

The series editors and consultants believe that the academic disciplines of history and theology are of vital importance to the spiritual vitality of the churches of the Baptist faith and order. The series sets out to discuss, examine and explore the many dimensions of their tradition and so to contribute to their on-going intellectual vigour.

A brief word of explanation is due for the series identifier on the front cover. The fountains, taken from heraldry, represent the Baptist distinctive of believer's baptism and, at the same time, the source of the water of life. There are three of them because they symbolize the Trinitarian basis of Baptist life and faith. Those who are redeemed by the Lamb, the book of Revelation reminds us, will be led to 'fountains of living waters' (Rev. 7.17).

Series Editors

Anthony R. Cross, Fellow of the Centre for Baptist History and Heritage, Regent's Park College, Oxford, UK

Curtis W. Freeman, Research Professor of Theology and Director of the Baptist House of Studies, Duke University, North Carolina, USA

Stephen R. Holmes, Lecturer in Theology, University of St Andrews, Scotland, UK

Elizabeth Newman, Professor of Theology and Ethics, Baptist Theological Seminary at Richmond, Virginia, USA

Philip E. Thompson, Assistant Professor of Systematic Theology and Christian Heritage, North American Baptist Seminary, Sioux Falls, South Dakota, USA

Series Consultant Editors

David Bebbington, Professor of History, University of Stirling, Scotland, UK

Paul S. Fiddes, Professor of Systematic Theology, University of Oxford, and Principal of Regent's Park College, Oxford, UK

Stanley J. Grenz, Pioneer McDonald Professor of Theology, Carey Theological College, Vancouver, British Columbia, Canada

Stanley E. Porter, President and Professor of New Testament, McMaster Divinity College, Hamilton, Ontario, Canada

To
Keith and Ruth Edwards,
for the joy of their fellowship over many years

'Andrew Fuller was in an eminent degree, possessed of the faculty of original perception; or that power of the mind which lays hold of truth by a rapid, instinctive, and unassisted grasp; of an unborrowed genius, assisted in a very small degree by the minds that had thought and pondered, and elicited the truth of things before him... To the study and practice of religion he brought his whole soul, and at the fountain of divine truth, his capacious mind drank deeply, till this water of life became in him as a well of water springing up into eternal life.'

William Ward (1815)

Contents

Contributors xv

Foreword
Tom Ascol xvii

Preface
Michael A.G. Haykin xix

Abbreviations xxi

Chapter 1
Peter Morden
Andrew Fuller: A Biographical Sketch 1
Introduction 1
Fuller's Ecclesiastical Context 2
   High Calvinism at Soham and in the Particular Baptist
   Denomination 2
Resistance to Revival Influences 4
Numerical and Spiritual Decline in Particular Baptist Life 5
Fuller's Conversion 5
Controversy at Soham 7
Call to Ministry and Weakening Commitment to High Calvinism 8
Difficulties at Soham and the Call to Kettering 10
The Influence of Jonathan Edwards 11
Fuller's Ministry at Kettering 13
   Fuller's Preaching 13
   Further Examples of Work at Kettering 15
   The Growth of the Church at Kettering 16
   Personal Struggles 18
Wider Ministry 20
   Theological and Apologetic Writing 20
   Fuller as a Theologian and Apologist 24
   The Prayer Call of 1784 27
   Fuller and the Baptist Missionary Society 31
      FULLER'S ROLE IN THE FORMATION OF THE BAPTIST MISSIONARY
      SOCIETY 32
      FULLER AS SECRETARY OF THE BMS 33
      FULLER'S CONTRIBUTION IN PROMOTING THE WORK OF THE BMS
      AND RAISING FUNDS AT HOME 34
Fuller's Death 39

Fuller and the Revival of Particular Baptist Life 40

Chapter 2
Gerald L. Priest
Andrew Fuller, Hyper-Calvinism, and the 'Modern Question' **43**
An Evangelical Baptist Response to Hyper-Calvinism 47
The Gospel Worthy of All Acceptation 49
   Formative Influences and Basic Propositions 49
   What Constitutes Saving Faith? 53
   The Scripture Calls Faith a Duty 56
   Jonathan Edwards and Dichotomous Ability 58
   Fuller's Inability/Ability Doctrine 63
An Evaluation: Consensus and Dissensus 66
A Summary Resolution 72

Chapter 3
Curt Daniel
Andrew Fuller and Antinomianism **74**

Chapter 4
Clint Sheehan
Great and Sovereign Grace: Fuller's Defence of the Gospel against Arminianism **83**
Introduction 83
Fuller as an Opponent to Arminianism 85
Fuller's Opposition to Arminianism 91
Closing Remarks 120

Chapter 5
Michael A.G. Haykin
'The Oracles of God': Andrew Fuller's Response to Deism **122**
The Age of Reason (1794, 1795) 122
The Nature and Importance of an Intimate Knowledge of Divine Truth (1796) 125
The Gospel Its Own Witness (1799) 128
Letters on Systematic Divinity (1814) 134
Conclusion 137

Contents xiii

Chapter 6
Tom J. Nettles
**Christianity Pure and Simple: Andrew Fuller's
Contest with Socinianism** **139**
Fuller's Preparation for the Conflict 141
Motivation for the Confrontation 143
Fuller's Polemical Method..146
Fuller's Method of Argument...149
The Argument in Action...150
    The Conversion of Profligates 151
    Love of Christ..155
    Veneration for the Scriptures..159
    Examples of other Conclusions...161
Responses to Fuller...164
    Socinian Responses...164
    Friendly Responses 168
Conclusion 169

Chapter 7
Barry Howson
Andrew Fuller and Universalism..**174**
History and Theology of Universalism..176
William Vidler's Universalism..180
Fuller's Letters to Vidler against Universalism 186
    Letter I..186
    Letter II...187
    Letter III 189
    Letter IV...190
    Letter V...192
    Letter VI...194
    Letter VII 196
    Letter VIII..198
Summary of Fuller's Particularism 200
Conclusion 201

Chapter 8
Robert W. Oliver
Andrew Fuller and Abraham Booth..**203**
The Warrant of Faith...204
    The Area of Debate...206
    The Significance of the Debate...208
Controversy on the Atonement 209
    The Course of the Controversy...209

The Issues..210
    IMPUTATION 210
    SUBSTITUTION 214
    PARTICULAR REDEMPTION..................................217

Chapter 9
Michael A.G. Haykin
Andrew Fuller and the Sandemanian Controversy............223
Sandemanianism and the Nature of Saving Faith......................225
An Initial Response by Fuller..228
Strictures on Sandemanianism (1810)......................................230
Conclusion..235

Chapter 10
Peter Morden
Andrew Fuller as an Apologist for Missions.......................237
Introduction..237
Fuller as Missionary Theologian 239
Fuller as Missionary Apologist..241
'The Instances, Evil, and Tendency of Delay' 242
Arguments in Favour of World Mission....................................243
Fuller and Carey 245
Growth and Opposition...246
The Vellore Mutiny and its Aftermath......................................247
Fuller's *Apology for the Late Christian Missions to India*......249
Fuller on Toleration...251
A Missionary's Attitude to the Authorities 252
The Great Commission..254
Conclusion..255

A Select Bibliography of Primary and Secondary Sources
Greg Meadows...257

Subject Index..269

Person Index..273

Contributors

Tom Ascol has served as Pastor of Grace Baptist Church in Cape Coral, Florida, since 1986. He is also the Executive Director of Founders Ministries and Editor of the Founders Journal. He has contributed to numerous journals and books and is the author of *From the Protestant Reformation to the Southern Baptist Convention: What Hath Geneva to do with Nashville?* (1996). He has also edited *Reclaiming the Gospel and Reforming Churches: The Southern Baptist Founders Conference 1982–2002* (2002) and *Dear Timothy: Letters on Pastoral Ministry* (2004), all published by Founders Press. He and his wife Donna have six children.

Curt Daniel is a graduate of Central Bible College (BA), Fuller Theological Seminary (MDiv) and The University of Edinburgh (PhD). He has been Pastor of Faith Bible Church, Springfield, Illinois, USA, since 1995. He has published articles in several books and journals, and is presently writing on the history and theology of Calvinism.

Michael A. G. Haykin is the Principal of the Toronto Baptist Seminary and Bible College, Senior Fellow, The Jonathan Edwards Centre for Reformed Spirituality, and Adjunct Professor of Church History at The Southern Baptist Theological Seminary, Louisville, Kentucky. He is the author of several books, including *The Spirit of God: The Exegesis of 1 and 2 Corinthians in the Pneumatomachian Controversy of the Fourth Century* (Leiden: Brill, 1994), *One Heart and One Soul: John Sutcliff of Olney, His Friends, and His Times* (Darlington: Evangelical Press, 1994), and *The Armies of the Lamb: The Spirituality of Andrew Fuller* (Dundas, ON: Joshua Press, 2001). He and his wife Alison, and their two children, Victoria and Nigel, live in Dundas, Ontario. They attend Trinity Baptist Church, Burlington, Ontario, where he and his wife are members, and where he serves as an elder.

Barry Howson (PhD McGill University) is the Director of Religious Studies at Heritage College, Cambridge, Ontario, Canada. He is the author of *Erroneous and Schismatical Opinions: The Question of Orthodoxy Regarding the Theology of Hanserd Knollys (c.1599–1691)* (Leiden: Brill, 2001), and has contributed several articles to books and journals. He and his wife Sharon and their two daughters, Natalie and Shawna, live in Cambridge, Ontario.

Greg Meadows is presently working on a reflection-oriented study of Philippians 2:5-11 and another volume focusing on the will of God. He has served in pastoral and teaching capacities since his graduation from

Heritage Theological Seminary. He lives in Woodbridge, Ontario, with his wife Jessica and their daughter Kayla. Their home church is King Bible Church in King City, Ontario.

Peter Morden is the Senior Pastor of Shirley Baptist Church, near Solihull, England. He is author of *Offering Christ to the World: Andrew Fuller (1754–1815) and the Revival of Eighteenth Century Particular Baptist Life* (Studies in Baptist History and Thought, 8; Carlisle: Paternoster Press, 2003).

Tom J. Nettles currently serves as Professor of Historical Theology at The Southern Baptist Theological Seminary, Louisville, Kentucky. He has published several works on the history of Baptist theology, including *By His Grace and For His Glory* (Grand Rapids, MI: Baker, 1986) and *Baptists and the Bible* (Nashville: Broadman Holman, 1999).

Robert W. Oliver is currently pastoring a Baptist church in Bradford on Avon, England, where he has served since 1971. After research into early English Strict Baptist History under the supervision of Harold Rowdon and Barrie White, he was awarded a PhD at London Bible College by the Council for National Academic Awards in 1987. Since 1989 he has also been Lecturer in Church History at the London Theological Seminary and is also currently Adjunct Professor of Church History, Westminster Seminary, Philadelphia (John Owen Centre, London).

Gerald L. Priest is Professor of Historical and Practical Theology at Detroit Baptist Theological Seminary, Allen Park, Michigan. He has written for various Baptist publications, including the Detroit Seminary's own journal. He is currently working on a Baptist history text book. Dr Priest received his PhD from Bob Jones University and has pursued studies in Baptist and American history at Wake Forest University and the University of North Carolina at Greensboro.

Clint Sheehan is the former Pastor of Faith Fellowship Baptist Church in Ingersoll, Ontario, and is currently Assistant Professor of Physics at Ouachita Baptist University in Arkadelphia, Arkansas. He has published papers in the disciplines of Old Testament Studies and Molecular Physics. He completed a PhD in Physics at The University of Western Ontario in 2000 and plans to commence work on a PhD in Old Testament Studies in the near future.

Foreword

The Evangelical Revival that swept across Great Britain in the middle part of the eighteenth century did not immediately impact large numbers of Particular Baptists. This was due primarily to an uneasiness with the Arminianism of some of the prominent leaders in the movement. The fear of unacceptable theology caused some Particular Baptists even to look upon the Calvinistic George Whitefield as preaching in an 'Arminian dialect' and having semi-Pelagian tendencies. For many years the benefits that the Revival brought to different groups largely passed by the Particular Baptists, who, for the most part, remained in a state of decline with their tendencies toward 'High Calvinism'.

The winds of change finally began to blow across their low-burning embers in the last quarter of the century. These same Baptists who had lost much of their spiritual fervor and theological vitality became, by the end of the century, world leaders in the foreign missionary enterprise. The man whose writings, above all others, provided the theological underpinnings for this reversal was Andrew Fuller.

Much of Fuller's later usefulness can be traced to his early experiences among the Particular Baptists. From the age of six he attended the Baptist church at Soham and was under the ministry of its pastor, John Eve. According to Fuller, Eve was '*high* in his sentiments, or tinged with false Calvinism' and therefore had little concern to call the unconverted to Christ. Under the sort of preaching which these sentiments produced, Fuller was never challenged to consider his standing before God. The deadening effects of this theological emphasis contributed to his lengthy and painful struggle for conversion. Once he was converted, though, it provoked his thinking about the operation of saving grace, particularly regarding the notion of a 'warrant of faith'.

From the very outset of his Christian life Fuller's convictions were forged in the furnace of doctrinal controversy. As a newly converted teenager he became embroiled in a church fight that shaped not only his future theological writings but also his life's vocation as a gospel minister. The Soham church where he was a member erupted in debate over the question of whether or not people have the power to keep themselves from sin and to do the will of God. The controversy, which ultimately resulted in the severance of Pastor Eve's relationship with the church, left an abiding impression on Fuller's mind. At this early stage of his spiritual pilgrimage he was forced to think seriously about sin, grace, salvation and law—themes that would receive more careful attention in his later writings.

After the church at Soham called him to be their minister in 1775, Fuller began to work his way out of High Calvinism. He was helped along the path by three other Baptist pastors: John Sutcliff of Olney, John Ryland, Jr., of Northampton, and Robert Hall of Arnesby. Through their influence Fuller became acquainted with the writings of Jonathan Edwards and found in the New England theologian a helpful teacher of evangelical Calvinism.

Fuller's writings demonstrate an intense love to declare and passionate desire to defend revealed truth. Unfortunately, he died before completing a work on systematic theology. Much of what he did write was provoked by doctrinal error. Consequently, many of his most useful works have an apologetic or polemic tone. These treatises were more 'born' than written and provide a study in the pastoral duty of using sound doctrine to refute those who 'subvert whole households, teach things which they ought not' (Titus 1:9-11).

His treatments of High Calvinism, Sandemanianism, Deism, antinomianism, Socinianism, universalism and Arminianism are, in many respects, models of apologetic theology. Together with his writings on behalf of the Baptist Missionary Society they reveal the heart of one who was Valiant for Truth in his day.

All who recognize that some of the finest gifts Christ has given to his church are saints of earlier generations will appreciate the following essays. Those who are particularly interested in the people called Baptists are especially indebted to Michael Haykin and the contributors to this volume for shedding light on one of the greatest champions ever to serve that denomination.

Pastors, scholars and students alike will find in the pages following much information that is both personally informative and ecclesiastically helpful. The controversial issues that confronted Fuller confront us still. The truths for which he contended need continued defense today. May his devotion to those truths and his zeal for the Savior in contending for and making them known be kindled afresh among gospel ministers of this generation.

Thomas K. Ascol
Cape Coral, Florida, USA
March 2004

Preface

As a young man Andrew Fuller had what he called 'an athletic frame' and 'a daring spirit'. This daring and physical prowess showed itself in a number of ways, but especially, we are told, in a love of wrestling.[1] After his conversion, though, Fuller came to consider wrestling as a sinful sport. It may well have been the pugnacious spirit, so needful for wrestling, that Fuller came to regard as the sinful element in wrestling. But though he gave up wrestling, a certain degree of pugnaciousness never completely left him. In later years, this character trait was turned in a very different direction as he did battle for Christian orthodoxy and resisted vigorously what he saw as distortions of scriptural teaching. A host of errors confronted Christians in the eighteenth century, and Fuller tackled most of them, ranging from the dire heresies of Deism and Socinianism to the problems generated by Sandemanianism and Arminianism.

It is often remarked that the eighteenth-century Evangelical Revivals failed to produce, at least in the British Isles, a first-class theologian. Well, this is not exactly true, for Fuller was such a theologian. And his apologetic works form an important part of his rich theological corpus. Although deeply influenced by the New England divine Jonathan Edwards, who died when Fuller was four, Fuller called no man master. In a covenant that he made with his Lord in 1780, we learn how it was that he determined before God

> to take up no principle at second-hand; but to search for every thing at the pure fountain of thy word... One thing in particular I would pray for; namely that I may not only be kept from erroneous principles, but may so love the truth as never to keep it back.[2]

When he made this covenant, Fuller surely had little inkling of where it would lead him. This volume seeks both to lay out and to understand, but also to celebrate, the way that Fuller was indeed led as he sought for Christian truth 'at the pure fountain of thy [i.e. God's] word'.

This book has been a long time in the making, and I wish to thank all of the authors for both their respective chapters and their patience. A big thank-you is also due Anthony R. Cross, Fellow of the Centre for Baptist History and Heritage, Regent's Park College, Oxford, for his many kindnesses along the way in producing this volume. His unfailing

---

[1] Andrew Gunton Fuller, 'Memoir', in *The Complete Works of the Rev. Andrew Fuller* (ed. and revised Joseph Belcher; 3 vols; Harrisonburg, VA: Sprinkle Publications, 1988 [3rd edn, 1845]), I, pp. 4, and 105-106, n. *].

[2] Fuller, 'Memoir', I, p. 20.

encouragement and editorial skills, his help in tracking down references and production of the indices have all been deeply appreciated. I am also extremely grateful to the staff of Paternoster Press for publishing this volume in their series in Baptist history and thought.

I have dedicated this book to two close friends, Keith and Ruth Edwards. Like Fuller, I have been blessed with a circle of good friends, and I count Keith and Ruth among the dearest of them and their fellowship in the gospel a sweet joy.

Michael A. G. Haykin
Peasedown St John, Bath,
12 May 2004

Abbreviations

BMS	The Baptist Missionary Society
BQ	*The Baptist Quarterly*
CMS	The Church Missionary Society
DNB	*The Dictionary of National Biography*
LMS	The London Missionary Society

CHAPTER 1

Andrew Fuller: A Biographical Sketch

Peter Morden

Introduction

Andrew Fuller (1754–1815) was one of the foremost English Baptist ministers of his day. His ministry, which began in 1775 and lasted until his death, coincided with what Michael Haykin has termed the 'profound revitalization' of the Particular Baptist denomination, the denomination of which Fuller was a part.[1] Perhaps best known for his theological treatise *The Gospel Worthy of All Acceptation* and for being the founding secretary of the Baptist Missionary Society, he in fact published a wide range of theological and apologetic works, as well as spending the whole of his ministerial career as a local church pastor. By any standards he was a significant figure, one whose life and work have continuing relevance today.

Andrew Fuller was born on 6 February 1754 at Wicken, a village near Ely in Cambridgeshire, the youngest son of Robert Fuller (d.1781) and Philippa Gunton (d.1816).[2] Robert was a tenant farmer, working a

---

1   M.A.G. Haykin, 'A Habitation of God, Through The Spirit: John Sutcliff (1752–1814) and the Revitalization of the Calvinistic Baptists in the Late Eighteenth Century', *BQ* 34.7, (July, 1992), p. 306.

2   See J. Ryland, Jr., *The Work of Faith, the Labour of Love, and the Patience of Hope Illustrated in the Life and Death of the Rev. Andrew Fuller* (London: Button and Son, 2nd edn, 1818), pp. 8-10, for this and other biographical details in this paragraph. Ryland's official 'tombstone' biography (the first edition appeared in 1816), is the most important source for Fuller's life. All references are from the 2nd edn unless otherwise stated. Also significant is John W. Morris, *Memoirs of the Life and Writings of the Rev. Andrew Fuller* (High Wycombe, 1816), with an important 2nd edn (London: Wightman and Cramp, 1826), both of which are cited in this chapter. Fuller's son, Andrew Gunton Fuller, adds a number of personal family reminiscences to supplement these two in his *Men Worth Remembering: Andrew Fuller* (London: Hodder and Stoughton, 1882), a much more detailed work than the brief memoir attached to Fuller's collected works. More

succession of small dairy farms, and in 1761 he moved his family a distance of two and a half miles to a new situation in the village of Soham. Both parents were Dissenters and Baptists, although Robert appears to have been less committed than his wife. Philippa became a member of the Particular, or Calvinistic, Baptist church at Soham, and the whole family attended regularly. Her own mother, also called Philippa, had actually been one of the founding members of the church. In 1775 her son Andrew, despite having little by way of formal education, would become its pastor.

Fuller's Ecclesiastical Context

High Calvinism at Soham and in the Particular Baptist Denomination

The Baptist meeting at Soham was small, isolated and struggling. The minister, John Eve, was committed to High or 'hyper' Calvinism, the prevailing theology among most Particular Baptists for much of the eighteenth century.[3] Fundamental to High Calvinism was the belief that the unconverted had no duty to repent and believe the gospel. That total depravity rendered them incapable of doing so without the regenerating influence of the Holy Spirit was not in dispute amongst eighteenth-century Calvinists. But High Calvinism effectively held that unbelievers had no *moral* obligation to believe, since they could not justly be held accountable for not doing what they were unable to do. The logical outworking of this position was that what were termed 'indiscriminate exhortations to faith and repentance' could not be addressed to the unconverted. To do so would be a nonsense, because it could not be the 'duty' of the unregenerate to do 'anything spiritually good'. Fuller himself summed up the practical effects of High Calvinism: nothing was

---

recently there is Gilbert Laws, *Andrew Fuller: Pastor, Theologian, Ropeholder* (London: Carey Press, 1942), but this adds little to the earlier biographies.

3   I have referred to 'High' rather than 'hyper' Calvinism in this chapter, but Fuller used both terms interchangeably, also referring to 'false' and 'pseudo' Calvinism. The major work charting the development of High Calvinism is probably still P. Toon, *The Emergence of Hyper-Calvinism in English Nonconformity, 1689-1765* (London: Olive Tree, 1967). Toon states, pp. 144-45, that 'Hyper' Calvinists 'placed excessive emphasis on the immanent acts of God—eternal justification, eternal adoption and the eternal covenant of grace. In practice this meant that "Christ and him crucified", the central message of the apostles, was obscured.' In addition, High Calvinists often made no distinction between the secret and revealed will of God. Also on High Calvinism, see Peter Naylor, *Calvinism, Communion and the Baptists: A Study of English Calvinistic Baptists from the Late 1600s to the Early 1800s* (Studies in Baptist History and Thought, 7; Carlisle: Paternoster Press, 2003), pp. 164-82.

to be said to 'sinners...inviting them to apply to Christ for salvation'.[4] Eve, who was pastor at Soham from 1752 to 1771, typified this trend. As Fuller was later to write, 'Mr Eve...had little or nothing to say to the unconverted. I, therefore, never considered myself as any way concerned in what I heard from the pulpit.'[5] The first systematic exposition of High Calvinism had been published in 1707 by Joseph Hussey, appropriately entitled *God's Operations of Grace, but no Offers of Grace*. But in mid-eighteenth century Particular Baptist circles it was strongly associated with the views of two London pastors, John Brine (1703–65) and John Gill (1697–1771).[6]

A number of questions regarding High Calvinism and Particular Baptist life cannot be followed up here. One of these is the extent to which Gill, whose influence through his voluminous writings was huge, was truly a 'High Calvinist'.[7] But one point is worth emphasizing. This is the extent to which High Calvinism had spread amongst the denomination. Roger Hayden has stressed that, throughout the first half of the eighteenth century, a warmer, more expansive brand of Calvinism was kept alive by successive tutors at the Bristol Baptist Academy. He also highlights what he terms the 'inspirational fellowship' provided by the Western Association of Baptist churches, also based around Bristol, during this period. High Calvinism, he argues, did not dominate Particular Baptist life in the way that has often been suggested.[8]

Undoubtedly some Baptist historians have been prone to overstatement when describing the so called 'dark ages' of the mid-eighteenth century,[9] and Hayden does a thorough job in correcting this strain of Baptist historiography. But I believe he overestimates the influence of Bristol, and underestimates that of the London ministers, which in some parts of

---

4　　Ryland, *Andrew Fuller*, pp. 31-32.
5　　Ryland, *Andrew Fuller*, p. 11.
6　　For Hussey see Toon, *Hyper Calvinism*, p. 70. For Gill, see O.C. Robison, 'The Legacy of John Gill', *BQ* 24.3 (July, 1971), pp. 111-25.
7　　For a negative, but balanced assessment of Gill, see Robison, 'The Legacy of John Gill', esp. p. 120; for a much more positive view see T.J. Nettles, *By His Grace and for His Glory: A Historical, Theological, and Practical Study of the Doctrines of Grace in Baptist Life* (Grand Rapids: Baker Book House, 1986), pp. 73-107. The matter is well discussed by M.A.G. Haykin, *One Heart and Soul: John Sutcliff of Olney, His Friends and His Times* (Durham: Evangelical Press, 1994), pp. 17-19.
8　　R. Hayden, 'Evangelical Calvinism among Eighteenth Century Particular Baptists with Particular Reference to Bernard Foskett, Hugh and Caleb Evans and the Bristol Baptist Academy 1690-1791' (PhD thesis, Keele University, 1991). See, e.g., pp. 305-306, 360.
9　　E.g., W.T. Whitley, *History of the English Baptists* (London: Charles Griffin, 1923), p. 258: 'in the dark ages of the eighteenth century there were not ten learned men by whose reputation the [Baptist] denomination might be redeemed'.

the country was all pervasive.[10] The Particular Baptist denomination was experiencing numerical and spiritual decline, in the West as elsewhere, with High Calvinism undoubtedly a contributing cause. To be sure there were other factors which had also led to this decline, for example, the legal and social discrimination which Dissenters still faced, even after the 1669 Act of Toleration, and the geographical isolation of many of the churches.[11] But High Calvinism helped foster a very insular concept of the church, which went hand in hand with a stubborn resistance to forces associated with the Evangelical Revival, which was then sweeping Britain.

Resistance to Revival Influences

The two key figures in the Revival were John Wesley (1703–91) and George Whitefield (1714–70). Wesley was clearly beyond the pale for Particular Baptists because of his aggressive Arminianism, together with the caustic comments he made, together with his brother Charles, about the 'people called anabaptists'. But the Calvinistic Whitefield was regarded with grave suspicion too. This was partly because many Particular Baptists, certainly those tinged with High Calvinism, doubted his adherence to the 'doctrines of grace', and spoke dismissively of his 'Arminian dialect'. But it was also because High Calvinists were deeply concerned with questions of church order, questions in which Whitefield had almost no interest. Many Particular Baptists proudly described themselves as 'a garden enclosed', quoting from one of their favourite texts, Song of Solomon 4.12.[12] All the main Revival leaders (Howell Harris in addition to the Wesleys and Whitefield), were from the Church of England which was regarded as an apostate church. Some Calvinistic Baptists were more open to Whitefield, but they were few and far between.[13] As long as High Calvinism held sway, most Particular Baptists would remain 'a garden enclosed', shut off from any Revival influences. Some Calvinistic Baptist churches actually excommunicated members for associating with Methodists. There is no evidence that this happened at Soham—but then there is no evidence that forces linked with the Revival ever touched the church during Eve's pastorate.

---

10   For example, Norfolk and Suffolk, Northamptonshire and Cambridgeshire. For London's influence in much of the North of England, see J. Fawcett, Jr., *An Account of the Life, Ministry and Writings of the late Rev. John Fawcett, DD* (London: Baldwin, Craddock and Joy, 1818), pp. 97-102.

11   For these and other factors contributing to decline, see Haykin, *One Heart and Soul*, pp. 15-33.

12   Haykin, *One Heart and Soul*, pp. 26-28

13   See R.W. Oliver, 'George Whitefield and the English Baptists', *Grace Magazine* 5 (October, 1970), pp. 10-11.

Numerical and Spiritual Decline in Particular Baptist Life

That numerical decline was taking place is certain.[14] Between 1715 and 1718 there were approximately 220 Calvinistic Baptist churches in England and Wales. But by 1750 this figure had dropped to 150.[15] To speak of a parallel spiritual decline is, of course, based on more subjective evidence. But there is little doubt that this was happening. Even in the Western Association the annual newsletters regularly bemoaned the low spiritual temperature of their churches. Isaac Hann, who was responsible for the letter of 1761, appeared close to despair as he wrote: 'We are almost at a loss to know what we can say further for the stirring up of sleepy professors.' Those who read Hann's words were exhorted to take heed 'lest they sleep the sleep of death'. He went on to plead with his readers: 'Look over the letters which of late you have had from us...hearken to the counsel and advice of those who would not cease to warn every one with tears.'[16] It is hard to disagree with Fuller's own trenchant assessment: 'Had matters gone on but a few years longer', he wrote, 'Baptists would have become a perfect dunghill in society.'[17] Later Fuller was to decisively reject High Calvinism, and his public disputes with those who continued to defend it are the subject of chapter 2. Suffice to say here that the church in which Fuller grew up was one where High Calvinism was the prevailing theology, a church with an insular ecclesiology which was not engaged in evangelistic work. In this Soham was fairly typical of the denomination as a whole.

Fuller's Conversion

Fuller was converted in 1769, following a long period of intense struggle. This was not because of any change in the church at Soham, or in Eve's preaching. Indeed, there is no evidence that his pastor was of any help to Fuller as he wrestled with guilt and crippling doubts as to whether he was one of the 'elect'. It was not that Eve, and ministers like him, did not believe in conversion, but those who were among the elect would eventually be brought to realize their position by an inner persuasion of the Holy Spirit, classically described in High Calvinist teaching as a

---

14   See also, P.J. Morden, *Offering Christ to the World: Andrew Fuller (1754–1815) and the Revival of Eighteenth Century Particular Baptist Life* (Studies in Baptist History and Thought, 8; Carlisle: Paternoster Press, 2003), pp. 7-10.

15   For these figures, see Haykin, *One Heart and Soul*, p. 25.

16   J.G. Fuller, *A Brief History of the Western Association* (Bristol, 1843), pp. 44-45. Cf. R. Brown, *English Baptists of the Eighteenth Century* (A History of the English Baptists, 2; London: Baptist Historical Society, 1986), pp. 77-78.

17   Cited by Morris, *Andrew Fuller*, 1st edn, p. 267.

'warrant' to believe. In 1766 Fuller began, by his own account, to see himself as a 'poor sinner'.[18] But he believed that he was not 'qualified' to come to Christ, not possessing the subjective 'warrant of faith' convincing him that he was one of the elect. In the years following 1766 he came under increasing conviction, but simply did not know what to do. In popular High Calvinist teaching, the 'warrant' often took the form of a particular text of Scripture suggesting itself forcibly on a person's mind. Fuller thought he had experienced this in 1767, when the text 'Sin shall not have dominion over you, for ye are not under the law, but under grace' (Romans 6.14) came strongly to him. But despite this and further 'impressions', he found that the 'bias of his heart' was not changed.

Fuller was eventually encouraged by the Old Testament examples of Esther, who went in to see the King without being invited, and Job, who threw himself on God's mercy with the words, 'Though he slay me, yet will I trust him' (Job 13.15). Through these rather unlikely texts, Fuller found release from the agonies of conviction. Gunton Fuller describes his father's conversion experience:

> He...came to this resolve, 'I must, I will—yes, I will—trust my soul, my sinful, lost soul, in his hands; if I perish, I perish.' As he looked away from self, and fixed his eyes upon a crucified Saviour, his guilt and fears began to dissolve...and he found how true were the words of Christ, 'Come unto me all ye that labour and are heavy laden, and I will give thee rest.'[19]

By his own reckoning, Fuller had been struggling with 'guilt' and 'fears' for at least three years previous to this. It was not until the autumn of 1769, when he was sixteen years old, that 'his troubled soul' finally found this 'rest'. Eve at least accepted Fuller as a genuine convert, and he was baptized in April 1770, joining the church at Soham. Fuller's conversion experience, as he and his biographers related it, was in the classic Evangelical pattern of 'agony, guilt and intense relief'.[20] It resulted in serious theological reflection on what he described as the 'erroneous views of the gospel', which had kept him in 'darkness and despondency for so long'. He was clear, for example, that he would have come to faith sooner, if he had not 'entertained the notion of...having no warrant to come to Christ without some previous qualification'.[21] The delay had been intensely painful and, as he now saw it, quite unnecessary.

---

18   Unless otherwise stated the details and quotations describing Fuller's conversion, in this and the following two paragraphs, are taken from Ryland, *Andrew Fuller*, pp. 12-20.
19   Gunton Fuller, *Men Worth Remembering*, p. 28.
20   D.W. Bebbington, *Evangelicalism in Modern Britain: A History from the 1730s to the 1980s* (London: Unwin Hyman, 1989), p. 5.
21   Ryland, *Andrew Fuller*, p. 30; Gunton Fuller, *Men Worth Remembering*, p. 28.

Fuller was full of joy at his new found faith, but that joy was to be short lived.

Controversy at Soham

Gunton Fuller, commenting on the 'straitness' and 'sluggishness' of the Soham church, nevertheless noted one 'redeeming feature'. There was, he believed, a good family spirit of 'brotherly affection' amongst the small membership.[22] But in 1771 even this was lost as the small church was split by a dispute which caused Fuller great pain, and which he was later to refer to as the 'wormwood and gall of my youth'. By his own admission it was to have a formative influence on his thought.[23]

The conflict began in 1770, when Fuller himself discovered that a member at Soham had been guilty of excessive drinking. Fuller saw the man and challenged him on 'the evils of his conduct'. The man answered in a way that suggests that the 'antinomianism' or lawlessness, that often went hand in hand with High Calvinism, was present at Soham. To Fuller's consternation, the man explained that he could not help his drinking, and that he did not have the power to keep himself from sin. Fuller considered this a 'base excuse', and told him that 'he *could* keep himself from sins such as these, and that his way of talking was merely to excuse what was inexcusable'. The man's behaviour was promptly reported to the church, and the result was that Eve commended Fuller, with the man being excluded from membership. In the course of this dispute, however, Eve appears to have made a comment to the effect that, although people had no power in and of themselves to do anything spiritually good, they had the power to obey the will of God 'as to outward acts'. This seemingly innocuous statement was to open up a more general debate, and eventually lead to Eve's resignation.

Leading members of the church, including Joseph Diver (d.1780), an older man who Fuller was close to, challenged Eve concerning his assertion about believers' ability to do God's will. Fuller, who had also taken this view, was readily excused as a 'babe in religion', but their pastor 'should have known better'. Believers did not have the power to keep themselves from evil, but should constantly pray for 'keeping grace'. Scriptures that Eve was referred to included Psalm 19.13 ('Keep back thy servant also from presumptuous sins; let them not have dominion over me: then shall I be upright, and I shall be innocent from the great transgression') and Jeremiah 10.23 ('the way of man is not in

---

22 Gunton Fuller, *Men Worth Remembering*, pp. 32-33.
23 For the details contained in the next two paragraphs, see Ryland, *Andrew Fuller*, pp. 23-28.

himself: it is not in man that walketh to direct his steps'). Fuller initially agreed with his pastor, but as the dispute continued, found it increasingly difficult to see how Eve's opponents could be answered. With obvious pain and great reluctance he switched sides. The dispute was never properly resolved, and Eve was eventually forced to resign from Soham in 1771, leaving for a church in Wisbech. Eve's High Calvinism had not been consistent enough for the majority of his church members.[24]

The dispute is clearly revealing of the type of theology, attitudes and concerns prevalent at Soham, but it also left Fuller with a major problem. To what extent, and in what sense, was it someone's 'duty' to do the will of God? Fuller was increasingly dissatisfied with High Calvinism, but was unable to articulate clearly what was wrong, or say how the problems could be resolved.

Call to Ministry and Weakening Commitment to High Calvinism

Following Eve's resignation, Joseph Diver, who had been elected a deacon of the church, preached most Sundays at Soham.[25] But, with Diver's encouragement, Fuller began to take occasional services himself. Fuller was unhappy with his first attempts at preaching, but by early 1774 the church was becoming increasingly convinced that God was calling him to be their pastor. After a trial period of just over a year, he was finally ordained and inducted on 3 May 1775, Robert Hall, Sr. (1728-91), the minister from Arnesby Baptist Church, taking a lead part in the service. Fuller was just twenty-two years of age.

1775 was a significant year for two additional reasons. Firstly, on 8 June the Soham church applied to join the Northamptonshire Association of Particular Baptist churches.[26] The new Association had been formed in 1764 and was, according to John Briggs, the 'archetype of the new Associations, born out of the Evangelical Revival'.[27] This brought Fuller into contact with John Sutcliff (1752-1814), who had recently settled at the Baptist church at Olney, and with his future biographer, John Ryland, Jr. (1753-1825), who was then at Northampton. Fuller wrote that in them

---

24 Cf. the comment of M.R. Watts, *The Dissenters*. Volume 1: *From the Reformation to the French Revolution* (Oxford: Clarendon Press, 1978), pp. 459-60.

25 See Ryland, *Andrew Fuller*, pp. 29-31, for the details in this paragraph.

26 Morris, *Andrew Fuller*, 1st edn, p. 31. Soham was, of course, in Cambridgeshire, but the Northamptonshire Association accepted churches from neighbouring counties. Hall's church at Arnsby was in Leicestershire. For the Northamptonshire Association, see T.S.H. Elwyn, *The Northamptonshire Baptist Association* (London: Kingsgate Press, 1964).

27 J.H.Y. Briggs, *The English Baptists of the Nineteenth Century* (A History of English Baptists, 3; Didcot: Baptist Historical Society, 1994), p. 203.

he found 'familiar and faithful brethren', who 'partly by reflection, and partly by reading the writings of Edwards, Bellamy, Brainerd, &c' had rejected High Calvinism as a system.[28] The significance of this move would prove to be great, as we shall see.

Secondly, on a visit to London later that year, Fuller read a pamphlet that he was to refer to as crucial to the development of his thought.[29] The tract was entitled *The Modern Question*, and it was written by Abraham Taylor, a Congregational Minister. 'The Modern Question' which concerned Taylor was 'whether the unconverted have a duty to believe the gospel', and he was quite clear that they did.[30] This was clearly relevant to Fuller's concerns, and he read Taylor's tract carefully. The Congregationalist's style—Philip Doddridge had accused him of 'bigotry'[31]—was unlikely to endear itself to Fuller. Indeed, by his own account he was 'but little impressed with [Taylor's] reasonings'. That was until he came to a passage where Taylor cited a series of biblical texts, specifically some of those where John the Baptist, the apostles and Christ himself directly addressed the unconverted. Taylor was able to show, in a way that Fuller was unable to answer, that New Testament figures repeatedly challenged the 'ungodly' to spiritual repentance and faith. The impact this had on Fuller was clearly great. In the following months he read and reflected theologically on the relevant Scripture passages. 'The more I read and thought', he said, 'the more I doubted the justice of my former views.' Fuller could not forget these texts, nor help feeling that they exposed his preaching as 'anti-scriptural and defective in many respects'.[32]

In 1776 Fuller married Sarah Gardiner from Burwell, Cambridgeshire, who was a member of the church at Soham, and settled into the work of pastoral ministry. Fuller's commitment to High Calvinism was clearly beginning to weaken but this did not immediately affect his preaching, as his continuing uncertainty concerning 'indiscriminate offers of the gospel', together with his innate caution and a certain degree of apprehension, all combined to hold him back. In his own words: 'I...durst not, for some years, address an invitation to the unconverted to come to Jesus.'[33] But by the late 1770s his position was changing and

---

28   Ryland, *Andrew Fuller*, p. 35. Fuller first met Sutcliff on 28 May 1776 at an Association meeting at Olney; see Morris, *Andrew Fuller*, 2nd edn, p. 33.

29   Ryland, *Andrew Fuller*, pp. 34, 37.

30   G.F. Nuttall, 'Northamptonshire and *The Modern Question*: A Turning Point in Eighteenth-Century Dissent', *Journal of Theological Studies* 16.1 (January, 1965), p. 102, who covers the development of the dispute in some detail, pp. 101-23.

31   Nuttall, 'Northants and *The Modern Question*', p. 115.

32   Ryland, *Andrew Fuller*, pp. 34, 37.

33   Ryland, *Andrew Fuller*, p. 32. Fuller's comment is made regarding where he stood at the end of 1774.

Fuller introduced a new evangelistic note of direct appeal into his public ministry. The result, unsurprisingly, was consternation and dissatisfaction at Soham, although the exact extent of the opposition is unclear.[34] Ryland, working with free access to all Fuller's private papers, was able to date the beginning of this opposition precisely to December 1779.[35] Fuller was now publicly moving away from High Calvinism.

Difficulties at Soham and the Call to Kettering

Fuller's difficulties at Soham continued, although by the early 1780s he was beginning to see moderate success, with some conversions and an increased number coming to Sunday worship. But opposition to him was hardening too, and Fuller found himself increasingly unhappy, not just, it has to be said, because of his evangelical preaching. One of the central problems was that the church was poor and struggled to support their pastor. Fuller's stipend of £13 a year, despite an extra £5 from the Particular Baptist Fund in London, was woefully inadequate. Attempts to supplement this, first by a small shop and then a school, failed. Fuller, now with a growing family, found he was simply unable to manage. Even the success of his preaching was a source of frustration, as the meeting house was not large enough to accommodate those who wanted to come, and the people were unwilling to look for a more suitable place of worship, even when their landlord raised the rent.[36] Fuller's unhappiness regularly surfaced in his diary, and against this background some, who through the Northamptonshire Association had become his friends, began to suggest that he should seek a move to a new church.

The protracted negotiations which surrounded Fuller's eventual acceptance of the call to the pastorate of the 'Little Meeting' at Kettering in 1782, a call that had originally come over a year earlier, occupy considerable space in all the early biographies.[37] Fuller was clearly torn between loyalty and love for his church and the prospect of a pastorate which would be more supportive, both for his ministry and his family. But whatever struggles he was going through, he would not compromise his newly found evangelistic principles. Indeed, these were principles to which he was becoming increasingly committed. Fuller had by now

---

34   Morris, *Andrew Fuller*, 2nd edn, p. 34, was more negative than Ryland, *Andrew Fuller*, p. 44, who only spoke of 'the unkindness of a few'.

35   Ryland, *Andrew Fuller*, p. 44.

36   A. Gunton Fuller, *Memoir of the Rev. Andrew Fuller*, in *The Complete Works of the Rev Andrew Fuller, With a memoir of his Life by the Rev. Andrew Gunton Fuller* (ed. A.G. Fuller; rev. edn J. Belcher; 3 vols; Harrisonburg, VA: Sprinkle Publications, 1988), I, pp. 18-19. All subsequent references to Fuller's *Works* are from this edition.

37   See, e.g., Gunton Fuller, *Memoir*, pp. 19, 24-34.

moved decisively away from High Calvinism, embracing an evangelical Calvinism which still affirmed God's sovereignty, while also emphasizing human responsibility. His new found evangelical theology would find full expression in his most effective theological work, *The Gospel Worthy of all Acceptation*, originally published in 1785. A detailed analysis of all the reasons behind his 'theological conversion', together with a summary of the work itself and his continuing battles with High Calvinism, are contained in chapter 2 of this book. Some of the reasons for Fuller's change will already have been hinted at, but it is important to note here that the most significant extra biblical influence on Fuller was certainly Jonathan Edwards (1703–58). Particularly important was Edwards' *A Careful and Strict Enquiry into the Modern Prevailing Notions of the Freedom of Will*, which was originally published in 1754.[38]

The Influence of Jonathan Edwards

That Fuller read 'Edwards on the will' had been suggested to him as far back as 1775, by Robert Hall, Sr., at his ordination. Fuller initially obtained the wrong book, *Veritus Redux* by an 'Episcopalian Calvinist', Dr John Edwards, and it was not until 1777 that he discovered his mistake and rectified it.[39] The most relevant section of the *Freedom of the Will* is headed 'Of the distinction of Natural and Moral Necessity and Inability'.[40] As the title of this suggests, Edwards drew a clear distinction between what he termed 'natural' and 'moral' inability. The fact that no one was able to respond to the gospel without the electing grace of God was fundamental to Edwards. But crucially, this helplessness was *not* because of a lack of 'natural' powers. Rather, a person's 'inability' to respond was wholly of the 'moral' or 'criminal' kind. Put simply, a person could not come because they would not come. Anyone who did not respond was therefore criminally culpable. All had the natural powers to respond, but they refused to do so.

The importance of Edwards to Fuller will be made clear at many points in this book, but perhaps no more so than here. Fuller's theology and practice had been decisively refashioned with help from the man who stood at the 'headwaters of the Evangelical Revival'.[41] Fuller had been opened up to evangelical influences, which had previously been absent from Soham, particularly through his friends in the Northamptonshire Association. He now fully embraced an Edwardsean evangelical

---

38   For the text see J. Edwards, *Freedom of the Will*, in *The Works of Jonathan Edwards* (ed. P. Ramsey; New Haven: Yale University Press, 1957), I, pp. 135-440.

39   Ryland, *Andrew Fuller*, p. 36.

40   Edwards, *Freedom of the Will*, pp. 156-62.

41   Bebbington, *Evangelicalism in Modern Britain*, p. 5.

Calvinism, a theology which was to undergird the whole of his future life and ministry. By the time of his actual induction at Kettering, on 7 October 1783, the personal statement of faith he offered to the church contained an article that was both a statement of his theology and a declaration of intent for his future work. It is worth quoting in full:

> I believe it is the duty of every minister of Christ plainly and faithfully to preach the gospel to all who will hear it; and, as I believe the inability of men to spiritual things to be wholly of the moral, and therefore of the criminal kind,—and that it is their duty to love the Lord Jesus Christ, and trust in him for salvation, though they do not; I therefore believe free and solemn addresses, invitations, calls, and warnings to them, to be not only consistent, but directly adapted as means, in the hand of the Spirit of God, to bring them to Christ. I consider it as part of my duty that I could not omit without being guilty of the blood of souls.[42]

This part of Fuller's personal confession indicates that a sea change had taken place in both his theology and his practice. With its distinction between natural and moral inability and its warm practical tone, his statement reads like a summary of the main arguments of *The Gospel Worthy*, still two years away from publication, although by now basically ready in manuscript form. Fuller had moved far from his inherited High Calvinism.

Fuller would remain as pastor at Kettering until his death, although as we have already noted, Fuller's ministry developed both national and international dimensions. He became the denomination's foremost theologian and apologist, and he was involved in the 1784 'Call to Prayer' which paved the way for the formation of the Baptist Missionary Society, working tirelessly on behalf of the fledgling society. Indeed Fuller was an important figure in all the developments which historians have usually focused on when describing the revitalization of Particular Baptist life which took place in the latter half of the eighteenth century. There is no doubt he was a hugely significant figure, and all this presents anyone seeking to sketch Fuller's life with a problem. After some thought I have decided not to deal with the rest of his life and work in strict chronological sequence, but focus instead on some of the different areas of ministry in turn, beginning with his work as a local church pastor. This aspect of his work is actually a key to understanding Fuller, particularly the practical thrust of all he did, and it is here that the outline of Fuller's post 1783 ministry begins.

---

42 Ryland, *Andrew Fuller*, p. 68.

Fuller's Ministry at Kettering

Fuller's Preaching

According to his son, Fuller gave himself, with 'constitutional ardour' to the work at Kettering.[43] Examples of his regular Sunday preaching from the early period of his ministry at the church do not survive, or only as shorthand notes. In fact many of Fuller's sermons in his *Works* are recorded only in note form, and these notes are often brief. But a sermon preached in 1784, entitled 'The Nature and Importance of Walking by Faith', was later published. Although this was not preached at Kettering, but at a meeting of the Northamptonshire Association at Nottingham,[44] because it survives in a more complete form, it is likely to give a better impression of Fuller's general style and approach. His text was 2 Corinthians 5.7, 'We walk by faith, not by sight', and he dealt with his subject carefully and systematically yet with passion. Two short passages will serve to give a flavour of Fuller in the pulpit. As he began to deal, in the second section of his message, with the importance of 'walking by faith', he spoke passionately of God's glory:

> O brethren, let the *glory of God* lie near our hearts! Let it be dearer to us than our dearest delights! Herein consists the criterion of true love to him. Let us, after the noble example of Joshua and Caleb, "follow the Lord fully." Let us approve of everything that tends to glorify him. Let us be reconciled to his conduct, who "suffers us to hunger, that we may know that man lives not by bread alone but by every word that proceedeth out of the mouth of God." If he should bring us to hard and difficult situations...let us remember that it is that he may give us an opportunity of glorifying him, by trusting him in the dark. The more difficult the trial, the more glory to him that bears us through, and the greater opportunity is afforded us for proving that we can indeed trust him with *all* our concerns—that we can trust him even when we cannot see the end of his present dispensations.

Fuller concluded his message with a stirring appeal:

> Christians, ministers, brethren, all of us! let us realise the subject. Let us pray, and preach, and hear, and do everything we do with eternity in view! Let us deal much more with Christ and with invisible realities. Let us, whenever called, freely deny ourselves for his sake, and trust him to make up the loss. Let us not faint under present difficulties, but consider them as opportunities afforded to us to glorify God. Let us be ashamed that we derive our happiness so much from things below, and so little from things above. In one word, let us fight the good fight of faith, and lay hold on eternal life!

---

43   Gunton Fuller, *Memoir*, p. 34. On his pastoral ministry at Kettering, see Morden, *Offering Christ to the World*, pp. 103-27.
44   *Works*, I, pp. 117-134 (originally published, Northampton: T. Dicey, 1784). The following quotations are on pp. 132-34.

Some of Fuller's evident power in the pulpit survived the transfer of his sermon to the printed page. His deep concern for God's glory is self evident, as is his desire that both he and his hearers give themselves in service to God. Ryland commented on Fuller as a preacher, saying that he 'loved men' and had 'an evident unction from the Holy One'. Although there were some who excelled him for 'fluency' and popular appeal (Ryland was thinking particularly of Samuel Pearce [1766–99], the minister at Cannon Street in Birmingham), Fuller was an effective, extempore preacher.[45] Some critical remarks concerning Fuller's preaching do appear in the other biographies. Hayden summarizes some of these comments. Fuller lacked 'easy elocution', and his voice although 'strong' could also be 'heavy'.[46] In addition, he seems to have spent little time in preparation for some of his weekly local church preaching, and Gunton Fuller could comment that 'it was not often that Mr Fuller's preparations for the pulpit were elaborate'.[47] Time would increasingly be at a premium for Fuller as his ministry grew. Nevertheless he could certainly rise to the occasion for something like the Nottingham meeting, and he was clearly a popular speaker. Certainly, there is little difficulty in believing his son's comment: 'Sleepy hearers were not often found in Mr Fuller's congregation.'[48]

Fuller engaged in a range of pastoral work and covered a variety of topics in his preaching at Kettering. At one stage Fuller kept a book, *Families that attend at the Meeting*, where details of members, their names, families and 'particular cases' were noted. Fuller added that a 'review of these may help me in my preaching'. Significantly this book dates from the period before he began work as secretary of the BMS, after which his time would be squeezed.[49] His sermons included expository preaching which was specifically designed to build up more mature believers, in addition to textual preaching that might be described as more 'inspirational' and more suited to occasional 'hearers'. Ryland listed the biblical books he systematically covered from the time when he began his habit of regular expository preaching on a Sunday morning in April 1790.[50] His *Expository Discourses on the Book of Genesis* stand as an example of this type of preaching, as do his *Expository Discourses on*

---

45   Ryland, *Andrew Fuller*, p. 144.
46   R. Hayden, 'The Life and Influence of Andrew Fuller', in R.L. Greenall (ed.), *The Kettering Connection: Northamptonshire Baptists and Overseas Missions* (Leicester: Department of Adult Education, University of Leicester, 1993), p. 5; cf. Morris, *Andrew Fuller*, 2nd edn, pp. 81-82.
47   Gunton Fuller, *Men Worth Remembering*, p. 61.
48   Gunton Fuller, *Men Worth Remembering*, p. 80.
49   August 1788. Ryland, *Andrew Fuller*, p. 381.
50   Ryland, *Andrew Fuller*, p. 382.

the Apocalypse.[51] Particularly when expounding Revelation, Fuller took more time in preparation than was his normal practice.[52] By this stage he had been decisively influenced by Edwards' post-millennial eschatology, although he always rejected some of the more speculative aspects of Edwards' thinking. Nevertheless he was ready to believe that great success would 'attend the preaching of the gospel' even before the millennium dawned.[53] This would be a time 'full of wars and struggles', and yet also of great victories.[54] An appreciation of Fuller's post-millennialism is important to understanding several aspects of his ministry. What is clear is that Fuller delighted in, and looked forward to, the spread of the gospel.

Further Examples of Work at Kettering

One further aspect of Fuller's ministry at Kettering worth highlighting is the work he did with young people. Every year, from at least the early 1790s, he would preach a new year's sermon particularly aimed at children and 'youth'. On these occasions, according to Ryland, Fuller would 'pour forth all his heart...exhorting and charging every one, as a Father doth his children.'[55] One of these sermons, entitled 'Advantages of Early Piety', gives an example of what was said on those occasions.[56]

Fuller took as his text Psalm 90.14: 'O satisfy us early with thy mercy, that we may rejoice and be glad all our days', which he preceded to interpret as a prayer on behalf of the youth of Israel. He continued: 'I hope I need not say that this prayer...is expressive of the desires of your minister and your parents; you know it is so. Oh that it might express your own!' He concluded by pleading with his hearers to come to Christ:

> What shall I say more? Will you, my dear young people, will you drink and be satisfied at the fountain of mercy; a fountain that is wide open and flows freely through our Lord Jesus Christ? You cannot plead the want of sufficient inducements. Ministers, parents, Christians, angels, the faltering voice at death, the solemn assurance of a judgement to come, and, above all, the sounding of the bowels of Jesus Christ, all say, Come.

---

51   *Works*, III, pp. 1-198; pp. 201-306 (originally published in 1806 and 1815 respectively).
52   Gunton Fuller, *Men Worth Remembering*, p. 61. Cf. *Works*, III, pp. 201-202.
53   A. Fuller, *Discourses on the Apocalypse* (London, 1815), in *Works*, III, e.g., pp. 293-94.
54   Fuller to John Saffery, 14 October 1811, Angus Library, Regent's Park College, Oxford (II/273).
55   Ryland, *Andrew Fuller*, p. 383.
56   *Works*, I, pp. 421-26, esp. 425-26. The sermon is undated.

Ryland recorded that 'many young people' who later believed 'traced their first serious impressions' to these occasions.[57] Fuller wrote to Ryland in March 1810 that he had begun a weekly meeting in his vestry at Kettering for 'earnest' young people, and there were now four waiting for baptism. At one stage he appears to have been meeting with them on both Monday and Friday nights, times that, he said, were 'much thronged'.[58] Fuller appeared to have a particular concern for younger people, something that was also shown in his letters to his own children.[59]

Fuller's evangelistic impulses also drove him to reach out to those who were beyond the immediate orbit of the church. Gunton Fuller recorded that, some time in the 1800s (a period when Fuller had very little time for pastoral work amongst his members), his father was devising a scheme to evangelize among young lacemakers who worked in Kettering. This involved getting hold of some of the white wrapping paper the girls used and printing some 'little hymns' on them, some of which he planned to compose himself. In a letter to a friend quoted by Gunton Fuller, his father enthused about the plan: 'Every child who comes for a small quantity of thread will find it wrapped up in a paper containing a short impressive hymn addressed to its heart.'[60] Not the most plausible of Fuller's schemes, it is unlikely this was ever implemented. But the Kettering pastor's evangelistic concerns are clear.

The Growth of the Church at Kettering

During his pastorate at Kettering, the 'Little Meeting' grew slowly but steadily. When Fuller arrived there were eighty-eight members, and when he died in 1815 this had increased to 174.[61] Certainly this was not spectacular, but we especially need to note the large number of hearers—those who attended who were not in membership—who often swelled the congregation to 1,000 strong.[62] A number of these who came regularly walked in from surrounding villages.[63] The meeting house had to be enlarged twice to accommodate those who were now coming—steps the Kettering church were more willing to take than their counterparts at Soham had been.[64] Moreover, throughout the period of Fuller's ministry,

---

57 Ryland, *Andrew Fuller*, p. 383.
58 Ryland, *Andrew Fuller*, pp. 251-52.
59 Gunton Fuller, *Men Worth Remembering*, pp. 70-73; Ryland, *Andrew Fuller*, pp. 297-307.
60 Gunton Fuller, *Men Worth Remembering*, p. 88.
61 Ryland, *Andrew Fuller*, p. 374.
62 Ryland, *Andrew Fuller*, p. 246.
63 Ryland, *Andrew Fuller*, p. 383.
64 In 1786 and 1805. Ryland, *Andrew Fuller*, p. 374.

Kettering remained a small and relatively poor market town with a population of no more than 3,300.[65] In addition the Congregational church was strong, with Ryland describing the minister, Thomas Toller, as 'justifiably popular'. The town also boasted a congregation of Wesleyan Methodists, and towards the end of Fuller's time, evangelical preaching in the Church of England.[66] Toller, reflecting back on this period in his farewell sermon, commented that in the early years of the nineteenth century, Kettering was known as 'the Holy Land' because almost everyone seemed to attend some place of worship.[67] The evidence strongly suggests that in this comparatively small and declining market town, with significant competition from other churches, Fuller was an effective pastor.

Nevertheless there were problems. The failure to translate the large number of hearers to a more significant increase in the membership was not uncommon in the context of the time, but the likelihood is that Fuller had less time for personal 'follow up' or in-depth pastoral work than most ministers. This was certainly true from 1792 onwards when he was away for up to three months of the year, travelling round the country on behalf of the BMS. Ryland noted that Fuller admitted that these journeys were 'some impediment to his Pastoral duties'. Morris was stronger when he said 'that in discharging the duties of the Pastoral Office, Mr Fuller was not (entirely) successful... His numerous and, perhaps still more important engagements did not afford him sufficient opportunity.'[68] Fuller admitted as much himself. In October 1794 he wrote to Ryland lamenting the extent to which his role with the BMS was 'interfering' with his work at Kettering. 'I long to visit my congregation', he said, 'that I may know of their spiritual concerns and preach to their cases'.[69] There is little doubt that, as Brian Stanley notes, his work for the BMS was both to the 'detriment' and 'regret' of the church, although they were

---

65 R.L. Greenall, 'After Fuller: Baptists in 19th Century Kettering', in Greenall (ed.), *The Kettering Connection*, pp. 33-46. By the time of Fuller's death in 1815, Kettering was actually in severe economic decline. The collapse of the eighteenth century staple trades of wool combing and worsted weaving had badly effected the town (see especially p. 33). Fuller described Kettering as 'a place of but little wealth and of only 3000 inhabitants', Fuller to James Deakin, 25 October 1812, in E.A. Payne (ed.), 'Letters to James Deakin' *BQ* 7.8 (October, 1935), p. 368.

66 Ryland, *Andrew Fuller*, p. 383.

67 Greenall, 'Baptists in Kettering', p. 35. A religious census of 1828 could discover only 40 'of no sect'.

68 Ryland, *Andrew Fuller*, p. 155; Morris, *Andrew Fuller*, 1st edn, p. 74.

69 Ryland, *Andrew Fuller*, p. 155. Cf. comments of Ryland's own, *Andrew Fuller*, p. 381.

generally supportive of the mission work.[70] It was only from 1811 that Fuller had an assistant at Kettering, the Rev. John Keen Hall, the nephew of his old friend Robert Hall, Sr.[71] Suffice to say that given the pressures he was under, it is remarkable that Fuller saw the growth in his congregation that he did, and was as loved a pastor as he seemed to be.

Personal Struggles

Despite the growth Fuller saw in his church, and despite the opening up of wider opportunities for ministry, the years 1783–92 were difficult for Fuller personally. Fuller's diary entries show that he had struggled with assurance of salvation for much of this time. For example, on 12 September 1780, while still at Soham, he wrote:

> Very much in doubt respecting my being in a state of grace... The Lord have mercy on me, for I know not how it is with me. One thing I know, that if I be a Christian at all, real Christianity in me is inexpressibly small in degree. O what a vast distance is there between what I ought to be, and what I am! If I am a saint at all, I know I am one of the least of all saints. I mean, that the workings of real grace in my soul are so feeble, that I hardly think they can be feebler in any true Christian... I think of late, I cannot in prayer consider myself as a Christian, but as a sinner casting myself at Christ's feet for mercy.[72]

In 1786 this spilled over into full blown spiritual depression. His final surviving diary entry for 1786 was made on Sunday 11 June. Fuller had recently heard Robert Hall, Sr., preach, taking as his text Proverbs 30.2: 'Surely I am more brutish than any man.' Fuller was convinced these words were far more applicable to him than to his friend and mentor, so he proceeded to preach on them himself that Sunday. The next diary entry that Ryland could discover was dated 3 October 1789, over three years later. Ryland recorded that between sixteen to eighteen leaves had been torn out (presumably by Fuller himself), but in his 3 October entry the Kettering pastor also confessed to having written nothing for 'about a year and a half', for, he said, 'it seemed to me that my life was not worth writing.' Fuller described it as a time of 'lukewarmness', 'backsliding' and much 'hardness of heart'. Looking back on this period in 1796, in a letter to the missionary John Thomas in India, he wrote of 'a deep dejection' that had gripped him, which although he 'strove to throw it off

---

70   B. Stanley, *The History of the Baptist Missionary Society, 1792–1992* (Edinburgh: T&T Clark, 1992), p. 20.
71   Laws, *Andrew Fuller*, p. 8.
72   Ryland, *Andrew Fuller*, p. 78. Cf. p. 119: 'I have a fountain of poison in my nature...and am far from a spiritual frame of mind.'

in company' returned as soon as he was in private.⁷³ For a period of over three years, Fuller was, by his own reckoning, struggling as a Christian and struggling with depression.

Fuller's diary does not necessarily give a totally rounded picture of his spiritual life. Bruce Hindmarsh, in his study of John Newton, comments that because his subject's diary was used as a means of 'disciplined self examination' in the Puritan tradition, its confessional and sometimes 'self recriminatory' tone are not necessarily reflective of his spirituality as a whole. In other words, taken on its own, the diary is likely to be a distortion of Newton's spiritual life, a distortion created by the medium itself.⁷⁴ The same is likely to be true for Fuller, and Hindmarsh's words of caution need to born in mind, particularly as Fuller's diary is the primary source for understanding his spiritual state. Probably his state of mind was often brighter than the extract quoted, and many others like them, would lead us to believe. Nevertheless there is every reason to think that his struggle for assurance and lack of joy were very real, exacerbated by Fuller's High Calvinist background, with its tendency to introspection. The recommencement of his diary at the end of 1789 did not signal any great change, although reading Jonathan Edwards' sermons seemed to bring some relief. Nevertheless it was not until after 1792 that his mood changed decisively.

Throughout his married life, Fuller experienced a series of personal tragedies. Doubtless these contributed to his depressed spiritual state, although Fuller himself tended to treat the two as separate issues. Eight of the eleven children from his marriage to Sarah Gardiner died in infancy or in early childhood. Fuller particularly grieved for a six year old daughter who died in 1786, immediately before the onset of his severest depression. 'I lay before the Lord', he said, 'weeping like David and refusing to be comforted.'⁷⁵ Sarah herself was to die in distressing circumstances in 1792. For about three months before her death Sarah, heavily pregnant, was 'seized with hysterical afflictions' which 'deprived her of her senses'.⁷⁶ Despite occasional periods where she was calmer, she often failed to recognize her husband, and sometimes had to be restrained by force when violent attacks came on. 'I...was overcome with grief', recorded Fuller, 'I wept with her.' She died on 23 August, the same day as she had given birth to her eleventh child, Bathoni, who only

---

    73   See Ryland, *Andrew Fuller*, p. 119, and p. 159 for Fuller's letter to J. Thomas, 16 May 1796.

    74   B. Hindmarsh, *John Newton and the English Evangelical Tradition: Between the Conversions of Wesley and Wilberforce* (Oxford: Clarendon Press, 1995), p. 222.

    75   Gunton Fuller, *Memoir*, p. 51.

    76   These and other details relating to Sarah's illness and death are taken from a letter written by Fuller to his wife's father, 25 August 1792, cited by Gunton Fuller, *Memoir*, pp. 59-60.

survived a few weeks. Such was life for lower middle class families at the end of the eighteenth century.

After 1792, Fuller found some happiness in his personal life. In December 1794 he was married again, to Ann Coles, a minister's daughter from Maulden, Bedfordshire.[77] Fuller's comment in his diary, that 'this day will probably stamp my future life with increasing happiness or misery', does not sound particularly optimistic. But the marriage was a happy one, although three of the six children Ann bore also died in infancy. But his eldest son from his previous marriage, Robert, caused his father great grief. Robert Fuller rejected the Christian faith and left home to join the navy. After a spell on merchant ships, he was press ganged into naval service once again in 1801. Later he was flogged for desertion in Ireland, and eventually died, at sea in 1809, being buried somewhere off the coast of Spain. Fuller's letters to his son convey some of the pain and anguish he felt. The Sunday following Robert's death, Fuller wept in the pulpit, and some of those in his congregation who knew what had happened wept with him. An article in *The East Midland Baptist Magazine* for 1895, written by a Rev. D. McPherson, gives an account of a talk the writer had with an old lady in Kettering, a Mrs Toon, who was eight years old at the time of Fuller's death. Mrs Toon remembered 'Fuller's greatest grief'. It was, she said, that 'a prodigal son had gone abroad and sorrowful tidings came back respecting him. The father was distracted and filled with shame.'[78] All of this means that Fuller accomplished much of his most significant work in the midst of spiritual struggles and personal tragedy.

Wider Ministry

Theological and Apologetic Writing

Fuller clearly loved his family and gave himself, as well as he was able, to his work at Kettering. But it was for his wider ministry that he was known by the Christian world at large, of which his published works form a highly significant part.[79] These included a biography of his friend Samuel Pearce, who died in 1799,[80] in addition to various volumes of sermons, some of which were published posthumously. But of far greater

---

77   For this and details relating to Robert, see Gunton Fuller, *Memoir*, pp. 66, 69-73.

78   Cited by A.H. Kirkby, 'The Theology of Andrew Fuller and its Relation to Calvinism' (PhD thesis, Edinburgh University, 1956), p. 24.

79   Cf. Morden, *Offering Christ to the World*, pp. 23-76. On Fuller's theology in his published works, see also Naylor, *Calvinism, Communion and the Baptists*, pp. 205-19.

80   *Memoirs of the Rev Samuel Pearce MA*, in Fuller, *Works*, III, pp. 367-446.

significance were the theological and apologetic works which appeared during his own lifetime. The chapters in this book set out to give detailed consideration to this important and sadly neglected body of work. Details of the respective controversies, Fuller's protagonists, and the arguments Fuller deployed will all be given in the respective chapters. In this section I will give outline details of the various disputes only. Page references from the edition of Fuller's *Works* published by Sprinkle show where his contributions to the different debates can now be found, but I have omitted full publishing details of the original works, which, once again, can be found in the relevant chapters. The aim of this overview of Fuller's theological and apologetic work is to locate the contours of the individual disputes on the larger map of his life and ministry, as well as making some general points about his overall approach and method.

Fuller's first published work was *The Importance and Nature of Walking by Faith*, which was quoted from earlier as an example of Fuller's preaching style. This will be referred to again in relation to the so called 'Prayer Call' of 1784.[81] *Walking by Faith* went on to have far reaching implications, but even this would be eclipsed by *The Gospel Worthy of All Acceptation* which Fuller finally, after much hesitation, had delivered to the press for publication in 1785. The main thrust of Fuller's argument was accurately conveyed by the subtitle of the second edition, published in 1801 (II, pp. 328-416). It was, Fuller contended, 'the duty of men to believe in Jesus Christ'. This work, a clear and direct challenge to High Calvinism, was important in Particular Baptist life partly because it helped crystallize the thinking of others who had already moved in the same direction as Fuller. But it also influenced many others as yet uncertain. In the words of E. F. Clipsham, 'it provided a theology such as thinking men were seeking'.[82]

Not everyone accepted Fuller's arguments, indeed, as a result of publishing *The Gospel Worthy*, Fuller would become engaged in a series of controversies, both with High Calvinists and Arminians. Fuller had to contend with High Calvinist opposition from both inside and outside his denomination. He responded in print to two High Calvinist opponents,

---

81   For all the publishing details contained in this and the following paragraphs in this section, see Ryland, *Andrew Fuller*, pp. 132-43. I have generally only given the short titles of works mentioned.

82   E.F. Clipsham, 'Andrew Fuller's Doctrine of Salvation' (BD thesis, University of Oxford, 1961), p. 281. See also E.F. Clipsham, 'Andrew Fuller and Fullerism: A Study in Evangelical Calvinism,' *BQ* 20.3-6 (July–October, 1963 and January–April, 1964); '1: The Development of a Doctrine', '2: Fuller and John Calvin', '3: The Gospel Worthy of All Acceptation', '4: Fuller as a Theologian', pp. 99-114, 146-54, 214-25, 268-76. Clipsham's comment is cited by R.W. Oliver, 'The Emergence of a Strict and Particular Baptist Community Among the English Calvinistic Baptists, 1770–1850' (PhD thesis, CNAA [London Bible College], 1986), p. 85.

William Button (1754–1821) and John Martin (1741–1820). Both were Particular Baptists and both, significantly, were London pastors. Fuller published two works in response to these arguments, the first focusing on Button's work, in 1787 (II, pp. 417-511). The details of these disputes are covered in chapter 2. Fuller effectively restated his position, seeking to respond to specific points made by his two opponents. But in addition to High Calvinist opposition, there were also those in the wider Christian world who thought that Fuller had not gone far enough in modifying his theology. In 1786 Dan Taylor (1738–1816), leader of the Arminian New Connexion of General Baptists, published his own 'Observations' on *The Gospel Worthy*, under the pseudonym Philanthropos. These were friendly towards Fuller, but strongly defended the Arminian position. Fuller's reply was coupled with the one to Button. But this particular controversy was to continue. Taylor dropped his use of 'Philanthropos' for his two further pamphlets, published under his own name in 1787 and 1790 respectively. Fuller did the reverse, adopting a *nom de plume* of his own, 'Agnostos', in replying to Taylor's second tract in 1788 (II, pp. 512-60). By the time this dispute began Taylor was an established and respected figure in the wider evangelical world, a respect that was certainly shared by Fuller himself. This dispute is dealt with in chapter 4.

Controversies that related, directly or indirectly, to *The Gospel Worthy* would dog Fuller for the rest of his life. But despite these continuing disputes, there is good evidence that the majority of Particular Baptists accepted what came to be dubbed 'Fullerism'. Certainly *The Gospel Worthy* was the most influential text in weaning Particular Baptists away from High Calvinism. Ryland cited the example of an older minister, Joshua Thomas, who initially opposed *The Gospel Worthy*, but 'came over to Mr Fuller's views at last'.[83] He would have been one of many. Of course there were others who had held and propounded the same views as Fuller before 1785, not least Ryland himself. But nevertheless, it was the Kettering pastor who had provided evangelical Calvinism with its most developed statement in an English Baptist context, and who was most closely associated with the theology typified by the resurgent Northamptonshire Association. Kirkby quotes a letter written in 1797 to the Evangelical Baptist pastor Joseph Kinghorn, from deacons in a church in Hull. The Hull church wanted Kinghorn to help them to find a minister and specified the sort of man they were looking for. Among other things they specified that he was to be a 'lively, zealous and affectionate preacher' and 'orthodox'. The letter has a marginal note explaining the meaning of 'orthodox'. It says: 'of Mr Fuller's

---

83   Ryland, *Andrew Fuller*, p. 131.

sentiments'.[84] Fuller's achievement in writing and effectively defending *The Gospel Worthy* was considerable.

Fuller also published two apologetic works opposing Socinianism, a term Fuller used in preference to Unitarianism. The first of these was *The Calvinistic and Socinian Systems Examined and Compared, as to Their Moral Tendency* and it appeared in 1792 (II, pp. 108-242). Fuller followed this up in 1797 with *Socinianism Indefensible on the Ground of its Moral Tendency*, replying to a number of articles that had appeared in response to his original work (II, pp. 243-91). This time, although Unitarians were clearly stung by these arguments, there were few criticisms of these works from anyone who really mattered to Fuller. Indeed, he wrote that his *Calvinistic and Socinian Systems Compared* had, in fact, 'procured an unusual tide of respect and applause'. Yet Fuller saw this as potentially as great a test for him as being attacked, and was 'apprehensive' in case God saw his heart 'too elated'. Yet his reputation as an apologist was clearly enhanced by this work, which was quickly reprinted. The disputes with Socinians are dealt with in chapter 6. *The Gospel its Own Witness* was published in 1800 (II, pp. 1-107). In it Fuller challenged Deism, one of the supreme examples of eighteenth-century rationalism. Fuller's work dealt in particular with Thomas Paine (1737–1809), whose book *The Rights of Man* first appeared in 1791, two years after the ferment caused by the French Revolution. Once again, Fuller's work was warmly received by the wider evangelical world. *The Gospel its Own Witness* is dealt with in chapter 5.

Further works followed. As already noted, the second edition of *The Gospel Worthy* was published in 1801. This was thoroughly revised and contained some important changes, although Fuller's central argument remained the same. It is this second edition which appears in Fuller's *Works*. One addition to the original work was an appendix where Fuller dealt with 'Sandemanianism' (II, pp. 393-496). Fuller was contending with Archibald McLean (1733–1812), a Scottish Baptist who had, amongst other things, a very intellectualized view of faith.[85] Fuller corresponded with McLean and the two remained on reasonably good terms, which is more than could be said for some of those he disputed with. Their generally good relationship is hinted at in the title of Fuller's follow up work, *Strictures on Sandemanianism, in Twelve Letters to a*

---

84   Kirkby, 'Andrew Fuller', p. 11. Kirkby is citing from a letter dated 23 March 1797, from deacons at George Street Baptist church in Hull, to Kinghorn, who was pastor of St Mary's Baptist Church, Norwich. The original is held in the archives at St Mary's. Cf. Watts, *The Dissenters*, I, who states that 'Fullerism became the new orthodoxy of the [Particular Baptist] denomination', p. 460.

85   Cf. B.R. Talbot, *The Search for a Common Identity: The Origins of the Baptist Union of Scotland 1800–1870* (Studies in Baptist History and Thought, 9; Carlisle: Paternoster Press, 2003), p. 268.

Friend, which was published in 1810 (II, pp. 561-646). The disputes with McLean are examined in chapter 9. Fuller's *Letters to Mr Vidler, on the Doctrine of Universal Salvation* was published in 1802 (II, pp. 292-327), following an earlier engagement with Vidler's views in *The Evangelical Magazine*, where Fuller wrote anonymously using the pen name of 'Gaius'. Fuller also wrote on antinomianism, the subject that had caused such controversy at Soham many years previously, particularly in his *Antinomianism Contrasted with the Religion Taught and Exemplified in the Holy Scriptures* (II, pp. 737-62). These works are considered in chapters 7 and 3.

One final dispute needs to be recognized, one that caused him particular pain. This was a controversy involving Abraham Booth (1734–1806),[86] a highly respected London Particular Baptist pastor and not a High Calvinist, at least not in the accepted sense of the term. Fuller and Booth had begun to disagree over regeneration as early as 1796. But their principal controversy, which centred on the atonement, began after the publication of the second edition of *The Gospel Worthy*. Booth was particularly unhappy with what he saw as the influence of some American theologians of the so called New Divinity School on Fuller. These included Joseph Bellamy (1719–90), Samuel Hopkins (1721–1803) and Jonathan Edwards, Jr. (1745–1801), who were disciples of Jonathan Edwards (Edwards, Jr, was in fact his son), but who also adopted, to varying degrees, a more 'governmental' view of the atonement. These issues will be dealt with in chapter 8. Much of the dispute with Booth was carried on in private, although it appears that many Particular Baptists became increasingly aware that the two men did not agree (for Fuller's relevant published works, see II, pp. 680-715).

Fuller as a Theologian and Apologist

A few general comments on Fuller's work are worth making here. Firstly, taking Fuller's theological and apologetic writing as a whole, it becomes clear that he engaged with all the major deviations from orthodox belief current in the late eighteenth and early nineteenth centuries, and that he did so with what his contemporaries recognized was considerable effectiveness. His achievement was, by any standards, a remarkable one and it is easy to forget Fuller's modest background and lack of formal education. Fuller's writings show him to be a theologian and an apologist of real stature.

Secondly, the use Fuller continually makes of Jonathan Edwards should be noted. By the 1790s Fuller had read most of Edwards' major

---

86   See Morden, *Offering Christ to the World*, pp. 77-102.

works and many of his sermons, and what he learned he employed in his own writing. Fuller used quotation sparingly, but there are specific references to Edwards in all the main works cited in this section, and there is little doubt the New England theologian profoundly influenced him.[87] As is clear from his dispute with Booth, he also highly respected a number of Edwards' disciples in the New Divinity Movement. By the late 1790s he was corresponding with some of them, particularly Hopkins, although he was always careful to read their works critically. But it is his debt to Edwards that was central. On 28 April 1815, as he lay dying, Fuller dictated a letter to Ryland which included the following:

> We have heard some, who have been giving out of late that 'if Sutcliff and some others had preached more of Christ and less of Jonathan Edwards, they would have been more useful.' If those who talk thus, preached Christ half as much as Jonathan Edwards did, and were half as useful as he was, their usefulness would be double what it is.[88]

The vital importance of Edwards for Fuller should be clear.

But one further comment as to theological method needs to be made. Fuller always sought to test everything by the Scriptures and so have a theology that was thoroughly biblical. His resolve, to search the Scriptures before accepting that something was true, was commented on by a number of his biographers.[89] But this commitment also appears in Fuller's private papers, particularly in a solemn and private 'Covenant' with God discovered by Ryland after his subject's death. The 'Covenant' was clearly not intended for publication, or indeed to be seen by anyone but the author. Ryland dated it as probably written in January 1780, occasioned by Fuller's having read a piece 'written at the time of the controversy between the Calvinistic and Arminian Methodists'.[90] Having read tracts written by both sides, with texts thrown back and forth in support of diametrically opposing views, Fuller was acutely aware of how difficult a thoroughgoing biblicism is in practice. He knew that there were many who professed 'to be searching after truth [and] to have Christ and the inspired writers on their side'. He was afraid, he wrote, 'seeing I am as liable to err as other men'. And yet he was determined to go back to the Bible, which he regarded as the very 'oracles of God'. At the heart of his 'Covenant' is the following passage:

---

87 See *Works*, II, pp. 74, 123, 330, for just three examples.
88 Ryland, *Andrew Fuller*, pp. 353-56.
89 For example, Ryland, *Andrew Fuller*, p. 43.
90 See H.D. Rack, *Reasonable Enthusiast: John Wesley and the Rise of Methodism* (London: Epworth Press, 1989), pp. 198-202, for some of the details of this dispute.

> Let not the sleight of wicked men, who lie in wait to deceive, nor even the pious character of good men (who yet may be under great mistakes), draw me aside. Nor do thou suffer my own *fancy* to guide me. Lord, thou hast given me a determination to take up no principle at second hand; but to search for everything at the pure fountain of *thy word*.[91]

This is especially valuable for being heartfelt and private, and also because of the humility before God that it revealed. Certainly Fuller's reading of Scripture was influenced by his background and his times. But, as the text of *The Gospel Worthy* shows in particular, Fuller was ready to submit his theological system to a rigorous biblical critique and revise it accordingly, at great personal cost. The rest of his writing, closely reasoned and returning repeatedly to the Scriptures, contains clear evidence that his desire as a young man 'to search for everything at the pure fountain of [God's] word' never left him. Fuller's theology cannot be understood if this is forgotten.

Fuller's power and importance as a theologian was recognized by his own denomination, and by the end of the eighteenth century Fuller was acknowledged, at least by evangelical Calvinists, as their premier theologian. Ryland, a significant thinker in his own right, considered Fuller 'the most judicious and able theological writer that ever belonged to the Baptist denomination'.[92] Joseph Ivimey, writing soon after Fuller's death, believed that the Kettering pastor enjoyed a high and, in many ways, an 'unrivalled station' as the denomination's theologian.[93]

But Fuller was also recognized by those who were not Particular Baptists, and on both sides of the Atlantic. Perhaps especially noteworthy were the honorary doctorates he was urged to accept from two prestigious New England Colleges. Fuller declined them both. Writing to Samuel Hopkins in 1798, he expressed his gratitude at the honour he had heard the New Jersey College had conferred on him earlier that year. It was, he said, 'such a token of respect'. He continued: 'I esteem it as coming from that quarter which, beyond any other in the world, I most approve.' But he did not, he believed, have the 'qualifications which are expected to accompany such titles' and in addition thought all such 'titles in religion' to be contrary to Jesus' words in Matthew 23.8: 'Do not be called Rabbi...for you are all brothers.'[94]

---

91   A. Fuller, 'Sermons...in shorthand, with occasional meditations in longhand [Books 1–5 bound in 1 vol.]', Bristol Baptist College library (G95A). Book 3, pp. 2-3, contains the original of the Covenant. See also Ryland, *Andrew Fuller*, p. 129.

92   Cited by Clipsham, 'The Development of a Doctrine', p. 99.

93   J. Ivimey, *A History of the English Baptists* (4 vols; London: Isaac Taylor Hinton/Holdsworth and Ball, 1811–30), IV, p. 532.

94   Fuller to S. Hopkins, 17 March 1798, Fuller Letters, Angus Library (4/5/1).

If Timothy Dwight (1752–1817), the President at Yale, had heard of Fuller's views about titles, it did not stop him writing to the Kettering pastor in 1805 informing him that 'The corporation of Yale College at the last public commencement conveyed on you the degree of Doctor of Divinity'. The President stated that, 'As this act is the result of the knowledge of your personal character and your published works only, and as such degrees are not inconsiderately given by this body, I flatter myself that it will be regarded by you in the light of a sincere testimony of respect to you.' The letter and testimony were handed to him personally by a Mr Silliman, Professor of Chemistry at Yale, who was in England, presumably on College business. Once again Fuller was courteous in declining the honour, and yet the esteem in which he was held is clear.[95] Fuller had made a significant impact in North America. Other aspects of his wider ministry were to have far reaching, global implications.

The Prayer Call of 1784

The so called 'Call to Prayer' was issued in 1784 by the Northamptonshire Association, following meetings at Nottingham on 2 and 3 June. It directly resulted in the establishment of monthly prayer meetings in many churches specifically to pray for revival throughout the known world, and it was crucial in paving the way for the formation of the BMS.[96] Fuller's involvement in the 'Call' represents an important aspect of his wider ministry. John Sutcliff was the key figure in issuing the call to prayer to the Northamptonshire Association,[97] but Fuller had an important role too, and the following account seeks to bring this out.

In considering the background to the prayer call, Jonathan Edwards is once again a central figure. In April 1784 John Ryland received, from a regular correspondent, John Erskine of Edinburgh, a parcel of books which included a treatise written by Edwards. This was entitled *A Humble Attempt to Promote Explicit Agreement and Visible Union of God's People in Extraordinary Prayer.*[98] Edwards' *Humble Attempt* was rooted in the movement to establish regular prayer meetings for revival, a movement which had begun in the 1740s and which criss-crossed the

---

95   Gunton Fuller, *Memoir*, pp. 84-85.
96   Stanley, *History of the BMS*, pp. 4-6.
97   E.A. Payne, *The Prayer Call of 1784* (London: Kingsgate Press, 1941), *passim*; Haykin, *One Heart and Soul*, pp. 153-71.
98   Originally published in Boston, 1748. For the text see, *The Works of Jonathan Edwards* (London, 1834, reprint 2 vols; Edinburgh: Banner of Truth, 1974), II, pp. 280-312. T. George, *The Life and Mission of William Carey* (Leicester: Inter-Varsity Press, 1991), p. 50, wrongly infers that the pamphlet was sent to Sutcliff.

Atlantic.⁹⁹ The 'Concert of Prayer' actually began in Scotland, where a number of ministers who were part of the growing transatlantic evangelical network with Edwards had committed themselves and their churches to pray for revival.¹⁰⁰ Edwards sought to set up something similar in New England, and a sermon he preached on the subject in 1747 was later revised, expanded and published as the *Humble Attempt*. Ryland was deeply impressed with what he read, and lost no time sending the work to Sutcliff and Fuller.¹⁰¹

In his treatise Edwards urged that regular prayer meetings be established, specifically so that 'fervent and constant' prayer to God could be made for the 'effusions of the blessed Spirit' which would lead to the rapid growth of God's kingdom.¹⁰² His appeal was based solidly on Scripture, but he also referred in detail to the times in which he and his readers were living. Edwards viewed his age both as 'one of great apostasy' and as a 'day of the wonderful works of God'. Examples of 'spiritual calamities' included the persecution of the Huguenots in France, and what he saw as a general 'deluge of vice and immorality'. Examples of God's works of 'power and mercy' included the British defeat of French forces in North America, and especially the spiritual revivals which had recently occurred in both Europe and the New World. Edwards believed that these 'late remarkable religious awakenings... [should] justly encourage us in prayer for the promised glorious and universal outpourings of the Spirit of God'. The balance between divine sovereignty (God sending his Spirit), and human responsibility (the need to appropriate God's blessing through prayer), was typical of Edwards. By 1784 it had become increasingly typical of Fuller too.

A phrase like 'the promised glorious and universal outpourings of the Spirit of God' hints at Edwards' postmillennial eschatology, and his accompanying belief in the imminence of 'the latter day glory'. This was allied with some speculative interpretations of biblical prophecy. He

---

99   For details see M.J. Crawford, *Seasons of Grace, Colonial New England's Revival Tradition in its British Context* (Oxford: Oxford University Press, 1991), pp. 229-31.

100   See Susan O'Brien, 'Eighteenth Century Publishing in Transatlantic Evangelicalism', in M.A. Noll, D.W. Bebbington and G.A. Rawlyk (eds), *Evangelicalism: Comparative Studies in Popular Protestantism in North America, the British Isles and Beyond, 1700–1990* (Oxford: Oxford University Press, 1994), pp. 41, 45, for the transatlantic Evangelical network.

101   Ryland, *Andrew Fuller*, p. 98 n. *The Memoir of Edwards* by Sereno Dwight, written in 1830, contains a letter from Edwards to Erskine where he promises to send him a copy of the *Humble Attempt*. See *Edwards' Works* (Banner of Truth edn), I, p. xcv.

102   *Edwards' Works* (Banner of Truth edn), II, p. 312. All the following quotations from the *Humble Attempt* are from pp. 280-312. Cf. Haykin's summary, *One Heart and Soul*, pp. 159-62.

projected that the purity of the Protestant church would be restored between 1750 and 1800, Roman Catholics would embrace the gospel between 1800 and 1850, and that Christ's millennial reign could possibly begin round about the year 2000.[103] The Northamptonshire men wanted to distance themselves from these aspects of Edwards' thinking. Later, when Sutcliff brought out an English edition of the *Humble Attempt* in 1789, he took the opportunity to make this explicit. 'As to the author's ingenious observations on the prophecies', he stated, 'we entirely leave them to the reader's judgement.'[104] Nevertheless Fuller, Ryland and Sutcliff broadly shared Edwards' postmillennialism and his belief that God was about to do something hugely significant.[105] Fuller himself would later express his views in his expository series on Revelation. The belief that the sovereign God was about to work in an unprecedented way proved a great motivation to prayer and action.[106]

Whatever minor reservations they may have had, the Association's key men were clearly struck by the central appeal of the *Humble Attempt*, and were determined to respond to what they had read. The breakthrough came at the annual meetings of the Association at Nottingham already mentioned. Fuller preached the message already referred to earlier in this chapter on the opening day, 2 June, which was later published as *The Nature and Importance of Walking by Faith*.[107] The message was wide ranging, but contained two elements that are particularly worth noting. The first was a strong challenge to those present to be concerned for 'the interest of Christ' in the whole world. The prophecies of the Bible teach the church to look forward to a time 'when the earth shall be full of the knowledge of the Lord, as the waters cover the sea'. The situation in the world was currently very different from this. But there was no place for despair. 'God forbid!' declared Fuller, 'The vision is yet for an appointed time... Let us take encouragement, in the present day of small things, by looking forward.' The similarities between Fuller's preaching and the general argument in the *Humble Attempt* are striking.[108]

---

103 For a detailed discussion of Edwards' millennial views, see J.A. De Jong, *As The Waters Cover the Sea, Millennial Expectations in the Rise of Anglo–American Missions, 1640–1810* (Kampen: J.H. Kok NV, 1970), pp. 124-37.

104 Sutcliff's Preface to the English edition of the *Humble Attempt* is printed in *Edwards' Works* (Banner of Truth edn), II, pp. 278-79.

105 See further, Morris, *Andrew Fuller*, 1st edn, pp. 249-61.

106 For the connection between post-millennialism and the late eighteenth century missionary movement, see De Jong, *As the Waters Cover the Sea, passim*, and I.H. Murray, *The Puritan Hope, Revival and The Interpretation of Prophecy* (Edinburgh: Banner of Truth, 1971), pp. 131-55, who deals with the BMS in some detail.

107 *Works*, I, pp. 131 and 134.

108 Cf. Haykin, *One Heart and Soul*, p. 163. Clearly the *Humble Attempt* made a big impression on Fuller.

The second element of Fuller's address to highlight is his call to 'earnest and united prayer'. He appealed to his hearers:

> Let us pray much for an outpouring of God's Spirit upon our ministers and churches, and not upon those only of our own connexion and denomination, but upon all that in every place call upon the name of Jesus Christ our Lord, both theirs and ours!

Fuller's world vision was once again clearly evident, as was a growing evangelical 'catholicity'. Fuller was echoing Edwards' 'Call to Prayer' and applying it strongly to his own context. Fuller concluded his message with his passionate appeal, already quoted, that all Christians 'do everything we do with eternity in view', considering present difficulties as opportunities to glorify God, to 'fight the good fight of the faith, and lay hold of eternal life!'[109]

The following day, after having referred directly to Fuller's sermon, Sutcliff launched the Association's own 'Prayer Concert'. Member churches were urged to establish meetings on the first Monday of each month, the 'grand object' of which would be prayer for revival. Less than two months had passed between Ryland receiving the *Humble Attempt* to the setting up of this call being issued. When he returned to Kettering, Fuller was ready to lead his own church in response to the call.

Fuller quickly set up a monthly meeting along the lines suggested. For the first few of these Fuller sought to stir up those who had come by reading passages from the *Humble Attempt*. This was followed by opportunities for singing and for extempore prayer focused on the overarching theme of revival. There are a number of references to these meetings in his diary, and it appears that Fuller found these times to be both a challenge and an encouragement. On 6 December 1784 he recorded that they had an 'affecting meeting of prayer' for the 'revival of real religion'. On this occasion he found 'much pleasure in singing', and also 'freedom to God in prayer'. On 7 March 1785 he wrote that he enjoyed divine assistance at the monthly prayer meeting, in speaking on continuing in prayer, and in going to prayer, 'though I felt wretchedly cold before I began'.[110] Within a few years the 'Call to Prayer' had spread beyond the boundaries of the Northamptonshire Association. For example, in 1786 it was taken up by the Warwickshire churches, and 1790 by the Western Association. The re-igniting of the 'Concert of Prayer' had led to a significant movement. It was yet another sign of the life and vigour that was to increasingly characterize Particular Baptist life, not just in the Northamptonshire Association but in many other places too.[111] As far as Fuller himself was concerned, his horizons were clearly

---

109 See p. 13 above.
110 Ryland, *Andrew Fuller*, pp. 103-105; George, *Faithful Witness*, pp. 48-49.
111 Payne, *Prayer Call*, p. 11.

broadening. His growing world vision would lead, in 1792, to his involvement in the formation of the BMS.[112]

Fuller and the Baptist Missionary Society

On 2 October 1792 at least fourteen men crammed themselves in the back parlour of a home belonging to Martha Wallis in Kettering (the dimensions of the room were twelve feet by ten).[113] She was the widow of a deacon, Beeby Wallis, who had been influential in Fuller first coming to the 'Little Meeting'. In addition to Fuller, one of his current deacons, Joseph Timms, was also present, probably acting as the nominal 'host'. As Fuller would later say: 'There was little or no respectability amongst us, not so much as a squire to take the chair.'[114] Those who had gathered agreed to the formation of the 'Particular Baptist Society for Propagating the Gospel Among the Heathen'. Of the fourteen men present, thirteen pledged an annual subscription. The only one who did not, William Carey (1761–1834), was in fact the greatest enthusiast for overseas mission present. Probably the minimum subscription required (half a guinea) was beyond Carey's limited financial means, although it must have stretched some of the other ministers present. Fuller was the 'natural choice' to act as the society's first secretary, and was duly appointed at this meeting.[115] Carey was to become its first missionary arriving in India aboard the Danish East Indiaman the Kron Princessa Maria on 7 November 1793.

The BMS may have begun in seemingly inauspicious circumstances, but the significance of this event in the history of cross-cultural missionary work is vast. Carey is famously described as the 'father of modern missions', a title that, as Stephen Neill points out, is misleading. Nevertheless the formation of the BMS represents the beginning of a new chapter for Protestant missions, marking 'the entry of the English speaking world on a large scale into the missionary enterprise'.[116] The issues are dealt with more fully in chapter 10. Suffice to say here that by 1792 the Particular Baptists were growing strongly and no longer in danger of becoming the 'dunghill' that Fuller had once feared. From

---

112 On which, see also Morden, *Offering Christ to the World*, pp. 128-56.

113 For details in this paragraph, see S.P. Carey, *Memoir of William Carey, DD* (London: Hodder and Stoughton, 1923), pp. 88-93; Stanley, *History of the BMS*, pp. 10-11. Both Ryland and Sutcliff were present.

114 Quoted by S.P. Carey, *William Carey*, p. 90

115 E.F. Clipsham, 'Andrew Fuller and the Baptist Mission', *Foundations* 10.1 (January, 1967), p. 5.

116 Stephen Neill, *A History of Christian Missions* (Pelican History of the Church, 6; Harmondsworth, Middlesex: Penguin, 1964), p. 261.

this position of renewed strength and vigour, they were about to be involved in something of global significance.

FULLER'S ROLE IN THE FORMATION OF THE BAPTIST MISSIONARY SOCIETY

Carey was the central figure in the formation of the BMS, as both Ryland[117] and Fuller himself acknowledged. 'The origins of the society', Fuller said, 'will be found in the workings of our brother Carey's mind'.[118] Carey and Fuller first met at the 1782 Association at Olney, when Carey was only twenty-one years old and 'still feeling his way to the Baptist position'.[119] It does not appear that Fuller had a central role in the theological formation of the younger man. By the time *The Gospel Worthy* was published, Carey had already imbibed the warm evangelical Calvinism by then prevalent among the leading figures of the Northamptonshire Association. Robert Hall, Sr's *Help to Zion's Travellers*, published in 1781, was more significant. 'I do not remember ever to have read a book with such raptures', Carey said, and years later he was to inform Fuller that 'its doctrines are the choice of my heart to this day'.[120]

This is not to say that Fuller was not a significant figure in the genesis of the BMS. At an Association ministers' meeting held at Clipstone on 27 April 1791, Fuller preached a message the original title of which was 'The Instances, Evil, And Tendency of Delay, in the Concerns of Religion'. Before giving his stirring evangelistic appeal, Fuller had something to say to those who said that 'the time has not yet come' for active engagement in the cause of world mission. This message, which was later published, will be dealt with in more detail in chapter 10. The same day John Sutcliff preached a sermon, later published together with Fuller's message and entitled *Jealousy for the Lord of Hosts Illustrated*, that was also relevant to world mission.[121] Against this background, after dinner that evening, Carey proposed that something should be done immediately to set up a mission society. The fact that this did not happen there and then has been portrayed by some of Carey's biographers as showing that the leading Northamptonshire ministers, including Fuller,

---

117 Ryland, *Andrew Fuller*, pp. 147-48.

118 *Periodical Accounts Relative to the Baptist Missionary Society* (Clipstone: J.W. Morris, 1800 (1794]), I, p. 1, quoted in Payne, *Prayer Call*, p. 1; Clipsham, 'Fuller and the Baptist Mission', p. 4.

119 Payne, *Prayer Call*, p. 4.

120 M.A.G. Haykin, 'The Elder Robert Hall and his Help to Zion's Travellers: 1', *Banner of Truth Magazine* 343 (April, 1992), p. 20. Carey probably read *Help to Zion's Travellers* in 1782–83.

121 This appears to be Sutcliff's only extant sermon, published later in 1791. Haykin, *One Heart and Soul*, reprints the text of the whole sermon in an appendix, pp. 355-65.

were dragging their feet. Indeed, 'they would not rise and build the Lord's house', according to S. Pearce Carey.[122] But, as Brian Stanley points out, this is inherently unlikely in view of what had just been preached. The delay was almost certainly more due to practical considerations, although Carey was doubtless frustrated by it.[123] After the Clipstone meeting another key moment came in May 1792 when, following the active encouragement of Fuller, Ryland and Sutcliff, Carey was ready to publish himself on the subject of world mission.

Carey's famous pamphlet was entitled *An Enquiry into the Obligations of Christians to use Means for the Conversion of the Heathens*, and first appeared early in 1792.[124] He went on to preach his celebrated sermon on Isaiah 54.2-3 at the annual Association Meeting at Nottingham, on Wednesday, 30 May 1792. The title of this has passed into Baptist folklore as 'Expect Great things from God; Attempt great things for God', but probably the shorter title, 'Expect great things; attempt great things', is strictly accurate.[125] At the business meeting the following morning it seemed once again that no firm proposal to form a society would be made. But, with Carey's prompting, it was Fuller who submitted the following resolution: 'that a plan be prepared against the next ministers' meeting at Kettering, for forming a Baptist society for propagating the Gospel among the Heathen.'[126] Fuller's role in the formation of the BMS had been a significant one. The part he would play in the following years would be greater still.

FULLER AS SECRETARY OF THE BMS

Fuller was the unpaid secretary of the BMS from its inception to his death in 1815. His own self understanding of the task is revealed in an image that would be picked up by most biographers, both of Fuller and Carey. Ryland recorded that Fuller, whilst on a journey with a 'confidential friend', had remarked that:

---

122 S.P. Carey, *William Carey*, p. 69.
123 See the discussion in Stanley, *History of the BMS*, pp. 10-11.
124 Originally published, Leicester: Ann Ireland, 1792. A facsimile edition was printed later (London, 1961) and the text is also reproduced in George, *William Carey*, pp. E.1-57.
125 See E.A. Payne, 'John Dyer's Memoir of Carey', *BQ* 22.6 (April, 1968), pp. 326-27; A.C. Smith, 'The Spirit and the Letter of Carey's Catalytic Watchword. A Study in the History of Baptist Tradition', *BQ* 33.5 (January, 1990), pp 226-36, although Ryland, *Fuller*, p. 150, has the longer title.
126 J. Rippon (ed.), *The Baptist Annual Register* (London: Dilly, Button, Thomas, 1790–93), I, pp. 375, 419, quoted by Stanley, *History of the BMS*, p. 14.

> Our undertaking to India really appeared to me, on its commencement, to be somewhat like a few men, who were deliberating about the importance of penetrating into a deep mine, which had never before been explored. We had no one to guide us; and while we were thus deliberating, Carey, as it were, said, 'Well, I will go down, if you will hold the rope.' But before he went down...he as it seemed to me, took an oath from each of us, at the mouth of the pit, to this effect—that 'while we lived, we should never let go of the rope'.[127]

The phrases 'as it were' and 'as it seemed to me' probably indicate that the rope holding image originated with Fuller rather than Carey. Certainly it was Fuller, out of the original founders, who took his role in this respect most seriously. As William H. Brackney puts it, he was the key 'executive', who became the 'voluntary superintendent in the operation of the society'.[128]

As secretary, Fuller issued the regular *Periodical Accounts* of the Society[129] and supplied missionary news to John Rippon's *Baptist Annual Register*, in addition to the *Evangelical Magazine* and *Baptist Magazine*.[130] He also took the lead role in the selection of missionaries, and wrote regularly to those in the field.[131] All this was in addition to his work promoting the society, through voluminous letter writing and regular speaking engagements. These included short visits to individuals and churches, and also longer tours, which, as we shall see, were to take him all over the country. He also 'championed' the cause of Christian missions during a time in which the right to engage in missionary work overseas was regularly under serious threat.

FULLER'S CONTRIBUTION IN PROMOTING THE WORK OF THE BMS AND RAISING FUNDS AT HOME

One of Fuller's first tasks when he became secretary at the inaugural meeting in 1792 was to raise some funds. Given that the subscriptions and promises of money, collected in Fuller's snuffbox, amounted to £13.2s.6d, this was his most pressing task.[132] One of a number of letters he wrote in January 1793 to promote the work was to John Fawcett

---

127 Ryland, *Andrew Fuller*, p. 157. The 'confidential friend' was probably Ryland himself.

128 W.H. Brackney, 'The Baptist Missionary Society in Proper Context: Some Reflections on the Larger Voluntary Religious Tradition', *BQ* 34.8 (October, 1992), p. 370.

129 Although this was originally done by Samuel Pearce until his death in 1799, Ryland, *Andrew Fuller*, p. 147.

130 See the (incomplete) list of articles in Ryland, *Andrew Fuller*, 1st edn, p. 230-35. Ryland omitted this list from the second edition.

131 The bound volume containing the transcriptions of Fuller's Letters to Serampore (Angus Library, III/170) is 600 pages long.

132 Ryland, *Andrew Fuller*, p. 150.

(1740–1817) of Hebden Bridge in Yorkshire. Fuller had never met Fawcett, but this did not stop him making a strong appeal for support: 'Any sums of money conveyed...will be thankfully received. The sooner the better, as the time is short.' Carey was still in the country at this stage, and Fuller wrote that the prospective missionary would in fact be in Fawcett's county within the next few weeks to 'visit a relation'. If Fawcett were to 'hear him preach', Fuller assured him, 'he would certainly give him a collection'.[133] Fawcett became an enthusiastic supporter of the BMS. As Fuller wrote to him in 1793: 'My heart rejoices that you have so cordially entered into the mission business.'[134] Fuller would continue to write letters to promote the society, often spending ten hours a day at his desk, mostly giving himself to the work of the BMS. He would also visit individuals to solicit support and pay one off visits to churches for the same purpose. But it was his longer tours that probably did most to raise awareness and support for the mission.

In fact, Fuller was regularly away from Kettering for up to three months of each year, travelling huge distances on behalf of the society. As late as 1814, by which time his health was deteriorating rapidly, he was working at an extraordinary pace. Morris recorded Fuller's itinerary for May to July of that year. In May and June he was due to go to Olney, Bedford, Leicester, Essex and London, although Fuller noted he had to be in Kettering on 26 June, 'which is our Lord's Supper day'. In July he was in the north of England, on successive Sundays in Liverpool, Manchester, Leeds, Newcastle and Hull. As Fuller surveyed this forthcoming programme, it is little surprise that he wrote: 'May the Lord strengthen me for these labours.'[135] Stanley notes that during this year, Fuller travelled 600 miles in one month alone, collecting, by his own reckoning, about £1 a mile.[136] In all he travelled many times to London, and at one time or other visited most of the counties in England, including one journey into the High Calvinist bastion of Norfolk.[137]

---

133 Fuller to J. Fawcett, n.d., but from early 1793, in Fawcett, Jr., *John Fawcett*, p. 296.
134 Fuller to J. Fawcett, 28 January 1792, in Fawcett, Jr., *John Fawcett*, p. 294.
135 Morris, *Andrew Fuller*, 1st edn, p. 156.
136 Stanley, *History of the BMS*, p. 20, citing a letter from Fuller to W. Ward, 5 September 1814. Cf. Fuller to J. Deakin, August 14 1812, in Payne (ed.), 'Letters to James Deakin', p. 365. Fuller estimated that a journey to Wales was also 'about a 600 miles excursion'. He raised what he usually aimed for—'my old price, a pound a mile'.
137 Fuller to J. Deakin, August 14 1812, in Payne, 'Letters to James Deakin', p. 365.

But even more remarkable were journeys between 1799 and 1813 to Wales, to Ireland (in 1804), and several trips to Scotland. The extensive Scottish journeys are the best documented of all his tours on behalf of the mission. Fuller kept a journal of his first journey which includes details of travel arrangements, preaching engagements and people met, together with various observations on the life of the Scottish churches. Information concerning the other trips can be extracted from various letters recorded by Ryland.[138] In all he visited Scotland five times—in 1799, 1802, 1805, 1808 and 1813—producing what was described as a 'hallowed excitement' and enjoying great personal popularity.[139] After 1799 Fuller aimed to make his visits 'triennial'. But at the very end of his life this would be something that even he would fail to manage.

His trips to Scotland can be taken as an example of how Fuller worked. Fuller canvassed support from a range of churches, bringing him into contact with a much wider network of ministers and other friends than he had previously experienced. He was very positive about many non-Baptist evangelicals in Scotland, and they in turn welcomed him. In Edinburgh in 1799 he had his first face to face meeting with his own and Ryland's correspondent, John Erskine, whom he described as 'an excellent old man'.[140] Fuller was also impressed with a number of other ministers 'in the Kirk', as he also was by the Independents James and Robert Haldane. Early in 1799 James Haldane had accepted ordination to the pastorate of an Independent congregation which met at the former Circus building in Edinburgh until a large purpose built tabernacle was opened in 1801. The Haldanes, especially Robert, were men of means and built sizeable 'tabernacles' in other major centres, including Glasgow. These were free of pew rents and designed to reach the underprivileged classes. Together the brothers stood for a robust evangelicalism with a strong commitment to mission both at home and abroad. In fact, in 1796 Robert had actually attempted to undertake a self financed evangelistic tour to Bengal.[141] It was at their instigation that

---

138 Ryland, *Andrew Fuller*, pp. 164-83, reproduced the bulk of the journal, and also included much primary material from the other Scottish tours, pp. 184-212.

139 F.A. Cox, *History of the Baptist Missionary Society of England from 1792 to 1842* (London: T. Ward, 1842), p. 21, cited by Brackney, 'The BMS in Context', p. 370; Ryland, *Andrew Fuller*, p. 156. On his first journey to Scotland he was accompanied by Sutcliff, on the last for some of the time by William Steadman. See also Talbot, *Search for a Common Identity*, *passim*.

140 See Ryland, *Andrew Fuller*, pp. 168-69, for the information in the next two paragraphs.

141 D.M. Lewis (ed.), *Dictionary of Evangelical Biography 1730–1860* (2 vols; Oxford: Blackwell, 1995), I, pp. 500-503. Their movement was later severely weakened by internal tensions.

Fuller had come to Scotland, and they and their churches were to prove fertile soil for the message concerning the BMS.

Fuller was welcomed into the pulpits of the Haldanes' growing connexion, and preached at the Circus on his first visit. He recorded his initial impressions in his journal: 'Certainly these appear to be excellent men, free from the extravagance and nonsense which infect some of the Calvinistic Methodists in England; and yet trying to imbibe and communicate their zeal and affection.' Fuller was less positive about the Scotch Baptists, many of whom had been influenced by Sandemanianism. Their intellectualized view of faith accounted, Fuller believed, for the arid nature of many of their churches which were not sufficiently committed to the spread of the gospel.

The tours to Scotland, in common with the vast majority of the others that Fuller undertook, were financially successful. As such they made a vital contribution to the continuing work of the BMS. Wherever Fuller preached he took collections, and he also solicited money by visiting ministers and prominent Christian laypeople house to house. He often preached to thousands, for example to over 4,000 at the Haldanes' tabernacles in Edinburgh and Glasgow on his second tour in 1802 (these estimates are, of course, Fuller's own). These were extraordinary experiences for Fuller, but the verdict of his hearers on these occasions appears to have been extremely positive. As far as collecting money was concerned, Ryland commented that 'he always disliked violent pressing for contributions...he chose, rather, to tell a plain unvarnished tale; and he generally told it with good effect'. Nevertheless he was never coy about fund raising. To help the Bible translation work at Serampore, and as an inducement for Fuller to visit Scotland, Robert Haldane had arranged for £100 to be transferred to BMS funds, probably early in 1799. Suitably encouraged, Fuller agreed to embark on his first tour later that year. Ryland recorded that during that one evening during that first journey, a lady commented: '"O sir, why did you not come here before?" Fuller (with his tongue perhaps only slightly in his cheek), responded: "Why madam, every man, as Sir Robert Walpole said, has his price; and till that gentleman there (Robert Haldane) sent me a hundred pounds, I did not know it would be worthwhile to visit you."'[142]

These tours also highlight the exhausting pace at which Fuller worked. An extract from a letter to his wife, Ann (written from Lancaster, in the north of England, 1 August 1805), gives a flavour of what was happening. Fuller was on his way home from his third visit to Scotland:

---

142 This anecdote is also in A. Haldane, *The Lives of Robert and James Haldane* (London: Hamilton, Adams, 3rd edn, 1853), pp. 298-99.

> The last letter I write you, was from Glasgow, Tuesday, July 23. (This letter is wanting.) Since then, I have preached at Paisley, Greenock, Saltcoats, Kilmarnock, Kilwinning, Air (sic), and Dumfries. I am now on my way to Liverpool, I have not been in bed till tonight, since Lord's Day night, at Irvine, in Scotland. I have felt my strength and spirits much exhausted; yet hitherto the Lord hath helped and my health is good.

This sort of punishing schedule was not at all unusual for Fuller in Scotland. A typical day would see him travel upwards of forty miles, visit, preach and collect (on a Sunday usually three times), and then stay up into the evening talking with ministers. Nor was he always able to report to his wife that his health was bearing up. As early as 1793, Fuller had suffered what he termed a 'paralytic stroke'. One side of his face was left temporarily paralysed, and, though he recovered, from this point on he was to suffer severe headaches for the rest of his life. The letters give ample evidence that the tours were further sapping his strength. The open air preaching that he was sometimes asked to do can hardly have helped, particularly when the weather was poor.[143] For all his illnesses, the remedies of the day, such as hot tiles wrapped in a flannel and applied to the stomach when he was in pain, could only give temporary relief.[144]

All this needs to be set alongside the other demands of his ministry. Fuller had many other duties as secretary of the BMS. He also continued to write and pastor the church at Kettering. One of his letters, from as early as 1801, captures the dilemma he was increasingly facing.

> Pearce's memoirs are now loudly called for. I sit down almost in despair... My wife looks at me with a tear ready to drop, and says, 'My dear, you have hardly time to speak to me.' My friends at home are kind, but they also say, 'You have no time to see us or know us, and you will soon be worn out.' Amidst all this there is 'Come again to Scotland—come to Portsmouth—come to Plymouth—come to Bristol'.[145]

After 1792 Fuller had never been happier, as he gave himself to the work of the mission and found that as he did so it was a means of 'reviving his soul'. As Fuller engaged in wholehearted evangelical action, he became less introspective (indeed, he must have had little time for this). As he worked for the BMS he found he now felt 'more genuine love to God and his cause' than at any previous time in his life.[146] This new found joy never really left him, but sometimes the dynamic he had discovered—that for him activity in God's service led to greater

---

143 Ryland, *Andrew Fuller*, e.g., pp. 196-97, 202, 207, gives ample evidence that these tours were affecting his health.
144 E.A. Payne 'Andrew Fuller as a Letter Writer', *BQ* 15.7 (July, 1954), p. 293.
145 Gunton Fuller, *Men Worth Remembering*, pp. 91-92. The letter is from 'March 1800'.
146 Ryland, *Andrew Fuller*, p. 155, quoting from Fuller's diary for 18 July 1794.

happiness—was stretched to breaking point by the pace at which he worked. The demands on Fuller certainly contributed to regular and often severe illness. In 1801, Robert Hall, Jr., having heard that Fuller had recently visited Plymouth and Bristol, expressed his fears for Fuller's health in a letter to Ryland: 'If he is not more careful he will be in danger of wearing himself out before his time. His journeys, his studies, his correspondencies (sic) must be too much for any man.'[147] In fact from 1800 onwards Fuller was rarely well, yet it never seems to have occurred to him to slacken his pace. A member of the Kettering congregation wrote to Ryland: 'Mr F.'s exertions are too much for his health... Dear sir, pray for us, that so valuable a life may yet be continued.'[148] When advice to slow down was given, Fuller felt unable to heed it. Against this background, perhaps the remarkable thing is not that 'his exertions proved greater than nature was able to sustain, and [that] he sunk under them into a premature grave', but rather that he managed to survive until 1815.[149]

Fuller's Death

On 4 September 1814 Fuller was taken seriously ill with a 'disordered liver' after preaching at Kettering.[150] Fuller was in bed for two weeks and never really recovered his strength. By March 1815 he was conscious he was dying, and on 2 April he preached for the last time, from Isaiah 66.1-2: 'Thus saith the Lord, the heaven is my throne, and the earth is my footstool...' As he presided at communion with his people, speaking slowly and haltingly, 'he seemed absorbed in the contemplation of a crucified, risen exalted Redeemer'. He was confined to bed soon after this, made arrangements for his own funeral service (Ryland was to preach on Romans 8.10) and was nursed by his family. Among his last words were, 'my hope is such that I am not afraid to plunge into eternity'. He died on 7 May, aged sixty-two. When news of his death reached India William Ward, one of the original 'Serampore trio', spoke of Fuller having had 'as large a share as any man on earth' in the establishment and promotion of the mission, and having 'left no living

---

147 R. Hall, Jr., to J. Ryland, Jr., 25 May 1801, G.F. Nuttall, 'Letters from Robert Hall to John Ryland, 1791–1824', *BQ* 34.3 (July, 1991), p. 127. The original is held in the Library of the Selly Oak Colleges, Birmingham.
148 Ryland, *Andrew Fuller*, p. 344.
149 Ryland, *Andrew Fuller*, p. 381. Fuller nevertheless 'rejoiced in all his labours'.
150 For details in the next two paragraphs, see Gunton Fuller, *Memoir*, pp. 99-102

person who can fill his place'.[151] It was a fitting epitaph, as was the comment of J.W. Morris: 'He lived and died a martyr to the Mission.'[152]

Fuller and the Revival of Particular Baptist Life

By the time of Fuller's death, the decline in Particular Baptist life had been decisively reversed. Indeed, as early as 1793 Fuller wrote a letter detailing 'the state of religion in Northamptonshire', which hinted at major changes that had already taken place.[153] Out of twenty-one churches in the county, there were now only four or five who embraced 'what is called the High Calvinist scheme'. The rest, according to Fuller, made 'no scruple' about openly 'exhorting' people to believe the gospel. The county with which both Gill and Brine were linked, was now coming down on what we saw Fuller had termed the 'affirmative side' of 'The Modern Question'. Ministers could and should offer the gospel indiscriminately to all.[154] But the letter also indicated something else. The churches which embraced what Fuller here termed 'Moderate Calvinism', were growing. Fuller spoke of a 'readiness discovered in many parts of the county for hearing the gospel', and of a 'considerable increase' among the churches. Indeed he could be more specific. 'Seven or eight new churches have been raised amongst (us) within the last 20 years.' There is no reason to doubt the figures Fuller gave, particularly as he expected his correspondent, possibly a General Baptist layman, to publish them. When we put this together with the number of people regularly coming to hear Fuller in Kettering (over 1,000), the figures indicate that something highly significant was taking place.

Nor was this growth confined to Northamptonshire. The 1790s saw the publication of several volumes of John Rippon's *Baptist Annual Register*,[155] which provides what Nuttall describes as a 'fine contemporary record of (English Particular Baptist) churches'.[156] The formation of

---

151 Quoted Clipsham, 'Fuller and the Baptist Mission', p. 10.

152 Morris, *Andrew Fuller*, 2nd edn, p. 49.

153 G.F. Nuttall, 'The State of Religion in Northamptonshire (1793) by Andrew Fuller', *BQ* 29.4 (October, 1981), pp. 177-79. The original letter from Fuller to Mr Josiah Lewis is now held in Dr Williams's Library, London. All quotations and information in this paragraph and the next are from Fuller's letter and Nuttall's brief introductory remarks.

154 Nuttall, 'Northants and *The Modern Question*', *passim*.

155 On which, see Ken R. Manley, *'Redeeming Love Proclaim': John Rippon and the Baptists* (Studies in Baptist History and Thought, 12; Carlisle: Paternoster Press, 2004), ch. 5.

156 G.F. Nuttall, 'The Baptist Churches and their Ministers: Rippon's Baptist Annual Register', *BQ* 30.8 (October, 1984), pp. 383-87.

such a comprehensive survey was in itself an indicator of the health of the denomination. In the list that appears in volume three (1798–1801) of the *Register*, 361 churches are recorded by Rippon. This figure can be compared with the one we quoted earlier in this chapter, suggesting that in the 1750s there were only 150 Calvinistic Baptist churches in England and Wales. If these statistics are even approximately right (the complete accuracy of the 1750s figure is open to some question), then it is surely correct to say that a revitalization of Particular Baptist life in England had taken place.

Fuller, as the denomination's leading theologian, and one of its leading figures overall, had a significant place in that story. Fuller made an important contribution to the revitalization of the denomination. But this renewal did not only lead to growth at home, but also, as Nuttall states, 'in vigorous mission and interest across the oceans'.[157] By 1815 there was a thriving work in India and the BMS was working in other areas too, for example the West Indies.[158] Many of his contemporaries and colleagues had little doubt of his importance in the overall story of Particular Baptist life and growth. After Fuller's death Robert Hall, Jr., paid tribute to his friend saying that Fuller 'endeared himself to his denomination by a long course of most useful labour'. Moreover: 'by his excellent works...as well as his devotion to the cause of missions, he laid the world under lasting obligations'. Joseph Belcher, the editor of the American edition of Fuller's works, wrote in similar vein: 'Andrew Fuller was providentially raised up at a period when coldness benumbed some parts of the Christian church, and errors obscured the glory of others... The wonder is, that one short life should have accomplished so much.'[159] Later commentators have been no less fulsome. W.T. Whitley spoke of him as a 'great theologian', and E.A. Payne referred to 'Fullerism' as a 'revivifying impulse, north, south, east and west'.[160]

In his *Narrative of Surprising Conversions*, Jonathan Edwards, the mentor Fuller never met, wrote that 'Persons after their own conversion, have commonly expressed an exceeding great desire for the conversion of others. Some have thought that they should be willing to die for the conversion of any soul.' Edwards' words fit Fuller perfectly, as do the those of the evangelical authoress Hannah More, from the beginning of the nineteenth century: 'Action is the life of virtue', she wrote, 'and the world is the theatre of action'.[161] Although Fuller never went further

---

157 Nuttall, 'Baptist Churches and their Ministers', p. 383.
158 Stanley, *History of the BMS*, pp. 46-56, 68.
159 For both these quotations, see *Works*, I, pp. 106-107.
160 All comments cited by Clipsham, 'The Development of a Doctrine', pp. 99-100.
161 Both Edwards' and More's comments are quoted by Bebbington, *Evangelicalism in Modern Britain*, pp. 10, 12.

afield than Britain and Ireland, in a very real sense, the 'world' *had* become 'his theatre of action', as he developed a ministry that was influential and respected around the world, and which continues to have real relevance today.

CHAPTER 2

Andrew Fuller, Hyper-Calvinism, and the 'Modern Question'

Gerald L. Priest

Can and should the gospel of salvation be offered to sinners without distinction? Is unregenerate man under moral obligation to repent of sin and believe in Christ upon hearing the gospel? Is there any sense in which he is *able* to do so? And is the minister of the gospel obligated to call upon the unregenerate to exercise faith and repentance? These queries collectively constitute the so-called 'modern question' of Andrew Fuller's day, which we can reduce to simply—*is faith a duty*?[1] The question was first raised by the Congregational minister Joseph Hussey (1660–1726) in 1707 with his publication of *God's Operations of Grace: but No Offers of His Grace*,[2] in which he took the hyper-Calvinist[3]

---

1 Those answering these questions in the affirmative would be advocates of what might be called 'duty faith', i.e., the obligation of everyone to believe the gospel of Christ.
2 This was reprinted by Primitive Publications, Elon College, NC, in 1973.
3 Some prefer the less pejorative term 'high' Calvinism/Calvinists. I mean to use the terms 'hyper' and 'high' synonymously. While it is true that hyper-Calvinism has been interpreted in a variety of ways, we should consider how the expression was applied in the eighteenth century to opponents of Andrew Fuller and his fellow moderate or evangelical Calvinists. The term was directed against those who normally advocated the following positions or variations of them: (1) a supralapsarian decree of election; which would include (2) reprobation or what John Gill called 'pre-damnation'; (3) eternal justification, the doctrine that God decreed the elect *for* justification before the fall; a corollary of this logically being (4) passive faith (i.e., God grants his elect faith apart from active human volition); (5) a divine warrant or indication (usually conviction of sin) that an individual was elect prior to conversion; and (6) a distinction between preaching the gospel indiscriminately and *offering* it to those *sensible* to it (i.e., those who have a warrant that they are elect). David J. Engelsma, *Hyper-Calvinism and the Call of the Gospel: An Examination of the 'Well-Meant Offer'* (Grandville, MI: Reformed Free Publishing Association, rev. edn, 1994), pp. 15–16, actually defines hyper-Calvinism in terms of a denial of duty faith: 'Hyper-Calvinism is the denial that God in the preaching of the gospel calls everyone who hears the preaching to repent and believe. It is the denial that the church should call everyone in the preaching. It is the denial that the

position that to offer the gospel indiscriminately would imply that the natural man had the innate ability to respond to it. Hussey admitted that, as far as he was able to determine, no authorities had raised the question before, but he felt constrained to do so in the face of Arminianism[4] and its rationalist counterparts, Deism and Socinianism. All of these humanistic systems, Hussey believed, were a major threat to the doctrines of grace. The following quote from Hussey's work reflects the high Calvinism that prompted an evangelical response from more moderate Particular Baptists, such as Andrew Fuller (1754–1815):[5]

---

unregenerated have a duty to repent and believe. It manifests itself in the practice of the preacher's addressing the call of the gospel, 'repent and believe on Christ crucified', only to those in his audience who show signs of regeneration, and thereby of election, namely, some conviction of sin and some interest in salvation.' Cf. C. Samuel Storms, *Chosen for Life: An Introductory Guide to the Doctrine of Divine Election* (Grand Rapids, MI: Baker, 1987), pp. 116–18. No one would have been called hyper-Calvinist who held to the five points of Dort (TULIP). In fact, those who departed from those points usually incurred the charge of Arminianism. Hyper-Calvinists went beyond Dort and made their own tenets the test of Calvinism, so that when Fuller, in agreement with Dort, taught that the atonement was sufficient for all the world, but efficient only for the elect, he was accused of being Arminian. See 'Canons of the Synod of Dort,' in Philip Schaff (ed.), *The Creeds of Christendom* (3 vols; Grand Rapids, MI: Baker, 1983), p. 586. See also Iain H. Murray, *Spurgeon v. Hyper-Calvinism: The Battle for Gospel Preaching* (Edinburgh: Banner of Truth Trust, 1995), pp. 50–51, where Murray writes: 'So-called 'Fullerism' represented an emphasis not only to be found in the Reformers and Puritans but supremely in Scripture itself'.

4   Arminianism was a term that carried a wide variety of meanings in Fuller's day. At the least, and according to normal historical usage, it applied to those who embraced the teachings of Jacobus Arminius (1560–1609) as expressed in the controversial five points of the Dutch Remonstrance of 1610. The Remonstrants attempted to define predestination in terms of foreknowledge and conditioned salvation on man's free will. All men can be saved, grace can be resisted, and those saved may not persevere in the faith but could fall from grace. Because of their emphasis on the unlimited atonement (Christ suffered for all men), they were often accused of teaching universalism. Arminius and true Arminians have taught that all men possess original sin, but that God in the atonement extended an ability by means of a prevenient grace for all men to be saved. Prevenient grace negated the disabling effects of original sin. Those who denied original sin were frequently called Arminian, but in actuality they were Pelagian. Because of its stress on human ability, Arminianism has frequently degenerated into latitudinarianism and liberalism, including Unitarianism. This is why some Unitarians, like John Taylor of Norwich, were referred to as Arminian. The Arminian General Baptists of Great Britain were almost wholly taken over by Socinianism, a form of Unitarianism, by the mid-1700s. One must realize this context when considering why Particular Baptists tended to lump Arminians, Arians and Socinians together as the common enemy of orthodox Christianity.

5   For an overview of Fuller's life and a brief evaluation of his theology, see Phil Roberts, 'Andrew Fuller', in Timothy George and David S. Dockery (eds), *Baptist*

> By offers of grace, tenders and proffers of salvation, it is evident, men do thereby imply that free grace and full salvation is [sic] propounded, tendered, and offered to all sinners within the sound [of the gospel]... Is not this a piece of robbery against the Holy Spirit?...does not the plea confine the operation of the Holy Spirit to common and eternal workings? Wherein does your plea give Jehovah the Spirit His due honour in the internal and mighty workings of His grace on sinners' hearts, that sinners may believe, repent, and be saved?[6]

The main problem of the gospel's indiscriminate offer for Hussey is that it failed to consider the imputation of Christ's righteousness to the elect, who *only* could respond in faith: 'The Spirit will not, and cannot honourably work without the imputation of Christ; but offers of Christ...without a due regard of the imputation of his righteousness, or the work of the Spirit, therefore are not fit means to work this ability [i.e., the ability to close with Christ].'[7] Hussey said that it is all right to preach the gospel, just do not make it an offer, since the non-elect have no ability in them to respond to it; otherwise, you rob the Spirit of his power, degrade the gospel, and flatter men that they have some ability to receive it.[8] One can understand why this view was charged with antinomianism when it seems to tell man that he has no duty to respond because he has no ability. Therefore, he has no moral obligation to obey God's revelation. What Hussey (and most hyper-Calvinists) attempted to do was guard the gospel against the Arminian assertion of human ability and the Socinian view of universalism.

The modern question was revisited in 1739 by the posthumous publication of Congregationalist minister Matthias Maurice's *The Modern Question Affirm'd and Proved* in which he forsook his earlier high Calvinism to proclaim the duty of all hearers to believe the gospel of Christ. The book included a testimony of his church at Rowel (Rothwell) to the effect 'that God does in his Word make it the *Duty* of poor unconverted Sinners, who hear the Gospel preach'd, to be truly

---

Theologians (Nashville, TN: Broadman, 1990), pp. 121–39. Roberts gives a comprehensive bibliography of works by and about Fuller, making it unnecessary to repeat them here.

6 Cited in Alan P.F. Sell, *The Great Debate: Calvinism, Arminianism, and Salvation* (Grand Rapids, MI: Baker, 1983), p. 53. An avowed Calvinist himself, John Newton cautioned John Ryland, Jr., that Hussey's high Calvinism had made many 'rather wise than warm, rather positive [dogmatic] than humble, rather captious than lively, and more disposed to talk of speculations than experience.' When reading Hussey, Newton found that his writings contained 'more bones than meat', and 'are seasoned with much of an angry and self-important spirit'. See Newton's letter to Ryland, 16 January 1772, cited in Michael A.G. Haykin, *One Heart and One Soul: John Sutcliff of Olney, His Friends and His Times* (Durham: Evangelical Press, 1994), p. 81.

7 Sell, *Great Debate*, pp. 53–54.
8 Sell, *Great Debate*, p. 54.

concern'd for their Souls, and believe in *Jesus Christ* for Salvation.'[9] This inaugurated a pamphlet battle between the high and moderate Calvinists in which the Particular Baptists engaged most vociferously. The quarrel really heated up when John Gill (1697–1771) entered the fray with the republication in 1751 of John Skepp's 1721 work, *The Divine Energy: or the efficacious operations of the Spirit of God in the soul of man, in his effectual calling and conversion: stated, proved, and vindicated. Wherein the real weakness and insufficiency of moral persuasion, without the super-addition of the exceeding greatness of God's power for faith and conversion to God, are fully evinced. Being an antidote against the Pelagian plague*[10]—the title providing a virtual synopsis of the work! Sell states:

> So persuaded was Skepp that God must have all the glory, and that man could do nothing, that he, like Hussey before him, refused to *offer* the gospel lest it be thought that any but God's Holy Spirit could apply it to the heart, or that sinful man had the moral ability to respond. This was the position which Gill and [John] Brine [Gill's close friend] strenuously defended against the supporters of Mathias Maurice....[11]

Baptist historian Joseph Ivimey viewed with concern this high Calvinist trend among Particular Baptists as a significant shift from an earlier evangelicalism:

---

9   Cited in Peter Naylor, *Picking Up a Pin for the Lord: English Particular Baptists from 1688 to the Early Nineteenth Century* (London: Grace Publications, 1992), p. 154.

10   Skepp was Gill's close friend and mentor. He had been a member of Gill's ordination council and encouraged Gill in his pursuit of Hebrew studies. Sell, *Great Debate*, p. 78, reminds us that 'above all, Skepp had been a member of Hussey's church at Cambridge and his own theological stance is adequately described by the title of his book' [cited above]. It was to Skepp that Joseph Ivimey, *A History of the English Baptists: Comprising the Principal Events of the History of Protestant Dissenters, from the Revolution in 1668 till 1760; and of the London Baptist Churches, During That Period* (4 vols; London: B.J. Holdsworth, 1823), III, p. 267, attributed the introduction of the non-invitation, non-application scheme among the Baptists, a scheme that had 'plentifully watered our churches'.

11   Sell, *Great Debate*, p. 78. Attempts to make Gill less the hyper-Calvinist than either Skepp or Brine have been unconvincing. The latter two ministers may have been more dogmatic in drawing a contrast between gospel preaching and offer, but as Walter Wilson, *History and Antiquities of Dissenting Churches...in London* [1808–14], II, pp. 574–75, stated, both Gill and Brine enjoyed 'a perfect congeniality of views upon religious subjects'. Cited by Geoffrey F. Nuttall, 'Northamptonshire and *The Modern Question*: A Turning-Point in Eighteenth-Century Dissent', *Journal of Theological Studies* 16.1 (April, 1965), p. 117: 'Their common inspirer was John Skepp'. Cf. Naylor, *Picking Up a Pin*, p. 155, in which he states: 'Of the three Baptist high Calvinists, Brine, Skepp and Gill, Gill was held as the greatest'.

> The manner of preaching the gospel, by some of the Baptist ministers, to unconverted sinners, had been greatly altered [during the mid 1700s]... From the zeal which they displayed for the peculiar doctrines of Calvinism, and their tenaciousness for the sentiment that *salvation is of the Lord*, and by grace alone, without human endeavours, they were led into an extreme, so as to deny that all who hear the gospel are called to that exercise of repentance and faith which is connected with salvation; thus taking the negative side of what was then called the modern question, 'Whether it be the duty of all men to whom the gospel is published, to repent and believe in Christ?' So far as I have been able to discover, this subject had never been made a question by our ministers [previous to 1727, the end of George I's reign].[12]

An Evangelical Baptist Response to Hyper-Calvinism

In reacting to this extreme Calvinist approach, several Particular Baptists of a more evangelistic bent 'wished both to resist Arminianism, and to proclaim the gospel more experimentally and generously than the stricter Calvinism seemed to permit'.[13] Among these were John Sutcliff, John Ryland, Jr., and Robert Hall, Sr., of Arnesby, whose Northamptonshire Association sermon, *Help to Zion's Travellers*, was put into print in 1781. Hall's comment that 'the way to Jesus is graciously open for everyone who chooses to come to him' made a favorable impression on Andrew Fuller and his zealous young friend, William Carey.

What especially aroused Fuller's attention to the issue was his reading of *The Modern Question Concerning Repentance and Faith Examined*, first published in 1735 by Particular Baptist and duty faith advocate Abraham Taylor. Fuller, having been reared in a strict Particular Baptist church whose pastor was 'noninvitational', began wrestling with the modern question in earnest. He was not at all satisfied with Gill and Brine's separate rebuttals of Taylor's work in 1738 and 1743 respectively. Gill was intent on clearing himself and his high Calvinist party of antinomianism: 'For my part I have been traduced as an Antinomian, for innocently asserting that the essence of justification...lies in the will of God—I *abhor* the thoughts of setting the law of God aside as the rule of walk and conversation; and constantly affirm...that all who believe in Christ for righteousness should be careful to maintain good works, for necessary uses.'[14] But he was hard put to throw off the yoke of antinomianism especially due to his promotion of two distinguishing marks of supralapsarian Calvinism—reprobation and eternal just-

---

12   Ivimey, *A History of the English Baptists*, III, pp. 259–60.
13   Sell, *Great Debate*, pp. 54–55.
14   John Rippon, *A Brief Memoir of the Life and Writings of the late Rev. John Gill, D.D.* (London: n.p., 1838), p. 56.

ification.¹⁵ Gill was suggesting that if God had chosen and condemned the non-elect before the Fall, and had not only determined the elect but justified them in eternity past, then what is the point of *offering* the gospel indiscriminately? By this extreme view Gill was trying to buttress his case for perseverance of the saints against John Wesley's denial of it and accusations against him (Gill) of antinomianism. Not only was Gill unable to shake free of Wesley but he faced similar accusations from his own Particular Baptist denomination. What troubled Robert Hall and certainly Andrew Fuller was the fact that, for all his assertions of *proclaiming* the gospel to everyone, Gill undervalued the *general* call when insisting upon the *effectual* call. As E.F. Clipsham put it: 'Gill...went to great lengths to explain away the meaning of "all" wherever it occurs in connection with the universal proclamation of the gospel, and studiously avoided the direct commands and exhortations in

---

15   There have been fairly recent attempts from two different camps to rescue John Gill from the charge of hyper-Calvinism: those who are evangelical Calvinists who wish to see in Gill an essential theological kinship with Fuller, and those hyper-Calvinists who disdain Fullerism in favor of Gill, who they believe was a consistent Calvinist. The first group, associated with the Founders movement within the Southern Baptist Convention, is represented by Tom Ascol, Timothy George and Tom Nettles. See respectively, 'The Doctrine of Grace: A Critical Analysis of Federalism in the Theologies of John Gill and Andrew Fuller' (PhD thesis, Southwestern Baptist Theological Seminary, 1989); 'John Gill', in George and Dockery (eds), *Baptist Theologians*, pp. 77–101; and *By His Grace and for His Glory: A Historical, Theological, and Practical Study of the Doctrines of Grace in Baptist Life* (Grand Rapids, MI: Baker, 1986), pp. 73–107. See also Haykin, *One Heart and One Soul*, pp. 17–19. The second group is represented by the Strict Baptist Historical Society and the *Gospel Standard* in Great Britain. Most notable among them is George M. Ella, e.g., *John Gill and the Cause of God and Truth* (Durham: Go Publications, 1995), where he attempts to exonerate Gill from the charge of hyper-Calvinism. A more defensible interpretation of Gill is by Robert W. Oliver, 'John Gill (1697–1771)', in Michael A.G. Haykin (ed.), vol. 1 of *The British Particular Baptists 1638–1910* (3 vols; Springfield, MO: Particular Baptist Press, 1998–2003), I, pp. 144–65, where he gives evidence that Gill was indeed a hyper-Calvinist. See also his critique of Nettles's view of Gill with 'By His Grace and for His Glory', *Banner of Truth* 284 (May, 1987), pp. 30–32. The most exhaustive treatment in favor of Gill's hyper-Calvinism is Curt Daniel, 'Hyper-Calvinism and John Gill' (PhD dissertation, University of Edinburgh, 1983). While it could be argued that Gill did not go beyond what Calvin himself taught on reprobation, he nevertheless cannot be excused from promoting a spirit at odds with the missionary mandate. Gill's successor, Charles Spurgeon, *Commenting and Commentaries* (London: Passmore & Alabaster, 1876), p. 9, could recommend his predecessor's orthodoxy as a corrective to heresy, but could also acknowledge the chilling effect this 'Coryphaeus of hyper-Calvinism' had on evangelism.

the Bible [for all men] to repent and believe on Christ and be saved.'[16] Since Gill believed that Christ died only for the elect, then the 'all' of Scripture should be interpreted as all the elect (or those justified from eternity past), not all the world.[17]

The Gospel Worthy of All Acceptation
Formative Influences and Basic Propositions

For Fuller and his evangelical friends, 'all' meant *all* men! As a devout Particular Baptist, he had to be careful how he approached the subject, however. He wanted to give no quarter to Arminians or Socinians by even suggesting universalism. And he definitely was not happy with Gillism, which was killing evangelism, yet he wished to maintain the doctrines of Reformed soteriology in no uncertain terms.[18] He had struggled long and

---

16   E.F. Clipsham, 'Andrew Fuller and Fullerism', *BQ* 20 (July, 1963), p. 102. Clipsham is citing Gill's *Cause of God and Truth* (London: n.p., 3rd edn, 1772), pp. 42, 53, 72, 317, 339.

17   For example, Gill, *Cause of God and Truth*, pp. 42–43, wrote on 2 Cor. 5.14–15: 'That the text does not say that Christ died for *all men*, but for *all*; and therefore, agreeable to other scriptures [Mt 1.21; Jn 10.15; Eph. 5.25; Heb. 2.9-10], may be understood of all *the people* whom Jesus saves from their sins... That it is said in the latter part of the text, that those for whom Christ died, for them also he rose again; who therefore ought to live... Christ died for no more nor for others than those for whom he rose again; such for whom he rose again, he rose for their justification; if Christ rose for the justification of all men, all men would be justified, or the end of Christ's resurrection would not be answered; but all men are not, nor will be justified; some will be condemned: it follows, that Christ did not rise from the dead for all men, and consequently did not die for all men'.

18   Despite Fuller's attempt at precision, he only muddied the doctrinal waters of soteriology when he sought to describe the atonement in terms that suggested a moral or governmental, rather than a penal, view. In opposition to the Anselmian commercial theory, one that fit hyper-Calvinist particularism quite well, Fuller defines atonement as Christ's 'obedience unto death', answering 'every end of moral government, and [opening]...a way by which God could honorably...pardon the sinner'. 'Sin is only a debt in a metaphorical sense; properly speaking, it is a *crime*, and satisfaction for it requires to be made, not on pecuniary, but on moral principles.' See Fuller, *Atonement of Christ and Justification of the Sinner, arranged from the writings of the Rev. Andrew Fuller by the editor of his complete works* (New York: American Tract Society, 1854), pp. 72–73. A close examination of Fuller's writings, however, indicates that he was opposing a literal numericalism in favor of a penal suffering which gave infinite moral value to the atonement sufficient to expiate the sins of the whole world. Fuller's problem is more semantic than substantive. Although, for a more critical discussion of Fuller's moralist view of the atonement, see Michael A.G. Haykin, 'Particular Redemption in the Writings of Andrew Fuller (1754–1815)', in D.W. Bebbington (ed.), *The Gospel in the World:*

hard with the modern question, and finally produced his version of it in a landmark work that helped launch the modern missions movement—*The Gospel Worthy of All Acceptation*.[19] In his preface Fuller candidly listed the various influences which prompted him to write what he knew would be a controversial work.

1) Reading the missionary exploits of John Eliot and David Brainerd, missionaries to the American Indians. Their apostolic witness to the heathen was forceful and indiscriminate—all needed to be saved.

2) A respected friend's view of unbelief as willful rejection of the revealed truth of God.

3) His own personal deliberate conclusion that the opposite of unbelief was a sure 'persuasion of the truth of what God has said' in his Word.

4) Reaction to Sandemanianism that faith is only a general or formal assent to Christian doctrine. And probably most decisive, was the influence of

5) Jonathan Edwards's *Freedom of the Will* in which Edwards made a distinction between natural and moral ability. Fuller 'found much satisfaction in this distinction'.[20]

Fuller also listed seven premises which would form the structure of his argument. Wisely, he juxtaposed them against those positions he held in common with his fellow Particular Baptists:

International Baptist Studies (Studies in Baptist History and Thought, 1; Carlisle: Paternoster Press, 2002), pp. 118–22, where, p. 121, he writes: 'From the mid-1790s on, Fuller regularly used governmental language in describing the atonement.' A similar problem exists in Fuller's attempt to explain imputation as figurative, rather than 'proper or real'. But, again, his comments must be taken in the context of opposition to hyper-Calvinists, some of whom made of Christ an *actual* guilty criminal and the justified sinner a possessor of inherent, rather than imputed, righteousness. Fuller's mistake was in his unfortunate use of terms, not in teaching heresy. Among those who are critical of Fuller's doctrine are William Rushton, *A Defense of Particular Redemption, wherein the doctrine of Andrew Fuller relative to the Atonement of Christ is tried by the Word of God* (Elon College, NC: Primitive Publications, rev. edn, 1973), and George M. Ella, *Law and Gospel in the Theology of Andrew Fuller* (Durham: Go Publications, 1996). Although not without its problems, a plausible explanation in support of Fuller's orthodoxy may be found in Nettles, *By His Grace and For His Glory*, pp. 121–30.

19   The full title is *The Gospel Worthy of All Acceptation, or the Duty of Sinners to Believe in Jesus Christ*. The first edition was published in 1785 and the second revised edition appeared in 1801. If Carey's *Enquiry Into the Obligations of Christians to Use Means for the Conversion of the Heathen* (1792) was the ethical impetus for the missions movement, Fuller's *Gospel Worthy* was the doctrinal basis for it. Whereas Fuller made it a duty for sinners to accept the gospel, Carey obligated Christians to take the gospel to them.

20   From the 1801 edition of *Gospel Worthy* in *The Complete Works of the Rev. Andrew Fuller with a Memoir of His Life* (ed. Andrew Gunton Fuller; London: Henry G. Bohn, 1856), p. 151. Hereafter this edition will simply be referred to as *Works*.

1) His argument was not against unconditional election, the cause of salvation, but the cause of damnation—man's own unwillingness to be saved. Man is an unbeliever because 'he will be so'.

2) Only the redeemed are entitled to the blessings of the gospel; the unredeemed are presently under the curse of sin.

3) 'The question is not whether men are bound to do any thing more than the law requires, but whether the law, as the invariable standard of right and wrong, does not require every man cordially to embrace whatever God reveals', beginning with the greatest commandment of loving God wholeheartedly.

4) 'The question is not whether men are required to believe any more than is reported in the gospel, or any thing that is not true; but whether that which is reported ought not to be believed with all the heart, and whether this be not saving faith.'

5) And surely the crux of his entire argument: 'It is no part of the controversy whether unconverted sinners be able to turn to God, and to embrace the gospel; but what kind of inability they lie under with respect to these exercises; whether it consists in the want of natural powers and advantages, or merely in the want of a heart to make a right use of them.'[21]

6) It is not an issue as to the requirement of faith for justification, but whether or not faith is the divinely 'appointed *means* of salvation'.

7) 'Finally, the question is not whether unconverted sinners be the subjects of exhortation, but whether they ought to be exhorted to perform spiritual duties.'[22]

These positions clearly place Andrew Fuller in the camp of evangelical Calvinism. Yet the hyper-Calvinists would take issue with most of them, building their case on the supposition that, since man is incapable of responding to the gospel, that is, he *cannot* be saved, then he is not duty bound to obey it. Faith, therefore, is not a duty, it is only and absolutely a supernatural gift. Otherwise, saving faith is the work of a dead man. Nettles states that, unlike Hussey and Brine, Gill did consider it the duty of lost persons to be saved; in other words, Gill taught duty faith. However (and Nettles admits this), the duty is in the obligation of the unregenerate to receive the revelation they hear, not in the minister to *offer* them the gospel. Nettles writes of Gill: 'Although no minister has the authority to offer salvation to any,... "yet they may preach the gospel of salvation to all men, and declare, that whosoever believes shall be saved..." The relation between an "offer of grace" and the proclamation

---

21 With this premise Fuller advances what I believe is a false assumption. He suggests that in order for man to be obligated to accept the gospel he must have the ability to do so. It is this issue that I plan to address in the following pages.

22 *Works*, p. 151.

of the gospel is another important aspect of understanding Gill.'[23] Indeed, it is! According to Gill, ministers can only preach the gospel, not offer it to their listeners. That distinction is exactly what Fuller was combating. It can be further clarified by George's two citations from Gill. The *first* quote is from an admonition to young ministers to 'preach the gospel of salvation to all men'. George then compares this to a *second* comment by Gill, a charge to an ordination candidate: 'Some sensible to sin and danger,...are crying out, What shall we do to be saved? You are to observe, and point out Christ...to them... Your work is to lead men, under a sense of sin and guilt, to the blood of Christ.'[24] But for Gill these statements have two entirely different applications: the first has to do with preaching the gospel to all men, the second with offering it to those who are *sensible* to it, that is, the elect. Oliver's observation of this difference is a very important one, in that it helps explain how Gill can be 'evangelistic' and at the same time hyper-Calvinistic.[25] If this distinction between indiscriminate preaching and limited offer is not made then we have Gill in a gross contradiction. Gill was *not* teaching duty faith in the same sense as Fuller. Indeed, Fuller was combating the very thing Gill was advocating.[26] Fuller believed that on his side was the strongest defense of all—the argument of Scripture wherein all unregenerate men are constantly exhorted to trust in a living Savior. Fuller did not endear himself to the Gill camp when he added: 'If, therefore, there be any professors of Christianity who question the propriety of this, and who would have nothing said to them, except that, "if they be elected they will be called," they are not to be reasoned with, but rebuked, as setting themselves in direct opposition to the word of God.'[27] He then proceeded to remove any possible doubt as to his final intention:

> The greater part of those who may differ from the author on these subjects, it is presumed, will admit the propriety of sinners being exhorted to duty; only this duty

---

23 Nettles, *By His Grace and For His Glory*, pp. 99–100.

24 George, 'John Gill', pp. 93–94.

25 See Oliver's review, 'By His Grace and For His Glory', pp. 31–32; cf. Nettles, *By His Grace and for His Glory*, pp. 94–97.

26 What is interesting is that, while Gill rests his argument on the particularist view of the atonement, Fuller's full offer/full obligation view is based on a provisionally unlimited atonement. The difference can be understood this way: Gill—if Christ died only for the elect, then one should not offer the gospel indiscriminately; Fuller—if Christ died effectually for the elect but sufficiently for the whole world, then we can and should offer the gospel to everyone.

27 *Works*, p. 152. No doubt Fuller had in mind in his second edition of the *Gospel Worthy* the now famous response to Carey's proposal to take the gospel to the heathen nations at a Northampton ministers meeting in 1787. John Ryland, Sr., replied, 'Young man, sit down! When God pleases to convert the heathen, He will do it without your aid or mine.'

must, as they suppose, be confined to merely natural exercises, or such as may be complied with by a carnal heart, destitute of the love of God. It is one design of the following pages to show that God requires the heart, the whole heart, and nothing but the heart; that, instead of its being true that sinners are obliged to perform duties which have no spirituality in them, there are no such duties to be performed; and that, so far from their being exhorted to every thing excepting what is spiritually good, they are exhorted to nothing else. The Scriptures undoubtedly require them to read, to hear, to repent, and to pray, that their sins may be forgiven them. It is not, however, in the exercise of a carnal, but of a spiritual state of mind, that these duties are performed.[28]

What constitutes a major difference between Fuller and the hyper-Calvinists is that he believed that the general call, not the effectual call, required the duty to respond to the gospel. Only the effectual call enabled one to do so. In Part I of his treatise, Fuller seeks to prove this from such Scripture passages as John 20.31 and 1 Peter 2.7. To those who would regard the obligation of sinners to believe the gospel a subject of little importance, Fuller countered that the very intent of gospel promulgation is that men 'should believe that Jesus is the Christ, the Son of God, and, believing, have life through his name'. 'If believing be a commandment, it cannot be one of the *least*.'[29] Believing on Christ is not merely an offer but an obligation. To Fuller revelation itself is tantamount to commandment, and therefore revelation includes obligation. He reasoned 'that [if] it is the duty of every man to believe what God reveals', then every man has the duty to accept the gospel, especially since this is God's *greatest* revelation.[30] This allows him to utilize gospel offer passages in the Bible as scriptural injunctions (e.g., Jn 3.16; 12.36; Rom. 10.9). Duty faith is the constant refrain throughout *The Gospel Worthy* and it forms the heart of 'Fullerism'.

What Constitutes Saving Faith?

Fuller rightly states that salvific faith is not primarily concerned with personal security or happiness, but its grand object, Jesus Christ and his glory. 'It is the peculiar property of true faith to endear Christ.'[31] He also refutes the hyper-Calvinist view that there must be an obvious 'warrant' or interest in salvation by the elect prior to conversion. Such a warrant would amount to a type of prevenient grace before saving

---

28 *Works*, p. 152. This paragraph is the summary thesis of Fuller's entire work, the *Gospel Worthy*.
29 *Works*, p. 152. All italicized words in Fuller's quotations are his own.
30 *Works*, p. 152.
31 *Works*, p. 153.

grace.³² 'The gospel contains no *gift* or *grant* to mankind in general... It warrants every sinner to believe in Christ for salvation, but no one to conclude himself interested in salvation till he has believed; consequently, such a conclusion, even where it is well-founded, cannot be faith, but that which follows it.'³³ Fuller identifies faith quite specifically. He admits of Abraham Booth's definition that 'faith in Christ [is] a *dependence* on him, a *receiving* him, a *coming* to him and *trusting in him* for salvation'. But this is not precise enough for Fuller. He prefers to see these elements not as integral to faith, but as 'immediate effects of faith itself'.³⁴ And this leads us to a second consideration: what constitutes saving faith for Fuller? Faith is, first of all, an activity of the mind—an active, not a passive, mind. He bases this on Hebrews 11.6. 'Here are three different exercises of the mind: First, believing *that God is*; Secondly, believing that he is *a rewarder of them that diligently seek him*; Thirdly, *coming* to him: and the last is represented as the effect of the former two. The same may be applied to Christ.'³⁵ Fuller prefers the term *trust* to capture the essence of saving faith. This term is best adapted 'to express the confidence which the soul reposes in Christ for the fulfillment of his *promises*'.³⁶ Fuller argues that trust has an essential relation to revealed truth. To call into question, or in this case to not believe, God's revelation is to impugn the integrity of his promises. 'And from hence it will follow, that trusting in Christ, no less than crediting his testimony, is the *duty* of every sinner to whom the revelation is made,'³⁷ Warrant, then, for Fuller is the gospel offer itself, which makes incumbent an obligation to be saved, not evidence that one will be saved.

But secondly, if faith is a duty, it must be exercised in a way pleasing to God; this demands that it be godly. 'God requires nothing of intelligent creatures but what is holy.'³⁸ If it is holy, then it will be genuine faith, and sufficient to carry us to heaven. By identifying faith this way, Fuller is combating the error of Sandemanianism, espoused by Scottish Baptist Alexander McLean, who taught that faith is a mere profession, or intellectual assent to the gospel. Saving faith must be holy in nature, that is, there must be a godly disposition of the heart for it to be genuine. This active inclination of the heart is wrought supernaturally by the gracious work of the Holy Spirit which gives glory to God. To be a holy

---

32   It is this kind of reasoning by the hyper-Calvinists that places them ironically in agreement with the Arminians! Fuller frequently takes advantage of this paradoxical relationship to prove that hyper-Calvinists are in reality *pseudo*-Calvinists.
33   *Works*, p. 153.
34   *Works*, p. 156.
35   *Works*, p. 156.
36   *Works*, p. 156.
37   *Works*, p. 156.
38   *Works*, p. 180.

propensity it must necessarily include repentance, 'for repentance without faith could not please God'.[39]

Finally, the only way for faith to be holy is for God through his Word to regenerate the heart prior to believing; regeneration must precede faith. He writes,

> The...question is in what *order* these things are caused. Whether the Holy Spirit causes the mind, while carnal, to discern and believe spiritual things, and thereby renders it spiritual; or whether he imparts a holy susceptibility and relish for the truth, in consequence of which we discern its glory, and embrace it. The latter appears to me to be the truth. The following are the principal grounds on which I embrace it.[40]

Fuller then proceeds to lay out his reasons for regeneration preceding faith and repentance:

1) 'The Scriptures represent the dominion of sin in the heart as *utterly inconsistent* with a spiritual perception and belief of the gospel... Hence it will follow that the Holy Spirit must remove the obstacle of unbelief, so that spiritual things may be spiritually discerned.'

2) 'Though holiness is frequently ascribed in the Scriptures to a spiritual perception of the truth, yet that...perception itself...is ascribed to the influence of the Holy Spirit upon the heart: "The Lord *opened the heart* of Lydia, and she attended to the things which were spoken of Paul".' In addition, Fuller cites as proof texts 2 Cor. 4.6, 1 Jn 2.27, and 1 Jn 2.20.

3) 'Every thing which proves spiritual perception and faith to be holy exercises also proves that a change of heart must of necessity precede them, as no holy exercise can have place while the heart is under the dominion of carnality.'[41]

Faith, then, is the effect of the spiritual influence of God upon the heart, which influence (i.e., regeneration) enables the carnal heart to have a holy sensibility toward God. If otherwise, Fuller contends, we have the absurdity of an *ungodly believer*. Yet, in the final analysis, 'the truth appears to be, these things [regeneration and faith] are inseparable; and when promises are made to one, it is as connected with the other. The priority contended for is rather in order of nature than of time... No sooner is the heart turned towards Christ [by regeneration] than Christ is embraced [in faith].'[42]

---

39   *Works*, p. 181.
40   *Works*, p. 187.
41   *Works*, pp. 187-88.
42   *Works*, p. 189.

The Scripture Calls Faith a Duty

In Part II of *The Gospel Worthy*, Fuller seeks to prove duty faith by calling upon Scripture passages that command belief. Psalm 2, clearly a messianic passage, tells rulers of the heathen (i.e., the nations or Gentiles) to 'serve the Lord with fear, and rejoice with trembling: kiss the Son, lest he be angry, and ye perish from the way... [B]lessed are all they that put their trust in him (vv.11–12). This instruction includes not only the promise of blessing to all the nations who accept the Lord's Anointed, but it explicitly commands that they *should* do so, and includes a severe warning for any who reject him. In Acts 4.27, Herod and Pontius Pilate are singled out as representatives of kings and rulers who had taken their stand against the Lord (Ps. 2.2). They should therefore be included as objects of the psalmist's warning to 'kiss' (literally, do homage) to the Son, which can mean nothing less than 'to be reconciled to him, to embrace his word and ordinances, and bow to his sceptre'.[43] Here then is a specific case of unconverted sinners being commanded to believe in Christ for salvation, plainly a spiritual duty. Fuller then turns to two other Old Testament passages, Isaiah 55.1-7 and Jeremiah 6.16. Isaiah proclaims: 'Let the wicked forsake his way, and the unrighteous man his thoughts: and let him return unto the Lord, and he will have mercy upon him; and to our God, for he will abundantly pardon.' Fuller concludes that this is the language of divine invitation to the unregenerate, an invitation which implies an obligation to accept it. Likewise, Jeremiah insists that ungodly men walk in 'the good way', the same way in which the godly patriarchs walked, which was the way of faith in the promised Messiah.[44]

Fuller then directs his readers to the New Testament, which 'is still more explicit than the Old' in the matter of duty faith.[45] John 12.36, for example, is Christ's address to a group of unbelievers to 'believe in the light, that ye may be the children of light'. The 'light' to which he refers is himself, as indicated in the context: 'I am come a light into the world' (v. 46). Compliance with his invitation would have resulted in them becoming 'children of light', that is, true believers in Christ. Another instance Fuller cites is John 6.29: 'This is the work of God, that ye believe on him whom he hath sent.' Those whom the Lord addresses are unbelievers (v. 36) who follow him out of greed, 'because ye did eat of the loaves, and were filled' (v. 26). He knows their mercenary motives and exhorts them instead to 'labor not for the meat which perisheth, but for that meat which endureth unto everlasting life, which the Son of man

---

43   *Works*, p. 157.
44   *Works*, p. 157.
45   *Works*, p. 158.

shall give unto you' (v. 27). When these unbelievers ask Christ what they can do to 'work the works of God' (v. 28), his answer is to believe on him whom God has sent (v. 29). Here is an indiscriminate offer of eternal life to unregenerate sinners based on the sole condition of simple faith in the Son.

John Gill, on the other hand, had taken quite a different approach to duty faith passages. Peter Naylor notes a 'puzzling feature' of Gill's idea of faith and repentance in explaining such passages as John 5.34 ('but these things I say, that ye might be saved'), and Ezekiel 18.30-31 ('repent...cast away...your transgression...and make you a new heart and a new spirit'). According to Gill, since it is not in the power of man to effect genuine faith and repentance, what he calls 'evangelical repentance', these scriptural exhortations must refer to 'legal repentance', a kind of national or social reformation. Even more strained is Gill's treatment of Acts 3.19—'Repent ye, therefore, and be converted.' While insisting correctly that this passage does not suppose repentance and conversion lay in the power of men, he completely negates the intent of its message by suggesting that 'the conversion here pressed unto us is not an internal conversion of the soul to God...but an outward reformation of life'.[46] In instance after instance Gill distorts the plain meaning of duty faith passages to fit his system. This fallacy of legal repentance fell under the censure of Fuller. To him, there are no duties required by God that were not spiritual; rather, all duties were to be performed in 'a spiritual state of mind... [A]ll the precepts of the Bible are only the different modes in which we are required to express love to him [God].' Unregenerate sinners, then, are constantly exhorted to evangelical faith and repentance, that is, that which is 'spiritually good'.[47] While Fuller allows Gill the courtesy of establishing his [Fuller's] principles 'when his system was out of sight',[48] the problem is that Gill's opposing principles were obviously the focus of his biblical hermeneutics. All in all, Fuller proved to be the better exegete.

In concert with Gill, the hyper-Calvinist John Brine had complained that declaring to unregenerate sinners the necessity of belief for salvation is far short of making it a duty. Fuller responded that if believing were an act pleasing to God, and pleasing God by believing was necessary and acceptable to God, how could it be otherwise than a duty? As evidence, he cited John 5.23—'The Father hath committed all judgment unto the Son, that all men should honour the Son, even as they honour the Father. He that honoureth not the Son honoureth not the Father which hath sent him.' Fuller contended that it is impossible to honor the Son if we reject

---

46 Naylor, *Picking Up a Pin*, pp. 167–68.
47 *Works*, p. 152; cf. Naylor, *Picking Up a Pin*, p. 194.
48 *Works*, p. 163.

his offices and neglect his salvation.⁴⁹ Duty faith is further illustrated in the case of Simon Magus, a man unquestionably unregenerate and having no 'warrant' of election, yet Peter admonished him to 'repent and pray to the Lord, if perhaps the thought of his heart might be forgiven him'. His warrant was simply to receive Christ and it would be a sin if he did not, 'for all disobedience consists in a breach of duty'.⁵⁰ The question remains as to whether Simon *could* not repent and receive Christ or that he *would* not. Fuller's answer to this question was perhaps the most controversial issue in his soteriology, and is the moral crux of the modern question of duty faith.

Jonathan Edwards and Dichotomous Ability

In order to make men fully responsible for their duty to accept Christ, Fuller borrowed Jonathan Edwards's principle of dichotomous (moral versus natural) ability. Edwards was posing this doctrine in the context of his opposition to the Arminianism of John Taylor of Norwich, who rejected the Reformed belief of the imputation of Adam's sin to his posterity. The denial of immediate imputation of Adam's guilt (original sin) in favor of mediate imputation is basic to Arminian semi-Pelagian anthropology. To Taylor, Adam's sin had only natural, not moral or penal consequences. Edwards countered with just the opposite view. natural man was morally corrupt, and faced the consequences of his inherent moral depravity, but his natural (mental and physical) faculties remained unchanged by the fall. However, in opposing Arminian indeterminism, Edwards did not want to resort to fatalism and deprive man of free agency. His solution was moral determinism. Man will always choose that which is selfish and sinful because of a fixed moral inclination to do so as the result of original sin. Edwards kept fallen man's freedom intact by defining it as ability to choose without natural necessity to do otherwise.⁵¹

Perhaps a further explanation of how Edwards arrived at his principle of dichotomous ability will help us understand Fuller's own argument, which he claimed was derived from Edwards. Upon his removal in 1750 from Northampton to Stockbridge, Massachusetts, Edwards began writing some of his most important theological work. One of his very first treatises, published in November 1752 as *Misrepresentations Corrected*, was a refutation of his cousin's understanding of church membership. Solomon Williams insisted that 'at the level of "moral sincerity" the

---

49   *Works*, p. 158.
50   *Works*, pp. 158–60.
51   The concept of natural necessity will be further explained below.

unregenerate can consent to the gospel and that this can be an effective step to their receiving the grace of God'. Such were acceptable as church members.[52] Edwards rightly answered that this view undermines the doctrine of conversion and gives the communicant a false sense of security. Edwards saw in Williams's teaching a crediting of the unregenerate with ability to be accepted before a holy God—the old heresy of Pelagius.[53] This was the immediate catalyst for Edwards to write what many consider his most important theological work, *A Careful and Strict Inquiry into the Modern Prevailing Notions of that Freedom of Will which is supposed to be Essential to Moral Agency* or simply, *Freedom of the Will* (1754).[54] The purpose of the treatise was to explain that the doctrine of human responsibility was scriptural, that 'necessity—the determination of the human will...—is not inconsistent with a reasonable concept of freedom or moral accountability'.[55] Edwards wanted to 'demolish any suggestion that the human will is "self-determined" or possessing within itself its own autonomous power of deliberating [or] choosing'. The Arminian doctrine of belief in man's ability to determine his own will is unscriptural.[56]

The problem Edwards attempted to address is a perennial one and crucial to soteriology: if man is without power to repent and turn to God, how can he be held responsible for remaining in sin? If human inability is true, so it seems, then man is no longer a free agent but acts under compulsion. Edwards's answer is that man is free in the sense of possessing the faculties of moral agency—mind, will, emotion (which Edwards assimilates into 'affections')—and is therefore a responsible agent. However, man is incapable of spiritual good because of the constitutional disposition of those faculties—they are inherently and thoroughly corrupt.[57] The acts of man's will are always dictated by his

---

52   Iain Murray, *Jonathan Edwards: A New Biography* (Edinburgh: Banner of Truth Trust, 1987), p. 424.

53   This view closely resembles the Roman Catholic doctrine of condign merit.

54   One of the most insightful interpretations of Edwards's *Freedom of the Will* is C. Samuel Storms, 'Jonathan Edwards on the Freedom of the Will,' *Trinity Journal* 3 (Fall, 1982), pp. 144–45. An expansion of this article may be found in chapter 4 of Storm's more comprehensive work, *Tragedy in Eden: Original Sin in the Theology of Jonathan Edwards* (Lanham, MD: University Press of America, 1985), pp. 151–290.

55   Allen C. Guelzo, 'The Return of the Will', in Sang Hyun Lee and Allen Guelzo (eds), *Edwards in Our Time: Jonathan Edwards and the Shaping of American Religion* (Grand Rapids, MI: Eerdmans, 1999), p. 89.

56   Guelzo, 'The Return of the Will', p. 89. Cf. Storms, 'Jonathan Edwards on the Freedom of the Will', pp. 148–56.

57   When Edwards speaks of the freedom of the will, he is actually speaking of the freedom of the willer, since the will is not indigenously free, see Conrad Cherry, *The Theology of Jonathan Edwards: A Reappraisal* (Bloomington: Indiana University Press, 1990), p. 132.

moral disposition. 'The will, in every instance, acts by moral necessity... A man is truly morally unable to choose contrary to a present inclination.'[58] Man's choices are determined by his fallen nature. This inability, says Edwards, is thoroughly consistent with accountability wherein man's 'exceeding guilt and sinfulness in the sight of God most fundamentally and mainly consist'.[59] Man will never 'will' to be pleasing to God and love Him until God first acts upon him. Regeneration was God's act; man's acts were repentance and faith. Until or unless God acted man would not. Edwards completely exploded the Pelagian notion that somehow man could apprehend God by works.

However, Edwards stops short of saying man 'cannot' come to Christ because of his allowance for natural ability.[60] The bondage of man is voluntary—'he *will* not be saved'. Edwards writes: 'We may learn the reason why natural men will not come to Christ: they *do* not come because they *will* not come.' Man has the natural capacity to make free choices: 'the will is plainly, that by which the mind chooses anything', so that 'an act of the will is the same as an act of choosing or choice'. Assuming that there is nothing extrinsic to man compelling him in his choices (what Edwards calls natural necessity), he is volitionally free. Liberty is simply 'being free from hindrance and impediment in the way of doing', so that 'let the person come by his volition or choice how he will, yet, if he is able, and there is nothing in the way to hinder his pursuing and executing his will, the man is fully and perfectly free, according to the primary and common notion of freedom'.[61] Freedom, then, is the absence of whatever is extrinsic to my will that would compel me to do otherwise.

Man has a will that can choose. He is by nature a volitional being. He can make right choices if he wills to do so. However, he will not make the right choices because of moral corruption. The fall made him morally but not naturally corrupt, according to Edwards. There is '*no other necessity* of sinning than a moral necessity'.[62] There is true choice but never contrary choice, that is, contrary to the inclinations. Otherwise, if man is naturally unable to choose the good, then he cannot be found guilty of sin. He cannot say before the judgment seat, 'I could not

---

58 Edwards, *Freedom of the Will*, in *The Works of Jonathan Edwards* (2 vols; Edinburgh: Banner of Truth Trust, reprint edn, 1974), I, p. 50, hereafter cited as *Edwards's Works*.

59 *Edwards's Works*, p. 52.

60 In fairness to Edwards, he never states in *Freedom of the Will* that man possesses natural ability. This is inferred from his denial of natural inability.

61 Edwards, *Freedom of the Will*, in *The Works of Jonathan Edwards* (ed. Paul Ramsey; New Haven: Yale University Press, 1957–), I, pp. 163–64.

62 Edwards, *Freedom of the Will*, in *Works of Jonathan Edwards* I, p. 432.

respond to the truth.' He will have to admit, 'I would not respond to it.'⁶³ His will, to be free, cannot be coerced either toward sin or righteousness, but it is determined by motive, which, again, is morally corrupt. And so practically speaking, and Edwards admits this elsewhere, man has two wills—the rational will and the will of the appetite.⁶⁴ 'Our first parents were...perfectly free agents with respect to their rational will; the inclinations, which we call appetites, were not above, did not keep it [sic] in subjection.'⁶⁵ The rational will had 'sufficient' but not 'efficient' grace to prevent the will of the appetite to be exercised in disobedience.

No amount of natural ability can save a soul because of the moral impossibility to do so. 'Hence we may learn that *it is impossible for men to convert themselves* by their own strength and industry, with only a concurring assistance helping in the exercise of their natural abilities and principles of the soul, and securing their improvement.'⁶⁶ We have no final ability 'to make ourselves holy or work any holy inclination or affections or exert any one holy act any more than a dead body can raise itself to life'.⁶⁷ ''Tis entirely in man's power to submit to Jesus Christ as a Saviour if he will, but the thing is, it never will be he should will it, except that God works it in him: It depends on will not on power. Many things are in our power that are impossible because of our disposition.'⁶⁸ However, by suggesting that man is morally but not naturally incapable, Edwards appears to be teaching partial depravity.⁶⁹ If Edwards only

---

63   Pelagians, like Finney, would say that natural man *should* (moral duty) and *can* respond (natural and moral ability).

64   Edwards, Misc. 436, *Works of Jonathan Edwards*, XIII, p. 484.

65   Edwards, Misc. 436, *Works of Jonathan Edwards*, XIII, p. 485.

66   Edwards, *Treatise on Grace*, pp. 37–38, cited in John Gerstner, *Rational Biblical Theology of Jonathan Edwards* (3 vols; Powhatan, VA: Berea Publications, 1991–93), II, p. 355.

67   Edwards, unpublished MS sermon on Rom. 5.6, cited in Gerstner, *Rational Biblical Theology of Jonathan Edwards*, II, p. 356.

68   Edwards, Misc. 710, cited in Gerstner, *Rational Biblical Theology of Jonathan Edwards*, II, p. 271.

69   Gary Long, 'The Doctrine of Original Sin in the New England Theology from Jonathan Edwards to Edwards Amasa Park' (ThD dissertation, Dallas Theological Seminary, 1972), p. 64, n. 4, disagrees that Edwards's distinction between natural ability and moral inability locks him into partial depravity. 'Though Edwards did distinguish natural ability from moral inability, he meant nothing by it than the fact that man, in the fall, did not lose any of his constitutional faculties—a truth maintained by all Reformed theologians... Shedd, one of the best theological interpreters of Edwards, says that "natural *ability* for Edwards, is the possession of the requisite mental faculties viewed *apart* from their moral state and condition."... It is not denied that Edwards' abstract distinction between natural ability and moral inability has led to ambiguity among those who professedly followed him.' Long, however, does not cite Shedd accurately. After the single comment Long mentions above, Shedd adds, 'In so viewing them [man's faculties]

cracked open the doorway of human ability, the New Divinity men opened it wider until Nathaniel Taylor took the door of inability off its hinges and cast it aside.

Did Edwards really teach *partial* depravity? In his treatise on *Original Sin* and elsewhere he boldly declares for *total* depravity.

> They [unregenerate men] are totally corrupt, in every part, in all their faculties; in all the principles of their nature, their understanding, and wills; and in all their dispositions and affections. Their heads, their hearts, are totally depraved; all the members of their bodies are only instruments of sin; and all their senses, seeing, hearing, tasting, &c. are only inlets and outlets of sin, channels of corruption.[70]

Such a statement seems to leave no room for partial depravity. Then why make a distinction between moral and natural ability at all? Shedd explains:

> The real question is, whether the sinner can originate the 'thing that is wanting' in order to obedience: namely, 'a being willing,' or a disposition to obey. Edwards always and everywhere asserts that he cannot; but for the purpose of meeting the objection that if the sinner is unable to obey he is not obligated to obey, he contends that it is improper to call the inability to 'be willing' or inclined, an inability, because the mere existence of the faculty of will without the power to change its disposition constitutes ability. 'To ascribe a non-performance,' says Edwards, 'in these things, to the want of power is not just; because the thing wanting is not a being able, but a being willing. There are faculties of mind, and a capacity of nature, and everything sufficient but a *disposition*.' But the absence of a disposition to obey is fatal.[71]

Edwards maintains natural ability because he wants to make each man *personally* responsible for his own sin. Man will never be able to say, 'I could not respond to the gospel.' Natural ability gives man a choice; moral inability determines what choices he will make—the wrong ones. What Edwards did not want to do is to give any room for man excusing himself from turning to Christ because he *could* not do so.

> It is no excuse, that you cannot receive Christ of yourself, unless you *would* if you could... Certainly if persons would not if they could, it is just the same thing as to

---

he [Edwards] differs from the elder Calvinists, who regarded a mental faculty and its moral condition as inseparable. Edwards conceives of the will abstractly and separate from its inclination, and as so conceived contends that it is 'naturally able' to obey the law of God. The elder Calvinists denied that the will can be so conceived of'. See William G.T. Shedd, *Dogmatic Theology* (3 vols; Grand Rapids, MI: Zondervan Publishing House, reprint edn, 1969), II, p. 220, cf. 219–29.

    70   Edwards, Discourse IV: 'The Justice of God in the Damnation of Sinners,' in *Edwards's Works*, I, p. 670.

    71   Shedd, *Dogmatic Theology*, II, p. 223.

the blame that lies upon them, whether they can or cannot. If you were willing, and then found that you could not, your being unable would alter the case, and might be some excuse; because then the defect would not be in your will, but only in your ability. But as long as you *will* not, it is no matter, whether you have ability or no ability... If you are not willing to accept Christ, it follows that you have no sincere willingness to be willing.[72]

What, then, is the answer to the objection why man is to blame for what he cannot do? 'Men are under no such inability to any moral good required of them as is owing to any defect in the capacity of their nature.'[73] Again, 'No man is condemned properly not because he is unable but because he is unwilling.'[74]

Because Edwards was so adamantly opposed to any form of human indeterminism and autosoterism and because he strongly affirmed total depravity in *Original Sin*, some theologians have argued that he should not have ever written *Freedom of the Will*.[75] He did not need to; the former treatise was sufficient to combat Arminianism. Positing a dichotomy between natural and moral ability only served to create confusion among interpreters of Edwards. In attempting to resolve the difficulty and perhaps risking the charge of presumption, Gerstner proposes that what we end up with in Edwards is no real dichotomy at all, but a compatibility.

> Edwards' assertion notwithstanding,...in his thought moral inability is a natural inability. His whole psychology is based on the fact that we must have an inclination in order to choose in a particular way. His doctrine of the fall and the complete obliteration of the moral image in man means that the inclination to virtue has been totally erased. That is the same thing as to say man no longer has any natural ability to incline to God. Edwards keeps insisting that he does have a natural ability 'if he will.' But the 'if he will' implies if he is inclined, but he cannot incline without an inclination. This inclination is totally lacking according to Edward's own view of man the sinner.[76]

Fuller's Inability/Ability Doctrine

Whereas Edwards was attempting to guard Calvinist orthodoxy against Arminianism, Fuller was arguing his case for moral necessity on two

---

72 *Edwards's Works*, p. 676.
73 Edwards, unpublished MS sermon on Rom. 5.6, cited in Gerstner, *Rational Biblical Theology of Jonathan Edwards*, II, p. 356.
74 Edwards, unpublished MS sermon on Rom. 5.6.
75 Cf. Storms, 'Jonathan Edwards on the Freedom of the Will', p. 141.
76 Gerstner, *Rational Biblical Theology of Jonathan Edwards*, II, p. 357.

fronts: against the hyper-Calvinists on the one hand (represented by the followers of Gill and Brine) and the Arminians on the other hand (represented by Dan Taylor, leader of the New Connexion General Baptists). And whereas Edwards appears to have been influenced by Williams Ames's dichotomous arrangement of theology (which Ames called technometry) in his *Marrow of Theology* (..date..),[77] Fuller was persuaded by both Edwards and Edwards's pupil, Joseph Bellamy, to accept the moral inability/natural ability model.[78] What both Edwards and Fuller were combating was essentially the same thing: the antinomian element of the modern question, that is, 'if there be no power in fallen man to keep the divine law there is no obligation to keep it'.[79] In order to disprove this premise, Fuller adapted Edwards's dichotomous ability model as a basis for his validation of duty faith.

Guiding Fuller's thought in much of his argumentation is the concept that all virtue consists of benevolence (or unselfish love, a prominent feature of New England theology), and sin is the absence of benevolence. Such statements as the following appear frequently in *The Gospel Worthy*: 'It is owing to a want of love to God that any man continue impenitent or unbelieving.'[80] It is due to man's unwillingness to love

---

77 Edwards often began with the thought of William Ames. For example, he found Ames' discussion of assurance and true humility in worship in *Cases of Conscience* (1639) to be helpful in his writing of *A Treatise Concerning Religious Affections* (Part II, Section XI and Part III, Section X). His principle of dichotomous ability in *Freedom of the Will* could very well have been influenced by Ames.

78 Michael Haykin, 'Andrew Fuller (1754–1815) and the Free Offer of the Gospel', *Reformation Today* 182 (July–August, 2001), p. 25, calls this distinction a *physical* ability versus a moral inability, because Fuller himself equates the natural and physical. Fuller considers man's rational processes (intelligence, reasoning, etc.) as essential elements of man's physical/natural divinely created being. He evidently follows Edwards by including the understanding as part of 'natural' (apart from 'moral') man. But it appears that Fuller fails to properly distinguish the mind as part of man's immaterial being (his soul), not his material (i.e., natural) body. This underscores a major flaw in the dichotomous ability model. No one would disagree that the natural man has physical abilities, but to include rational powers as part of them is to make the soul corporeal; man does not think with his body, but with his mind or soul. Moreover, this mind, while able to think rationally, cannot comprehend divine revelation. The natural understanding does place limitations on the will because it, too, is corrupted by original sin. If not, then man is only partially depraved. Man has rational ability but not when it comes to spiritual perception. One may note this distinction in a comparison of Rom. 1 with 1 Cor. 2. Man is capable of knowing God's truth, indeed, is responsible for it (Rom. 1.18-20), but he cannot understand its *significance* (1 Cor. 2.14) because of a *reprobate* mind (Rom. 1.24-32). Fuller, *Works*, p. 202; cf. p. 208, admits that the man of 1 Cor. 2.14 cannot receive spiritual truth but only because he is carnally, not naturally, depraved.

79 Shedd, *Dogmatic Theology*, II, p. 222.

80 *Works*, p. 161.

God, not any natural inability, that indicts him. In quoting John McLaurin's[81] *Essay on Grace* (1755), Fuller agrees that 'Where it [love] does not beget conviction, it is not owing to the weakness of men's capacities; but the strength of their prejudices and prepossessions.'[82] To Fuller, 'whatever is not a sinner's duty, the omission of it cannot be charged on him as a sin, nor imputed to any depravity in him'.[83] It follows, therefore, that the duty of loving God requires ability in order for man to be held accountable. He further argues that if the inability of sinners to believe in Christ (a virtual equivalent of loving God) be likened to the impossibility of a corpse to rise up and walk, 'it were absurd to suppose that they would...fall under the Divine censure'.[84] Here I must take exception with Fuller. The Bible states that this is precisely what sinners are—dead in trespasses and sins, according to Ephesians 2.1. Fuller states that 'no man is reproved for not doing that which is naturally impossible',[85] and yet Paul clearly tells us that dead sinners are under the wrath of God and deserving of his punishment (vv. 2–3). It is as much a miracle to regenerate a sinner as to resuscitate a corpse. And that is exactly what regeneration is, a monergistic miracle by a sovereign God to enable man to do what is otherwise impossible to do—love God. To allow man any vestige of human ability in salvation is to deny total depravity, the pervasive quality of guilt and sin, and the fact that salvation is totally of divine grace. Fuller, however, reasons that 'if sinners were naturally and absolutely unable to believe in Christ, they would be equally unable to disbelieve; for it requires the same powers to reject as to embrace'.[86] But this argument is a *non sequitur*, and Fuller uses it often. If the unbeliever is unable to believe, it is illogical to suggest that he could have some power to believe. The point is that the unbeliever has no facility to believe since he is wholly in a *state* of unbelief. Being unable to disbelieve (or simply to believe) is not an option in such a state. Using Fuller's line of reasoning we could just as easily say of the Pharisees, a group who would not accept the gospel, that they had at one time in their lives the ability and the willingness to receive it but had now *become* hardened to the point of wanting to reject it. They formerly had the power to believe, but having hardened their hearts, they lost the power. The point is they already stood before a holy God as guilty sinners, never having had any power. Their guilt is only compounded by their rejection

---

81 McLaurin, an evangelical pastor from the Scottish Lowlands, was instrumental in inaugurating the famous 'Concert or Prayer' for revival, beginning in 1744, see Haykin, *One Heart and One Soul*, p. 159.
82 *Works*, p. 161.
83 *Works*, p. 162.
84 *Works*, p. 162.
85 *Works*, p. 162.
86 *Works*, p. 162.

of him. But when did they become guilty? At the time of their rejection? Hardly. They were guilty not from their first moral act, but from conception (Ps. 51.5). To say otherwise is to beg the questions of total depravity and immediate imputation.

Fuller constantly defines sin and unbelief in terms of volitional transgression. Of course, sin is that, and Fuller builds his case on Scripture passages that affirm this, but he either misinterprets or neglects those passages which prove that the reason man will not believe is because he cannot do so. For example, he states that 'a voluntary and judicial blindness, obstinacy, and hardness of heart, are represented as the bar to conversion'. This is true but it fails to consider *original* sin—the sin with which we are all born, the imputed sin of Adam, that *causes* us to willingly commit sinful acts. It also fails to consider the *comprehensiveness* of sin as pervading all of man's faculties, not merely his moral capacity. Fuller goes so far as to say that 'nothing can be sin which is not a breach of duty'.[87] This is dangerously close to Taylorism, that limits sin to voluntary transgression of a known law. Once again, such a statement fails to consider the full implications of original sin. It also helps explain why Fuller tends to view the atonement as righting the moral breach of God's law; sin is limited to a legal offense rather than a product of natural sinfulness.

An Evaluation: Consensus and Dissensus

Fuller writes truly when he tells us that it is the duty of the unregenerate to trust Christ. Paul declares this emphatically in Acts 17.30—'Therefore having overlooked the times of ignorance, God is now declaring to men that all *people* everywhere should repent.'[88] But to suggest that duty requires human ability takes his argument beyond the bounds of orthodoxy, and overlooks the fact that we are all *born* sinners and come into this world having sufficient guilt to condemn us 'because all sinned' in Adam (Rom. 5.12). Andrew Fuller fails to properly acknowledge the *condition* of man due to original imputed sin. It is true that rejecting Christ, compounds man's guilt, but the reason he does not and, in fact, cannot receive Christ is because he comes into the world with the guilt of Adam and inherent moral depravity which has defiled *all* of his faculties, and which prevent him from responding. Is he still responsible even though he cannot respond? Most assuredly he is, and he stands guilty for

---

87   *Works*, p. 163.
88   Scripture citations are from the New American Standard Bible, 1995 update, with the exception of the passages from the Authorized (King James) Version quoted by Fuller. Amazingly, Fuller never once cites Acts 17.30 as a proof text in support of duty faith in *Gospel Worthy*.

not responding. But he became legally guilty when Adam, his federal representative head, sinned in the Garden. It is the doctrine of imputation that is so crucial to understanding man's culpability and his inability to respond to the gospel. And Fuller fails to adequately treat this. He instead falls back on moral inability and defines total depravity only in those terms, which leaves him open to the criticism of teaching partial depravity. But, in fact, we are accountable before a holy God for both original guilt and voluntary sin.[89] To neglect the former in favor of the latter is to make a serious concession to Pelagianism and mediate imputation, which is really no imputation at all. Yet Fuller attempts to rescue himself from such an indictment while answering the claims of Arminianism following the first publication of *The Gospel Worthy*. When Dan Taylor first read it, he thought he had a 'soul mate' in Fuller, and began publishing his sentiments under the pseudonym Philanthropos. Fuller, however, clarified that he was not in agreement with Taylor in a series of replies refuting Taylor's Arminianism. In doing so, Fuller does come out in favor of immediate imputation of Adam's sin to his posterity. Following this, he attempts in Edwardsean fashion to explain what he meant by natural inability in *The Gospel Worthy*:

> The depravity of our hearts is not owing to natural weakness, either of body or mind, nor yet to the want of opportunity to know and glorify God. When we speak of it as being the *sin of our nature*, we use the term in a very different sense from what we do when speaking of *natural* inability. By the *sin of our nature*, we mean not any thing which belongs to our nature as human, but what is, by the fall, so interwoven with it as if it were, though in fact it is not a part of it; and so deeply rooted in our souls as to become *natural*, as it were, to us.[90]

I believe we would be hard pressed to find a better, more orthodox, explanation of man's natural sinful condition than this. Edwards undoubtedly would have concurred. It preserves intact the *imago dei* in man but accounts also for the pervasive and pernicious effects of sin to the point that man is *naturally* a sinner. Yet when we compare this statement with a comment Fuller makes in a letter written in 1795, we find that he has forced himself into a serious contradiction. Fuller is describing total depravity to a friend and suggests correctly that men as

---

89   The justice of God's condemnation of men on the basis of original sin is born out by Zacharias Ursinus's argument, *The Summe of Christian Religion* (1645), Question 8, cited in Shedd, *Dogmatic Theology*, II, p. 222, n. 1: 'Objection 5. They who cannot but sin, are unjustly punished; but the unregenerate cannot but sin: therefore God doth unjustly punish them. Answer: They who necessarily sin are unjustly punished, except that necessity come *voluntarily*, and *by their own will*. But men have drawn upon them that necessity voluntarily in the first parents, and themselves do willingly sin. Therefore, God doth justly punish them.'

90   *Works*, p. 217.

rational beings are accountable for what they do, and are subjects of gospel address. He then adds, 'Nor can it be affirmed with truth that there are no *motives* for them on which they can be exhorted to cease to do evil, or learn to do well; the motives to these things exist in all their native force, independently of the inclination or disinclination of their hearts to comply with them.'[91]

We are left with the question of how can sin be so interwoven and so deeply rooted in our souls as to be *natural* to us and yet allow us to have a motive to respond to the gospel *independent* of the disposition of our hearts. To add to the confusion, Fuller, who has maintained all along that the sinner can but will not turn to Christ, states in the same letter something reminiscent of his own experience as a youth:

> A sinner is exhorted to repent and believe in Christ—he feels hardened in insensibility—he *cannot* repent—he has no desire after Christ. A consciousness of this kind, if it operate according to its native tendency, will lead him to reflect, What a state must I be in! Invited to repent and believe in Christ for the salvation of my soul, and cannot comply! Mine, surely, is the very heart of an infernal![92]

As ministers are we then to appeal to men who are totally depraved and insensible to the truth? Well, yes we are with the expectation that the power of the gospel through the agency of the Holy Spirit will awaken the guilty sinner to the truth we preach. But man's motives, if we can equate them with imaginations or rational powers, are only evil continually. We do not appeal to the motives, we appeal to the estranged sinner whose motives are thoroughly corrupt and wayward from God. We offer him the gospel in the hope that he will repent. We plead with him to turn to Christ with the understanding that, if he is to do that, God must transform him, that is, change his motives. But Fuller leaves us wondering what kind of motives men have that allow them to respond in faith to the gospel message and yet are incapable of doing so. Are they totally depraved or not? It is this kind of ambiguous reasoning that suggests to us that Fuller would have been better off in his struggle against the antinomianism of the hyper-Calvinists to have simply maintained the admittedly difficult paradox, but scriptural truth, that man is both guilty and responsible, that he is both obligated to turn to Christ but that he cannot do so—he is *totally* incapable of doing so unless and until God mercifully changes his heart. Such a view does not inevitably shut us up to antinomianism; it confirms man's obligation to a holy God.

There are definite points of agreement with Fuller. Surely he is right in saying that man has natural abilities—to think, to reason, to choose, to act. Without these elements of the image of God in man, man would not

---

91   *Works*, p. 305.
92   *Works*, p. 305.

be what he is. Whatever else he has become, he is still a man. I would agree that sin is an intrusion into the human race, and not an integral part of man's original constitution. As Machen so well put it, 'universal sinfulness of mankind is not something that belongs to man just because he is man. It is by no means a necessary part of human nature as such.'[93] Otherwise, Jesus would have had to be a sinner for the simple reason he was a man, and Adam would have had to be created a sinner, and the Christian would have no hope of one day being glorified as the culmination of his redemption from sin. No, Adam as representative man fell into sin by his own volition, and by doing so, plunged all of humanity into sin. Therefore, we can say with the Scriptures that every man has been thoroughly corrupted by it (Eph. 2.3; 4.17-19; Gen. 8.21; Ps. 51.5; Jer. 17.9). Every part of his person has been vitiated by wickedness and he is therefore incapable naturally of perceiving the revelation of God.[94] While we admit that man has natural abilities of reason, we must also realize that they are so entirely polluted by sin that they have become virtual *liabilities* as to understanding the significance of divine revelation. Do our words of proclamation fall on deaf ears? Of course they do! Dead men cannot hear. That is what makes salvation a miracle of God's grace. He resurrects the corpse and gives him the ability to hear. The divine instrument of that ability is the quickening gospel of Jesus Christ. Therein lies the power—not in man's faculties, but in the Word.

I would agree with Fuller that Scripture makes it clear that the gospel is something to be obeyed (Rom. 1.5, 6.17; 10.16), and faith therefore is a duty. But to say that man must have some ability for that duty to have relevance is to fail to understand the nature of sin. Its dominion renders man totally incapable, absolutely unable, to come to Christ. Fuller should have simply adhered to his denomination's *Second London Confession* (1677) on the matter of total depravity:

> 2. Our first Parents by this Sin, fell from their original righteousness and communion with God, and we in them, whereby death came upon all; all becoming dead in Sin, and wholly defiled, in all the faculties, and parts, of soul, and body,...the guilt of the Sin was imputed, and corrupted nature conveyed, to all their posterity... From this original corruption, whereby we are utterly indisposed,

---

93 J. Gresham Machen, *The Christian View of Man* (Edinburgh: Banner of Truth Trust, 1965), p. 208. Cf. Fuller, *Works*, p. 173.

94 It is interesting that Fuller, *Works*, p. 172, exempts infants and imbeciles from guilt because they have no natural ability to respond to the gospel. But how does this absolve them from original guilt? Are they somehow exempt from Adam's sin simply because of the absence of natural powers of reason? These are questions Fuller does not answer.

disabled, and made opposite to all good, and wholly inclined to all evil, do proceed all actual transgressions.[95]

It is not that man cannot because he will not, it is that he will not *and he cannot be saved*;[96] yet he is still a responsible agent, accountable for the righteous demands of a holy God. Asahel Nettleton, a Calvinistic evangelist and contemporary of the Pelagianist, Charles Finney, cites the greatest theologian who ever lived as affirming both the responsibility of man to receive Christ and his total inability to do so:

> There are many who think they see a great inconsistency in the preaching of ministers. 'Ministers,' they say, 'contradict themselves—they say and unsay—they tell us to do, and then tell us we cannot do—they call upon sinners to believe and repent, and then tell them that faith and repentance are the gift of God—they call on them to come to Christ, and then tell them that they cannot come.'
>
> That some do preach in this manner, cannot be denied. I well recollect an instance. A celebrated preacher, in one of his discourses used this language: '*Come unto me, all ye that labour and are heavy laden, and I will give you rest.*' In another discourse, this same preacher said: 'No man *can come unto me* except the Father which hath sent me draw him.' Now, what think you, my hearers, of such preaching, and of such a preacher? What would you have said had you been present and heard Him? Would you have charged Him with contradicting himself? This preacher, you will remember, was *none other than the Lord Jesus Christ!* And, I

---

95   From chapter VI, 'Second London Confession', in William L. Lumpkin (ed.), *Baptist Confessions of Faith* (Valley Forge, PA: Judson Press, rev. edn, 1969), pp. 258-59. Neither this statement, nor the one found in the Westminister Confession, from which it is taken, make any distinction between moral and natural ability/inability.

96   This is the affirmation of both Dort (1619) and Westminster (1647). The 'Third and Fourth Heads of Doctrine: *Of the Corruption of Man, his Conversion to God, and the Manner thereof*, *The Canons of the Synod of Dort, A.D. 1619*, in Schaff (ed.), *Creeds of Christendom*, III, p. 588 (italics added):

> ART. III. Therefore all men are conceived in sin, and are by nature children of wrath, incapable of any saving good, prone to evil, dead in sin, and in bondage thereto; and, without the regenerating grace of the Holy Spirit, *they are neither able nor willing to return to God*, to reform the depravity of their nature, nor to dispose themselves to reformation.

See 'Chapter IX, *Of Free Will*', *Westminister Confession of Faith, 1647*, in Schaff (ed.), *Creeds of Christendom*, III, p. 623 (italics added):

> III. Man, by his fall into a state of sin, hath wholly lost all ability of will to any spiritual good accompanying salvation; so as a natural man, being altogether averse from that good, and dead in sin, *is not able*, by his own strength, to convert himself, or to prepare himself thereunto.

It is difficult to imagine any expression of human communication that could be more clear in declaring the total inability of man to respond to the gospel.

have no doubt, that many ministers have followed His example, and been guilty of the same self-contradiction, if you call it such.[97]

In addition to Nettleton's citation, the Scripture is replete with 'cannot' passages. For example, in Matthew 7.18, Jesus states emphatically that a bad tree is incapable of producing good fruit. The word for 'bad' is *sapros*, which carries the idea of rottenness, and in this context probably refers to that which is unserviceable or of little worth. The bad tree is the corrupt sinner who can only produce fruit or works which are bad, that is, *poneros* (*'evil'*) fruit. Whatever else we may say about the 'badness' of the fruit, we can legitimately maintain that Jesus is teaching that bad people are absolutely incapable of producing a good product (cf. Jn 15.4–5; 1 Cor. 2.14). In John 14.17, Jesus is announcing to his disciples that another paraclete will come to enable an understanding of the truth, which the natural man cannot receive. 'The world cannot receive [Him], because it does not see Him or know Him.' The world is the order of men in rebellion against God, who are not only unwilling to accept the truth the Spirit offers, but *cannot* (οὐ δύναται, literally, 'are not able to') receive it. If it could, it would cease being the 'world'.[98] The Spirit is the same who convicts this world of sin and righteousness and judgment (Jn 16.8), that is, he shows the world that what it does is evil, and he does so in connection with the gospel of Christ. The Holy Spirit so convinces the world of its guilt that 'the world's unbelief not only ensures that it will not receive life, it ensures that it cannot perceive that it walks in death and *needs* life'.[99] Finally, Romans 8.7-8 tells us that the unregenerate mind, the 'mind set on the flesh, is hostile toward God'. Paul states that this carnal mind not only refuses to subject itself to the law of God (willfulness), but 'is not even able to do so' (inability). His conclusion? 'Those who are in the flesh cannot please God.' In other words, as John Murray incisively explains, it is impossible for the unregenerate to please God. 'The apostle does not leave his readers to inference; he expressly states...that it is a *moral* and *psychological* impossibility for those who are in the flesh to do anything that elicits the divine approval and good pleasure. Here we have nothing less than the doctrine of total inability of the natural man.'[100]

Adamic immediate imputation is the only solution to this problem of rendering the unregenerate guilty on the basis of total depravity.

---

97 David B. Calhoun, 'Faith and Learning', in *Princeton Seminary* (2 vols; Edinburgh: Banner of Truth Trust, 1994), I, pp. 225–26.

98 D.A. Carson, *The Gospel According to John* (Grand Rapids, MI: Eerdmans, 1991), p. 500.

99 Carson, *Gospel According to John*, p. 537.

100 John Murray, *Epistle to the Romans* (New International Commentary on the New Testament; Grand Rapids, MI: Eerdmans, 1968), pp. 286–87, italics added.

'Therefore, just as through one man [Adam] sin entered into the world, and death through sin, and so death spread to all men, because all sinned' (Rom. 5.12). All men are condemned and spiritually dead because of Adam's sin, which is man's sin. But the Apostle Paul does not leave men in despair: 'For if by the transgression of the one, death reigned through the one, much more those who receive the abundance of grace and of the gift of righteousness will reign in life through the One, Jesus Christ' (Rom. 5.17).

A Summary Resolution

One of the principal objections to 'Gillism', or hyper-Calvinism, is its antinomianism: man is under no obligation to obey the gospel since he *cannot* do anything spiritually good. 'Fullerism', or moderate Calvinism, countered with duty faith: every man *is* obligated to accept Christ predicated on his ability to do so; the only reason he cannot is because he will not. Both of these views are unscriptural. The resolution to the problem is found in man's constitutional relationship to Adam. The Fall left man without ability but not accountability. 'All men are corrupt throughout the *totality* of their being with every part, power, and faculty of their nature—mind, intellect, emotions, will, conscience, body—being affected by the Fall.'[101] Such depravity leaves man altogether unable to come to Christ. In answer to the objection, 'How [then] can the teaching of total depravity and total inability be reconciled with God's commands? Do not the very commands of God presuppose the human ability to do them? Can a man justly be required to do that for which he has not the necessary ability?' Robert Reymond responds: 'God deals with man according to his *obligation*, not according to the measure of his ability. Before the Fall, man had both the obligation and the ability to obey God. As a result of the Fall, he retained the former but lost the latter.'[102] What is the natural man left to do? He can only cast himself on the mercies of God, realizing that there is absolutely nothing he can do to save himself, but that divine grace is fully adequate to pardon the repentant sinner on the basis of an all-sufficient atonement.

If it is incumbent upon all men to repent and turn to Christ for salvation, it is likewise the duty of every Christian to take the gospel of God's salvation to them. The warrant of the gospel is not to be found in some sign in the unregenerate that he is elect; it is to be found in the promise that 'whoever will call on the name of the Lord will be saved'

---

101 Robert Reymond, *A New Systematic Theology of the Christian Faith* (Nashville, TN: Thomas Nelson, 1998), p. 452.
102 Reymond, *A New Systematic Theology*, p. 454.

(Rom. 10.13). But 'how will they hear without a preacher?' (Rom. 10.14). It is God's own mandate that we, as believers 'make disciples of all the nations' (Mt. 28.19-20), that God might draw to himself such as should be saved (Acts 2.47). The revival of this divine commission was the practical beginning of the modern missions movement, inspired by the burden of men like Andrew Fuller and his companion in the faith, William Carey. Carey shared his friend's vision of reaching *all* men with the gospel of Christ. He persisted ('plodded', as he called it) in summoning his fellows' attention to what God had commanded as a *faith duty*: 'Go into *all* the world and preach the gospel to *all* creation' (Mk 16.15, italics added).[103]

> Since the apostolic age many...attempts to spread the gospel have been made, which have been considerably successful, notwithstanding which a very considerable part of mankind is still involved in all the darkness of heathenism. Some attempts are still being made, but they are inconsiderable in comparison with what might be done if the whole body of Christians entered heartily into the spirit of the divine command on this subject... Pity,...humanity, and much more Christianity, call loudly for every possible exertion to introduce the gospel amongst them [the heathen]... Let then everyone in his station consider himself as bound to act with all his might and in every possible way for God... [W]hat a 'treasure,' what a 'harvest' must wait such characters as Paul, and Elliott, and Brainerd, and others, who have given themselves wholly to the work of the Lord... Surely it is worth while to lay ourselves out with all our might in promoting the cause and kingdom of Christ.[104]

---

103 This verse is not found in the best manuscripts, but its truth is undeniable (cf. Mt. 28.19–20; Lk. 24.46–49; Acts 1.8).
104 William Carey, *An Enquiry into the Obligations of Christians, to Use Means for the Conversion of the Heathens* (Leicester: Ann Ireland, 1792), pp. 4, 8, 55, 57.

CHAPTER 3

Andrew Fuller and Antinomianism

Curt Daniel

Andrew Fuller was an extremely busy man. In addition to pastoring a church, he was a key figure in the growing missionary movement. Somehow he found the time to write a good number of books, sermons and pamphlets.[1] He was positively involved in missions; he was also negatively involved in controversy. Several of those controversies had a direct bearing on missions from a Calvinistic point of view as expressed in his major book, *The Gospel Worthy of All Acceptation.*

One area of controversy was the ongoing question of the law of God. As I have discussed elsewhere,[2] antinomianism had special reference to Calvinism. There were three main 'calvinistic antinomian' controversies in the seventeenth century (1640s and 1690s in England, 1630s in New England). In the eighteenth century, the first controversy centered around John Gill's reprinting the works of Tobias Crisp.[3] But it did not end with Gill's death. The controversy took on two main fronts, and Fuller replied to both of them.

The first front was the Deist–Socinian challenge. Fuller staunchly defended Reformed orthodoxy against the double threat in a series of short books and articles. In his *The Gospel Its Own Witness* (1800), he included a section entitled 'The Holy Nature of the Christian Religion Contrasted with the Immorality of Deism'.[4] He then used similar arguments against Socinianism in a longer work, *The Calvinistic and Socinian Systems Examined and Compared as to Their Moral Tendencies*

---

1   I will be quoting from the reprinted three-volume edition Joseph Belcher (ed.), *The Complete Works of the Rev. Andrew Fuller* (3 vols; Harrisonburg: Sprinkle Publications, 1988).

2   Curt Daniel, 'Hyper-Calvinism and John Gill' (PhD dissertation, University of Edinburgh, 1983; 'John Gill and Calvinistic Antinomianism', in Michael A.G. Haykin (ed.), *The Life and Thought of John Gill (1697–1771): A Tercentennial Appreciation* (Leiden: Brill, 1997), pp. 171-90.

3   Gill reprinted Crisp's collected works as *Christ Alone Exalted* (London, 1755), and added explanatory footnotes to exonerate Crisp from the charge of Antinomianism.

4   *Works*, II, pp. 8-57.

(1792),[5] and also in a short work entitled *Socinianism Indefensible on the Ground of Its Moral Tendency* (1797).[6]

Fuller's argument to both heresies is basically the same. He says that both Deists and Socinians err greatly in charging Calvinists with holding to a theological system that encourages immorality. The contrary is actually the case, both in doctrine and example.[7] He argues that both systems deny the absolute validity of God's holy law. This is doctrinal antinomianism. Both systems also produce ungodly behavior. This is practical antinomianism. A system can legitimately be judged by its fruits, and both systems are notorious for the immorality of their proponents and adherents. He points out the utter inconsistency and error of their opinion that 'Calvinism, it seems, must be immoral, though Calvinists be virtuous; and Socinianism must be amiable, though Socinians be vicious!'[8] Since they cannot prove Calvinists are immoral, and Fuller can prove that the Deists and Socinians are indeed immoral, this clinches the argument. Fuller does not resort to a cheap form of *ad hominem* argument, but a detailed argument in which he cites their lives as consistent examples of what is taught and approved of by their systems of belief (or, as Fuller would say, unbelief). Which is the thing to be proved (*QED*).

However, this presented Fuller with an unexpected problem. In defending Calvinism from the charges of antinomianism, he then had to address those hyper Calvinists who were promoting and extending the views of John Gill and Tobias Crisp. In sum, he contended that historic Calvinism was not antinomian, but hyper Calvinism[9] was not historic Calvinism. Fuller's own views of the law are basically in keeping with historic Reformed orthodoxy.[10] As he replied to the arguments of hyper Calvinism in *The Gospel Worthy of All Acceptation*, so he felt the need to say something about the tendency of hyperism towards antinomianism.

The old hyper Calvinists were dead. Gill was gone, and John Rippon, his successor, had abandoned hyperism to work closely with Fuller and Carey in the great missionary movement. John Brine was dead. But hyper Calvinism was by no means dead. A new champion arose by the name of

---

5   *Works*, II, pp. 108-242.
6   *Works*, II, pp. 243-87.
7   *Works*, II, pp. 141-153.
8   *Works*, II, p. 149.
9   Fuller usually preferred the term 'high Calvinism'.
10 A good summary and analysis is found in Thomas Kennedy Ascol, 'The Doctrine of Grace: A Critical Analysis of Federalism in the Theologies of John Gill and Andrew Fuller' (PhD dissertation, Southwestern Baptist Theological Seminary, 1989), pp. 220-55. Ernest Kevan gives the best study of the Puritans' view of the Law in his highly acclaimed *The Grace of Law* (Grand Rapids, MI: Baker Book House, 1964).

William Huntington.[11] Gill and Brine were hyper Calvinists, but could be exonerated from the charge of doctrinal antinomianism. On the other hand, Huntington went further than both and explicitly and repeatedly taught doctrinal antinomianism. His views were inextricably associated with his hyper Calvinism. Therefore, Andrew Fuller felt the need to reply, both to defend biblical truth and to remove obstacles among Particular Baptists who would be kept from supporting the missionary movement because of both hyperism and antinomianism.

Fuller was careful not to directly charge Gill and Brine with antinomianism. His problem was Huntington. Still, he refrained with naming him except in a few places. Fuller did not give a detailed refutation of Huntington's writings on the subject; he left that to others.[12] He gave a brief and favorable review of an anonymous anti-Huntington work named *The Voice of Years*.[13] Fuller did not so much address Huntington's beliefs as his spiritual standing. His 'good qualities', said Fuller, could appear even in an outward manner in an unbeliever. On the other hand, Huntington's 'bad qualities' indicate 'a spirit which is not of God'. The two are irreconcilable in Huntington, whose whole ministry drew attention to himself and not to Christ. As for his doctrinal antinomianism, Fuller commented: 'if the obedience and death of Christ were in honour of the Divine law, we do not understand how Christ could be either believed in or preached, while the law was denigraded'. Using an argument similar to his critique of Deism and Socinianism, Fuller concluded with serious doubts as to whether Huntington was even a regenerate man. He had no doubts, however, that his antinomianism was unbiblical and dangerous. His friend and biographer John Ryland, Jr., would later quote Fuller's scathing criticism of Huntington's writings: 'I have never read anything more void of any thing like true religion.'[14] The followers of the two men carried on the debate for years in the same tone. The self-styled 'Huntingtonians' derided the 'Fullerites' as dangerous unbelieving Arminians who disguised themselves as Calvinists.

---

11   The literature on Huntington is very large, but usually not recent. George M. Ella has written a highly sympathetic biography entitled *Huntington: Pastor of Providence* (Darlington: Evangelical Press, 1994). The short bibliography is useful. The bibliography in my 'Hyper-Calvinism and John Gill' contains still more entries.

12   See the preceding footnote for specifics. Critics included mainstream Calvinists and even some hyper Calvinists who resisted the invitation into doctrinal antinomianism.

13   *Works*, III, pp. 762-64.

14   Quoted by John Ryland, Jr., *The Work of Faith, the Labour of Love, and the Patience of Hope Illustrated in the Life and Death of the Reverend Andrew Fuller* (London, 1st edn, 1816), p. 387.

Even today, those who admire Huntington pour scorn on the memory of Fuller as a Judas, and Fullerites as not much better.[15]

Fuller rarely referred to Huntington or his defenders by name elsewhere. But it is apparent that he had them in mind when he penned *Antinomianism Contrasted with the Religion Taught and Exemplified in the Holy Scripture* (1817).[16] He says they are not Socinians, Arians or Arminians, but proponents of 'a system of false religion which has arisen and grown up among us under the names and forms of orthodoxy'. They do not plead with lost sinners.[17] He gets to the heart of their problem: 'The distinguishing feature of this special religion is selfishness.'[18] They lack 'love of Christians as Christians',[19] let alone love for sinners. Instead, they love themselves. Moreover, they even lack love for God as God. In a masterful conclusion, Fuller reasons, 'If we be not under the moral law as a rule of life, we are not obliged to love either God or man, and it is no sin to be destitute of love to both.'[20] Thus, they are consistent, but thereby expose their own error.

Fuller goes on. Believers commit sin. But sin is defined as being a transgression of the law. If the law does not apply to believers, then there is no such thing as sin for them.[21] The same is true with knowing one's sin.[22] Jesus did not abolish the law.[23] Christian liberty does not mean license to disregard the law.[24] Believers are not under the law in the hands of Moses to condemn, but in the hands of Christ to rule.[25] These hyper Calvinists are obsessed with the decrees of God to the exclusion of the commands of God, including the command to offer the gospel to all men. 'When the revealed will of God is disregarded as a rule of life, it is common to be much occupied about his secret will, or his decrees, as a substitute for it.'[26] That is why they neglect preaching to and praying for lost sinners.[27] They stand self-condemned.

---

15   E.g., George M. Ella, *Law and Gospel in the Theology of Andrew Fuller* (Eggleston: Go Publications, 1996).
16   *Works*, II, pp. 736-62.
17   *Works*, II, p. 738.
18   *Works*, II, p. 738.
19   *Works*, II, p. 738.
20   *Works*, II, p. 748.
21   *Works*, II, p. 748.
22   *Works*, II, p. 748.
23   *Works*, II, pp. 748-49.
24   *Works*, II, p. 749.
25   *Works*, II, p. 750. This was a popular phrase used by the Puritans, but disowned by the hyper calvinist antinomians, who professed admiration for the Puritans.
26   *Works*, II, p. 760.
27   *Works*, II, p. 760.

Fuller also addressed Huntingtonian antinomianism in *The Moral Law the Rule of Conduct to Believers*.[28] He argued that all Ten Commandments are still valid for believers. They are summed up in the commands to love God and men. Our relationship as children of our heavenly Father is defined in terms of love from and to God.[29] Christ and Paul denied that they abolished the law.[30] God requires believers to have brotherly love. If there is no law, there is no love. If there is no law, then we are without law and therefore are lawless. If so, then there is no such thing as sin, which is defined by the law.[31] Nor does the gospel set aside or replace the law in its proper place. 'Sometimes they will profess to make the Gospel their rule; but the Gospel, strictly speaking, is not a rule of conduct, but a message of grace, providing for our conformity to the rule previously given. To set aside the moral law as a rule, and to substitute the gospel in its place, is making the gospel a new law, and affords a proof how Antinomianism and Neonomianism, after all their differences, can occasionally agree.'[32] Finally, if the influence of the Holy Spirit takes the place of the law as a rule, then believers are without sin, for there is no law and they are always led by the Spirit.[33]

Fuller briefly defended the moral law against antinomianism in his *Dialogues and Letters Between Crispus and Gaius*.[34] In another short work, *Picture of an Antinomian*,[35] Fuller related how he was appalled by his hearing an antinomian (Huntingtonian) hyper Calvinist preacher.

In several places, Fuller associated hyper Calvinism and antinomianism. Hyperism's rejection of the doctrines of free offers and duty faith is inherently antinomian. He knew full well that Gill and Brine were not technically doctrinal antinomians, but he argued that their hyper Calvinism opened the door to doctrinal antinomianism. Gillism led to Huntingtonianism. Was he right? The evidence strongly suggests so.

This was a recurring theme in his *magnum opus*, *The Gospel Worthy of All Acceptation*.[36] At the start, he sets aside peripheral matters and points upon which all parties agree. Among the central points that define the state of the question, Fuller stated his case: 'The question is not whether men are bound to do any thing more than the law requires, but whether the law, as the invariable standard of right and wrong, does not require every man cordially to embrace whatever God reveals', including the

---

28 *Works*, III, pp. 585-88.
29 *Works*, II, p. 586.
30 *Works*, II, p. 586.
31 *Works*, II, p. 587.
32 *Works*, II, p. 587.
33 *Works*, II, p. 589.
34 *Works*, II, pp. 647-80.
35 *Works*, III, pp. 829-31.
36 *Works*, II, pp. 328-416. This is the 2nd edn of 1801, 1st edn 1785.

gospel.[37] This is the core of his argument and is crucial to understanding Fuller's views of both hyper Calvinism and Huntingtonian antinomianism.[38] His argument is based on several key points. 'Every man is bound cordially to receive and approve whatever God reveals.'[39] The gospel is revealed, therefore every man is bound to believe it. 'Though the Gospel, strictly speaking, is not a Law, but a message of pure grace; yet it virtually requires obedience and such an obedience as includes saving faith.'[40] The gospel is to be 'obeyed', according to Romans 1.5, 6.17, 10.16 and 2 Thessalonians 1.8-9. Unbelief is a great sin.[41] God threatens punishment to those who do not savingly believe in Christ.[42] Other spiritual exercises inextricably related to saving faith in Christ are also duties.[43]

Fuller also replied to the hyper Calvinist use of federal theology to bolster their case.[44] He refuted Brine's argument that the covenant of works says, 'Do and Live' and the covenant of grace says 'Believe and be saved', therefore the gospel and the law are irreconcilable. Fuller replies that believers are under the law as a rule of conduct, not as a covenant of works. 'Faith in Christ [is] a requirement of the moral law.'[45] All obligations must arise from some law. Unbelief is a sin, defined as the transgression of the law. Therefore, the existence of unbelief proves that the moral law requires faith in Christ.[46] Also, 'If love to God includes faith in Christ wherever he is revealed by the gospel, then the moral law, which expressly requires the former, must also require the latter.'[47] 'Unbelievers will be accused and convicted by Moses; their unbelief must, therefore, be a breach of the law of Moses.'[48] This is the case he brings against antinomianism in *The Gospel Worthy*.

There is a brief but poignant passage in Fuller's lesser known work entitled *The Reality and Efficacy of Divine Grace, with the Certain Success of Christ's Kingdom*.[49] In Letter VII, he again addresses the question whether saving faith in Christ is required by the moral law. He

---

37 *Works*, II, p. 331.
38 I am indebted to Ascol, 'The Doctrine of Grace', *passim*, for this observation.
39 *Works*, II, p. 349.
40 *Works*, II, p. 352.
41 *Works*, II, pp. 354-58.
42 *Works*, II, pp. 358-60.
43 *Works*, II, pp. 360-66.
44 On Fuller's acceptance of federalism, see Ascol, 'The Doctrine of Grace', e.g., pp. 261-63.
45 *Works*, II, pp. 483-88.
46 *Works*, II, p. 486.
47 *Works*, II, p. 486.
48 *Works*, II, p. 486.
49 *Works*, II, pp. 512-60.

carefully notes that he does not state that 'the law expressly, but radically, or remotely, to require faith'.⁵⁰ Rather, the love which the law requires leads a person to embrace the gospel. Baptism and the Lord's Supper are not expressly stated as being part of the moral law, but are certainly demanded of believers by God. There is a difference between 'positive' and 'moral' law. Positive law arises from the will of the lawgiver and not from the nature of things. Faith in Christ is based on our moral relation to God as lawgiver. Thus, one might say, duty faith is not explicitly stated in the law, but is implicitly assumed. Similarly, one might add, Christ and the gospel are not explicitly stated in the law *per se*, but are implicitly set forth in divine revelation and carry the force of moral law. There is no moral neutrality to Christ and the gospel.⁵¹

Fuller denied that he was teaching Baxterianism (neonomianism), as charged by Abraham Booth.⁵² While he agreed with some of Baxter's views, he rejected those views that are usually cited as being distinctive to his erroneous system, especially on justification and the gospel as a 'New Law'. Lest any Huntingtonian think Fuller was an Arminian, he explicitly disagreed with Baxter's notion that Arminianism and Calvinism are reconcilable. Fuller repeatedly confessed his allegiance to historic Calvinism. If Baxter erred on one side of the road towards Arminianism, then Huntington erred on the other side of the road towards antinomianism.

In appendices to later editions of *The Gospel Worthy of All Acceptation*, Fuller replied to two critics who defended hyper Calvinist views. John Martin wrote *Thoughts on the Duty of Man Relative to Faith in Jesus Christ, in Which Mr. Andrew Fuller's Leading Propositions are Considered*.⁵³ William Button wrote *Remarks on a Treatise Entitled, The Gospel Worthy of All Acceptation*.⁵⁴ Their arguments were similar to those advanced by Gill and Brine during the so-called 'Modern Question' debate regarding duty faith. Soon, William Gadsby would take Huntington's hyper Calvinism and antinomianism and develop them into the distinctive beliefs of the Gospel Standard branch of the Strict and Particular Baptists.⁵⁵ This group is the major group today that teaches and defends both the hyper Calvinism of John Gill and the doctrinal

---

50   *Works*, II, pp, 539-40.
51   *Works*, II, pp. 539-40.
52   *Works*, II, pp. 714-15. On the controversy with Booth, see ch. 8.
53   London, 1788. Fuller's reply is in *Works*, II, pp. 716-36.
54   London, 1785. Fuller's reply is in *Works*, II, pp. 417-59.
55   On Gadsby, see his son John Gadsby's *A Memoir of the Late William Gadsby* (London: J. Gadsby, 1870); B.A. Ramsbottom, *William Gadsby* (Harpendon: Gospel Standard Trust Publications, 2003). Gadsby's works were collected in *The Works of the Late William Gadsby* (2 vols; London, 1851).

antinomianism of William Huntington.[56] Another branch of nineteenth century English Baptist hyper Calvinism—the so-called 'Earthen Vessels' who followed John Stevens—rejected Huntington's antinomianism, but continued to reject the notion of duty faith.[57] A major contribution from this group was *Remarks on Duty Faith* by John Foreman.[58] Theological descendants of Huntington continue to defend 'the Celebrated Coalheaver'. They also continue to oppose the legacy of Andrew Fuller in the strongest terms.

The whole matter, it seems to me, is over the idea expressed in the word 'duty'. Hyper Calvinism has been historically defined as that extreme form of Calvinism that does not believe in 'offers' of the gospel. Most hyper Calvinists also reject the idea that unbelievers have the 'duty' to savingly believe in Christ. Their basic argument is that all duty belongs to the law. Law and gospel are irreconcilable. To say that unbelievers have the duty to believe is to give them the law, not the gospel. That would be Galatianism, not Paulinism. It would mean they are saved by their work of duty, not by the grace of God. William Gadsby wrote: 'If the faith of God's elect is a duty required by the law of works, then real faith in Christ must be a work of the law...then God's people are saved by the works of the law.'[59] Fullerism, therefore, is seen as legalism. Fuller and mainstream Calvinists disagree, and turn the argument on its head. Hyper Calvinist rejection of duty faith becomes antinomian.

Related to this point is the matter of the relation of faith to the law as the covenant of works. To be precise, does the moral law require faith?[60] Hyper Calvinists usually appeal to Galatians 3.12:'The Law is not of faith.' Gill commented: 'the law does not consist of faith in Christ, nor does it require it...it is the Gospel that reveals the righteousness of Christ, and directs and encourages men to believe in him and be saved.'[61] '[A]s the law is not of faith, so faith is not of the law. There is a faith indeed which the law requires and obliges to, namely, faith and trust in God, as the God of nature, and providence...but as for special faith in Christ as a Saviour, or a believing in him to the saving of the soul; this the law knows nothing of, nor does it make it known...but it is a blessing of the covenant

---

56   For a useful history, see B.A. Ramsbottom, *The History of the Gospel Standard Magazine 1835–1985* (Carshalton: Gospel Standard Societies, 1985).
57   See my 'Hyper-Calvinism and John Gill', *passim*.
58   London, 1860, reprinted by Ossett: Christian Bookshop, 1995.
59   Gadsby, *Works of the Late William Gadsby*, I, p. 251.
60   This has been discussed in various works of biblical theology. For example, Daniel P. Fuller, *Gospel and Law: Contrast or Continuum?* (Grand Rapids, MI: Eerdmans, 1982), e.g., p. ix.
61   John Gill, *An Exposition of the New Testament* (6 vols; London: William Hill Collingridge, 1852–53), II, p. 381.

of grace'.[62] Fuller and mainstream Calvinists agree only to a point. They contend that the law is a schoolmaster that points to Christ (Gal. 3.24). Whatever God commands is a duty and therefore comes under the heading of moral law. As Fuller noted, duty faith is not expressly part of the moral law, but is an extension of it. This is not to mingle law and gospel, or works and grace. To deny the duty of saving faith is not merely over-emphasizing divine sovereignty, it is minimizing or eliminating human responsibility. The result is the same as antinomianism: relieving men of all moral responsibility in this area. Thus, Fuller rests his case. Hyper Calvinism is a kind of antinomianism in itself, and produces the explicit doctrinal antinomianism propounded by William Huntington.

---

62   John Gill, *A Complete Body of Doctrinal and Practical Divinity* (Paris, AR: Baptist Standard Bearer, 1984), p. 376.

CHAPTER 4

Great and Sovereign Grace: Fuller's Defence of the Gospel against Arminianism

Clint Sheehan

Introduction

Preparing an analysis of Andrew Fuller against Arminianism is both a daunting and an enjoyable task. It is daunting because Fuller himself never wrote a formal apologia on the subject. He does, however, express his views on the subject in a wide range of writings and so this project requires pulling together information from a wide range of sources. His controversies with Dan Taylor are certainly the prime source, although all others must be considered. The challenge is in synthesizing these thoughts in a manner that would fairly and accurately represent the argument that Fuller would have presented had he been so inclined. Before Fuller's arguments can be assessed they must first be systematized. This paper, therefore, is as much a construction of the apologia that Fuller never wrote as it is an analysis of it. That Fuller did not engage Arminianism on every conceivable point is not symptomatic of any weakness in his position, but rather indicative of his lack of desire to squander his time on this controversy. It is clear that in those points of engagement that Fuller did select, he was unquestionably decisive.

And as daunting as this task was, it was equally enjoyable. Reading Fuller, it is difficult not to be impressed by his intellect, humility, and godliness. One can even read Fuller expounding a view contrary to one's own, disagree, and still be impressed by him. It was a unique combination of knowledge, abilities and temperament that rendered Fuller a peculiarly skilful apologist for the great truths of God's Word. J.W. Morris, a close friend of Fuller, noted that Fuller's 'powerful understanding was equally distinguished by a rapidity of exercise, grasping a subject almost intuitively, and fixing on the point of an argument with singular precision intuitively, and fixing on the point of an argument with singular precision and accuracy'.[1]

Andrew Fuller's success as an apologist was as much a product of his temperament as of his abilities. To be successful, an apologist must be humble and gracious. The most skillfully crafted argument is of no effect if the intended audience takes offence and ceases reading. Fuller took great care to try to avoid offending his readers. At the same time, Fuller gave no quarter and thus avoided any appearance of weakness. John Ryland, Jr., perhaps the man who knew Fuller the best, observed that Fuller's 'natural temper might occasionally lead him to indulge too much severity, especially if it were provoked by the appearance of vanity or conceit. But to the modest and diffident, I never knew him otherwise than tender.'[2]

This combination of humility and steadfastness was not merely a front presented in his writings; it was constituent of his very nature. Appearances are easily maintained in times of comfort, but such falsehoods tend to be laid bare by adversity. That Fuller was genuinely humble and yet unwavering is evidenced by words spoken as death was unmistakably near. Shortly before his death, Fuller said, 'I am a great sinner, and if I am saved, it must be by great and sovereign grace—by great and sovereign grace.'[3] Taken alone, this could be evidence either of humility, or of fear and weakness. That this is indicative of the former is certain given that as death drew nearer he remarked, 'My hope is such, that I am not afraid to plunge into eternity.'[4] Clearly Fuller possessed an uncommon balance of strength and humility.

Fuller was too wise to ever let his confidence give way to complacency. He wrote: 'it becomes me to watch against every thing that might lead me aside from the simplicity of the gospel'.[5] Neither did he let his confidence give way to arrogance. 'If the querist imagines that we profess to have embraced a system which answers all difficulties, he should be reminded that we profess no such thing.'[6]

---

1   J.W. Morris, *Memoirs of the Life and Writings of the Rev. Andrew Fuller* (Edinburgh: T. Hamilton, Paternoster Row; and Oliphant, Waugh, and Innes, 1816), p. 262.

2   John Ryland, *The Work of Faith, the Labour of Love and the Patience of Hope Illustrated in the Life and Death of the Reverend Andrew Fuller* (London: Button and Son, Paternoster Row, 1816), p. viii.

3   Morris, *Memoirs*, p. 460.

4   Morris, *Memoirs*, p. 461.

5   Andrew Fuller, *A Defence of A Treatise Entitled the Gospel of Christ Worthy of All Acceptation* in *The Complete Works of the Rev. Andrew Fuller* (ed. Joseph Belcher; 3 vols; Philadelphia: American Baptist Publication Society, reprinted 3rd edn, 1845), II, p. 457. All subsequent citations of Fuller, unless otherwise noted, are to this volume.

6   Fuller, *Accountability of Man* in *Answers to Queries* in *Works*, III, p. 766.

Fuller's humility also ensured his comfort with the deep mysteries found in God's Word. He was never so vain as to believe that his own understanding was the final arbiter of the veracity of any particular doctrine. What Fuller understood Scripture to assert, Fuller accepted as truth, even where this gave rise to counterintuitive or seemingly paradoxical conclusions. 'If God hath done thus and thus, it is not for us to object that it is inconsistent with his character, but to suspect our own understanding, and to conclude that, if we knew the whole, we should see it to be right.'[7]

Fuller as an Opponent to Arminianism

Early in his theological development, Fuller was heavily influenced by John Gill's *Body of Divinity*.[8] This helped provide Fuller with a solid foundation. At the same time, however, Fuller was prone to hyper-Calvinistic tendencies. These tendencies were first tempered by the writings of Dr. Abraham Taylor, which led him to doubt his belief that the gospel should not be preached to sinners.[9] Ultimately, the writings of John Bunyan, John Owen, and some of the elder Puritans extinguished these erroneous tendencies.[10] Fuller found the decisive factor to be the fact that John the Baptist, Christ, and the apostles often addressed 'the impenitent and the ungodly, and the object of their address was to excite them to flee from the wrath to come—to repent and live—to believe and be saved'.[11]

If the writings of Gill, Bunyan and Owen were instrumental in the development of Fuller's theological foundation, the writings of Jonathan Edwards were instrumental in the development of his theological maturity.[12] Fuller was introduced to the work of Edwards by John Sutcliff and John Ryland.[13] This influence of Edwards on Fuller and his friends was no secret. Morris commented: 'Mr. Fuller and his connections certainly had a very high esteem for the writings of President Edwards, and others of the New England school.'[14] Fuller himself, in a dying letter

---

7   *Accountability of Man*, p. 767.
8   Ryland, *Work of Faith*, p. 59.
9   Ryland, *Work of Faith*, p. 60.
10 Morris, *Memoirs*, p. 25.
11 Morris, *Memoirs*, p. 27.
12 Ryland, *Work of Faith*, lists some of Edwards' works that were influential to Fuller: 'Edwards on the Will', p. 58; 'Edwards on the Affections', p. 133; 'Attempt to Promote Prayer for the Revival of Religion', p. 152; 'Original Sin', p. 357; 'Free Grace and Atonement', p. 365; and various sermons, p. 189.
13 Morris, *Memoirs*, p. 28.
14 Morris, *Memoirs*, p. 28.

to Ryland wrote: 'We have some who have been giving it out of late, that "if Sutcliffe and some others had preached more of Christ, and less of Jonathan Edwards, they would have been more useful." If those who talk thus, preached Christ half as much as Jonathan Edwards did, and were half as useful as he was, their usefulness would be double what it is.'[15]

Although Fuller held certain earlier divines in high esteem, he did not believe any of them were infallible, nor did he consider himself a follower of any of them. 'I never mean to set up any man as a standard of faith.'[16] He hesitantly identified himself as a Calvinist, not because he agreed with Calvin on every point, nor because he desired to be identified as a follower of Calvin, but simply to 'avoid any unnecessary circumlocution'.[17] On whatever points Calvin and Fuller might disagree, without question they shared the same understanding of soteriology.

Fuller was a strong advocate for the doctrines of grace, but he also defended the preaching of the gospel to all without distinction. Not surprisingly, therefore, he came under attack from hyper-Calvinist, or pseudo-Calvinists as he called them, and from Arminians. Fuller believed this was because the principles he maintained were 'equally repugnant to Arminianism as to Pseudo-Calvinism'.[18] This is doubtlessly true, although it seems that the primary reason is that Fuller had an uncanny ability to reflect the balance found in Scripture. Here is an example of his humility allowing him to feel comfortable with the mysteries of God's Word. He saw no need to compromise the teachings of Scripture concerning either the sovereign grace of God or the universal offer of the gospel. Both were plainly asserted in the pages of Scripture and so both must be true even if they appear mutually exclusive to many.

That Fuller affirmed the universal preaching of the gospel has rendered him prone to charges of Arminianism, particularly from pseudo-Calvinists. This charge is, of course, patently false and cannot be maintained by anyone who has actually read the writings of Fuller. If the Canons of Dort (1619) are any judge in the matter, soteriologically Fuller was unquestionably a Calvinist. He was firmly convinced of the total depravity of man. 'I believe that men are now born and grow up with a vile propensity to moral evil, and that herein lies their inability to keep God's law, and as such it is a moral and a criminal inability.'[19] Also, 'being wholly under the dominion of sin they have no heart remaining

---

15 Morris, *Memoirs*, p. 459.
16 Fuller, *Reply to the Observations of Philanthropos*, in *Works*, II, p. 459.
17 *Reply to the Observations of Philanthropos*, p. 459.
18 Fuller, *The Reality and Efficacy of Divine Grace, with the Certain Success of Christ's Kingdom CONSIDERED IN A Series of Letters: Containing Remarks Upon the Observations of the Rev. Dan Taylor on Mr. Fuller's Reply to Philanthropos*, in *Works*, II, p. 513.
19 Ryland, *Work of Faith*, pp. 101-102.

for God, but are full of wicked aversion to him'.[20] Fuller believed in unconditional election. 'I believe in the doctrine of eternal, personal election and predestination' and that 'in the choice of the elect God had no motive out of himself'.[21] He believed in a limited atonement, although he preferred the expression 'particular redemption'. If 'eternal, personal, and unconditional *election* be a truth, that of a special design in the death of Christ must necessarily follow'.[22] To Fuller, particular redemption and election were inseparable. 'I consider particular redemption as merely a branch of election, or as the great design of election running through all the works of God.'[23] Fuller believed in the doctrine of irresistible grace. 'I believe in the necessity of an almighty work of God the Spirit, to new model the whole soul; to form in us new principles or dispositions, or, as the scriptures call it, giving us a *new heart* and a *new spirit.*'[24] Furthermore, the 'influence of the Spirit of God in this work, I believe to be always effectual'.[25] He also believed in the final perseverance of the saints. 'I believe all those who are effectually called of God never fall away so as to perish everlastingly; but persevere in holiness till they arrive at endless happiness.'[26]

Without question, Fuller believed that Calvinism represented an accurate synopsis of the teachings of Scripture concerning soteriology. While contemplating the writing of a systematic theology, Fuller stated that three of the leading doctrines of the gospel were election, the atonement, and the influence of the Holy Spirit.[27] This explains why Fuller was so tenacious in his defence of Calvinism against pseudo-Calvinism and Arminianism.

To Fuller pseudo-Calvinism went 'as far *above* or *beyond* Calvinism as Arminianism falls below it'.[28] Ultimately, both pseudo-Calvinism and Arminianism lead to the conclusion that 'men are obliged to just as much of duty as they are inclined to'.[29] Although he perceived these systems as direct attacks on the true gospel, his gracious spirit was such that he took great pains to avoid questioning the character or godliness of others *solely* because of the profession of these views.[30]

---

20 Ryland, *Work of Faith*, p. 102.
21 Ryland, *Work of Faith*, p. 103.
22 *Reply to the Observations of Philanthropos*, p. 493.
23 Morris, *Memoirs*, p. 408.
24 Ryland, *Work of Faith*, p. 105.
25 Ryland, *Work of Faith*, p. 105.
26 Ryland, *Work of Faith*, p. 106.
27 Fuller, *Letter II*, in *Letters on Systematic Divinity* in *Works*, I, p. 685.
28 Ryland, *Work of Faith*, p. 51.
29 Morris, *Memoirs*, p. 276.
30 Ryland, *Work of Faith*, p. 57.

As gracious as Fuller attempted to be towards the professors of these views, he was without mercy to the views professed. He explicitly called Arminianism a form of false religion.[31] He classified Arminianism as heterodoxy and seemingly placed it on a par with Arianism.[32] Fuller believed that Arminianism was based on a flawed idea of human depravity or blameworthiness.[33] He believed that Arminianism was rooted in pride.[34] 'Their scheme appears to me to undermine the doctrine of salvation by grace only, and to resolve the difference between one sinner and another into the will of man.'[35] In other words, anyone professing Arminianism claims ultimate credit for their own salvation because it was the exercise of *their* will that resulted in their closing with Christ. In their scheme, the only difference between why one is saved and not another lies exclusively in the advantageous exercise of their own faculties. Christ made salvation a possibility, but *we* make it a reality. Fuller dealt with this sophistry in detail in his discussions of grace and depravity.

Fuller was at once an eager and a reluctant apologist for Calvinism against Arminianism. Considering Arminianism as gross doctrinal error, and an attack on the true gospel, Fuller did not hesitate to express his opposition to this error whenever fitting. If these common, but often brief, volleys against Arminianism evidence his eagerness, the fact that he never penned a complete systematic refutation of their scheme evidences his reluctance. It is not clear exactly why he never undertook such a project. It does seem reasonable to infer that this reluctance arose in part from his belief that too much had already been written on the subject.[36]

The closest Fuller came to a systematic refutation of Arminianism is found in his correspondence to the Rev. Dan Taylor. It is an error, however, to read this correspondence in the first instance as an anti-Arminian treatise. That these writings provide the core of a skilful refutation of the Arminian scheme is purely incidental. Fuller's purpose was strictly to counter the theological perspectives of Dan Taylor. This is obvious in light of Fuller's statement that whether Taylor 'is an Arminian

---

31 Fuller, *Dialogue VII—Antinomianism*, in *Dialogues and Letters Between Crispus and Gaius*, in *Works*, II, p. 661.
32 Fuller, *Antinomianism Contrasted with the Religion Taught and Exemplified in the Holy Scriptures*, in *Works*, II, p. 737.
33 *Dialogue VIII—Depravity*, in *Crispus and Gaius*, p. 662.
34 Ryland, *Work of Faith*, p. 356.
35 Fuller, *Letter VI—Baxterism*, in *Six Letters to Dr. Ryland Respecting the Controversy with the Rev. A. Booth*, in *Works*, II, p. 715.
36 See, e.g., the editorial remarks in the preface to *The Reality and Efficacy of Divine Grace*, p. 512. While these editorial remarks were specifically directed to the writing of this series of letters, they nevertheless provide insight into Fuller's thoughts on the matter.

or not is of very little account with me'.³⁷ Had Taylor held some other collection of views, it is entirely likely that we would not now possess some of Fuller's key arguments against Arminianism.

This may appear a subtle and inconsequential observation. In fact, this is pivotal in laying bare the full force of these writings. If read as primarily an anti-Arminian polemic, this correspondence to Taylor is acutely inadequate. Fuller makes no effort to answer all major Arminian objections to Calvinism. In fact, in his correspondence to Taylor, Fuller addresses only four key issues. Of these, only three are of particular importance to a general response to Arminianism. Moreover, he does not attempt to construct either a systematic defence of Calvinism or refutation of Arminianism. Fuller's primary focus is on the logical flaws within Taylor's system. Fuller maintains that, when taken to their logical conclusion, many of Taylor's principles are at best nugacity and at worst heresy.

When read as intended, Fuller's correspondence to Taylor is a powerful testament to his skill as an apologist. Since these writings will provide the core of the construction of Fuller's refutation of Arminianism, it is appropriate to provide a brief biography of Dan Taylor. Dan Taylor was born to Azor Taylor, by his second wife Mary, on 21 December 1738 at Sourmilk Hall, Northowram, in the West Riding of Yorkshire.³⁸ Azor was a pitman at the local coalmine and Dan joined his father there at five years of age.³⁹ Dan's brother John recounted that from childhood Dan held Arminian beliefs.⁴⁰ His first denominational affiliation was Methodist, and the theological influence of Wesley remained evident throughout Taylor's life. Taylor was primarily self-educated. His combination of knowledge, zeal and a sharp mind resulted in a call to preach, which he accepted.⁴¹ Obviously highly motivated, Taylor maintained a schedule that would be unbearable to most.⁴² In addition to ministry commitments, he held employment outside the church, and devoted a considerable portion of each day to study.⁴³

---

37 *Reply to the Observations of Philanthropos*, pp. 459-60.
38 George Smith, *The Dictionary of National Biography: From Earliest Times to 1900* (ed. Sir Leslie Stephen and Sir Sydney Lee; Oxford: Oxford University Press, 1963–64), XIX, p. 405.
39 Smith, *DNB*, XIX, p. 405.
40 Frank W. Rinaldi, 'The Tribe of Dan: The New Connexion of General Baptists 1770–1891' (PhD thesis, Glasgow University, 1996), p. 19 (forthcoming as *'The Tribe of Dan': A Study of the New Connexion of General Baptists 1770–1891* [Studies in Baptist History and Thought, 10; Carlisle: Paternoster Press, 2005]).
41 Frank Beckwith, 'Dan Taylor (1738–1816) and Yorkshire Baptist Life', *Baptist Quarterly* 9.5 (January, 1939), p. 300.
42 Beckwith, 'Dan Taylor', p. 302.
43 Rinaldi, 'Tribe of Dan', pp. 14-15.

Theology aside, Taylor's motivation and commitment were worthy of admiration. His defence of the Bible as the inspired Word of God is also to be commended.[44] In an age where it was fashionable to reject the veracity and authority of Scripture, Taylor did not accept such compromise.[45] This zeal for the Word of God frequently led Taylor into the arena of apologetics.[46] One cannot help but feel a certain heaviness of heart when reading about Taylor. He appeared to be sincere, motivated, and diligent in his service to God; unfortunately this is marred by the errors he professed. The apostle's lament in Rom.10.2 could be applied to Taylor.

A combination of a change of heart about infant baptism and concerns over Methodist polity led Taylor out of the Methodist denomination and to the General Baptists.[47] Not entirely satisfied with the state of affairs among the General Baptists, Taylor was instrumental in the formation of a new denomination, the New Connexion of General Baptists.[48]

Fuller's reluctance to exert a concentrated effort against Arminianism is further demonstrated in that it was Taylor who first engaged Fuller. Fuller was in the midst of a controversy with Mr. Button in which Fuller was defending Calvinism against pseudo-Calvinism. Seeing that Fuller held to some points that appeared sympathetic to Taylor's own position,[49] Taylor, writing under the name *Philanthropos*, set out to win Fuller away from Calvinism. Fuller's response was not an attempt to prove Arminianism in error, but merely to show Taylor that he was in error.

To place Fuller's correspondence to Taylor in context, a review of the relevant aspects of Taylor's theology is necessary. Although he left the Methodists, Taylor remained Wesleyan in his soteriology.[50] Since Wesley's theology is an accurate reflection of evangelical Arminianism, Fuller's response to Taylor can be directly integrated into a general apologetic against Arminianism.

While not intended as a formal statement of faith, the theological beliefs considered most essential by Taylor and the New Connexion were summarized in *The Six Articles* (1770). The following are the most important to understanding the controversy between Fuller and Taylor. Taylor professed that 'Man's nature is depraved, his mind defiled and his powers weakened' to the end that 'No man naturally seeks after God, but

---

44   Rinaldi, 'Tribe of Dan', pp. 28-29.
45   Beckwith, 'Dan Taylor', pp. 303-304.
46   Rinaldi, 'Tribe of Dan', p. 21.
47   Smith, *DNB*, XIX, pp. 405-406.
48   Beckwith, 'Dan Taylor', pp. 301-302.
49   Especially the universal offer of the gospel.
50   Rinaldi, 'Tribe of Dan', pp. 12-13, 15.

wanders from him'.[51] Taken at face value, this much is certainly in agreement with the Calvinistic understanding of depravity. He taught that Christ 'suffered to make a full atonement for all the sins of all men'.[52] Taylor also believed that 'Man has the freedom to respond in faith'.[53]

For the sake of economy in his responses to Taylor, Fuller 'only selected the main subjects in debate, and attempted a fair discussion of them'.[54] To Fuller, the four main subjects in this debate were as follows.[55] Whether regeneration is prior to coming to Christ. Whether moral inability is excusable. Whether faith is required by moral law. Whether a universal offer of the gospel was consistent with a limitation of design in the death of Christ. Fuller addressed these subjects by focusing on the precedence of regeneration to faith, the inability of fallen man, and the extent of the design of the death of Christ.[56] The former two of these three were developed chiefly through the discussion of total depravity and irresistible grace.[57] Fuller was convinced that if total depravity were admitted, Taylor's scheme was useless.[58] If Taylor's scheme is shown to be in error, it follows that evangelical Arminianism is brought to naught.

Centered on Fuller's correspondence to Taylor, but drawing liberally from all of his works, the remainder of this chapter will be devoted to the construction and analysis of Fuller's defence of the gospel against Arminianism.

Fuller's Opposition to Arminianism

Since establishing the truth of the Calvinist understanding of total depravity alone is enough to bring down the Arminian scheme, this will be the starting point.

Depravity consists in 'the opposite to what is required by Divine law'.[59] Since the 'sum of Divine law is love:[60] the essence of depravity must consist in the want of love to God and our neighbour'.[61] Fuller summed up total depravity with the statement that 'the human heart is by

---

51   Rinaldi, 'Tribe of Dan', p. 24.
52   Rinaldi, 'Tribe of Dan', p. 25.
53   Rinaldi, 'Tribe of Dan', p. 25.
54   *The Reality and Efficacy of Divine Grace*, p. 514.
55   *Reply to the Observations of Philanthropos*, p. 461.
56   Morris, *Memoirs*, p. 281.
57   Of course all three of these issues are in direct response to the chief beliefs of Taylor presented in the prior paragraph.
58   *Reply to the Observations of Philanthropos*, p. 507.
59   *Dialogue VIII—Depravity*, p. 662.
60   E.g., Mt. 22.37-40.
61   *Dialogue VIII—Depravity*, p. 662.

nature totally destitute of love to God, or love to man as the creature of God, and consequentially is destitute of all true virtue'.[62] This is not to say that fallen man is destitute of love, but rather that the love possessed by fallen man is misdirected to selfish and evil ends. 'Private self-love seems to be the root of depravity...self-admiration, self-will, and self-righteousness are but modifications of it.'[63]

While the essence of depravity is defective and misplaced love, the outworking is much broader. 'A state of unregeneracy is a state of forgetfulness. God is forgotten. Sinners have lost all just sense of his glory, authority, mercy, and judgement; living as if there were no God, or as if they thought there was none.'[64] Total depravity means that unregenerate man loves sin rather than God, it does not mean he cannot sin more than he does.[65] The fact that the unregenerate are not, in general, as evil as possible, however, does not imply that they sometimes do good.[66]

In spite of the testimony of Scripture, some oppose this doctrine. Their argument is experientially and not scripturally founded. They concede that in Scripture God says that every inclination of the thoughts of the heart of man was only evil all the time; that there is not a righteous man on earth who does what is right; that the hearts of men, moreover, are full of evil and there is madness in their hearts while they live; and, see how each of you is following the stubbornness of his evil heart instead of obeying me. At the same time, their experience tells them that the unregenerate have performed a host of noble deeds throughout the ages. Both of these assertions, taken at face value, present a legitimate contradiction. At least one of these requires some interpretation to eliminate this contradiction. Those who reject total depravity must do so with the assumption that their experiences are more dependable than the Word of God. Even though these, and similar, passages are forceful and unambiguous, they cannot possibly mean what they say because that runs contrary to the experiences and observations of these individuals. No matter what Scripture says, no matter how plainly and forcefully it says so, no matter how frequently it says so, if it does not mesh with their experiences, it is Scripture and not their experiences that need reinterpreting. The response of Fuller to such people is that 'all which is called virtue in unregenerate men is not virtue in reality, and contains nothing in it pleasing to God, is no part of their duty towards him; but, on

---

62 *Dialogue VIII—Depravity*, p. 662.
63 *Dialogue VIII—Depravity*, p. 662.
64 Fuller, *Nature and Extent of True Conversion*, a sermon on Ps.22.27, in *Works*, I, p. 550.
65 *Dialogue VIII—Depravity*, p. 662.
66 At least not 'good' as God judges good. E.g., Rom. 3.12; Gen. 6.5.

the contrary is of the very nature of sin'.[67] Many unregenerate persons, and their actions, may outwardly appear virtuous but we are unable to judge the motives.[68] Fuller rightly notes that duties not performed in the love of God are not good works.[69] A 'mere external compliance with relative duties' is sin, although the omission is worse.[70] He also reminds the objector that God 'alone is able to judge of actions as perfectly to ascertain their motives'.[71]

Fuller's appeal[72] to the third chapter of Romans alone should be sufficient to establish the scriptural basis for his understanding of total depravity as defined above.[73] There was no need for Fuller to expend effort in a detailed scriptural defence of these principles since Taylor professed belief in the doctrine of total depravity. Everything put forth above from Fuller is perfectly consistent with Taylor's understanding of depravity as outlined in *The Six Articles*. In fact, the above discussion could seemingly be a joint Calvinist–evangelical Arminian defence of the doctrine of total depravity against the Pelagians. This concord, however, is merely an illusion. Taylor's description of total depravity is on the surface identical to Fuller's, their meanings on the other hand are radically different. Fuller argued that what Taylor and the evangelical Arminians professed concerning depravity was inconsistent with the rest of their system of soteriology.

Fuller believed that salvation is impossible in the Arminian scheme. No true Arminian would deny that there are only two categories of people, those who are 'in the flesh' and those who are 'in the Spirit'.[74] The regenerate are distinguished from the unregenerate in that they are indwelt by the Spirit of God. Appealing to Hebrews 11.6, Fuller noted 'without faith it is impossible to please God'.[75] Certainly no Arminian would dispute this. Fuller held that the stumbling block for the Arminian scheme comes with his next observation. Citing Romans 8.8, he observed that it is evident that those of 'a wicked mind' cannot believe in Christ because those 'that are in the flesh cannot please God'.[76] Taken in

---

67 Fuller, *Dialogue IX—The Total Depravity of Human Nature*, in *Crispus and Gaius*, p. 664.
68 Fuller, *Letter III—The Total Depravity of Human Nature*, in *Crispus and Gaius*, p. 670.
69 *Letter III—The Total Depravity of Human Nature*, p. 671.
70 *Letter III—The Total Depravity of Human Nature*, p. 671.
71 *Letter III—The Total Depravity of Human Nature*, p. 671.
72 E.g., *Dialogue IX—The Total Depravity of Human Nature*, p. 665.
73 These same sentiments are also put forth in Job 14.4; Jer. 13.23; and Mt. 7.18 for example.
74 E.g., Rom. 8.9.
75 *Dialogue IX—The Total Depravity of Human Nature*, p. 665.
76 *Reply to the Observations of Philanthropos*, p. 471.

connection, these verses clearly imply that those in the flesh cannot have faith.[77] By default, therefore, faith is the exclusive possession of those who are in the Spirit. Consequently, the unregenerate, if left to their own devices, will never receive the salvation of God in Christ.[78] Since the Arminians reject any special efficacious work of grace by God within individual unbelievers to bring them to faith in Christ, their scheme renders salvation impossible. The passages referenced here by Fuller on this matter are unambiguous and so the force of his conclusion cannot reasonably be avoided. If, as Taylor and the Arminians maintain, faith precedes regeneration, then since those who are in the flesh cannot have faith, no one will ever be saved. It is obvious why Fuller understood the priority of regeneration to faith as being one of the key issues in the debate.

The typical Arminian response, including Taylor's, to this consists of two points. First, they argue that this limits the free will of man. They assume that the certainty of a specific outcome is incompatible with free agency. Second, they maintain that if man is incapable of coming to Christ *unaided*, then there can be no accountability for sin. Fuller's treatment of these objections was masterful. He affirmed a view of free will to which surely no Arminian would object. By distinguishing between natural and moral inability he demonstrated that free will itself, and not the lack thereof, is the humanly insurmountable barrier to salvation.

If a person read no more of Fuller than his exposition of free will, they could easily mistake him for an Arminian. He advocated free will in the strongest logical sense. 'A free agent is *an intelligent being, who is at liberty to act according to his choice, without compulsion or restraint.*'[79] Man is absolutely free to do whatever he wills. Similarly, man does not sin by compulsion, or against his own will.[80] Fuller considered man as a free agent and that 'to deny this would be to deny that we are accountable to the God that made us'.[81] He believed free agency consisted '*in the power of following the inclination.*'[82] Furthermore, he believed 'we are free agents in all those matters which are inseparably connected with eternal salvation' because 'if otherwise, we should be equally incapable of rejecting, as accepting, the gospel way of salvation'.[83]

---

77 See also, e.g., 1 Cor. 2.14.
78 See, e.g., Jn 6.44.
79 *The Reality and Efficacy of Divine Grace*, p. 519.
80 *The Reality and Efficacy of Divine Grace*, p. 519.
81 Fuller, *Dialogue V—The Free Agency of Man*, in *Crispus and Gaius*, p. 656.
82 *Dialogue V—The Free Agency of Man*, p. 656.
83 *Dialogue V—The Free Agency of Man*, p. 656.

That the ability to accept and the ability to reject are inseparable was a critical observation. Fuller used this fact to argue that total depravity is not incompatible with a truly free will. No one will dispute that neither God, nor the angels and saints in heaven, can, or will, ever cease from doing good. 'If God, angels and saints in heaven be not free agents, who are?'[84] 'If an unaltered bias of mind to do good does not destroy free agency, neither does an unalterable bias of mind to evil.'[85] In like manner: 'If a bias of mind to evil, be it ever so deep-rooted and confirmed, tends to destroy free agency, then the devil can be no free agent, and so is not accountable for all his enmity against God.'[86]

What Fuller has advanced is sufficient to show that be a man's inclinations as wicked as possible, his free agency is not in the least diminished. The heart of free agency is not what a man's preferences are, but rather that he is free to act upon these preferences.[87] Herein lies true free will, that a person is free to do whatsoever they will at any instant in time. The Calvinist doctrine of total depravity is, therefore, consistent with the true free agency of man.

The second objection of Taylor's to address is that the Calvinist understanding of depravity leaves man unaccountable for sin. The argument is that if man cannot turn away from sin and towards God in faith and repentance, *in his own strength*, then he is not blameworthy for his sins. By distinguishing between moral and natural ability, Fuller shows that total depravity does not diminish the accountability of the sinner before God in the least.

The difference between what Fuller meant by moral and natural ability can be understood in the following way. Moral inability means that 'man cannot because he will not'. Natural ability means that 'man will not because he cannot'. This distinction is of great significance, and is not simply a matter of semantics as some might imagine. Fuller affirmed that the inability of the unregenerate is moral, not natural. 'We allow that men can come to Christ, and do things spiritually good, *if they will*.'[88] In other words, man has no intrinsic flaw or disability that bars a positive response to the gospel. The hindrance is strictly a lack of desire. 'The depravity of our hearts is not owing to natural weakness, either of body or mind.'[89] Men 'have the same natural ability to embrace Christ as to reject him'.[90] The presence of this natural ability is all that is required to make man

---

84   *Dialogue V—The Free Agency of Man*, p. 657.
85   *Dialogue V—The Free Agency of Man*, p. 657.
86   *The Reality and Efficacy of Divine Grace*, p. 519.
87   Logically, either all possible sets of inclinations and preferences are consistent with free will, or none are.
88   *Reply to the Observations of Philanthropos*, pp. 481-82.
89   *Reply to the Observations of Philanthropos*, p. 476.
90   *Reply to the Observations of Philanthropos*, p. 480.

accountable.[91] What a person likes or dislikes is of no consequence to their accountability.[92]

Fuller did not maintain that moral inability is such as to doom to failure all of the attempts of the unregenerate to overcome evil inclinations. Instead, 'sin hath such a dominion in their heart as to *prevent* any *real attempts* of that nature being made'.[93] Overcoming these inclinations to evil is a matter of choice. All are free to choose to follow these inclinations, or to choose to do good, but nobody chooses good. Fuller cites Romans 3.12 as foundational in this issue.[94] In the latter part of this verse, this idea is explicitly stated: 'There is none who does good. There is not even one.' The first portion of this verse makes it clear that this failure is by choice and not by compulsion. Were it by compulsion, the apostle would have written, 'All have *been turned* aside, together they have *been made* useless.' That he wrote, 'All have *turned* aside, together they have *become* useless' indicates that intentional choice is the cause of the failure.

Fuller, at this point, believes he has made a sufficient case to dismiss the Arminian objection that the Calvinist understanding of depravity is incompatible with personal accountability. It 'is of no account, as to the criminality of sin, whence it comes, or by whom or what we are tempted to it. If we choose it, it is *ours* and we must be accountable for it.'[95]

Just as, on the surface at least, both Taylor and Fuller espoused similar definitions of depravity, both also recognized that the grace of God was necessary for man to overcome depravity. Exactly what these two men, and the systems they represented, meant by this grace was radically different. Where Fuller believed that God administered grace in a discriminating and effectual manner to the elect, Taylor believed God dispensed grace in a general manner to all people.[96] Fuller powerfully demonstrated that what Taylor and the Arminians called grace was no grace at all.

Fuller not only demonstrated, contrary to the Arminian position, that free agency, accountability, and depravity are compatible, he also revealed the difficulties implied by the Arminian position. First, 'If blame does not lie in being the subject of an evil disposition, because as individuals we could not avoid, then, for the same reason, it cannot lie in

---

91 *The Reality and Efficacy of Divine Grace*, p. 521.
92 Otherwise, e.g., a dislike for paying taxes would be a sufficient justification for not paying them.
93 *Reply to the Observations of Philanthropos*, p. 477.
94 *Reply to the Observations of Philanthropos*, p. 478.
95 Fuller, *Discourse VI—Gen. iii.15-24*, in *Expository Discourses on the Book of Genesis*, in *Works*, III, p. 15.
96 Rinaldi, 'Tribe of Dan', p. 25.

the *exercise* of that disposition, unless that also can be avoided.'[97] If 'our native depravity' is blameless, so are all of the fruits of it.[98] Fuller convincingly argued that we always act according to our prevailing inclination.[99] At any instant, a person may be subject to a variety of inclinations. It is the strongest of these that will determine the person's actions. A rational person cannot do otherwise but act according to their prevailing inclination.[100] Some may object that people regularly act contrary to their inclinations. For example, it is not uncommon for a dinner guest to politely eat a meal they have an aversion to without complaint. This is true, but rather than being a counter example this establishes the truth of Fuller's contention. The dinner guest acted contrary to a possibly very strong inclination in eating the unsavoury meal. This was done, however, in response to their prevailing inclination, namely being gracious to their host. The strongest inclination at any instant dictates the course of action.

Even as a person can do no other but follow their prevailing inclination, they are also unable to alter their prevailing inclination. If a person could 'change his prevailing inclination, he must, in so doing, be either involuntary or voluntary'.[101] The former is not free agency, and the latter requires two simultaneously opposing *prevailing* inclinations, which is a contradiction.[102] Since a rational person will always act according to their prevailing inclination, and since total depravity implies that the prevailing inclination of the unregenerate is always opposed to God, then in the Arminian scheme the unregenerate are not accountable for their sins. Arminianism, taken to the logical conclusion at this point, teaches that even though man is free to do absolutely whatever he wills, he is not accountable for what he does provided that he is doing what he prefers or enjoys.

If, as Taylor claims, total depravity excuses people from accountability since they cannot do otherwise, then 'There is no need, surely, for *grace* to deliver men from a state wherein they are already *blameless.*'[103] So what does this general, or prevenient, grace of Taylor accomplish? Taylor believed, in the Arminian tradition, that this grace made men sensible to their sinful condition and the opened the door, for those who would, to respond to the gospel.[104] Fuller maintained that this Arminian grace accomplished something much more insidious from his point of view. If

---

97 *Reply to the Observations of Philanthropos*, p. 473.
98 *The Reality and Efficacy of Divine Grace*, p. 525.
99 Fuller, *Dialogue V—The Free Agency of Man*, in *Crispus and Gaius*, p. 657.
100 *Dialogue V—The Free Agency of Man*, p. 657.
101 *Dialogue V—The Free Agency of Man*, p. 657.
102 *Dialogue V—The Free Agency of Man*, p. 657.
103 *Reply to the Observations of Philanthropos*, p. 472.
104 Rinaldi, 'Tribe of Dan', pp. 30-34.

moral inability renders man blameless, and it is only this grace that makes men accountable, then this is no grace, but debt.[105] What these call grace is all that renders man accountable. Fuller lamented, 'this supposed grace, instead of being any real favour towards mankind, is the greatest curse that could ever befall them'.[106] Had Christ never come, man would never have been responsible. 'In consequence of his coming, and of *grace* being given them, to deliver them from something wherein they were never blame-worthy—now they lie exposed to inexcusable blame and everlasting ruin.'[107]

Is Fuller overstating this? He would answer no, and in support of this answer he appealed to excerpts from Taylor's letters. First, Taylor believed man was so reduced by the fall as to be *'really and totally unable to do good'*.[108] Second, Taylor taught that if man had been left in this condition he would not have been to blame, but that his inability would have been his excuse. Yea, 'let his practices have been as vile as they might, he would have been excusable'.[109] However, God has not left man in this condition. 'He has sent his Son to die for all men universally; and by giving, or at least offering, his Spirit to all men, he removes the inability which they derived from the fall; and they become accountable beings, and are inexcusable if they do not comply with things spiritually good.'[110] Under Taylor's scheme, 'if it were not for grace provided for them, they ought not to be punished *at all*'.[111] In fact, the 'greatest grace would have been to let them alone'.[112]

Fuller summarized the major problems of the Arminian position in the following statement: 'The Father sends his Son to atone for men's guilt, and deliver them from everlasting misery, from the consideration that there was nothing in that guilt, antecedently to his sending his Son and offering them grace, that properly deserved such misery, or indeed any misery at all!'[113] Under this scheme, the gift of Christ and the gospel is a damning curse upon the world.[114] Christ did not die for the sins of anyone if it was his death that first made us accountable.[115]

This has not yet exhausted what Fuller would regard as the flaws connected to the Arminian understanding of grace. Teaching that there is

---

105 *Reply to the Observations of Philanthropos*, p. 478.
106 *Reply to the Observations of Philanthropos*, p. 479.
107 *Reply to the Observations of Philanthropos*, p. 479.
108 *Reply to the Observations of Philanthropos*, p. 480.
109 *Reply to the Observations of Philanthropos*, p. 480.
110 *Reply to the Observations of Philanthropos*, p. 480.
111 *Reply to the Observations of Philanthropos*, p. 481.
112 *Reply to the Observations of Philanthropos*, p. 481.
113 *The Reality and Efficacy of Divine Grace*, p. 531.
114 *The Reality and Efficacy of Divine Grace*, p. 532.
115 *The Reality and Efficacy of Divine Grace*, p. 533.

'a provision made for the salvation of all', Taylor attempts to explain the fact that not all come to salvation.[116] This 'must be attributed to the depravity of men, not to any deficiency in the grace of God'.[117] This is a noble attempt by Taylor to defend the character of God, which has only been made subject to attack by Taylor's understanding of grace in the first place. Unfortunately for Taylor, this statement haplessly had the opposite effect. If the depravity of these individuals is so great as to not be conquered by the grace of God, then in Taylor's system these remain blameless since their depravity precludes them from acting otherwise. No one therefore is condemned for his sins. Those who reject the gospel are not condemned because their depravity is too strong to be overcome by grace, and so they remain in a blameless state. On the other hand, for those with a weaker depravity that grace is strong enough to overcome, their condemnation is removed because they have accepted the gospel that first brought them under condemnation.

As an aside, attention should be drawn here to the extraordinarily gracious character of Fuller. In spite of Fuller's dislike of Arminianism, he maintained a distinction between this theological perspective and the individuals who professed it. For example, in answering Taylor's objections that the Calvinist understanding of depravity must imply God cannot hold fallen man accountable, Fuller noted that Taylor's objections were reminiscent of those put forth in Romans 9.19. Fuller did not want anyone to think he was trying to compare the character of Taylor to that of the objectors addressed in this passage. He made it clear that he was exclusively speaking of Taylor's mode of reasoning, and not his character or person.[118] Fuller was without mercy to doctrinal error, but as we observe here, he was as gentle as possible with the professors of error where he was convinced they were sincere of motive.

That there is a difference between believers and unbelievers is beyond dispute. The question Fuller asked of Taylor and his system was '*Who maketh thee to differ?*'[119] An Arminian can maintain that man, of himself, cannot 'do anything spiritually good, it is all by the *grace* of God', but if this grace is given indiscriminately to all, 'it is no cause whatever of the *difference* between me and another'.[120] If the only divine agency is a 'sort of grace which is given to men in common' then this is 'no reason why one man believes rather than another; it is the man himself, after all, who is the proper cause of his own believing'.[121] What makes men to differ in this matter is either a discriminating and efficacious grace, or

---

116 Rinaldi, 'Tribe of Dan', p. 25.
117 Rinaldi, 'Tribe of Dan', p. 25.
118 *The Reality and Efficacy of Divine Grace*, p. 513.
119 *Reply to the Observations of Philanthropos*, p. 467.
120 *Reply to the Observations of Philanthropos*, p. 467.
121 *Reply to the Observations of Philanthropos*, p. 463.

that some are intrinsically prone to believing while others are not. It is either by God's doing, or by mine, that I am in Christ.[122] The Arminian scheme ultimately professes the latter. Fuller commented that this leads the Arminian believer to reflect that 'owing to himself...the good work is begun; and then God promises to carry it on to the day of Jesus Christ'.[123] While intending to further demonstrate the problems that arise from the Arminian scheme, this may actually be a statement many would own. It seems that Fuller has missed the true irony with his paraphrase of Philippians 1.6. In that verse the apostle is convinced that he who began the good work would also be the one to complete, or perfect, it. Obviously Paul intended that God both initiates and perfects our salvation.[124] The irony missed by Fuller is that if it is man who initiates his own salvation,[125] it is man himself who will perfect this until the day of Jesus Christ. What should be one of the most reassuring truths in scripture is reduced by the Arminian system to a frightening prospect. Rather than taking comfort that the God who actively brought us first to salvation will safely keep us there, the Arminian system would have us believe that God is sitting at the finishing line, cheering us on but leaving our safety to our own devices.

Not only can Arminianism not account for the salvation of a single individual, it cannot account for various circumstances surrounding salvation. Fuller observed: 'if the Spirit of God is not the cause why one sinner believes in Christ rather than another, then he is not the cause why there are more believers at one period of time than another'.[126] As a consequence, passages promising mass conversions in the latter days[127] are not sure promises of God, but rather hopeful predictions. Only if these future events depended on the sovereign exercise of the grace of God, rather than the unpredictable exercise of human wills following the prevailing inclinations, which are only directed towards evil, could the outcomes be certain. In fact, all revivals would be inexplicable if the will of man and not the grace of God was the effective first cause of salvation. It is curious that Taylor, himself a product of revival,[128] never made this connection. How, apart from an unusual working of the Spirit of God, could genuine revivals be explicable?

A similar dilemma surrounds the fact that at times it is the worst of sinners that is converted first. 'The chief of sinners are frequently brought to believe in Christ before others, who are far behind them in

---

122 The unmistakable answer is found in 1 Cor. 1.30.
123 *Reply to the Observations of Philanthropos*, p. 463.
124 This *exact* sentiment is also expressed plainly in Gal. 3.3, and Heb. 12.2.
125 By an unaided act of his own will.
126 *Reply to the Observations of Philanthropos*, p. 464.
127 Fuller had Isa. 60 in mind here in particular.
128 Beckwith, 'Dan Taylor', p. 300.

iniquity.'[129] The conversion of Saul is certainly one instance of this. Other examples offered by Fuller are Jerusalem, which killed Christ, and Corinth, which was a 'sink of abomination'.[130] In spite of being two of the leading centers of iniquity, they were two of the earliest centers of believers. 'How this can be accounted for, but upon the supposition of sovereign and invincible grace is difficult to say.'[131] Logically, 'the greater the depravity of any man is, the more improbable must be his conversion'.[132] Therefore, the worst of sinners believing first is inexplicable under the Arminian system.

Fuller believed that the reason one believed in Christ, while another did not, was divine agency alone.[133] This is diametrically opposed to the tendency of Arminianism to ascribe this difference to the creature.[134] Where Fuller's argument against the Arminian view of grace focused primarily on the internal inconsistencies and its logical conclusions, his defence of his own system relied heavily on appeals to Scripture. Fuller deserves recognition for his great wisdom in this approach. Too many trees have given themselves in vain to sustain this seemingly interminable debate between the Calvinists and the Arminians. Volumes have been written in support of both sides in this debate. Unfortunately, this debate has often not been a debate at all but rather a competition to determine which side could compile the lengthiest list of proof-texts. Each side is satisfied that they have the superior catalogue of proof-texts and therefore they hold the truth. Fuller knew that giving the world yet another treatise in which attempts were made to demonstrate that the Arminian system was incompatible with Calvinist proof-texts would be worthless. Instead, as detailed above, he allowed the Arminians their postulates and then proceeded to show that these were mutually contradictory, and that they lead to problems when taken to their logical conclusions. By doing this he was able to argue that the Arminian system was untenable.

1 Peter 1.1-2 was foundational to Fuller's position. Here election and the sanctification of the Spirit are identified as proper causes of obedience.[135] God chooses us for obedience and then fits us for it. The key to his position was in establishing links between faith and obedience. This was accomplished with the recognition that 'faith in Christ is not only the root of evangelical obedience, but that itself, being a duty is *a part* of obedience. Hence it is that believing in Christ is called *obeying*

---

129 *Reply to the Observations of Philanthropos*, p. 465.
130 *Reply to the Observations of Philanthropos*, p. 465.
131 *Reply to the Observations of Philanthropos*, p. 465.
132 *Reply to the Observations of Philanthropos*, p. 465.
133 *The Reality and Efficacy of Divine Grace*, p. 515.
134 *The Reality and Efficacy of Divine Grace*, p. 516.
135 *Reply to the Observations of Philanthropos*, p. 466.

him, (Rom. x.16; vi.17; i.5; Heb. v.9) and the contrary is represented as *disobeying* him (2 Thes. i.8, 9; 1 Pet. iv.17).'[136] This is also the explicit teaching of John 3.36 where believing in the Son is connected to eternal life and not obeying him is connected to condemnation.[137] From these, it is evident that faith and obedience are inseparable. Where there is no faith, there is no obedience. Where there is no obedience, there is no faith. 'It follows, then, that if election and the sanctification of the Spirit are the causes of our obedience, they must be the cause of our believing, and consequentially must precede it, since the cause always precedes the effect.'[138]

Fuller did not mean 'that there is a distinct principle wrought in the heart, which may be called a principle of *faith*, in distinction from other graces; but rather a new turn or bias of mind, previously to all acts or exercises whatsoever, internal or external, which are spiritually good'.[139] Whatever the cause, such a change of bias is obviously necessary because 'it will hardly be said that the same thoughts and temper of mind which lead a man to despise and reject the Saviour will lead him to esteem and embrace him!'[140] This production of a new bias of mind involves the replacement of the prevailing inclinations that were averse to God with new ones that are attracted to God. Just as the unregenerate exercise their free will in rejecting the gospel, the regenerate exercise their free will in accepting the gospel. Fuller noted that the precise method of regeneration is not clear. It may be the giving of a spiritual discernment, or possibly a divine energy attending the Word itself, but the answer does not alter the issue.[141]

The gospel, in and of itself, cannot be the agent of regeneration. This is evident considering that not all who hear the gospel respond in faith.[142] Scripture bears testimony to this. 'Christ did not pray that the truth might sanctify men, but that God would sanctify them *by* his truth.'[143] The apostles prayed for the effectiveness of the Word.[144] We are told not that the Word of God, but the Spirit of God was 'sent *to convince the world of*

---

136 *Reply to the Observations of Philanthropos*, p. 465.
137 This is the same argument developed in the third and fourth chapters of Hebrews.
138 *Reply to the Observations of Philanthropos*, p. 467. Recall that it was shown earlier that Fuller established the priority of regeneration to faith through the connection of Heb. 11.6 and Rom. 8.8.
139 *Reply to the Observations of Philanthropos*, p. 462.
140 *Reply to the Observations of Philanthropos*, p. 462.
141 *Reply to the Observations of Philanthropos*, p. 462.
142 If the power were within the gospel itself then the fact that some do not respond in faith would imply that the power of God is not always sufficient to overcome evil. The rebuttal to this is parallel to the one used above to refute the Arminian idea of grace.
143 *Reply to the Observations of Philanthropos*, p. 463 (cf. Jn 17.17-19).
144 *Reply to the Observations of Philanthropos*, p. 464 (cf. 2 Thess. 3.1).

sin'.[145] The Word is instrumental in our sanctification, but the *agency* is of the Holy Spirit.[146] If the Word brings about salvation, it is by the *power of God* to that end.[147]

The power of God to this end is not employed through the mere provision of assistance to the unregenerate, but rather through the regeneration of the unregenerate. The old unregenerate man, along with the prevailing inclinations to evil, is done away with and replaced by a newness of life with a new set of holy prevailing inclinations.[148] 'The work of *turning a sinner's heart must be altogether of God and of free grace*. If a sinner could return to God of his own accord, or even by Divine influence *helping* or *assisting him*, it must be upon the supposition of his having some will, wish, or desire to set about it.'[149] In fact, 'if men are *totally* alienated from God, all desire after him must be extinct; and all the warnings, invitations, or expostulations of the word will be ineffectual; yea, Divine influence itself will be insufficient, if it falls short of renewing the heart.'[150] The problem, as discussed earlier, is that man will always act according to his prevailing inclinations and the prevailing inclinations of the regenerate are to evil. Only if the old prevailing inclinations to evil are replaced by a new set inclined to good will a man ever respond favourably to the gospel. This is what is meant by conversion, or regeneration, and it must be the work of God.

Fuller appealed to an array of passages to confirm his position that salvation, in the first instance, is a work of God.[151] Those who come to Christ have *first* heard and learned of the Father (John 6.45). Only those *drawn by* the Father come to Christ (John 6.44). No man can come to Christ save it is *given* to him of the Father (John 6.65). The grace of God, and not our faith, is ascribed as the first cause of our salvation (Eph. 2.8).[152] '*Faith* as well as love, joy...is a fruit of the Spirit.'[153] If faith is a

---

145 *Reply to the Observations of Philanthropos*, p. 464 (cf. Isa. 32.15; 53.1; Jn 14.12; 16.8).

146 *Reply to the Observations of Philanthropos*, p. 463.

147 *Reply to the Observations of Philanthropos*, p. 463 (cf. Jn 17.17; Rom. 1.16; 2 Cor. 3.18; 1 Thess. 1.5).

148 E.g., Gal. 2.20; Eph. 2.5; Col. 2.13.

149 Fuller, *Letter IV—Consequence Resulting From the Doctrine of Human Depravity*, in *Crispus and Gaius*, p. 675.

150 *Letter IV—Consequence*, p. 675.

151 *Letter IV—Consequence*, p. 675.

152 Whether or not this passage specifically teaches that faith itself is a gift of God is often debated. What these debaters miss is that the answer to this is irrelevant. The point that is beyond debate is that this passage teaches that grace, or namely the working of God, is the first cause of salvation. So whether that grace, in its working, gives us a new principle of faith or simply activates something already within us, the working of the grace is still prior to our faith. Therefore regeneration precedes faith.

153 *Letter IV—Consequence*, p. 675 (cf. Gal. 5:22-23).

fruit of the Spirit, the presence and operation of the Spirit must precede faith.[154] God has *begat* us anew to a living hope (1 Pet. 1.3). The children of God are not born of the *will of the flesh*, nor of the *will of man*, but *of God* (John 1.13). Our being raised with Christ through faith *is* the working of God (Col. 2.12). In both Acts 13.48 and 16.14, saving faith is directly attributed to a special work of God.

The position advanced by Fuller was sufficient to convince many that regeneration precedes faith, that this did not damage free agency, and that it was consistent with the doctrine of total depravity. 'There is a link, as some have expressed it, that unites the purposes of God and the free actions of men, which is above our comprehension; but to deny the fact is to disown an all-pervading providence; which is little less than to disown a God.'[155] Perhaps the best example of this interplay between the providence of God and the will of man in the accomplishing of God's plan is the crucifixion of Christ.[156]

To summarize Fuller's understanding of grace, 'it is by the *agency* of the Holy Spirit causing that word to be embraced by one person, as it is not by another, and so as to become effectual'.[157] Thus, we see 'regeneration preceding our coming to Christ, since the cause always precedes the effect'.[158]

Some may object that there are some passages that teach the Spirit is given after we believe.[159] Fuller responds that the Spirit is 'given in other respects as well as for the purpose of regeneration'.[160] The Spirit is given

---

154 This was an acute observation by Fuller. In the broader context of this passage, Paul contrasts the unique marks of those in the flesh with the unique remarks of those in the Spirit. Faith is advanced as a distinguishing mark of a person who is in the Spirit. If a person must be in the Spirit, rather than in the flesh, to possess faith, then the presence and working of the Spirit is prior to any faith. Once again proving that regeneration precedes faith. This can be obscured by some modern translations of this passage in which *pistis* is translated as 'faithfulness' rather than 'faith'. The problem is the modern tendency to understand 'faithfulness' as referring to loyalty, rather than to being full of faith. That the latter is the correct meaning is easily established. In 1 Kgs 18, 850 prophets of Baal and Asherah loyally served their false gods to the death. In recent times, terrorists loyal to their evil causes have targeted their perceived enemies with suicide attacks. Dying for a cause is the pinnacle of loyalty to that cause. No sane person, however, would argue that these are examples of people demonstrating the fruit of the Spirit. This is to the exclusion of the former understanding of 'faithfulness' and to the establishment of the latter.

155 Fuller, *The Fall of Man*, in *Answers to Queries*, in *Works*, III, p. 765.
156 Cf. Acts 2.23. A second unmistakable example is found in Rev. 17.17.
157 *Reply to the Observations of Philanthropos*, p. 463.
158 *Reply to the Observations of Philanthropos*, p. 463.
159 Passages typically cited include John 7.38-39; Eph. 1.13-14; Gal. 3.2, 14.
160 *Reply to the Observations of Philanthropos*, p. 468.

to endow believers with extraordinary gifts and grace.[161] The Spirit is also given as an enlightener, comforter, and sanctifier of true Christians.[162]

Another common Arminian objection is that under the Calvinist system a person must be both regenerated and condemned at the same instant. Fuller notes that this is false because there is no period of time between regeneration and coming to Christ in faith.[163] The ordering is strictly logical in the sense that the cause logically precedes the effect. The two events are temporally simultaneous. There is both an idea of passivity and of activity present in this. Regeneration 'is passive with respect to the agency of the Holy Spirit in producing change, so as to contribute nothing towards it; but the very nature of the change itself, being from a state of enmity to love, implies activity of mind'.[164] 'God turns us ere we turn to him. Sinners are said to be converted, as well as to convert.'[165] Being endued with spiritual life and becoming active are simultaneous. Fuller provided an effective illustration of this principle. 'A blind man must have his eyes opened *before* he can see; and yet there is no period of time between the one and the other.'[166] Furthermore, Arminians have it no better if they are allowed this form of reasoning. In their scheme a person can have believed and not yet received the Spirit 'but yet, not having the Spirit of Christ, he is none of his'.[167]

'If men be utterly depraved, they lie entirely at the discretion of God either to save or not save them. If any are saved, it must be by an act of free grace. If some are brought to believe in Christ, while others continue in unbelief, (which accords with continued fact,) the difference between them must be altogether of grace. But if God make a difference in time, he must have determined to do so for eternity; for to suppose God to act without a purpose is depriving him of wisdom; and to suppose any new purpose to arise in his mind would be to accuse him of mutability. Here, therefore, we are landed upon election—sovereign, unconditional election.'[168] With this statement Fuller has demonstrated that the doctrine of election is a corollary of a right understanding of depravity and grace. This is a significant observation on his part. He has already established the truth of his views of depravity and grace. Therefore, by establishing the doctrine of election as the logical complement of the doctrine of depravity and the doctrine of grace, he has established the truth of the

---

161 E.g., Acts 19.2; John 7.39.
162 E.g., Eph. 1.13-14.
163 *Reply to the Observations of Philanthropos*, p. 468.
164 Fuller, *Regeneration by the Word of God*, a sermon on 1 Pet. 1.23, in *Works*, I, p. 666.
165 *Regeneration by the Word of God*, p. 666.
166 *Reply to the Observations of Philanthropos*, p. 468.
167 *Reply to the Observations of Philanthropos*, p. 468 (cf. Rom. 8.9).
168 Fuller, *Letter IV*, in *Crispus and Gaius*, II, p. 675.

doctrine of election. This illustrates an important methodological element of his defence of the gospel. Fuller believed that all of the doctrines associated with salvation must be considered in connection with each other. Only then could they be rightly understood. For example, if we consider 'the doctrine of *election* as unconnected with other things, it may appear to us to be a kind of fondness without reason or wisdom. A charge of caprice would, hereby, be brought against the Almighty... But if it be considered in connexion with the great system of religious truth, it will appear in a different light. It will represent the Divine Being in his true character; not as acting without design, and subjection himself to the endless disappointment; but as accomplishing all his works in pursuance of an eternal purpose.'[169]

The humility of Fuller was evidenced in his treatment of unconditional election. He conceded that some apparently unanswerable questions attended this doctrine, but felt no need to have an answer to every question. The truth of this doctrine did not depend upon his being able to answer, or not answer any question. The ostensible problem was the relationship between election, free agency and accountability. 'A fleshly mind may ask, "How can these things be?" How can Divine predestination accord with human agency and accountableness? But a truly humble Christian, finding both in his Bible, will believe both, though he may be unable fully to understand their consistency; and he will find in the one a motive to depend entirely on God, and in the other a caution against slothfulness and presumptuous neglect of duty.'[170] In his response to this common Arminian objection Fuller in essence is arguing that there must be concordance between these three since all are taught in Scripture.

Another common Arminian objection is that under the Calvinist system, the salvation of some is impossible. To this Fuller replied, 'I admit that the salvation of some men is *impossible*, that it is *certain* they will perish.'[171] The problem of this particular Arminian objection lies hidden beneath the surface. When considering the doctrine of election, they envision scores of men coming weeping to Christ, broken and sincerely seeking salvation only to be turned away by a harsh and capricious God. But, as Fuller has demonstrated, the unregenerate have an aversion to God and so *not one* will come to God on their own. Furthermore, Fuller affirmed that God would accept anyone who truly came to Christ in faith. This issue will be addressed in more detail in connection with Fuller's view of the universal offer of the gospel.

---

169 Fuller, *The Nature and Importance of an Intimate Knowledge of Divine Truth*, a sermon on Heb. 5.12-14, in *Works*, I, p. 167.
170 Fuller, *Letter II*, in *Letters on Systematic Divinity*, in *Works*, I, p. 686.
171 Fuller, *Gospel of Christ Worthy of All Acceptation*, in *Works*, II, p. 452.

To support his position on the doctrine of election, Fuller appealed to a range of Scripture passages.[172] Two particularly important discourses on election are found in the ninth chapter of Romans, and the first two chapters of Ephesians.[173]

The customary Arminian explanation of election consists of an appeal to foreknowledge. In their scheme, God elects to salvation those individuals whom he foreknows will believe the gospel message and turn to Christ in faith. But as Fuller stated, 'Certain foreknowledge, therefore, implies a certainty of the event foreknown.'[174] That God precisely and exhaustively foreknew all future events before the foundation of the world establishes that all events that do occur were decreed unalterably by God, before the foundation of the world.[175] Moreover, it is clear that those chosen of God unto salvation cannot have been chosen based on his foreknowledge of their faith because God himself is the cause of our faith through our regeneration.[176] Election is rooted in the sovereign decree of God, and not the future actions of man. That we see the 'whole difference between the saved and the lost being ascribed to sovereign grace, the pride of man is abased'.[177]

In his defence of unconditional election Fuller possibly faced a more challenging task than with the earlier doctrines, although his treatment of this doctrine was no less skilful. Election was the more challenging doctrine to defend owing to the intrinsic mystery surrounding the concordance of unconditional election, free agency and accountability. Apart from leaving that issue open ended,[178] Fuller showed that unconditional election was a corollary of grace and depravity. He also provided ample scriptural support for his views.

---

172 Eph. 1.3; 2 Thess. 2.13; Jn 6.37; 15.16; Rom. 8.29; 9.15, 29; 11.5, 7; Acts 13.48; 18.10; 2 Tim. 1.9; Mt. 11.25; 1 Pet. 1.2.

173 Fuller, *Letter IV*, in *Crispus and Gaius*, p. 675.

174 *The Reality and Efficacy of Divine Grace*, p. 546.

175 The choice of God to create the universe he did, with its specific set of people and events, rather than a universe with a different specific set of people and events *is* the sovereign and unalterable decree of God. The decree of God establishes his foreknowledge. God foreknows the future because he decreed the future.

176 *Reply to the Observations of Philanthropos*, p. 493.

177 Fuller, *Letter II*, in *Letters on Systematic Divinity*, p. 686 (cf. Eph. 2.8-10; 1 Cor. 1.29-31).

178 If it was in fact left open ended can be debated. His answer was that all three must be compatible because Scripture teaches all three. That seems an appropriate response, although some will not accept it. These are the people that hold to either the Arminian scheme or the pseudo-Calvinist scheme depending on whether they compromise the teachings of Scripture on the sovereign decree of God, or on the free agency of man respectively. Curiously, these same people believe in the Trinity, and in both the perfect humanity and perfect divinity of Christ. Why they accept these latter two apparent paradoxes as mysteries, but not the former is itself a mystery, or a paradox.

The next logical piece in Fuller's defence of the gospel against Arminianism is the extent of the atonement. If 'eternal, personal, and unconditional *election* be a truth, that of a special design in the death of Christ must necessarily follow'.[179] Fuller's discussions of the extent of the atonement were as much against the pseudo-Calvinists as against the Arminians. This was necessary because with this doctrine each of these systems contains an element of truth and an element of error. The balance and precision of Fuller was powerfully illustrated here as he managed to make sense of both the universal and the limited aspects of the death of Christ as found in Scripture. The error of the pseudo-Calvinists is to ignore the former, while the error of the Arminians is to ignore the latter.

Taylor's sentiments echoed the traditional Arminian position. 'Christ suffered to make a full atonement for all the sins of all men.'[180] Christ 'tasted death for every man'.[181] The problem with this position lies in the claim that a *full* atonement was made for *all* the sins of *all* men. If this statement were true, no man would stand condemned before God because *all* sins have been *fully* atoned for. From this it follows that anyone sent to hell is sent there unjustly, after all, *all* of his sins have been *fully* atoned for.[182] At this point the Arminian will object that people have to receive the gift of salvation, and if someone is sent to hell it is because they refused to accept the free gift of salvation from God.[183] This objection, however, is of no avail. Whether or not anyone chooses to accept the gift of salvation from God does not alter the fact that, in this system, *all* of their sins have *actually* been *fully* atoned for by Christ. All guilt and consequent accountability has been removed from all people and there remain no just grounds for the condemnation of anyone. Further, suppose on their supposition that it is the refusal to receive the gift of salvation that condemns a person to hell. If Christ truly did *fully* atone for *all* of their sins, then prior to refusing the offer of the gospel a person would have no guilt. Since the act of refusal itself is allegedly the source of the guilt that would see them condemned to hell since, as the Arminians would have it, Christ *fully* atoned for *all* sins, then even this guilt would have been dealt with at the cross. In fact, in this system, there is no one can be guilty before God and subject to his condemnation. Therefore, in the Arminian scheme God has no just grounds to condemn anyone to hell. Only two logical conclusions are open to this system. One, since not a single sin falls outside the scope of the atonement, all

---

179 *Reply to the Observations of Philanthropos*, p. 493.
180 Rinaldi, 'Tribe of Dan', p. 25.
181 Rinaldi, 'Tribe of Dan', p. 33.
182 The wages of sin is death, but in this scheme Christ *actually* paid these wages for all. *All* debts for *all* sin have been *fully* paid.
183 E.g., Rinaldi, 'Tribe of Dan', p. 25.

people will ultimately be saved. Two, God malevolently and unjustly sends some to hell with no grounds for their condemnation.

Were the Arminians content to assert that the atonement of Christ made provision for the salvation of any sinner who would respond in faith to the gospel, Fuller would have had no dispute with them on this subject. In Scripture, Fuller saw both a universal and a particular aspect to the death of Christ.

Fuller was very focused in his treatment of this issue in his correspondence to Taylor. What Fuller 'meant to hold out was between what the death of Christ was in itself adapted to, and sufficient for, and what it was designed by the Father and the Son actually to accomplish'.[184] Fuller confessed he was not 'fully acquainted with the arguments used on either side',[185] consequently his goal was not to provide an exhaustive defence but simply to show that a particular redemption was consistent with a universal offer of the gospel.[186]

Fuller argued that the death of Christ was unlimited in the sense that God would accept any who truly came to Christ in faith.[187] 'It is, all along, supposed that eternal salvation is promised by a faithful God to any and every exercise of what is spiritually good; and that if every sinner who hears the gospel were truly to come to Christ for salvation, every such sinner would undoubtedly be saved.'[188] 'I never supposed it possible for a soul to apply to Christ, and be disappointed.'[189] 'The Scripture assures us of *the exceeding great and tender mercy of God, and of his willingness to forgive all those who return to him in the name of his Son.*'[190]

Fuller saw no limitation in the sufferings of Christ. 'The sufferings of Christ, in themselves considered, are of *infinite* value, sufficient to have saved all the world, and a thousand worlds, if it had pleased God to have constituted them the price of their redemption, and to have made them effectual to that end.'[191] He also did not doubt that God loved all mankind, 'but the question is whether he loves them *all alike*'.[192]

---

184 Morris, *Memoirs*, p. 402.
185 *Reply to the Observations of Philanthropos*, p. 488.
186 *Reply to the Observations of Philanthropos*, p. 488.
187 Since Taylor shared these sentiments, although he took them further, Fuller did not need to support these statements in the present controversy. This issue was developed in his interactions with the pseudo-Calvinist, but is irrelevant for the purposes of this paper.
188 *Reply to the Observations of Philanthropos*, p. 484.
189 *Reply to the Observations of Philanthropos*, p. 484.
190 Fuller, *The Backslider*, in *Works*, III, p. 653.
191 *Reply to the Observations of Philanthropos*, pp. 488-489.
192 *Reply to the Observations of Philanthropos*, p. 494.

Fuller saw the limitation of the atonement as lying in the 'sovereign purpose and design of the Father and the Son'.[193] A way is open for all without distinction but which is effectual only for those whom God has appointed.[194] 'The death of Christ has opened a way whereby God can consistently with his justice forgive any sinner whatever who returns to him by Jesus Christ.'[195] Owing to depravity, however, if this were the end no one would be saved. For even one to be saved, effectual provision must be made for the application of the atonement.[196] Here again Fuller established the intimate connection between the various doctrines related to salvation. 'I consider particular redemption as merely a branch of election, or as the great design of election running through all the works of God. In giving his Son to die, he kept the design in view. In sending the gospel, he does the same.'[197] Christ died so all *could* be saved but that the elect *would* be saved.

To demonstrate the truth of particular redemption to Taylor, Fuller reduced the matter to two questions. '*First*, Had our Lord Jesus Christ any *absolute determination* in his death to save any of the human race? *Secondly*, Supposing such a determination to exist concerning some which does not exist concerning others, is this consistent with indefinite calls and universal invitations?'[198] Fuller had very perceptively identified the nucleus of the issue. Affirmative answers to both are fully sufficient to prove particular redemption.

Concerning the first question, 'if it be shown that Christ *had* such an absolute purpose in his death; the limited extent of that purpose must follow of course'.[199] With God, 'an *absolute* purpose must be effectual'.[200] All that God purposes does come to pass.[201] Therefore, if this absolute purpose extended to all mankind, all would be saved, but all are not saved so we 'must either suppose a limitation to the absolute determination of Christ to save, or deny any such determination to exist'.[202]

It is not difficult to establish that such a determination exists. Fuller identified Isaiah 53.11 as a key verse to this end: 'by his knowledge shall my righteous servant justify many *for* he shall bear their iniquity'.[203]

---

193 *Reply to the Observations of Philanthropos*, p. 488.
194 *Reply to the Observations of Philanthropos*, p. 496.
195 *Reply to the Observations of Philanthropos*, p. 489.
196 *Reply to the Observations of Philanthropos*, p. 489.
197 Fuller, *Conversations between Peter, James and John*, in *Works*, II, p. 694.
198 *Reply to the Observations of Philanthropos*, p. 489.
199 *Reply to the Observations of Philanthropos*, p. 489.
200 *Reply to the Observations of Philanthropos*, pp. 489-90.
201 E.g., Isa. 14.24, 27; 46.8-11; Dan. 4.34-35; Pss 115.3; 135.6.
202 *Reply to the Observations of Philanthropos*, p. 490.
203 *Reply to the Observations of Philanthropos*, p. 490.

This led Fuller to ask, 'How could it be certain that Christ should *justify many*, if there was no effectual provision made that *any* should *know* and believe in him?'[204] In addition to this explicit statement that Christ *shall*[205] justify many by bearing their sins, Fuller presented a variety of other passages. 'Those for whom Christ laid down his life are represented as being his sheep prior to coming to the fold.'[206] 'It became him for whom are all things—in bringing many sons into glory, to make the Captain of their salvation perfect through sufferings.'[207] Jesus was said to die 'that he might gather together in one the children of God that were scattered abroad'.[208] In others words, there was a determination in the death of Christ to save some. Jesus was not said to die to gather together *all people* into one, but only the children of God scattered abroad.

Fuller's acute perceptiveness was demonstrated in his discussion of Ephesians 5.26-29.[209] Husbands are commanded to love their wives in a unique way based upon the example of the unique love of Christ for the church. We are told that this unique love of Christ for the church was demonstrated in that he gave himself for the church. That he gave himself for the church, out of his unique love for the church, was for the express purpose of sanctifying the church. Scripture could not express the notion of particular redemption in a more unequivocal manner. That Christ fully, uniquely and deliberately gave himself only for the church out of his unique love for the church is the standard by which husbands are to love their wives. It would be irreverent to state the implications for the interpretation of this passage based on the Arminian notion that Christ died to make a full atonement for all of the sins of all people without distinction.

Fuller has demonstrated that an absolute determination in the death of Christ is a recurring theme in Scripture. This, as argued earlier, is sufficient to establish the truth of particular redemption. Even so, Fuller bolstered his position with a discussion of the sacerdotal aspects of the

---

204 *Reply to the Observations of Philanthropos*, p. 490. Fuller's question is decisive considering total depravity renders it certain no unregenerate person will come to Christ on their own.

205 A person cannot more strongly express their determination to do a certain thing than by saying that they *shall do* the certain thing. The language here is forceful, and Christ is the one who *shall do* what is spoken of. This establishes that he had an absolute determination that, as shown above, must be an effectual provision.

206 *Reply to the Observations of Philanthropos*, p. 490 (cf. Jn 10.11, 15-16; Heb. 13.20.

207 *Reply to the Observations of Philanthropos*, p. 491 (cf. Heb. 2.10). Note that Christ *was* the author of their salvation before his sufferings and thus before the sons who were to be brought into glory were even born.

208 *Reply to the Observations of Philanthropos*, p. 491 (cf. Jn 11.52.

209 *Reply to the Observations of Philanthropos*, p. 491.

death of Christ. The sacrificial system under the old covenant was a shadow of the sacrifice of Christ.[210] Thus, the old system allows us insight into the death of Christ by way of analogy. Under the old system, 'every sacrifice had its special appointment, and was supposed to atone for the sins of those, and those only, on whose behalf it was offered'.[211] By analogy, the sacrifice of Christ atoned for the sins only of those on whose behalf it was offered.

Fuller noted the substitutionary nature of the death of Christ in the Scripture statement that 'He hath redeemed us from the curse of the law, being made a curse for us'.[212] As our replacement, Christ was a real substitute. If Christ were a substitute for all, all would be saved. All are not saved, therefore Christ was not a substitution for all. This is made more emphatic by Fuller's observation that this redemption includes the real forgiveness of sin.[213] Anyone for whom Christ was a substitute has forgiveness. Not all have forgiveness so Christ did not die for all. When Christ died, each person for whom he died had his 'old self' crucified with him and so are said to have died with him.[214] Further, those for whom Christ gave himself are called a peculiar people.[215] If Christ gave himself for all, the phrase 'peculiar people' can have no intelligible meaning. The saints in heaven are said to be redeemed from among men.[216] 'But if all of every kindred, and tongue, and people, and nations were bought by the blood of Christ, there could be no possibility of any being bought *from among* them.'[217]

Arminians object that it is not explicitly said in Scripture that Christ died only for some. Fuller conceded this,[218] but replied that Scripture deals in positives, not negatives.[219] In other words, Scripture deals with those Christ died for, not those for whom he did not. Scripture does not explicitly say that all men should not be baptized, but the Arminians do not argue from this that all men therefore should be baptized.[220]

Expressing a common Arminian complaint, Taylor believed that a limitation in the atonement must be indicative of a defect in the mercy

---

210 Cf. Heb. 10.1-10.
211 *Reply to the Observations of Philanthropos*, p. 491.
212 *Reply to the Observations of Philanthropos*, p. 491 (cf. Gal. 3:10-13).
213 *Reply to the Observations of Philanthropos*, p. 491 (cf. Eph. 1.7; Col. 1.14).
214 *Reply to the Observations of Philanthropos*, p. 491 (cf. Rom. 6.5-8).
215 *Reply to the Observations of Philanthropos*, p. 491 (cf. Tit. 2.13-14; 1 Pet. 2.7-10).
216 Cf. Rev. 5.9-10.
217 *Reply to the Observations of Philanthropos*, p. 494.
218 He admitted that the exact words are not found in Scripture, but he has soundly demonstrated that this exact idea is.
219 *Reply to the Observations of Philanthropos*, p. 495.
220 *Reply to the Observations of Philanthropos*, p. 495.

and love of God.[221] First, as Fuller noted, this presupposes God must do all he can for the salvation of all, consistent with his justice, or else be wanting in love.[222] Once again the Arminians have pinned themselves into a corner. God could have spread the gospel over all the earth, over all time since the fall, but he did not.[223] Even more problematic for the Arminian scheme is the fact that not only did God not spread the gospel to all, he actively *prevented* the spread of the gospel.[224] Similarly, not as much was done for the salvation of Tyre, Sidon, and Sodom as was for Chorazin, Bethsaida, and Capernaum.[225] Worse yet, had that much been done for those cities, we are told they would have turned to God in faith and repentance. What does this imply about God in their scheme?

This Arminian complaint is further undone by foreknowledge. If God foreknew all events, and that it would be better if some were never born, then in the Arminian scheme God is unloving and unmerciful by allowing them to be born.[226]

Another Arminian objection is that there are passages where the blessings of the cross are expressed in universal language and, therefore, must extend to all. Fuller responds with a list of passages in which various other blessings are expressed in universal language but that no one would consider as extending to all.[227] If the Arminians demand we *must* interpret universal language literally, these passages teach universalism.[228] Fuller rightly observed that the benefits of the cross are sometimes discussed in universal terms as a response to the belief of the Jews of the day that the Messiah would be for them only.[229]

The Arminians object that there are no passages in which 'whole world' is used to signify the elect. They insist this phrase must always be interpreted literally. If they are right, then there is at least one instance in which Paul was plainly wrong. If Paul is in error in any of his writings, scripture is not inerrant. Given that, we could no longer be confident that the Bible is the Word of God. The problem for their position is that in Romans 1.8 Paul commended the church at Rome because their faith was spoken of throughout the *whole world*.[230] This is a curious situation

---

221 *The Reality and Efficacy of Divine Grace*, p. 542.
222 *The Reality and Efficacy of Divine Grace*, p. 542.
223 *The Reality and Efficacy of Divine Grace*, p. 542.
224 Cf. Acts 16.6-7.
225 *The Reality and Efficacy of Divine Grace*, p. 542 (cf. Mt. 11.20-23).
226 *Reply to the Observations of Philanthropos*, p. 495.
227 *Reply to the Observations of Philanthropos*, p. 496. Fuller lists the following; Pss 22.27; 65.2; Isa. 40.5; 54.5; 66.23; Joel 2.28; Luke 3.5; John 12.32.
228 *Reply to the Observations of Philanthropos*, p. 496.
229 *Reply to the Observations of Philanthropos*, p. 497 (cf. Gal. 3.28; Jn 11.47-53).
230 *Reply to the Observations of Philanthropos*, p. 499.

considering the gospel had not yet spread over a large geographical area, nor had all of the countries of the world been discovered. How, for example, could people in North America have known about the faith of the Roman church? How, for example, could the apostle have known what the people in Australia spoke of? On the supposition of the Arminians, this passage destroys the inerrancy and reliability of Scripture. Fuller was right to conclude that here 'whole world' must signify *only* the believing part.[231] That the phrase is used in a limited sense in this passage does not imply that it must always be interpreted in this sense, only that this is a valid possible interpretation in other passages. Similarly, Matthew 13.33 must have believers in mind with the expression 'until the whole be leavened' since only believers are leavened by the gospel.[232]

Space does not permit a detailed study of Fuller's responses to all of the individual Arminian proof texts. These primarily involved applications of the arguments outlined above. The responses to the two chief Arminian proof texts do, however, warrant comment. Arminians interpret the phrase 'ransom for all' in 1 Timothy 2.6-7 as proof that Christ made atonement for all. Fuller confuted this with an examination of this passage within its broader context.[233] In the first verse, Paul urges that prayers be made in behalf of *all men*. This is a fine thought, but not necessarily practical. We could never pray in a specific way for each individual on the face of the earth.[234] At best we could pray in some general manner for *all men* collectively. Surely the apostle had the latter in mind. Thus, the *all men* in this verse has a general sense rather than a particular sense. In verse two, *all* is used again in a general rather than particular sense. We may not, or need not, know all who are in authority over us, we are simply instructed to pray for them as a class of people.[235] The sense of *all* in this passage is established by its use in the first two verses and since the context remains the same, the meaning must remain the same throughout. It follows that Christ gave himself a ransom for *all* in a general sense. He is the saviour for all nations and the only possible

---

231 *Reply to the Observations of Philanthropos*, p. 499.
232 *Reply to the Observations of Philanthropos*, p. 499.
233 *Reply to the Observations of Philanthropos*, pp. 497-98.
234 To demonstrate the absurdity of this interpretation, there currently are approximately five billion people living on the earth. If we decided to devote ten seconds of prayer for each, it would take us over 1,580 years, non-stop, to pray for each person once.
235 Of course, where possible it is preferable to pray for specific individual leaders. This passage simply reflects the fact that this is not always practical, and that the effectiveness of the prayers does not require this.

way to God.²³⁶ His death was of sufficient value to allow the salvation of all who come to Christ in genuine faith.²³⁷

The other favourite Arminian passage is 1 John 2.2 where Christ is called the propitiation for the sins of the *whole world*. As with Romans 1.8, it is necessary to determine if it is logical to interpret *whole world* literally here. First, if Christ was a propitiation for everyone then no one would be condemned and all would be saved. All are not saved so it is not logical to interpret *whole world* literally in this passage. Secondly, Romans 3.25 shows that this propitiation is through faith and thus 1 John 2.2 can hardly apply to unbelievers.²³⁸ Since many will never have faith, the propitiation was not for all, meaning that the literal interpretation of *whole world* is not logical. It seems that here, like in Romans 1.8, the best interpretation of the phrase is as a reference collectively to all believers of all times.

Fuller convincingly demonstrated that the death of Christ was of sufficient value to save any number of sinners if they would apply to Christ, but was limited in application such that only the sins of the elect were actually atoned for. Prior to exploring Fuller's demonstration of the concordance of particular redemption with universal invitations, it is appropriate to introduce some of his remarks to the pseudo-Calvinists.

Pseudo-Calvinists are as much in opposition to Fuller's understanding of the atonement as the Arminians are. They misunderstand the atonement as not only being limited in application, but also in value.²³⁹ They also have the misconception that their view of the atonement is the traditional Reformed view.²⁴⁰

Fuller observed that many who held the Calvinist doctrine of predestination have distinguished between the *sufficiency* and *efficiency* of Christ's death.²⁴¹ This distinction is found in *The Thirty-Nine Articles* (1571) of the English Reformers.²⁴² Owen distinguished between 'what the atonement of Christ is in itself *sufficient for*, and what it is as *applied*,

---

236 E.g., Gal. 3.28; Jn 14.6.

237 This is all that is required by a hermeneutically sound reading of this passage. Any more that the Arminians would like it to teach leads them straight back into the errors discussed earlier.

238 *Reply to the Observations of Philanthropos*, p. 498.

239 Fuller refuted the errors of this view in his disputes with Mr. Button (*Works*, II). An involved review of this is irrelevant for the purposes of this paper in which the focus is Arminianism.

240 No doubt if these individuals were anonymously provided certain passages from Calvin himself, they would accuse him of not being a Calvinist and of opposing Reformed theology.

241 *The Reality and Efficacy of Divine Grace*, p. 545.

242 *The Reality and Efficacy of Divine Grace*, p. 545.

under the sovereign will of God'.²⁴³ Fuller found support for his position with the Canons of Dort: 'The death of the Son of God is the only and most complete sacrifice and satisfaction for sins of infinite value, abundantly sufficient to expiate the sins of the whole world.'²⁴⁴ Calvin himself expressed this exact same understanding of the atonement. His comments on 1 John 2.2 are unmistakably clear. Concerning this verse some 'have said that Christ suffered sufficiently for the whole world, but efficiently only for the elect. This solution has commonly prevailed in the schools. Though I allow that what has been said is true, yet I deny that it is suitable to this passage.'²⁴⁵ Fuller's understanding of the atonement is exactly that of Calvin himself, namely Christ died sufficiently for the whole world but efficiently only for the elect.

Before examining Fuller's defence of the compatibility of particular redemption with universal invitations, it is worth examining Calvin's opinion of universal invitations.²⁴⁶ Concerning the use of 'world'²⁴⁷ in John 3.16, Calvin wrote: 'And he has used a general term, both to invite indiscriminately all to share in life and to cut off every excuse from unbelievers.'²⁴⁸ 'He nevertheless shows He is favourable to the whole world whom He calls all without exception to the faith of Christ.'²⁴⁹ 'Christ is open to all and displayed to all, but God opens the eyes only of the elect that they may seek Him by faith.'²⁵⁰

According to Fuller, 'That the gospel is an *embassy of peace*, addressed to sinners indefinitely, and that any sinner whatever has a warrant to apply to the Saviour, and a promise of acceptance on his application, is evident from the whole current of Scripture. To oppose Arminianism by the denial of this well-known truth must be an unsuccessful attempt. No Arminian, so long as he has a Bible in his hand, can ever be persuaded that the language of Scripture exhortations to repentance and faith in Christ is not indefinite... I believe such a way of

---

243 Fuller, *Letter III—Substitution*, in *Six Letters to Dr. Ryland*, in *Works*, II, p. 707 n..

244 Fuller, *Letter V—Calvinism*, in *Six Letters to Dr. Ryland*, p. 12.

245 John Calvin, *Calvin's Commentaries: The Gospel According to St. John 11–21; The First Epistle of John* (trans. T.H.L. Parker; Grand Rapids, MI: Eerdmans, 1988).

246 This is both that the Arminians would see what Calvin truly believed, and that the pseudo-Calvinists would be silenced.

247 Pseudo-Calvinists here misinterpret 'world' as signifying the elect, while Arminians misinterpret this passage as proof that Christ made a full atonement for everyone.

248 John Calvin, *Calvin's Commentaries: The Gospel According to St. John 1–10; The First Epistle of John* (trans. T.H.L. Parker; Grand Rapids, MI: Eerdmans, 1988), p. 74.

249 Calvin, *John 1–10*, p. 74.

250 Calvin, *John 1–10*, p. 75.

speaking amongst the Calvinists has been more than a little advantageous to the Arminian cause.'[251] No one needs to fear truly seeking God in vain. 'If they are *willing* to be saved *in God's way*, nothing shall hinder their salvation.'[252] 'All the comfort contained in the gospel is to be presented to the sinner in a way of invitation; but no comfort is afforded him in a way of promise, but as repenting and believing the gospel.'[253] 'In some sense, the salvation of every sinner is *possible* as no one knows what will be his end, every man while in the land of the living is in the field of hope.'[254]

The chief reason no inconsistency exists with the universal gospel invitations and a particular redemption is the unlimited sufficiency of the atonement. The gospel can be sincerely offered to all because the death of Christ was sufficient to provide salvation to all who respond in faith. It is certain that only the elect will respond in faith because they alone will be regenerated and thus willing. Since those who reject the gospel do so of their own free will, and not by compulsion, they alone are to blame for their condemnation. They had salvation sincerely offered to them but they freely decided they would have none of it. The fault lies with the ones being invited, not the one inviting. No one would question the goodness of a man who sincerely invited all of his family and friends to a banquet, even though he knew some would choose not to attend.[255] They were welcome to come, but did not want to come.

If a limited atonement renders a general invitation insincere, then the Arminian scheme has it no better. Following Arminian reasoning, it is insincere for God to invite people to accept the gospel that he foreknows will not.[256]

If universal invitations are insincere because only the sins of the elect were atoned for, then in fact universal invitations must be insincere under *all* theological systems. There is no forgiveness possible for those who have blasphemed the Holy Spirit so it must be insincere to preach the gospel to these people, yet the Arminians preach the gospel to all without distinction.[257] Whether certain individuals cannot be saved because they have blasphemed the Holy Spirit, or because they are not elect, the principle is the same. Either both systems have sincere universal invitations or they both have insincere universal invitations.[258]

---

251 *Gospel of Christ Worthy of All Acceptation*, p. 434.
252 *The Reality and Efficacy of Divine Grace*, p. 546.
253 Fuller, *Aspects of Gospel Promises to the Wicked*, in *Answers to Queries*, in *Works*, III, p. 773.
254 *Gospel of Christ Worthy of All Acceptation*, p. 452.
255 *The Reality and Efficacy of Divine Grace*, p. 543.
256 *The Reality and Efficacy of Divine Grace*, p. 543.
257 Cf. Mt. 12.31-32. See also 1 Jn 5.16.
258 *Reply to the Observations of Philanthropos*, p. 504.

To complete the study of Fuller's arguments against Arminianism, his understanding of the doctrine of the perseverance of the saints will be reviewed. Fuller was consistent throughout his works in his methodology. Here, too, he emphasized the connection between the various doctrines. 'The doctrines of *efficacious grace* and the *final perseverance of believers*, are in themselves of a humbling nature. They imply the utter depravity of the human heart, as being proof against every thing but omnipotent love, and the proneness of the best of men to draw back even to perdition, were it not that they are preserved by grace.'[259]

In perseverance, Fuller saw no perfection in the life of the believer. True Christians can and do backslide, but not everyone who makes a profession of faith in Christ is actually saved.[260] The problem is that at the time it is not evident which is the case.[261] 'The estimate we form of *character* must be regulated by the *habitual course* of life and conduct.'[262] 'All true repentance is followed by a *forsaking* of the evil, and where this effect is not produced, there can be no scriptural ground to hope for forgiveness.'[263] It is important not to mistake feelings of shame or sorrow over sins with true repentance.[264]

Like faith, repentance is the fruit of regeneration. It is a manifestation of the new and holy prevailing inclinations. This is the reason that conversion is evidenced by a new course of life. The new life, however, is not without stumbling. 'The stumbling of such persons is not that they should fall; but rather that they should stand with greater care and firmness.'[265]

With this, Fuller has laid the framework for understanding the passages that warn about falling away.[266] Arminians tend to interpret these passages as evidence that a person can lose their salvation. This seems a plausible interpretation when these passages are considered in isolation. In light of the Calvinist understanding of election, grace, and particular redemption, however, this interpretation is untenable. The traditional Reformed interpretation of these passages is that they are not describing true believers. There will always be some individuals within the church who are not truly saved, but think that they are. Passages such as these serve as a warning for all within the visible church to examine themselves

---

259 Fuller, *Antinomianism Contrasted with the Religion Taught and Exemplified in the Holy Scriptures*, in *Works*, II, p. 761.

260 *The Backslider*, pp. 635-36.

261 *The Backslider*, p. 637.

262 Fuller, *Character Not Determined By Individual Acts*, in *Answers to Queries*, p. 784.

263 *The Backslider*, p. 644.

264 *The Backslider*, p. 644.

265 *The Backslider*, p. 637.

266 E.g., Heb. 6.4-6; 10.26-31; 2 Pet. 2.20-22.

to be sure that they are truly saved.²⁶⁷ Evidence for salvation is not some decision made in the distant past, but rather a present and abiding faith that manifests itself in increasing holiness and obedience. No real challenge to the doctrine of final perseverance is found in these passages.

The more challenging passages are those that seem to teach that being saved in the present is no guarantee of forgiveness for sins committed in the future.²⁶⁸ Of all such passages, 1 John 1.9 may be the strongest.²⁶⁹ *If we confess our sins, God will forgive us.* It follows that if we do not confess our sins, God will not forgive us. The challenge, however, does not lie in the *if*, but in the *we*. Here 'we' includes John and his audience whom he addressed as his little children.²⁷⁰ This either intends all those who profess faith in Christ, or strictly those who have real faith in Christ. Since the former includes the latter it is unquestionably addressed, at least, to those already saved. That being the case, the forgiveness for sins committed by Christians depends upon the confession of those sins.²⁷¹

Fuller showed that these passages are fully consistent with Calvinism, although his solution may appear controversial to some. He did not try to circumvent the apparently plain meaning of 1 John 1.9. 'Yet to speak of sins as being pardoned before they are repented of, or even committed, is not only to maintain that on which the scriptures are silent, but to contradict the current language of their testimony.'²⁷² Fuller added that this is not at all 'inconsistent with the certain perseverance of true believers, or with the promise that they shall not come into condemnation'.²⁷³ 'The truth taught us in this promise is not that if after believing in Christ, we live in sin, and die without repentance, we shall nevertheless escape condemnation; but that provision is made in behalf of believers that they shall *not live in sin*, that they shall *not die without repentance*, but return to God, and so obtain forgiveness. The promise of non-condemnation includes that of repentance and perseverance. I will put my law in their hearts, and they shall not depart from me.'²⁷⁴

Fuller's argument followed the most natural reading of such passages. This approach is consistent with particular redemption and does not require any changes in understanding of the atonement. Christ did

---

267 Cf. 2 Cor. 13.5.
268 E.g., Mt. 6.14-15; 18.23-25; 1 Jn 1.9.
269 Mt. 18.23-25, which seems to teach God may revoke his forgiveness, makes as strong a statement. Owing to the similarities, the explanation of one such passage will serve for all.
270 E.g., 1 Jn 2.1; 5.21.
271 This is not only an apparent problem for the Calvinist doctrine of final perseverance, but also for all others who believe in 'the security of the believer'.
272 Morris, *Memoirs*, p. 236 (from a sermon on justification).
273 Morris, *Memoirs*, p. 237.
274 Morris, *Memoirs*, p. 237.

actually pay for all of the sins of the elect. The only change in understanding concerns the applications of the benefits of the atonement. The complete forgiveness of the elect for all sins, past, present and future, is not received in one lump sum at conversion, but rather in installments over the course of the believer's lifetime in response to the confession of sins committed.

This is consistent with the Calvinist understanding of grace. Just as the grace of God through the work of the Spirit regenerates the elect resulting in faith and repentance, the grace of God through the work of the Spirit is the cause of ongoing faith and repentance. It would be as wrong to think our perseverance depended upon our efforts as it would be to think that our regeneration depended upon our will. *God* who began the good work in us will perfect it until the day of Christ.[275] We are instructed to work out our salvation because it is God working in us to *will* and *work* for his good pleasure.[276] The perseverance of the elect is certain in this view because it is the Spirit who convicts of sin.[277]

Finally, this is consistent with election. God's decree not only includes the sure salvation of the elect,[278] but also their sure perseverance.[279] Since the perseverance of the elect is sure, so too is the timely confession of sins throughout the life of the believer, thus ensuring the full forgiveness of the sins of the elect. The same God who provided everything necessary for the salvation of the elect will also provide everything needed for the perseverance of the saints.

Closing Remarks

Considering the volumes of material written by Fuller, it is difficult to do him justice in such a short study. All of his chief arguments against Arminianism have been highlighted here. Fuller developed each in much more detail than was possible to convey here. If it seems that there are any holes in Fuller's anti-Arminian apologetics, the fault lies with the selection of material for inclusion and not with Fuller himself.

There has not been a better refutation of the Arminian scheme than that provided by Fuller. The shortcoming is that it was not provided in one systematic work, but rather must be found running throughout his works, although with its core in his controversy with Dan Taylor. When these various sources are collated, the skill of Fuller is abundantly obvious. His perceptiveness and tenacity are evident in the way he

---

275 Cf. Phil. 1.6. See also Gal. 3.3.
276 Cf. Phil. 2.12-13.
277 Cf. Jn 16.8.
278 E.g., Eph. 1.3-5.
279 E.g., Jn 6.7, 39-40, 44.

reduced the entire Arminian scheme to its foundational propositions, and then from those propositions sought to refute it. Over the course of his writings, he hoped to demonstrate that the Arminian scheme is not self-consistent. Moreover, Fuller attempted to prove that the Arminian objections to Calvinism do not stand up under scrutiny, and in fact, if allowed often defeat their own system. In addition to arguing that their system is untenable, he also maintained that it is unscriptural. One might be inclined to start with the latter approach, but Fuller chose wisely not to do so since that methodology inevitably deteriorates into a competition of the proof texts. He further demonstrated that the Arminian objections to Calvinism are invalid. He completed the defence by showing that the Calvinist system is solidly rooted in Scripture. His repeated emphasis on the interconnection between the various doctrines is worth remembering. Individual doctrines, when studied in isolation from all other related doctrines, are prone to distortion or even error.

The Arminian may not like what Fuller wrote, and he may not agree with it, but it will be difficult for him to refute it. On the other hand, the Calvinist should not be puffed up by what he reads in Fuller. It must be remembered that Fuller's target was the Arminian system, not those who professed it. As much as possible, he tried to demonstrate love and grace to his opponents. Similarly, that he charged Arminianism with heterodoxy is not to be interpreted as a charge against the individuals who held the system. He recognized that the majority of Arminians are sincere in their beliefs, hold a high view of Scripture and desire to honour Christ with their lives. It was for these very people that he wrote this material; with the hopes of turning them away from the views they held.

CHAPTER 5

'The Oracles of God': Andrew Fuller's Response to Deism

Michael A.G. Haykin

The Age of Reason (1794, 1795)

In the last few hundred years there have been few books which have generated as much controversy as *The Age of Reason* (1794, 1795) by Thomas Paine (1737–1809).¹ Its author was a warm advocate and brilliant popularizer of a variety of radical causes: the abolition of slavery, the American and French Revolutions, and Deism. Although Paine had been raised a Quaker, by the time he came to write the first part of *The Age of Reason* in 1794 he could state with regard to his religious views:²

> I believe in one God, and no more; and I hope for happiness beyond this life... I do not believe in the creed professed by the Jewish Church, by the Roman Church, by the Greek Church, by the Turkish Church, by the Protestant Church, nor by any church that I know of. My own mind is my own church.

The Deism which Paine sought to propagate by means of the popular press was certainly nothing novel in the 1790s. The first significant English work to advocate Deism had been *Christianity not Mysterious* by John Toland (1670–22), which was published in 1696. Paine's

---

1　*The Age of Reason* was published in two parts, the first part appearing in 1794 and the second in the following year. For a discussion of the details surrounding its publication, see Alfred Owen Aldridge, *Man of Reason: The Life of Thomas Paine* (London: Cresset Press, 1960), pp. 230-32.

2　Thomas Paine, *The Age of Reason* (introduction by Philip S. Foner; Secaucus, NJ: Citadel Press, 1974), p. 50. On the life and thought of Paine, see David Powell, *Tom Paine: The Greatest Exile* (London/Sydney: Croom Helm, 1985); Ian Dyck (ed.), *Citizen of the World: Essays on Thomas Paine* (New York: St. Martin's Press, 1988).

importance lies in the fact that he was the first to seek to communicate deistic beliefs to the common man.³

The leading proponents of Deism, men such as Toland, Anthony Collins (1676–1729) and Matthew Tindal (1655–1733), typified an age sick of and disgusted with the religious wars and controversies of the two preceding centuries. But, in regarding the Bible as the true source of these controversies and wars, these men went much further than most. They sought a religion shorn of its dependence on revelation and the miraculous, in which only that which could successfully weather rational criticism need be affirmed as religious truth. Moreover, the advent of Newtonian physics, with its understandable emphasis on rational inquiry, tended to bolster the confidence of the Deists in human reason.

The Age of Reason displays this deistic perspective to the full. Paine disputed Christianity's claim that it is founded directly upon divine revelation. Due to the fact that human language is regularly in a state of flux and because of the variety of problems presented by translation from one language into another, Paine believed that special revelation in a written form is simply not possible.

> The Word of God cannot exist in any written or human language... Human language is local and changeable, and is therefore incapable of being used as the means of unchangeable and universal information.⁴

But he goes on to assert:⁵

> There is a Word of God: there is a revelation. The Word of God is the creation we behold and it is in *this* word, which no human invention can counterfeit or alter, that God speaketh universally to man... The creation is the Bible of the Deist. He there reads, in the handwriting of the Creator himself, the certainty of His existence and the immutability of His power, and all other Bibles and Testaments are to him forgeries.

Consequently, all that can be known about God is to be obtained through the exercise of human reason in the examination of God's works in nature.⁶ Moreover, Paine regards the only sure foundation for such an examination to be the world-view of Newtonian science, in which God was viewed as the First Cause of the universe and a wise clockmaker, whose finished work needed only a little tinkering on rare occasions. In such a world-view the biblical affirmations about God's rule of and

---

3   Samuel Edwards, *Rebel! A Biography of Tom Paine* (New York/Washington: Praeger Publishers, 1974), pp. 186-87, 192-93; Edward Royle (ed.), *The Infidel Tradition from Paine to Bradlaugh* (London: Macmillan, 1976), p. 3.
4   Paine, *Age of Reason*, pp. 63, 68. See also pp. 97-98, 182.
5   Paine, *Age of Reason*, pp. 68, 185. See also pp. 69, 98.
6   Paine, *Age of Reason*, pp. 70, 187-88.

intervention in history seemed irrelevant to Paine, even blasphemous. As Paine asserts:[7]

> We can know God only through His works... The principles of science lead to this knowledge: for the Creator of man is the Creator of science, and it is through that medium that man can see God, as it were, face to face... It has been by wandering from the immutable laws of Science, and the light of reason, and setting up an invented thing called revealed religion, that so many wild and blasphemous conceits have been formed of the Almighty.

Moral and textual criticisms of the Scriptures especially abound in the second part of *The Age of Reason*. For instance, Paine cited the differing genealogies in Matthew and Luke as what appeared to him to be a glaring example of the falsity of Scriptures.

> If these men, Matthew and Luke, set out with a falsehood...in the very commencement of their history of Jesus Christ, and of whom and what he was, what authority...is there left for believing the strange things they tell us afterward? If they cannot be believed in their account of his natural genealogy, how are we to believe them when they tell us he was the Son of God begotten by a ghost, and that an angel announced this in secret to his mother?[8]

Underlying this criticism is Paine's belief that:[9]

> Truth is a uniform thing; and as to inspiration and revelation, were we to admit it, it is impossible to suppose it can be contradictory.

The only portions of Scripture which contain any truth about God are, according to Paine, certain chapters of Job and Psalm 19. In the words of Paine, they are:[10]

> True *deistical* compositions, for they treat of the *Deity* through His works. They take the book of creation as the word of God, they refer to no other book, and all the inferences they make are drawn from that volume.

---

7   Paine, *Age of Reason*, pp. 187, 188, 190.
8   Paine, *Age of Reason*, p. 158. For a plausible solution to the differences in these genealogies, see R.B. Nettelhorst, 'The Genealogy of Jesus', *Journal of the Evangelical Theological Society* 31 (1988), pp. 169-72.
9   Paine, *Age of Reason*, p. 158.
10 Paine, *Age of Reason*, p. 70. Paine presumably has in mind only the first six verses in Psalm 19. The subject of Psalm 19.7-11 is Scripture. On Paine's view of Psalm 19 as a 'Deistical Psalm', see also his 'To John Mason', in *The Complete Writings of Thomas Paine* (collected and ed. Philip S. Foner; 2 vols; New York: Citadel Press, 1969), II, p. 814 n. 21.

Paine's broadside against the scriptural foundations of Christianity did not go unanswered.[11] Franklyn K. Prochaska has noted at least thirty rejoinders which saw the light of day before 1800.[12] However, in listing these rejoinders and examining some of them, Prochaska curiously overlooks those made by the Calvinistic Baptist, Andrew Fuller.

The Nature and Importance of an Intimate Knowledge of Divine Truth (1796)

When, towards the close of 1794, John Ryland, Jr. (1753–1825) wrote and asked Fuller if he had yet seen *The Age of Reason* (presumably the first part), Fuller replied:[13]

> You ask, if I have seen Paine's *Age of Reason*. I have not. You do not know what reading is to me; one hour would bring on the headach. A newspaper is as much as I can read at a time. I could do many things, if strength would allow it. Plans of various works have entered my mind: but all must be dropped, or nearly so, for want of strength. Reading is worse to me, than thinking or writing.

'The headach' to which Fuller refers in this passage was a result of a minor paralytic stroke in 1793. This stroke left him with a tendency to severe headaches for the rest of his life. But by the middle of 1796 Fuller had found the strength to read and digest Paine's work. For on 1 June 1796, at the annual ministerial meeting of the Northamptonshire Association, Fuller preached a sermon which contained his first public response to Paine and *The Age of Reason*. Entitled *The Nature and Importance of an intimate Knowledge of Divine Truth*, it takes Hebrews 5.12-14 for its text.[14] At the very beginning of the sermon Fuller gives a

---

11 Paine maintained that he wrote *The Age of Reason* in order to stem the tide of atheism in revolutionary France, see *Age of Reason*, pp. 49-50; *Letter to Samuel Adams*, in *Complete Writings*, II, p. 1436. But most of it reads more like a diatribe against Christianity than against atheism.

12 Franklyn K. Prochaska, 'Thomas Paine's *The Age of Reason* Revisited', *Journal of the History of Ideas* 33 (1972), pp. 561-76. For another study of responses to Paine's *The Age of Reason*, see Richard H. Popkin, '*The Age of Reason* versus *The Age of Revelation*. Two critics of Tom Paine: David Levi and Elias Boudinot', in J.A. Leo Lemay (ed.), *Deism, Masonry, and the Enlightenment* (Newark: University of Delaware Press/London and Toronto: Associated University Presses, 1987), pp. 158-70.

13 Cited John Ryland, Jr., *The Work of Faith, the Labour of Love, and the Patience of Hope, illustrated: in the Life and Death of the Rev. Andrew Fuller* (London: Button & Son, 2nd edn, 1818), p. 227.

14 Andrew Fuller, *The Nature and Importance of an intimate Knowledge of Divine Truth*, in *The Complete Works of the Rev. Andrew Fuller* (ed. and revised Joseph Belcher; 3 vols; Harrisonburg, VA: Sprinkle Publications, 1988 [3rd edn, 1845]), I, pp. 160-74.

general statement about the nature of Scripture. Commenting on the phrase 'the oracles of God' (Heb. 5.12), he states that it is a phrase 'strongly expressive of [the] Divine inspiration and infallibility of the Scriptures'.[15] In them God speaks and conveys knowledge about himself which can be obtained from nowhere else.[16] Fuller thus implies that Paine is sadly mistaken if he thinks that his unaided reason can reflect on the realm of nature and thereby derive sufficient and accurate knowledge about God. 'Reason', Fuller insists, 'as it exists in depraved creatures, is not a proper standard of truth.' Thus, the need for a better standard, one that was infallible, 'the oracles of God'.[17] There are some truths about God and his work in the Scriptures which pose no substantial problems for the human reason to comprehend. Yet, there are others 'which utterly surpass our understanding, but which require to be believed as matters of pure revelation'.[18] Of the latter, Fuller sees the doctrine of the Trinity as a good example.[19]

Fuller proceeds to emphasize that the search for truth about God must begin at and be rooted in the Scriptures.

> Many religious people appear to be contented with seeing truth in the light in which some great and good man has placed it; but if ever we enter into the gospel to purpose, it must be by reading the word of God for ourselves, and by praying and meditating upon its sacred contents. It is 'in God's light that we must see light' [cf. Ps. 36.9]... The writings of great and good men are not to be despised, any more than their preaching; only let them not be treated as oracular. The best of men, in this imperfect state, view things *partially*, and therefore are in danger of laying an improper stress upon some parts of Scripture, to the neglect of other parts of equal, and sometimes of superior importance... If we adopt the principles of fallible men, without searching the Scriptures for ourselves, and inquiring whether or not these things be so, they will not, even allowing them to be on the side of truth, avail us, as if we had learned them from a higher authority. Our faith, in this case, will stand in the wisdom of man, and not in the power of God... Truth learned only at second-hand will be to us what Saul's armour was to David; we shall be at a loss how to use it in the day of trial.[20]

---

15   *Nature and Importance*, p. 160.
16   *Nature and Importance*, pp. 160-61.
17   *Nature and Importance*, p. 161.
18   *Nature and Importance*, p. 163.
19   *Nature and Importance*, p. 163. Fuller's choice of 1 John 5.7 at this point as biblical support for the doctrine of the Trinity is an unfortunate one, since this text is uniformly recognized as a later interpolation. Fuller is aware of the discussion about the authenticity of this text, but he believes it to be genuine. See his *Letters on Systematic Divinity*, in *Works*, I, pp. 708-709.
20   *Nature and Importance*, p. 164.

Fuller here differentiates between the views of fallible men, albeit good men, and the truth of God in Scripture. The views of fallible men are, at best, unable to provide nourishment necessary for genuine spiritual growth, partial perspectives on the truth, and inadequate to support the believer in a time of trial. By contrast, Scripture enlightens the believer, brings balance and perspective to his life, and provides him with a wholly adequate defence against the testings of life. Fuller clearly presupposes that the fallibility which characterizes the writings of all Christian authors is completely absent from Scripture.[21]

At the conclusion of this sermon, Fuller comments on the theological scene facing himself and his fellow pastors.

> The present age seems to be an age of trial. Not only is the gospel corrupted by those who hear the Christian name, but, of late, you well know, it has been openly assailed. The most direct and daring opposition has been made to the very name of Christianity.[22]

Fuller's audience would have had little difficulty in identifying the perpetrator and nature of this open assault on the Christian faith: Paine and his *The Age of Reason*. Indeed, only a few sentences later Fuller explicitly refers to Paine's book by name. Fuller believes that the reason for the popularity of Paine's book lies not so much in the book itself, but in the fact that 'the turn or temper of the present age is peculiarly in favour of infidelity'.[23] But Fuller has no fears for the ultimate safety of the church.

> I am not going to alarm you with any idea that the *church is in danger*; no, my brethren; the church of which we, I trust, are members, and of which Christ, and Christ alone, is the head, is not in danger; it is built upon a rock, and the gates of hell shall not prevail against it... Nevertheless, it becomes us to feel for the souls of men, especially for the rising generation; and to warn even good men that they be not unarmed in the evil day.[24]

Fuller's concern for 'the rising generation' found partial expression in the following year, when the Northamptonshire Association sent out its annual circular letter to its member churches. It was written by Fuller's close friend John Sutcliff (1752–1814), pastor of the Baptist church in

---

21 Cf. Fuller's statement in *On An Intimate and Practical Acquaintance with the Word of God*, in *Works*, I, p. 483: 'Learn your religion form the Bible. Let that be your decisive rule. Adopt not a body of sentiments, or even a single sentiment, solely on the authority of any man... Dare to think for yourself. Human compositions are fallible. But the Scriptures were written by men who wrote as they were inspired by the Holy Spirit.'
22 *Nature and Importance*, p. 172.
23 *Nature and Importance*, p. 172.
24 *Nature and Importance*, p. 172.

Olney,[25] and addressed the subject of *The Divinity of the Christian Religion*. In particular, the letter sought to display the divinely inspired nature of the Bible. Surely it is no coincidence that Sutcliff was requested by his colleagues, including Fuller, to draw up such a letter at this particular point in time. Addressed to the members of the Baptist churches in the Northamptonshire Association, it plays an important role in Fuller's desire decisively to repel Paine's attack against Christianity on the very field of battle which the latter had chosen, namely, the mind of the common man. Noteworthy are the following remarks on inspiration which Sutcliff makes near the beginning of the letter.

> Some will probably ask, 'What do you mean by inspiration?' To such we reply: it is a supernatural influence upon the mind of a rational creature, enabling him to think, and if necessary to speak, or write, in such a manner as he could not have done without it. True, it admits of various degrees. When the writer was treating upon a subject with which he was previously acquainted, he only needed the Spirit of inspiration to assist his recollection, and secure him from error and mistake. But on many occasions, the Divine Spirit suggested the thoughts and ideas immediately to the mind of the penman of the sacred page. How this was done, we know not. Nor is it necessary we should. We hear that a certain fact is asserted. The credit we give to it, is not founded on, or proportioned to, the case with which we comprehend it, but the evidence by which it is supported. What we here assert is, that the Bible was written under such an influence as we have now described. Should satisfactory evidence be given of this, the natural consequence will be, that it contains a revelation of the mind and will of God, and ought to be our guide in matters of religion.[26]

Fuller, as will be seen, fully concurred with Sutcliff's view that there are 'degrees' of inspiration and that the Holy Spirit so directed the writing of Scripture as to exclude the incorporation of error.

The Gospel Its Own Witness (1799)

A more complete expression of Fuller's concern for 'the rising generation' did not appear for another two years. But when it did appear as *The Gospel Its Own Witness*, it soon became one of the most popular of Fuller's books. It went through three editions by 1802, and was reprinted a number of times in the next thirty years. Wilberforce

---

25 For the life and ministry of Sutcliff, see Michael A.G. Haykin, *One Heart and One Soul: John Sutcliff of Olney, His Friends, and His Times* (Darlington: Evangelical Press, 1994).

26 John Sutcliff, *The Divinity of the Christian Religion* (Circular Letter of the Northamptonshire Association: Northampton: T. Dicy, 1797), p. 4.

regarded this work as the most important of all Fuller's writings,[27] while a more recent writer, E.F. Clipsham, has described it as the most outstanding of Fuller's apologetical works.[28]

> The strength of Fuller's apologetic was due largely to its positive character. Though he exposed rationalist inconsistency and absurdity with skill and incisiveness, his main concern was always to show the glory of the gospel.[29]

The work has two parts. The first compares and contrasts the moral effects of Christianity and Deism, while the second aims at demonstrating the divine origin of Christianity from the general consistency of the Scriptures.

> If the Scriptures can be proved to harmonize with historic fact, with truth, with themselves, and with sober reason, they must, considering what they profess, be Divinely inspired, and Christianity must be of God.[30]

In the first part Fuller reiterates that nature has limitations as a vehicle of revelation.

> It is one thing for nature to afford so much light in matters of right and wrong, as to leave the sinner without excuse; and another to afford him any well-grounded hope of forgiveness, or to answer his difficulties concerning the account which something within him says he must hereafter give of his present conduct... It is one thing to leave sinners without excuse in sin, and another thing to recover them from it. That the light of nature is insufficient for the latter, is demonstrated by melancholy fact... It was, I doubt not from a close observation of the different efficacy of nature and Scripture, that the writer of the *nineteenth Psalm* (a Psalm which Mr. Paine pretends to admire), after having given a just tribute of praise to the former, affirmed of the latter, 'The law of Jehovah is perfect, converting the soul' [Psalm 19:7].[31]

Paine's admiration of Psalm 19, Fuller implies, fails to take account of all its verses. According to Fuller, the Psalmist was cognizant of the need for other general and special revelation. Due to the inherent limitations of the created realm in displaying God' nature as Saviour, an inscripturated revelation, 'the law of Jehovah', was required.

---

27   According to Arthur H. Kirkby, *Andrew Fuller (1754–1815)* (London: Independent Press, 1961), pp. 13-14.
28   E.F. Clipsham, 'Andrew Fuller and Fullerism: A Study in Evangelical Calvinism. 4. Fuller as a Theologian', *Baptist Quarterly* 20.6 (April, 1964), p. 271.
29   Clipsham, 'Fuller as a Theologian', p. 272.
30   Fuller, *The Gospel Its Own Witness*, in *Works*, II, p. 58.
31   *The Gospel Its Own Witness*, p. 19.

In the second part of Fuller's treatise, he takes a close look at what Paine regards as inconsistencies in the scriptural record. Fuller notes that:[32]

> [The authors of Scripture] discover *no anxiety to guard against seeming inconsistencies*, either with themselves or one another. In works of imposture, especially where a number of persons are concerned, there is need of great care and caution, lest one part should contradict another; and such caution is easily perceived. But the sacred writers appear to have had no such concern about them. Conscious that all they wrote was true, they left it to prove its own consistency. Their productions possess consistency; but it is not a studied one, nor always apparent at first sight.

Scripture is indeed consistent with itself, but that consistency is not always readily apparent. Fuller was well aware of some of 'the sticky problems of biblical phenomena',[33] but the way in which these problems were approached was critical. As the above passage implies, there had to be a willingness to spend time in seeking a resolution for each of the apparent inconsistencies of Scripture.[34] More importantly, Fuller continued, the Scriptures had to be read from the right perspective, namely, that of a humble dependence on the teaching ministry of the Holy Spirit.

> Mr. Paine's spirit is sufficiently apparent in his pages, and that of the sacred writers in theirs. So far from writing as they wrote, he cannot understand their writings. That which the Scriptures teach on this subject is sufficiently verified in him, and all others of his spirit: 'The natural man receiveth not the things of the Spirit of God, neither can he know them, for they are spiritually discerned' [1 Corinthians 2.14].[35]

Fuller never disparaged the importance of scholarship in the study of the Scriptures,[36] but he regularly stressed its insufficiency if it were not

---

32 *The Gospel Its Own Witness*, p. 72.

33 L. Ross Bush and Tom J. Nettles, *Baptists and the Bible: The Baptist Doctrines of Biblical Inspiration and Religious Authority in Historical Perspective* (Chicago: Moody Press, 1980), p. 430. See, for instance, Fuller's *Passages apparently Contradictory*, in *Works*, I, pp. 667-84.

34 As Fuller said in another context, *Habitual Devotedness to the Ministry*, in *Works*, I, pp. 506-507 (from a sermon on 1 Tim. 4.15-16): 'You may read the Scriptures a hundred times over, and yet be only on the surface, far from having fathomed them... The Scriptures were always considered a deep mine, even when they consisted of only the five Books of Moses.'

35 *The Gospel Its Own Witness*, p. 73.

36 See, e.g., Fuller's *Habitual Devotedness to the Ministry*, p. 506, and *The Young Minister Exhorted to Make Full Proof of His Ministry*, in *Works*, I, p. 520 (from a sermon on 2 Tim. 4.5-6). See also the comment of John H. Watson, 'Baptists and the Bible as Seen in Three Eminent Baptists', *Foundations* 16 (1973), p. 248.

coupled with an openness to the Holy Spirit as the illuminator of his Word. For instance, at the ordination of a Robert Fawkner in 1787, Fuller addressed the newly ordained pastor thus:[37]

> The apostle exhorts that we 'be not drunken with wine, wherein is excess; but *filled* with the Spirit' [Ephesians 5.18]. The word 'filled,' here, is very expressive, it denotes, I apprehend, being *overcome*, as it were, with the holy influences and fruits of the blessed Spirit. How necessary is all this, my brother, in your work! Oh how necessary is 'an unction from the Holy One!' [1 John 2.20]. It is this that will enable you to enter into the spirit of the gospel, and preserve you from destructive errors concerning it... We shall naturally fall in with the dictates of that spirit of which we are full. It is for want of this, in a great measure, that the Scriptures appear strange, and foreign, and difficult to be understood... It is no breach of charity to say, that if the professors of Christianity had more of the Holy Spirit of God in their hearts, there would be a greater harmony among them respecting the great truths which he has revealed.

Again, in his criticism of some of the views of Robert Robinson (1735–90), one of the very few eighteenth century Calvinistic Baptists who strayed from orthodoxy,[38] Fuller stated:[39]

> There are truths in the Holy Scriptures—truths, too, which constitute the essence and glory of the gospel—truths the discernment and belief of which form the essence of true religion, which cannot be admitted without an answerable disposition; and...this disposition must be produced by the Holy Spirit.

Paine's attack on Christianity was not limited to the idea of an inscripturated revelation, but also encompassed some of the foundational truths of the Christian faith. For instance, he used current astronomical knowledge to attack the doctrine of the atonement.

---

37 Fuller, *The Qualifications and Encouragement of a Faithful Minister Illustrated by the Character and Success of Barnabas*, in *Works*, I, pp. 138-39 (from a sermon on Acts 11.24).

38 On the sad story of Robinson's theological career, see especially Graham W. Hughes, *With Freedom Fired: The Story of Robert Robinson, Cambridge Nonconformist* (London: Carey Kingsgate Press, 1955).

39 Fuller, *Strictures on Some of the Leading Sentiments of Mr. R. Robinson*, in *Works*, III, p. 604. Cf. the following statement made by Thomas Scott (1747–1821), the biblical commentator, on 24 May 1794 in a letter to John Ryland, Jr.: 'If we once think ourselves competent to understand the Bible by dint of our own sagacity, and skill in languages and criticism, without an immediate and continual dependence upon the teaching of the Holy Spirit, we are within a few paces of some dreadful downfall. Witness [Martin] Madan...and R. Robinson; who in their several publications...either expressly disavow, or tacitly pass by the mention of such a dependence.' Cited by John Scott, *The Life of the Rev. Thomas Scott* (London: L.B. Seeley, 1822), p. 247. See also Watson, 'Baptists and the Bible', pp. 248-49.

Our ideas, not only of the almightiness of the Creator, but of His wisdom and His beneficence, become enlarged in proportion as we contemplate the extent and the structure of the universe. The solitary idea of a solitary world rolling or at rest in the immense ocean of peace gives place to the cheerful idea of a society of worlds so happily contrived as to administer, even by their motion, instruction to man. We see our own earth filled with abundance, but we forget to consider how much of that abundance is owing to the scientific knowledge the vast machinery of the universe has unfolded.

But, in the midst of those reflections, what are we to think of the Christian system of faith that forms itself upon the idea of only one world, and that of no greater extent, as is before shown, then twenty-five thousand miles? An extent which a man walking at the rate of three miles an hour, for twelve hours in the day, could he keep on in a circular direction, would walk entirely round in less than two years. Alas! what is this to the mighty ocean of space, and the almighty power of the Creator?

From whence, then, could arise the solitary and strange conceit that the Almighty, who had millions or worlds equally dependent on His protection, should quit the care of all the rest, and come to die in our world, because, they say, one man and one woman had eaten an apple?

And, on the other hand, are we to suppose that every world in the boundless creation had an Eve, an apple, a serpent and a redeemer? In this case, the person who is irreverently called the Son of God, and sometimes God Himself, would have nothing else to do than to travel from world to world, in an endless succession of deaths, with scarcely a momentary interval of life.[40]

Paine admits that 'it is not a direct article of the Christian system, that this world that we inhabit is the whole of the habitable creation'.[41] Nevertheless, he is confident that:[42]

> To believe that God created a plurality of worlds, at least as numerous as what we call stars, renders the Christian system of faith at once little and ridiculous, and scatters it in the mind like feathers in the air.

In his reply to Paine's reasoning, Fuller does not attempt to controvert the hypothesis that God has created a multitude of inhabited worlds in the universe.

> Mr. Paine seems to wish to have it thought that the doctrine of a multiplicity of inhabited worlds is a matter of *demonstration*; but the existence of a number of heavenly bodies, whose revolutions are under the direction of certain laws, and whose returns, therefore, are the objects of human calculation, does not prove that

---

40 Paine, *Age of Reason*, pp. 88-90.
41 Paine, *Age of Reason*, pp. 84-85.
42 Paine, *Age of Reason*, p. 85.

'The Oracles of God' 133

they are all inhabited by intelligent beings. I do not deny that, from other considerations, the thing may be highly probable; but it is no more than a probability.[43]

Yet, if he is forced to choose between this hypothesis and the scriptural record, Fuller has no hesitations as to his choice. He would continue to affirm Scriptural infallibility, for:[44]

If it were even to prove fallacious, [it] has no dangerous consequences attending it, and...if it should be found a truth, [it] involves our eternal salvation.

But Fuller really does not believe it has to come down to such a choice; for while the Scriptures 'do not teach the doctrine of a multitude of inhabited worlds...neither do they teach the contrary'.[45] Scripture's silence on this matter well illustrates why the Scriptures were given.

They were not given to teach us astronomy, or geography, or civil government, or any science which relates to the present life only, therefore they do not determine upon any system of any of these sciences. There are things upon which reason is competent to judge, sufficiently at least for all the purposes of human life, without a revelation from heaven. The great object of revelation is to instruct us in things which pertain to our everlasting peace; and as to other things, even the rise and fall of the mightiest empires, they are only touched in an incidental manner, as the mention of them might be necessary to higher purposes.[46]

The Scriptures do not seek to provide mankind with a comprehensive volume of knowledge, but primarily deal with 'things which pertain to our everlasting peace'. What is included in the Scriptures is designed to enable men and women find salvation, and not to gratify their curiosity about a host of other subjects.[47] This scope and purpose of the Scriptures must consequently be kept in mind when they are being interpreted.

The Scriptures are written in a *popular* style, as best adapted to their great end. If the salvation of philosophers only had been their object, the language might possibly

---

43 *The Gospel Its Own Witness*, p. 86.
44 *The Gospel Its Own Witness*, p. 86.
45 *The Gospel Its Own Witness*, p. 88.
46 *The Gospel Its Own Witness*, p. 88.
47 Cf. Fuller's comments *a propos* Genesis 1 in his *Expository Discourses on the Book of Genesis*, in *Works*, III, pp. 2-3 (from a sermon on Gen. 1.1-4): 'The account given by Moses relates not to the *whole creation*, but merely to what it immediately concerns us to know. God made angels; but nothing is said of them. The moon is called on of the *greater* lights, not as to what it is in itself, but what it is *to us*. The Scriptures are written, not to gratify curiosity, but to nourish faith. They do not stop to tell you *how*, nor to answer a number of questions which might be asked; but tell you so much as is necessary, and no more.

have been somewhat different; though even this may be a matter of doubt, since the style is suited to the subject, and to the great end which they had in view; but being addressed to men of every degree, it was highly proper that the language should be fitted to every capacity, and suited to their common modes of conception. They speak of the foundations of the earth, the ends of the earth, the greater and less lights in the heavens, the sun rising, standing still, and going down, and many other things in the same way. If deists object to these modes of speaking, as conveying ideas which are inconsistent with the true theory of the heavens and the earth, let them, if they can, substitute others which are consistent: let them, in their common conversation, when describing the revolutions of evening and morning, speak of the earth as rising and going down, instead of the sun...and see if men, in common, will better understand them, or whether they would be able even to understand one another.[48]

Finally, although the primary emphasis of the Scriptures has to do with its saving truths, it does not follow that the veracity of other facts mentioned in Scripture is in any way lessened. They may not be as important, but they are just as true.

> A true believer, so far as he understand it, *does* believe all Scripture truth; and to discredit any one truth of the Bible, knowing it to be such, is a damning sin.[49]

The conclusion to *The Gospel Its Own Witness* weaves together a number of the main ideas which Fuller has been stressing throughout the book: the limitations of nature as a vehicle of revelation, the need for special revelation, the salvific purpose of God's Word.

> When you have ascended to the height of human discovery, there are things, and things of infinite moment too, that are utterly beyond its reach. Revelation is the medium, and the only medium, by which, standing, as it were, 'on nature's Alps', we discover things which eye hath not seen, nor ear heard, and of which it never hath entered into the heart of man to conceive.[50]

Letters on Systematic Divinity (1814)

The year before he died, Fuller began work on a systematic theology in the form of a series of letters to John Ryland, Jr. Due to ill health and the numerous demands on his time, Fuller never completed this 'connected

---

48   *The Gospel Its Own Witness*, pp. 88-89.
49   Cited by Norman H. Maring, 'Andrew Fuller's Doctrine of the Church', in Winthrop Still Hudson (ed.), *Baptist Concepts of the Church* (Philadelphia: Judson Press, 1959), p. 77.
50   *The Gospel Its Own Witness*, p. 97.

view of the gospel' as he described it.[51] But of the nine letters he did write, three of them specifically considered the issues raised in his rejoinder to Paine fifteen years earlier. The first, the fifth letter in the series, details 'The Necessity of a Divine Revelation'. Essentially Fuller reasserts what he had already expressed in both *The Nature and Importance of an Intimate Knowledge of Divine Truth* and *The Gospel Its Own Witness* regarding the relationship of nature and God's Word, and the insufficiency of the former to provide saving knowledge of God.[52] The second, the sixth letter in the series, is devoted to 'The Inspiration of the Holy Scriptures'. It begins by looking at what the human authors of Scripture profess their writings to be. From such texts as 2 Samuel 23.2-3, 2 Timothy 3.16 and 2 Peter 1.21, Fuller concludes:

> We must, therefore, either admit these writings to be the word of God, or consider them as mere imposture... If their writings be not what they profess them to be, they are imposture, and deserve to be rejected. There is no consistent medium between faith and unbelief.[53]

There are, though, Fuller continues, degrees of inspiration in the Scriptures.

> But though all Scripture is given by inspiration of God, it does not follow that it is so in the *same sense and degree*. It required one degree of inspiration to foretell future events, and another to narrate facts which fell under the writer's knowledge. The one required less exercise of his own judgement, the other more. Inspiration, in the latter case, might be little more than a Divine superintendence, preserving him from error, and from other defects and faults, to which ordinary historians are subject.[54]

Here, Fuller is essentially reproducing Sutcliff's statements in *The Divinity of the Christian Religion*. Fuller, like Sutcliff, emphasizes that the Scriptures are free from error and that the process of their inspiration was not a mechanical one. Elsewhere Fuller also states that the English translation of the Bible should be regarded as 'subject to imperfection' because it is 'a human performance'.[55] Consequently, his statement in the text cited above regarding the lack of error in the Scriptures probably should be understood as a reference to the autographs. Fuller's reiteration of Sutcliff's point regarding the 'degrees' of inspiration is also noteworthy. For a little further on in this same letter Fuller can speak

---

51 Fuller, *Letters in Systematic Divinity*, in *Works*, I, p. 684.
52 *Letters in Systematic Divinity*, pp. 696-97.
53 *Letters in Systematic Divinity*, p. 699.
54 *Letters in Systematic Divinity*, p. 699.
55 Fuller, *The English Translation of the Bible*, in *Works*, III, p. 810.

of the Old and New Testaments as being 'dictated' by the Spirit.[56] His earlier statement about the 'degrees' of inspiration certainly precludes a literal understanding of this latter expression. The way in which Fuller is using the term 'dictated' would appear to be very similar to the way that it was used by John Calvin (1509-64), for whom:[57]

> [The term 'dictated'] is simply a theological metaphor conveying the thought that what is written in Scripture bears the same relation to the mind of God which was its source as a letter written by a good secretary bears to the mind of the man who dictated it—a relation, that is, of complete correspondence, and thus of absolute authority.

Fuller proceeds to argue for the inspiration of the Scriptures from their truth, consistency, perfection, pungency, and utility. He concludes the letter with a few comments on Psalm 19.7-11. The choice of this scriptural text is not accidental. Paine, as we have seen, had a high admiration for the first six verses of this Psalm. Fuller, however, refuses to concentrate on these six verses to the exclusion of the next five. For verses 7-11 indicate that:[58]

> The book of nature declares the 'eternal power and Godhead' of the Creator; but that of Scripture represents his whole character; not only as the Creator; but as the Moral Governor and Saviour of men. Hence it is 'able to make us wise unto salvation, through faith which is in Christ Jesus' [2 Tim. 3.15]... The opinions of the greatest men, formed merely from the works of nature, are full of uncertainty, and but ill adapted to instruct the illiterate part of mankind in their best interests; but the sacred Scriptures contain the true sayings of God, which may be safely depended upon.

Fuller here links together a number of themes which we have already encountered in his earlier writings. The burden of the Scriptures is shown to be the doctrine of salvation. Then, the doctrine of scriptural infallibility is revealed to have salvific implications: because the Scriptures are a reliable source of divine truth, they are 'able to make us wise unto salvation'. The seventh letter also touches on this main purpose of the Scriptures. 'The sacred Scriptures are full of Christ, and uniformly lead us to him.'[59] Scripture is important to Fuller because it points him to Christ in a way that nothing else can.

---

56 *Letters in Systematic Divinity*, p. 700.
57 J.I. Packer, 'Calvin the Theologian', in G.E. Duffield (ed.), *John Calvin* (Grand Rapids, MI: Eerdmans, 1966), p. 163.
58 *Letters in Systematic Divinity*, p. 701.
59 *Letters in Systematic Divinity*, p. 703.

The significance of these *Letters on Systematic Divinity* should not be underestimated. They represent the fruit of a lifetime's reflections on the purpose and nature of Scripture.

Conclusion

In the second part of *The Age of Reason* Paine makes the following boast:[60]

> I have now gone through the Bible [that is, the Old Testament], as a man would go through a wood with an axe on his shoulder and fell trees. There they lie; and the priests, if they can, may replant them. They may, perhaps stick them in the ground, but they will never make them grow.

Twenty years later, Fuller assessed Paine's boast thus:[61]

> A few years ago, a certain infidel braggadocio pretended to have gone through the wood and cut down the trees, which the priests, he said, might stick in again, but they would not grow! And have the sacred Scriptures been less in request since that time than they were before? Rather have they not been much more so? Infidelity, by overacting its part, has given itself a wound; and its abettors, like Herod, have been eaten of worms, and have died. But the word of the Lord has grown and been multiplied.

The years between the publication of the second part of *The Age of Reason* in 1795 and the writing of these words in 1814 had seen great growth not only among the Baptists, but also among other denominations such as the Anglicans, Methodists and Congregationalists. And accompanying this growth was a corresponding demand for God's Word. The British and Foreign Bible Society was founded in 1804 to help meet this need, and by 1814 it had distributed over 950,000 Bibles.[62] But Fuller also has in view important events beyond the home front. For in India the translation projects of William Carey (1761–1834), Joshua Marshman (1768–1837) and William Ward (1769–1823) were beginning to bear fruit. In the year in which Fuller wrote the words cited above Carey sent him 'a list of twenty-six versions of Scripture, finished or then in the press, or in the course of translation'.[63] Thus Fuller could declare immediately preceding his assessment of Paine's boast: 'May the

---

60 Paine, *Age of Reason*, p. 156.
61 *Letters in Systematic Divinity*, p. 702.
62 Roger H. Martin, *Evangelicals United: Ecumenical Stirrings in Pre-Victorian Britain, 1795–1830* (Metuchen, NJ/London: Scarecrow Press, 1983), p. 92.
63 F. Deaville Walker, *William Carey: Missionary Pioneer and Statesman* (Chicago: Moody Press, n.d.), p. 232.

blessing of God attend the various attempts to translate and circulate the sacred Scriptures.'[64] This is the prayer of a man wholly committed to an infallible Word and fully aware that the extension of the Saviour's kingdom is intrinsically linked to that Word.

---

64 *Letters in Systematic Divinity*, p. 702.

CHAPTER 6

Christianity Pure and Simple: Andrew's Fuller's Contest with Socinianism

Tom J. Nettles

They were on a collision course. While Andrew Fuller (1754–1815) filled his diary with lamentation, repentance, deepening sorrow over his innate sinfulness and growing admiration for the atoning work of Christ, Joseph Priestley (1733–1804) coolly congratulated humanity on its rational powers and moral goodness and the deity for his benign placability toward sin and his generally benevolent considerations of the moral efforts of humanity.[1]

'Oh horridly deceitful and desperately wicked heart!', Fuller groaned as he meditated on an apparent spiritual duplicity. 'Surely I have little else in my religious exercises, but these workings', he continued. 'I am afraid of being deceived at last. If I am saved, what must the Son of God have endured!!!' The musings of June and July of 1780 continued with oppressive intensity and increasing transparency of introspection. 'O what an ocean of impurity have I still in me. What vain desires lodge in my sinful heart.' And, if so, forgiveness can be at no small price: 'Rich must be the blood that can atone, infinitely efficacious the grace that can purify, and inconceivable the love that can remain without the shadow of

---

1   Well-known are the facts of Priestley's move from the Calvinism of his family, to Arminianism, from that to Arianism and thence to Socinianism. Priestley never seemed to mind the link with Socinus but views him as having re-discovered in modern times the original view of Christ, sin, and salvation. Subsequent Unitarians disavowed the epithet 'Socinianism' but Fuller was loathe to grant them their longing, with the exception of one of his last pieces on the controversy. In 1812, Bogue and Bennet credited Priestley with being 'the champion of socinianism' who 'provoked a contest which is not yet terminated'. See David Bogue and James Bennet, *History of Dissenters from the Revolution in 1688, to the Year 1808* (4 vols; London: printed for the authors, 1808–12), IV, p. 248. Bogue and Bennet, IV, p. 249, believe that an early conviction of Priestley that the 'sacred writers sometimes reason in a false and inconclusive manner' served as the foundation 'to all his subsequent aberrations from evangelical principles'.

turning, amidst all this vileness.' What confidence can such a being have of persevering in God's will by native strength? None.

> Am not I a fool and slow of heart to believe? Notwithstanding all the scripture says of my impotency, all the experience I have had of it, and all my settled and avowed principles, how hard is it for me to believe that I am *nothing*! Ah! Can I live near to God, set or keep the springs of godliness a-going in my soul, or investigate the things of God, to any purpose? No, I cannot.[2]

Priestley, on the other hand, believed that such views of human sin and ability to be derogatory of the goodness of God, destructive of any sincere efforts at virtue, and fallacious as a view of human nature. After discarding the doctrine of atonement of any sort as having any connection with forgiveness of sins, Priestley admires the simplicity of the resulting conclusion.

> It is certainly a great satisfaction to entertain such an idea of the author of the universe, and of his moral government, as is consonant to the dictates of reason and the tenor of revelation in general, and also to leave as little obscurity in the principles of it as is possible; that the articles of our creed on this great subject may be few, clear, and simple. Now it is certainly the doctrine of reason, as well as of the Old Testament, that God is merciful to the penitent, and that nothing is requisite to make men, in all situations, the objects of his favor, but such moral conduct as he has made them capable of. This is a simple and a pleasing view of God and his moral government, and the consideration of it cannot but have the best effect on the temper of our minds and conduct in life.[3]

Priestley contended that those doctrines most dear to the heart of Fuller and most reflective of his intimate knowledge of himself, were, after all, only corruptions of pure Christianity. Putrid and gangrenous excrescences adhered to Christianity as a result of centuries of alien

---

2   Andrew Fuller, *The Work of Faith, the Labour of Love, and the Patience of Hope Illustrated; in the Life and Death of the Reverend Andrew Fuller* (ed. John Ryland; London: Published by Button & Son, 1816), pp. 114, 120.

3   Joseph Priestley, *A History of the Corruptions of Christianity* (in some parts abridged, with appendices by A[biel]. A[bbot] L[livermore]; Keene, NH: J. and W. Prentiss, 1838), pp. 154-55. The original publication was dedicated to Theophilus Lindsey and Priestley finished the dedication in November 1782. Bogue and Bennet, *History of Dissenters*, IV, pp. 249-50, remark concerning this work: 'Viewed as a historical defence of socinianism, or rather as a death stroke to the deity and atonement of Christ, which had been promised with some parade, it must strike every intelligent reader as the ridiculous birth of a mountain in labour... He must have had a monstrous faith in the credulity of his adherents, if he thought that such a work would be taken for a proof that their principles prevailed in the earliest ages; and if he supposed that such an attack would induce his opponents to abandon their faith, he must have imageined that they held it by a hair.'

growths on the pure and simple message of the man Jesus. As Fuller grew in his awareness of the content and tendencies of this self-proclaimed primitivist view of the faith, he found he had no option but to challenge it at the very point in which Priestley claimed its chief strength to lie—its tendency to reproduce the simple, unadulterated, moral vision of Jesus.[4]

Fuller's Preparation for the Conflict

In the first year of Fuller's ministry, 1775, a question was proposed to him as to whether Christ is called Son of God as to his eternal divinity or whether the title only refers to his having assumed human nature through a miraculous birth. He looked for Scriptures in which the title must refer to the eternal relation of Christ to the Father, and, to his satisfaction, found several that he felt could be interpreted no other way. Among the passages that seemed to demand this understanding was John 5.18, where the Jews understood Jesus as making himself equal to God by calling God his own Father. Galatians 4.4 teaches that 'God sent forth his Son, born of a woman, born under the Law'. He was the Son antecedent to his being born of a woman. He possessed sonship prior to his taking our human nature in the womb of the woman and becoming subject to the law. Other Scriptures he used were Hebrews 1.8, 5.8, 9, and 1 John 3.8. These Scriptures, plus others, formed the basis of an essay Fuller wrote later entitled 'On the Sonship of Christ'.[5] 'Had I not been initiated into these principles at an early period', Fuller recalls, 'I should not have been able to write the treatise against Socinianism, which I have no cause to regret having written.'

Fuller moved from the church in Soham to Kettering in October 1782. One year later his installation as pastor was formalized by a day of preaching, exhortation, prayer, testimony and the reading of a confession of faith by Fuller, written for the purpose. By this time, it is clear that he had been engaging the issues raised by the intrusion of Socinianism into English Dissent. Articles five through seven treat the fall and sinfulness of man. After speaking of the intrinsic wicked aversion of heart that fallen

---

4   The conflict considered from the standpoint both of its antagonists and the theological issues at stake is reminiscent of other theological turning points in the history of Christian thought. Augustine and Pelagius harboring parallel views of sin and self-confidence discussed many of these same issues. Luther and Erasmus entered into similar pools of conflict, as did Calvin and Pighius. These earlier struggles did not involve an attack on the deity of Christ as did that of Fuller.

5   Andrew Fuller, *On the Sonship of Christ*, in *The Complete Works of the Rev. Andrew Fuller* (ed. Joseph Belcher; 3 vols; Philadelphia: American Baptist Publication Society, n.d.), III, pp. 704-707.

humanity has toward God, Fuller notes certain implications of this view of depravity.

> These are subjects which seem to me of very great importance. I conceive that the whole Arminian, Socinian, and Antinomian systems, so far as I understand them, rest upon the supposition of these principles being false. So that if it should be found at last that God is an infinitely excellent being, worthy of being loved with all that love that his law requires; that as such, his law is entirely fair and equitable, and that for God to have required less would have been denying himself to be what he is; and if it should appear at last that man is utterly lost, and lies absolutely at the discretion of God;—than the whole of these systems I think it is easy to prove must fall to the ground. If men on account of sin lie at the discretion of God, the equity and even necessity of predestination cannot be denied; and so the Arminian system falls. If the law of God is right and good, and arises from the very nature of God, Antinomianism cannot stand. And if we are such *great sinners*, we need a *great Saviour*, infinitely greater than the *Socinian* Saviour![6]

The relation between the equity of the divine law and the Socinian concept of forgiveness gave focus to one of Fuller's major points of theological and moral critique of Socinianism. God would never give a law that was unjust, unduly harsh, or unworthy of enforcement. A refusal to enforce it or to require the punishment requisite upon its infraction would be equal to a confession that it originally lacked justice or wisdom, or both. God, in Fuller's biblical synthesis, never has forgiveness and mercy operate so as to exclude the execution of justice.

When Fuller started his formal interaction with literature for the purpose of writing against Socinianism, he recorded in his diary, 'I have lately been employed in reading several Socinian writers, Lindsey, Priestley, Belsham, &c. and have employed myself in penning down thoughts on the moral tendency of their system. While thus engaged, I found an increasing aversion to their views of things, and I feel the ground on which my hopes are built more solid than ever.'[7]

Fuller's engagement in the 'moral tendency of their system' arose from his experiential revulsion at the self-congratulatory implications of the Socinian enthralment with rationality and rewardable virtue. Nothing could be further from Fuller's own contemplations on the glory and power of Christian salvation. As he reviewed and meditated on the eternal Son of God taking our nature, obeying the law, dying under its curse for the sins of his elect, rising again, commissioning the preaching of the gospel to the whole world, interceding for and providentially ruling the world for the welfare of his own people he was overcome. 'I cannot reflect upon this glorious procedure, with it's [sic] all-glorious Author, without emotions of wonder and gratitude.' Fuller beamed in the glory

---

6   *Work of Faith*, pp. 102-103.
7   *Work of Faith*, p. 214.

of such a wise, loving and powerful display of grace. 'As a workman', Fuller spoke of Christ, 'he might be truly said to have *His work before him!* At once he glorified the injured character of God, and confounded the devil, destroyed sin, and saved the sinner!'[8]

Motivation for the Confrontation

Fuller's motivation sprung from several factors. The occasion which gave urgency to Fuller's polemic concerned an issue of civil rights in English society. Baptists had been thrown together with other Dissenters 'without respect to their doctrinal principles' to give a united front in their application for repeal of the Corporation and Test Acts. Though this arose purely as a plea for a civil right, Joseph Priestley and others used the common meetings as an advantageous time for propagation of Socinian principles. Orthodox Dissenters sat still so as not to interrupt the harmony of the meeting. In public statements, Socinians painted with a broad brush when they spoke as if 'the Dissenters' like the early Christians all 'worshipped one God' and 'knew nothing of the Nicene or Athanasian creeds'. They also spoke of dissenters as 'coming under the ANATHEMA OF THE ORTHODOX'. Fuller resented this misrepresentation of the numerical dominance of Socinianism, but even more did he recoil from the impression that their theology had a grip on all Dissent, or that the issue was between Socinians who worshipped one God as opposed to Trinitarians who worshipped three Gods. 'It is natural', observed Fuller, 'from such representations as these, for those who know but little of us, to consider the Socinians as constituting the main body of the Dissenters, and the Calvinists', which Fuller was quite happy to be called, 'as only a few stragglers, who follow these leading men at a distance in all their measures.'[9] Such certainly was not the case and any theological advantage sought by Priestley in this common civil contest should not be given over easily.[10]

---

8   *Work of Faith*, p. 104.
9   Fuller, *The Calvinistic and Socinian Systems Examined and Compared, as to their Moral Tendency*, in *Works*, II, pp. 109-10. This work of Fuller covers from pp. 108-242 in this edition of Fuller's *Works*. The work first was published in 1792, the same year that Carey sailed for India and Fuller assumed responsibility for generating support for the missionary endeavor of the Particular Baptists. A second edition appeared in 1802 from which the author is working.
10   While Andrew Fuller dealt with this issue by confronting the principles of Socinianism and comparing them to orthodoxy, a twenty-seven year old Robert Hall took the approach of defending freedom from the standpoint of orthodox Christianity. In the preface to 'Christianity Consistent with a Love of Freedom', Hall remarks, 'I have taken up more time in showing that there is no *proper connection* between the Unitarian

Fuller's concern to maintain the integrity of the theological identity of orthodoxy in the midst of Dissent conformed readily to Baptist precedent on this issue. When seventeenth-century English Particular Baptists found that their advocacy of believers' baptism brought with it false charges of erroneous and radical positions held by some continental Anabaptists, they acted immediately to counter the charges. Seven churches produced a confession of faith that refuted the report of 'holding Free-will, Falling away from grace, denying Originall sinne, disclaiming of Magistracy, denying to assist them either in person or purse in any of their lawfull Commands, doing acts unseemly in the dispensing the Ordinance of Baptism, not to be named amongst Christians'. All these charges they stated unequivocally as untrue and presented a confession that admirably established their Calvinistic orthodoxy.[11] Fuller had both reason and precedent in his desire to distance himself and his churches from the doctrinal reductionism of the Socinians, though both Baptists and the non-trinitarians held the common label of Dissent from the Established Church.

More than personal identity was at stake. Allusion has already been made briefly to Fuller's theological reasons for entering the discussion. He found the Socinian system so spiritually and theologically repulsive, that he simply could not let his witness remain silent on such an issue.

---

doctrine and the principles of liberty that the subject may seem to require; but this will not be thought superfluous by those who recollect that *that* idea seems to be the great hinge of Mr. C[layton]'s discourse, and that it appears among the orthodox part of the Dissenters to have been productive already of unhappy effects.' Early in his discussion, Hall remarks: 'If Mr. C[layton] had glanced only towards the history of England, he must have remembered, that in the reigns of Charles the First and Second, the chief friends of freedom were the puritans... It is to the distinguished exertions of this party, we are in a great measure indebted for the preservation of our free and happy constitution. In those distracted and turbulent times which preceded the restoration of Charles the Second, the puritans, who to a devotion the most fervent, united an eager attachment to the doctrines of grace, as they are commonly called, displayed on every occasion a love of freedom, pushed almost to excess; whilst the cavaliers, their opponents, who ridiculed all that was serious, and if they had any religion at all, held sentiments directly repugnant to the tenets of Calvin, were the firm supporters of arbitrary power. If the unitarians, then are at present distinguished for their zeal in the cause of freedom, it cannot be imputed to any alliance between their religious and political opinions, but to the conduct natural to a minority, who...are sensible they can only shelter themselves from persecution and reproach, and gain an impartial hearing from the public, by throwing down the barriers of prejudice, and claiming unlimited freedom of thought.' See Robert Hall, 'Christianity Consistent With a Love of Freedom', in *The Works of the Rev. Robert Hall* (2 vols; New York: G. & C. & H. Carvill, 1830), II, pp. 385, 393.

11   This confession of faith, written in 1644, may be found in William L. Lumpkin, *Baptist Confessions of Faith* (Valley Forge, PA: Judson Press, rev. edn, 1969), pp. 153-71. The quoted material comes from the preface, p. 155.

Theology and experience could not be separated in Fuller's mind or his ministry. The nature of God, the law, sin, depravity, the person of Christ, the atonement, justification, divine sovereignty—all these were tied to each other and the integrity of each individual part depended on a true apprehension of the whole.[12] Not only did this hold true for the cognitive aspect of Christian truth; Christian experience depended on a proper grasp of these issues. Spiritual affections could be high or low, pure or corrupt, in direct relation to the sincere embracing of these truths.

Fuller was well aware that a man's opinions might sometimes be other than his real principles, and, thus, his conduct might be better than his opinions would warrant. But ideas so pervasively antagonistic to the leading principles of orthodox Christianity cannot support either Christian profession or deportment. 'Socinianism is slippery ground', Fuller believed, and 'few will be able to stand upon it'. His image of the danger is vivid. 'A precipice indeed it is, or rather the declivity of a rock, bulging into the sea, and covered with ice; a few wary individuals may frame to themselves a kind of artificial footing, and so retain their situation; but the greater part must either climb the summit, or fall into the deep.'[13] The specific theological issues and their tendency toward decline will emerge in the subsequent discussion.

Further, Fuller had seen some fall down that precipice and he desired to do what he could to provide an escape. The most celebrated case of conversion from orthodoxy to Socinianism, at least apparently, was that of the Cambridge Particular Baptist pastor, Robert Robinson.[14] Fuller had

---

12   A.H. Newman notes the theological atmosphere of Fuller's response to Socinianism with the observation, 'His moderate, sane, Evangelical Calvinism was embodied in effective form in *the Calvinistic and Socinian Systems Examined and Compared as to Their Moral Tendency*, London, 1794.' This is in the article on Fuller in Samuel M. Jackson (ed.), *The New Schaff-Herzog Encyclopedia of Religious Knowledge* (12 vols; Grand Rapids, MI: Baker, 1977 [n.d.]), *s.v.*.

13   Fuller, *Reply to Dr. Toulmin*, in *Socinianism Indefensible on the Ground of it Moral Tendency: Containing a Reply to Two Late Publications; The One by Dr. Toulmin, entitled The Practical Efficacy of the Unitarian Doctrine Considered; The Other by Mr. Kentish, entitled The Moral Tendency of the Genuine Christian Doctrine*, in*Works*, II, p. 254.

14   *Calvinistic and Socinian Systems Examined*, pp. 222-24. See the discussion of this phenomenon and its danger also to Samuel Pearce and its success with James Lyons, in Michael A.G. Haykin, 'A Socinian and Calvinist Compared: Joseph Priestley and Andrew Fuller on the Propriety of Prayer to Christ', *Nederlands Archief voor Kerkgeschiedenis/Dutch Review of Church History* 73 (1993), pp. 196-98. Thomas Belsham, one of Fuller's antagonists, had begun his ministry as a Calvinist and lectured on the person of Christ with the hope of ending the threat of unitarianism among his students. Some of his students were converted to Socinian views in the process and eventually Belsham himself capitulated. See Michael R. Watts, *The Dissenters*. Volume

no fear that a true child of God would be finally destroyed nor that the church was susceptible to any final danger. The Lord knows those who are his. He was fully committed, however, that one should not look at the *end* to the exclusion of the ordained *means*.[15]

Fuller's Polemical Method

Fuller knew others who had engaged the Socinians at different points of their arguments. Volumes from both sides of the controversy had covered the ground from two standpoints. One, the various Scripture passages in dispute were investigated with all the linguistic and critical tools available until the writers had 'exhausted their genius, in reasoning upon the scope of the sacred writers, and in criticising upon the original language'.[16] When the contest seemed to go against them, however, the Socinians cashiered passages, sometimes whole chapters, as spurious, or their meaning as dubious or obscure. They often rejected the aptitude of Scripture writers to deal conclusively with some controverted questions in religion and morality. If the plain meaning of a text seemed repugnant to the plain dictates of Socinian rationality, the interpretation of a text must wait till a later date. Priestley's discussion of the biblical material on the atonement gives an excellent case in point on this tendency.

> For they must either be interpreted literally, according to the plain and obvious sense of the words, which will enforce the belief of proper vicarious punishments, or they must be interpreted *figuratively*; and then they will not oblige us to believe the doctrine of atonement in any sense, or that Christ died a sacrifice in any other manner, than as any person might be said to be a sacrifice to the cause in which he dies.
>
> It is now, certainly, time to lay less stress on the interpretation of particular texts, and to allow more weight to general considerations derived from the whole tenor of scripture, and the dictates of reason; and if there should be found any difficulty in accommodating the one to the other (and I think there is even less of this than might have been expected) the former, and not the latter, should remain unaccounted for.[17]

1: *From the Reformation to the French Revolution* (Oxford: Clarendon Press, 1978), 466-67.
    15   Fuller, *Letter I. The Importance of a True System*, in *Letters on Systematic Divinity*, in *Works*, I, p. 686.
    16   *Reply to Dr. Toulmin*, p. 244.
    17   Priestley, *Corruptions*, p. 154.

This disingenuous attitude toward Scripture Fuller would reserve for a special criticism later, but it served to drive him toward a different approach.

A second sphere of controversy concerned the development of doctrine in the church. Of particular interest was the early church, for Socinian reasoning was that the immediate post-apostolic age would have the purest grasp of what was seen as essential in Jesus' own generation. Words and concepts introduced since then could have no claim to be an element of true Christianity. Fuller did not feel qualified to enter into the details of this discussion, nor did he think it particularly profitable for his purposes since a man may err theologically in the second century as easily as in the eighteenth century.

Fuller chose to examine the issue by proposing this question: 'What is that doctrine in the present day which is productive of the best moral effects?'[18] He pointed to six reasons for settling on this particular approach. An answer to this question, Fuller argued, would settle better than either of the other two approaches which, Calvinism or Socinianism, came nearer apostolic doctrine. The one which produces the same fruit would of course be the same kind of tree. Second, this question allows one to test the truthfulness and godliness of the doctrine. If the fruit of Calvinism commends itself to the conscience, the Socinians, however aloof they may be from scriptural reasoning, dare not set themselves against morality. Third, this seemed to be an approach commended by Scripture itself when it says, 'By their fruits ye shall know them.' Fourth, he believed that this approach might be more intriguing as a test before the public mind since none other had taken such reasoning as ground for an argument. Fifth, common Christians might be more astutely involved in this investigation. The line of historical reasoning or the construction of a text of Scripture often left pious people in the churches a bit confused about the importance of certain aspects of an argument. They can well understand, however, the relation of doctrine to the enhancement or circumscription of true piety. Finally, Fuller recognized that the Socinians had already introduced this line of reasoning in their attack on Calvinism as 'gloomy', 'bigoted', 'licentious', 'averse to the love of both God and man', and 'an axe at the root of all virtue'.[19]

This final reason apparently gave the initial clue to Fuller as to the type of argument he should use. The first five reasons seemed to provide support as he went along in the argument. Priestley invited the comparison and Fuller unhesitatingly obliged. Priestley spoke of Christianity's 'dreadful corruptions' which 'debased its spirit' and virtually 'annihilated all the happy effects which it was eminently

---

18 *Reply to Dr. Toulmin*, p. 245.
19 *Reply to Dr. Toulmin*, p. 245.

calculated to produce'. The leading principles of Calvinism, including the 'Trinity of persons in the Godhead, original sin, arbitrary predestination, atonement by the death of Christ, and the plenary inspiration of the Scriptures', would have the inviolable tendency 'to relax the obligations of virtue'. Going over the same theological ground in another work, Priestley concludes: 'If any system of speculative principles can operate as an axe at the root of all virtue and goodness, it is this.' The number of those professing true Christianity, however, according to Priestley, grows regularly 'whose lives are the greatest ornament to it, and who hold it in so much purity, that, if it was fairly exhibited, and universally understood, it could hardly fail to recommend itself to the acceptance of the whole world, of Jews and Gentiles'.[20]

Fuller took up the task gladly to ascertain which of the systems, when 'fairly exhibited', would have the happiest effects of purity of life and conversion of the unbeliever. In his opening letter, Fuller made allowance for the reality of hypocrisy in either system, the restraining and apparently virtuous effect of certain vices, and the zeal one may have for a bad system simply because it is 'more consonant to the bias of their hearts than that was which they formerly professed'. In spite of these difficulties that seem to establish a lack of certainty, Fuller believed that a right method of discussion on particular issues could yield success in discerning the 'general spirit and conduct of men, by which to judge of the tendency of their principles'.[21]

---

20 Priestley, *Corruptions*, p. ix. See also Fuller, *Calvinistic and Socinian Systems Examined*, pp. 112-13, 142. Priestley introduces one of his analyses of Calvinism and its moral tendencies with the statement, 'I do not see...what motive a Calvinist can have to give any attention to his moral conduct', quoted by Fuller, *Calvinistic and Socinian Systems Examined*, p. 142, from Priestley's *Philosophical Necessity*, p. 154. Fuller, pp. 146-49, questions Priestley as to why he should have any hesitance about the consistency between responsible morality on the one hand and the certainty of events on the other. When Fuller, p. 147, says, 'Upon the whole, let those who are inured to close thinking judge whether Dr. Priestley's own views of philosophical necessity do not include the leading principle of Calvinism', he does not align himself with any kind of impersonal determinism or a necessarian philosophy that runs along mechanically outside the moral texture of human conduct. He simply shows that Priestley's argument for the reality of morality in his own system may just as easily show the defensibility of responsible moral conduct in a Calvinist system. It does this while still attributing more to God than to man and so, by Priestley's own admission, generates a higher degree of piety than a system that places more weight on the human rather than the divine activity.

21 *Calvinistic and Socinian Systems Examined*, p. 115. Priestley evoked a wide range of responses both to his religion and his politics during the last decade of the eighteenth century. Robert Hall, previously mentioned, writing in 1891 prior to the publication of Fuller's work, shows great admiration for Priestley's political principles and his overall genius, while disavowing his theology. He defends Priestley against a particularly unjust characterization and attack. 'The reader can be at no loss to determine,

Fuller's Method of Argument

Fuller had first to settle on a number of categories which all Christians would agree should be proper effects of true Christianity. Obviously, Fuller does not exhaust the possible categories that could be investigated, but his sampling is sufficiently broad to make accurate observations concerning the tendencies of the systems. He distributed his remarks among fifteen chapters that he called *Letters*. The following subjects seemed sufficiently diverse and comprehensive for a fair test of the respective systems: their tendency to convert profligates, their tendency to convert professed unbelievers, an examination of the number of converts to Socinianism, on the standard of morality, on the promotion of morality in general, love to God, candour and benevolence to men, humility, charity and the supposed charge of bigotry toward Calvinists, love to Christ, veneration for the Scriptures, happiness or cheerfulness of mind, motives to gratitude, obedience and heavenly-mindedness, and the tendency to religious infidelity.

After the categories for investigation were established, what method would yield the greatest likelihood of accurate appraisal? Fuller proposed a two-fold trial.

> There are two methods of reasoning which may be used in ascertaining the moral tendency of principles. The first is, comparing the nature of the principles themselves with the nature of true holiness, and the agreement or disagreement of the one with the other. The second is, referring to plain and acknowledged facts, and judging of the nature of causes by their effects. Both these methods of reasoning, which are usually expressed by the terms *a priori*, and *a posteriori*, will be used in this and the following *Letters*, as the nature of the subject may admit.[22]

Fuller was confident that the principles of the two systems, overall, differed so far from each other that conclusions reached from close

---

whom the author seems to regard with a more than *odium theologicam*, with a rancor exceeding even the measure of his profession. The religious tenets of Dr. Priestley appear to me erroneous in the extreme, but I should be sorry to suffer any difference of sentiment to diminish my sensibility to virtue, or my admiration of genius. From him the poisoned arrow will fall pointless. His enlightened and active mind, his unwearied assiduity, the extent of his researches, the light he has poured into almost every department of science, will be the admiration of that period, when the greater part of those who have favored. Or those who have opposed him, will be alike forgotten... Dr. Priestley has not in any instance displayed that dissatisfaction to government, with which he is charged so wantonly... Dr. Priestley has moreover defended with great ability and success the principles of our dissent, exposing, as the very nature of the undertaking demands, the folly and injustice of all clerical usurpations; and on this account, if on no other, he is entitled to the gratitude of his brethren.' Hall, *Works*, II, pp. 399-400.

22 *Calvinistic and Socinian Systems Examined*, p. 116.

reasoning would reveal the truth. The first part, therefore, of each discussion employs respective theological expositions with closely connected inferences drawn from each system. This *a priori* method of reasoning should create at least the expectation as to the kind of practical effect each system would have on its adherents. Fuller then looks at 'facts' as they are well-known in the public forum. These are gathered from the testimonies of devotees, admissions made by leaders, and observations that are open for all to make. This *a posteriori* method, in Fuller's expectation, should show a pattern of consistency, in general, between theory and practice. In that way the trial of the apparent truthfulness of the two systems might be fairly consummated. Since Priestley so vigorously denounced the moral tendency of Calvinism, Fuller embraced the assumption behind such denunciation as revealing a test by which his antagonist would be willing to abide. As Fuller stated it:

> There is one thing, however, in the above passage, wherein we all unite; and this is—*that the* VALUE *or* IMPORTANCE *of religious principles is to be estimated by their influence on the morals of men.* By this rule let the forementioned doctrines, with their opposites, be tried. If either those or these will not abide the trial, they ought to be rejected.[23]

The strength of this method is that Fuller gained the advantage of being able to describe the theological principles of the debate in detail. These principles were not compared, then, to texts that were in dispute but to Christian virtues, attitudes, and goals that were not in dispute. He could remove caricatures, correct misimpressions, and describe biblical ideas without those being the ground of controversy. He would seemingly grant the legitimacy of the Socinian emphasis on Christianity primarily as a system of virtue, and demonstrate its inferiority in accomplishing its own end.

The Argument in Action

In this section, we will examine Fuller's approach on three key issues in which he employs both the test of theory and the test of fact. Then we will point to several summary and conclusive points Fuller distils from his arguments on other issues. The three issues of more extended discussion are: (1) the conversion of profligates; (2) love of Christ; and (3) veneration for the Scriptures.

---

23 *Calvinistic and Socinian Systems Examined*, p. 113.

The Conversion of Profligates

Fuller argued that the Calvinist system had a greater tendency to convert profligate sinners that the Socinian system. He begins with the foundational issue of conversion for it is the commencement of holy life. He assumes that the proposition is self-evident that 'the system which affords the most enlarged views of the evil of sin must needs have the greatest tendency to promote repentance for it'.[24]

Having established that principle and given biblical examples of the depth of repentance described as characteristic of saints in Scripture, he describes the views of sin at the heart of each system. We may observe also how Fuller uses the comparison for a full, yet succinct, description of the theology of his two parties.

Calvinism affirms that though man was originally created holy and happy, he disobeyed God of his own accord and became vile. God is infinitely amiable, the moral center of all intelligence and rebellion against him, if allowed to operate according to its tendencies, would exclude God and righteousness from the universe and destroy universal good, create anarchy and endless mischief and is in itself an infinite evil deserving of eternal punishment. Whenever God exercises forgiveness, it is not without 'that public expression of his displeasure against it which was uttered in the death of his Son'. These influences to self-abhorrence have led multitudes to repent in dust and ashes.[25]

On the other hand, Socinianism 'entertains dimunitive notions of the evil of sin'. They view it virtually as intrinsic to finitude, a frailty to be pitied rather than an evil to strike horror into the conscience. Its main detraction is not from the glory of God but from the happiness of man. That which is threatened against sin is so trifling as to be no object of dread. 'Since God has created us for happiness', Priestley reasons, 'what misery can we fear?' Since we are intended for ultimate unlimited happiness, 'it is no matter to a truly resigned person, when, or where, or how'.[26]

Fuller does not then press the question as to which of these views is true, but which one has the greatest tendency to promote repentance. 'If repentance be promoted by a view of the evil of sin, this question, it is presumed, may be considered as decided.'[27]

Nor was this the only problem with the tendency of Socinianism to foster only shallow repentance through shallow views of sin. Socinians

---

24 *Calvinistic and Socinian Systems Examined*, p. 116.
25 *Calvinistic and Socinian Systems Examined*, p. 116.
26 *Calvinistic and Socinian Systems Examined*, p, 117. Fuller quoted from a treatise by Priestley on *Necessity* contained in his *Discourses on Various Subjects*.
27 *Calvinistic and Socinian Systems Examined*, p. 117.

questioned seriously whether every transgression would be punished, or even if every commandment should receive a just recompense. Their difficulty came with 'the equity and goodness of the Divine law'. Inflict punishment for *every* transgression! Only a 'merciless tyrant' would do so and, according to Thomas Belsham, we must 'be tempted to which that the reins of universal government were in better hands'.[28] Fuller contemplates the implications of this and puts his test of promotion of virtue to it.

> It seems, then, that God has given us a law by the terms of which he cannot abide; that justice itself requires him, if not to abate the precept, yet to remit the penalty, and connive at smaller instances of transgression. I need not inquire how much this reflects upon the moral character and government of God. Suffice it at present to say, that such views must of necessity preclude *repentance*. If the law which forbids, 'every instance' of human folly be unreasonably strict, and the penalty which threatens the curse of the Almighty on every one that continueth not in *all things* therein written be indeed cruel, then it must so far be unreasonable for any sinner to be required to repent for the breach of it. On the contrary, God himself should rather repent for making such a law than the sinner for breaking it![29]

A third aspect of conversion Fuller invokes is its relationship to faith in Christ. Truly, New Testament language indicates that conversion manifests itself in faith in Christ as the one whose blood we receive forgiveness and that there is no other name through whom this aspect of conversion can come. The language constantly pushes the sinner to faith in Christ. Socinian writers, however, denude such language of all its force to press the sinner to Christ and substitute instead a 'good moral life' as the ground of our hope. This is dangerous reductionism, even contradiction to the biblical language, and deserves a warning, which Fuller soberly provided. If it is finally shown that a propitiatory death provides the only avenue of acceptance with God, those who reject this will find themselves fighting against God. 'Meanwhile', Fuller concludes, 'it requires but little penetration to discover that whatever takes away the only foundation of a sinner's confidence cannot be adapted to promote it.'[30]

The *a priori* arguments, therefore, indicate that Calvinism by its doctrine has greater tendency to effect profound conversion and leave no person with a just excuse for his disobedience or any reason as to why he should not be punished eternally without a satisfaction being made to the righteous anger of God. Socinianism tends to minimize the need for conversion because of its diminished view of the severity of sin and its

---

28 *Calvinistic and Socinian Systems Examined*, p. 117. Fuller quotes from Thomas Belsham's sermon on the 'Importance of Truth'.
29 *Calvinistic and Socinian Systems Examined*, pp. 117-18.
30 *Calvinistic and Socinian Systems Examined*, pp. 119.

confidence that God himself will not require a full exactment of punishment for disobedience. Why should any sinner be terribly concerned about conversion under such a system?

Now Fuller pushes forward to an inquiry into 'matters of fact', that is, the *a posteriori* arguments. In the first place, Fuller points out that Priestley acknowledges a distinct difference between the results of his preaching and that of the apostles or even of the Methodists of his day. The great conversion evident in the case of the apostles, and the current Methodists, Priestley explained in terms of novelty and the shock effect it has on auditors who are ignorant. Priestley did not expect that his preaching would have like effect. As a matter of theory, Priestley admitted he was 'less solicitous about the conversion of unbelievers who are much advanced in life than of younger persons, and that because he [Priestley refers to himself in the third person] despairs of the principles of Christianity having much effect upon the lives of those whose dispositions and habits are already formed'.[31] As a matter of personal observation, Priestley remarks, 'Our people having in general been brought up in habits of virtue, such great changes in character and conduct are less necessary in their case.'

What could make Priestley so dubious about the expectation of radical, immediate, profound conversion of profligate sinners? Fuller surmises that the natural, and not uncandid, conclusion is that Priestley does not see 'any such effects arise from his ministry, or the ministry of those of his sentiments'.[32] How could Priestley develop a theory in opposition to regular experience?

The experience of those, however, who make the 'doctrines of human depravity, the Deity and atonement of Christ, justification by faith, and sanctification by the influence of the Holy Spirit' is quite different. In the past and in the present they regularly see the radical conversion of such as were described in the New Testament as 'fornicators, adulterers, thieves, covetous, drunkards, revilers, extortioners'. Both the Reformation and the Evangelical Awakening in England and North America in the mid-eighteenth century preached these doctrines and saw this species of conversion regularly. He noted that 'a considerable degree of the same kind of success has attended the Calvinistic churches in North America, within the last ten years; especially in the states of Virginia, the Carolinas, and Georgia'. When grand and holy effects attend the labors of pastors and other preachers that insist on these teachings that Priestley included among the 'corruptions of Christianity', they must be forgiven, and

---

31 *Calvinistic and Socinian Systems Examined*, p. 120. Fuller quotes Priestley from *Letters to a Philosophical Unbeliever*.
32 *Calvinistic and Socinian Systems Examined*, p. 120.

warrantably believed, when they ascribe them to the 'name of our Lord Jesus Christ, and to the Spirit of our God'.

Before letting this issue rest, Fuller gives six reasons that the success of Calvinistic preaching cannot be attributed to the power of novelty. Much of its most powerful effects of radical conversion have taken place in congregations where those converted have heard the principles for decades. The message was not novel, but the conversion, as in the case of Jonathan Edwards's preaching in Northampton, still proved radical. In addition, even with a novel teaching, its effects in general and over time will not be distinct from its principles. An exceeding degree of heat will still produce the effects of heat. The apostles, and their doctrinal successors, did not see fit to pass along the insight that Priestley observes. They did not attribute any of the lasting moral effects of their message to its novelty but to the working of the mighty power of the Holy Spirit. On top of that, those most disposed to embrace novelty, such as those at Athens, benefited the least from Paul's doctrine.

Finally, Fuller issues a twofold challenge to Priestley and his intellectual and spiritual comrades. First, since Mr. Belsham has admitted that rational Christians appear indifferent to practical religion, there might be a need for the kind of conversion Priestley resists. 'We may conclude', Fuller insists, 'that the generality of "rational Christians" are not so righteous as to need no repentance; and that the reason why their preaching does not turn sinners to righteousness is not owing to their want of an equal proportion of sinners to be turned'.[33]

Secondly, Fuller challenges Priestley to go into the highways and hedges, since his doctrines are admittedly just now *newly* rediscovered, and woo the profligate population in 'the love of God and holiness' with these new doctrines. If the errors of the enthusiastic Methodists have been so powerful as to civilize and christianize large parts of the land, what wonders might be expected from Mr. Priestley's truth. Given his views, though, of the working of the principles of virtue, he would have to preach in such a way as to call the righteous, not sinners, to repentance. He could hold out no hope for those whose habits in the path of vice are so strong that they cannot be amended. 'Happy for many a poor wretch of that description', Fuller says as he seeks to clinch his argument, 'happy especially for the poor thief upon the cross, that Jesus Christ acted on a different principle!'[34]

---

33 *Calvinistic and Socinian Systems Examined*, p. 124.
34 *Calvinistic and Socinian Systems Examined*, p. 124.

Love of Christ

Fuller considered the bare language of the New Testament conclusive that Christianity consists largely of love to Christ. Conformity to *morality* itself, if defined by the moral law of God, cannot exist apart from love to Christ. 'He that loveth me will be loved of my Father', Jesus said. Peter wrote to those to whom he brought the gospel about their attitude toward Christ, 'Whom having not seen, ye love.' Paul concluded, 'If any man love not the Lord Jesus Christ, let him be anathema.' The question to be answered, then, by the twofold test, is which view tends more to the love of Christ, that is, the kind of love manifest in the apostolic testimony.

Three questions serve to clarify the *a priori* aspect of the problem: which system tends most to exalt his character, which places his mediatorial work in the most important light, and 'which represents us as most indebted to his undertaking'.

Fuller's answer to the first question employs the reasoning of Jonathan Edwards in *The Nature of True Virtue*. Fuller summarizes: 'God, possessing infinitely more existence than all the creatures taken together, and being as good as he is great, is to be loved and revered without bounds, except those which arise from the limitations of our powers; that is, "with all our heart, and soul, and mind, and strength."'[35]

Given this reality, does a system which reveres Christ as God or one that views him as a mere man excite more of genuine love and truly virtuous feeling in connection with thoughts about him? The language and devotion of the biblical writers seems to be consistent with that of the Calvinists. They engage in the most exalted encomiums on the name of Christ which must be embarrassingly ludicrous should he prove after all to be merely human, nothing more.[36]

In the face of this biblical atmosphere, Priestley says, 'In no sense whatever, not even in the lowest of all, is Christ so much as called *God* in all the New Testament.' To this position Fuller posed the dilemma as to 'whether such love as the prophets and apostles expressed towards Christ could consist with his being merely a fellow creature, and their considering him as such'. Again, given the principles of the Socinians, could the manner in which they expressed their love to Christ have been considered anything other than 'the height of extravagance, and the

---

35 *Calvinistic and Socinian Systems Examined*, p. 189.
36 *Calvinistic and Socinian Systems Examined*, pp. 189-91. Fuller does not intend to do lengthy and technical exegesis on the passages that he mentions, but merely to show that the devotion of the apostles, as well as the prophets in prospect, was remarkably like worship. Their language engages in so much God-talk that the Socinians are left with a formidable task of explaining all this away either by interpretive sophistry or by denigrating the philosophical sophistication of the biblical writers.

essence of idolatry?' Fuller asks the reader to judge the moral tendency of the respective views.

> Judge also for yourselves, brethren, which of the systems in question has the greatest tendency to promote such a spirit of love to Christ as is here exemplified: that which leads us to admire these representations, and, on various occasions, to adopt the same expressions; or that which employs us in coldly criticising away their meaning: That which leads us, without fear, to give them their full scope; or that which while we are honouring the Son, would excite apprehensions, lest we should, in so doing, dishonour the Father.[37]

The second question for investigation concerns the importance of the mediation of Christ. That system which puts him in the most important place as a mediator would have a previous tendency to excite greatest love for him. The Socinian system has little use for Christ, as in worship, so as an atoning sacrifice. Christ as an atonement for sin is considered one of the major corruptions of Christianity, according to Joseph Priestley.[38] His rediscovery of the pristine purity of Christianity as it reflects the benevolence of God in his moral government one day will be dominant again in Christian thinking, according to Priestley. Virtue is the necessary means of the happiness God wishes for all his creatures and 'his displeasure at sin is sufficiently shown by the methods which he takes to promote the reformation of sinners'. These considerations should eradicate, in time 'whatever remains of the doctrine of atonement; a doctrine which has no foundation in reason, or in the scriptures, and is indeed a modern thing'. Christ's death should be considered a sacrifice in no other manner 'than any person might be said to be a sacrifice to the cause in which he dies'.[39]

Fuller saw no concordance between this and the passionate New Testament devotion to Christ on account of his crucifixion and his being the mediator of all heavenly blessings. All the redeemed will say 'Worthy is the Lamb that was slain', and Paul knew nothing but 'Christ crucified'. For the knowledge of Christ Jesus and for the righteousness that comes by faith in him Paul suffered the loss of all things and gladly counted them as dung. In his letter to the Ephesians, Paul represents Christ as the medium through which all the blessings of God are bestowed. The primitive gospel was full of Christ; he was its life and its center. No

---

37 *Calvinistic and Socinian Systems Examined*, p. 191. The major passages that Fuller quotes and to which he refers in this call to judgment are Jn 1.1-3, 10, 14; 20.24-28; Heb. 1 and other references throughout; and Paul in various passages including Rom. 9.4, 5 and Col. 1.13-17.
38 Priestley, *Corruptions*, pp. 90-155.
39 Priestley, *Corrputions*, p. 154.

blessings of the gospel reached their target apart from making their journey through Christ.

Fuller sets out the options again. 'Which of the systems in question is it which resembles that of the apostles in this particular', Fuller asks, 'and consequently has the greatest tendency to promote love to Christ?' Is it the Calvinistic system in which 'Christ is the All in all' or the Socinian system of Joseph Priestley and Thomas Belsham in which 'he is scarcely ever introduced, except for the purpose of representing him as a "mere fellow creature, a fallible and peccable man?"'[40]

The third question used to test if one has the kind of regard for Christ as the primitive Christians indicated is, 'Which of the two systems represents us as most indebted to Christ's undertaking?' Fuller investigates the maxim that those who have much forgiven will love much, while those who have little forgiven will love little. The Socinian system sees sin as hardly more than external irregularities. Each person has much more of virtue than he does of sin and the race in general has more of virtue than it does of sin. On the other hand, Fuller's system asserts that we 'are utterly depraved, our very nature totally corrupted; and consequently, that all our supposed virtues, while our hearts were at enmity with God, were not virtue in reality but destitute of its very essence'. A Calvinist's view of human depravity causes them to see themselves as utterly destitute of merit and virtue, lost and ready to perish, 'so that if we are saved at all, it must be by rich grace, and by a great Saviour'.[41]

The height of one's regard for Christ also considers the penalty of sin from which Christ has saved him. Socinians see all punishment as remedial and restorative, not as punitive. None, therefore, will be punished eternally. The Socinian believes that God's benevolence naturally moves him to forgive without the exactment of retributive justice, we have been forgiven little, and that our due amount of remedial punishment has in no sense been laid on Christ. This, according to Priestley, is 'a simple and a pleasing view of God and his moral

---

40   *Calvinistic and Socinian Systems Examined*, p. 193
41   *Calvinistic and Socinian Systems Examined*, pp. 193-94. The Socinian system seems congenial to Paul's pre-conversion understanding of righteousness, as Fuller evaluates it. Paul thought highly of his conformity to the law as long as he viewed it in terms of merely an external department. When its true spirituality came into view, however, that is, when the commandment rose up in all its glory and splendor, sin revived. Sin then became a 'mighty ocean, that swelled and swept off all his legal hopes'. The Socinians see sin as a mere spray which titillates the face while they ignore the roaring ocean of which the spray is a mere effusion. Consequently, their thought of forgiveness corresponds in weightlessness and they view it as virtually an obligation which the deity owes his creatures if they are to do him the favor of considering him benevolent.

government, and the consideration of it cannot but have the best effect on the temper of our minds and conduct in life'.[42]

The Calvinist, to the contrary, sees sin as infinite in its evil and therefore worthy of an unbearable and endless punishment. While maintaining his integrity and the most striking complement of attributes, the Father could well refuse to forgive anyone. He has, however, out of undeserved love and for reasons of his own pleasure and glory, given his beloved Son, Jesus the Christ, as an atoning sacrifice and has thus achieved a gracious forgiveness fully consistent with his eternal justice. This incapacity to forgive apart from a real demonstration of justice allows mercy to triumph without its being at the expense of law, justice, and the general good and does not, therefore, diminish the loveliness and benevolence of the Father. 'Such an incapacity rather infers a perfection than an imperfection in his nature', Fuller contends, 'and instead of diminishing our regard for his character, must have a powerful tendency to increase it.'[43] Given the earlier maxim, which of the systems tends to greater love for Christ, and thus more nearly reflects the primitive example of regard for Christ?

As for matters of fact, *a posteriori* evidence, that exists alongside the statement of their principles in their writings and the arguments against the deity and the atoning work of Christ in their sermons. The derogation of prayer to Christ, their reduction of his value from redeemer to martyr, and their accusation of idolatry toward those whose opinion of him moves them to worship serve as the factual evidence of their unapostolic-like minimizing of the importance of Christ. How could an anathema be placed on anyone who did not love the Lord Jesus Christ by a Socinian? How could a Socinian ever say 'For to me to live is Christ' with any sense of the passion and reverence involved in that exclamation for Paul? Can any Pauline, Johannine, or Petrine fervor for the preciousness of Christ be deduced from the following coolness of Priestley as he criticizes the Arian position as being too high for the purposes for which Jesus lived.

> Besides, if we once give up the idea of Christ having been the maker of the world, and content ourselves with supposing him to have been a being of a much more limited capacity [as the Arians did], why may we not be satisfied with supposing him to have been a *mere man*? The purposes of his mission certainly could not require more. For it cannot be said that any thing is ascribed to him, that a mere man (aided, as he himself says he was, by the power of God, his Father) was not equal to.[44]

---

42   Priestley, *Corruptions*, p. 155.
43   *Calvinistic and Socinian Systems Examined*, p. 195.
44   Priestley, *Corruptions*, p. 86.

This kind of judgment can only be possible if one has omitted the force of many specific teachings of Scripture, ignored its spirit and focus, beclouded its clarity, and reshaped it in accordance with a dictatorial spirit. That leads one to consider if the Socinians had the kind of veneration for Scripture as manifest by Jesus himself and his apostles.

Veneration for the Scriptures

Fuller establishes the premise of this letter in his first sentence: 'If we may judge of the nature of true piety by the examples of the prophets and holy men of old, we may conclude with certainty that an affectionate attachment to the Holy Scriptures, as the rule of faith and practice, enter deeply into the spirit of it.'[45] That love for Scripture did so animate the biblical writers Fuller demonstrates briefly, but sufficiently, and then shows that Priestley himself considers a high regard for 'proper Scripture authority' as a mark of true piety.

What, then, may a Christian consider a 'proper regard' for the writings of the Bible to be? If the writers of the Bible are good and honest men, should we receive their writings in the spirit in which they presented them to the world? If their view of piety included a submission to Scripture in all matters of faith and practice, can one be said to be pious who sets himself above the Scripture? If a person venerates the authority of Scripture he must receive it for what it professes to be and for all the purposes conceived in its composition. Fuller was certain that a candid investigation of all the pertinent facts would show that the whole body of Socinian divinity breathed 'a language unfriendly to the sacred writings, and carry in it something hostile to *every thought being subdued to the obedience of Christ*'.[46]

Old Testament prophets claimed to speak and write by the Spirit of God. New Testament writers claim the inspiration of the Old Testament and, in addition, see themselves as inspired and in continuity with that prophetic revelation. The language against those who do not receive their words as of God is severely denunciatory and unworthy of goodness and piety unless it be true. Fuller concludes, therefore, that biblical piety involves receiving the Bible itself as an 'infallible standard of faith and practice'.[47]

Working with several writings of Priestley, Thomas Belsham, and Theophilus Lindsey, Fuller systematically and relentlessly demonstrates

---

45   *Calvinistic and Socinian Systems Examined*, p. 195.
46   *Calvinistic and Socinian Systems Examined*, p. 196.
47   *Calvinistic and Socinian Systems Examined*, pp. 196-97. Fuller begins his discussion with this proposition as a possibility, it is clear that his intent is to demonstrate the certainty of the proposed possibility.

that the Socinian practice, arising from their implicit theory, is to place their own rationality and conscience above the plain teaching of Scripture. Priestley, specifically on several occasions, treats the writers of Scripture as fallible men susceptible to all the mistakes of other historians and witnesses of events. They also were subject to biases and were 'liable to make mistakes with respect to things of small moment, because they might not give sufficient attention to them'. He felt fully qualified to question and challenge the reasoning of the writers by 'due consideration of the propositions they advance, and the arguments they allege'. Priestley claimed that the assertion of biblical inspiration 'is a thing to which the writers themselves make no pretensions. It is a notion destitute of all proof, and that has done great injury to the evidence of Christianity.'[48]

What Priestley means by 'proper Scriptural authority' then includes the fallibility of the writers. His claim that their fallibility comes as a result of their being men assumes, according to Fuller, 'that it is impossible for God himself so to inspire a *man* as to preserve him from error without destroying his nature.' This view obviously extended to Christ himself since Priestley considered him 'fallible and peccable'. This fallibility infected not merely what they did in their every day activities as men, but in what they actually reported as true in their writings. This is because of their lack of attention to details and the lack of rational sophistication.

Priestley does think they were infallible in their view of Christ, not because they were inspired, but because they had adequate opportunity to observe, reason, and draw their own conclusions. This proves only that any person may be infallible in certain things if he has adequate opportunity to observe and draw conclusions. On this premise it is just as rational to assert the infallibility of Joseph Priestley as it the biblical writers. And we may just as easily accept Priestley's materialistic philosophy of the non-existence of the soul as the New Testament testimony to the deity of Christ. 'One is as much an object of the sense as the other.'

The apostolic conclusions, however, according to Priestley were that Jesus was a 'man approved of God' and nothing more. With this judgment, Fuller begins to point out how the Socinian writers decided what Scriptures could be honored as authoritative and which not. Their principles of interpretation as well as judgments of textual authenticity were guided by principles of human rationality that make the reason of the individual the sole umpire in matters of faith. It turns out that the

---

48 *Calvinistic and Socinian Systems Examined*, p. 197. Fuller quotes from the *Letters to Philosophical Unbelievers* as also *Letters to the Philosophers and Politicians of France.*

'Proper Scriptural authority' is not real authority at all. Everything in Scripture must finally be subject to the Socinian canons of criticism. 'If this be true', Fuller asks, 'to what purpose are all appeals to the Scriptures on controverted subjects?' Socinians certainly should not appeal to them and should honestly acknowledge 'that they do not learn their religion thence, and therefore refuse to have it tried at that bar!'[49]

After further detailed engagement with Lindsey, Belsham, and continental Socinians who verge even further toward infidelity, Fuller envisions a striking scenario in the art of theological controversy.

> If we must quote particular passages of Scripture after the manner in which our adversaries translate them, we must also avoid quoting all those which they object to as interpolations. Nor shall we stop here: we must, on certain occasions, leave out whole chapters, if not whole books. We must never refer to the *reasonings* of the apostles, but consider that they were subject to be misled by Jewish prejudices; nor even to *historical facts*, unless we can satisfy ourselves that the historians, independently of their being Divinely inspired, were possessed of sufficient means of information. In short, if we must never quote Scripture except according to the rules imposed upon us by Socinian writers, we must not quote it at all; not, at least, till they shall have indulged us with a Bible of their own, that shall leave out every thing on which we are to place no dependence. A publication of this sort would, doubtless, be an acceptable present to the Christian world, would be comprised in a *very small compass*, and be of infinite service in cutting short a great deal of unnecessary controversy, into which for want of such a criterion, we shall always be in danger of wandering.[50]

As Fuller closes this discussion, he does not return to the question as to which system both in theory and in practice inculcates proper veneration for the Scripture. He established it as an issue of piety at the beginning of the letter and spent the entire content in a vigorous polemical investigation of the blatant Socinian defects on this issue. Also, one must assume that Fuller and his Calvinist compatriots accepted Scripture as an infallible, sufficient, divinely-inspired, clear, revelatory authority in all of its propositions. Though he does not revisit the initial question and prompt the reader to a conclusion, he expects that the nature of the discussion makes the answer undeniable.

Examples of other Conclusions

On the conversion of 'Professed Unbelievers' such as Jews, 'Mahometans', and skeptics Priestley argued that maintaining the deity of Christ with its concomitant the Trinity served as a great stumbling-

---

49 *Calvinistic and Socinian Systems Examined*, p. 203.
50 *Calvinistic and Socinian Systems Examined*, p. 205.

block. Fuller observed: 'We may so model the gospel as almost to accommodate it to their taste', but in so doing Christians would be 'more converted to them, than they to us.' Rather than being ineffective, however, the history of missions shows that poor benighted Trinitarians have not only been zealous but used effectually in conversion work. Finally, given the whole emphasis of the Socinian system, Fuller believes that it tends to 'render men indifferent to this great object', on the one hand, and to make 'conversion' involve virtually no change at all, on the other. 'The result is this', concluded Fuller, 'Socinianism so far from being friendly to the conversion of unbelievers [previously established as a goal of genuine piety] is neither adapted to the end nor favourable to the means—to those means, at least, by which *it has pleased God to save them that believe.*'[51]

Concerning a standard of morality, Fuller finds Socinian principles decidedly inferior and their practice self-professedly more worldly. Though Socinians expressed concern that Calvinism gave wrong impressions of the moral government of God and tended to relax the obligations of virtue, Fuller countered with a full investigation of the real tendencies of both systems under discussion. In reality, Socinianism relaxed obligation to virtue in several ways. God never intended to invoke the full rigor of the law, Socinianism claimed, but always intended to make allowance for human error and imperfection and accept simple repentance and sincere obedience instead of strict conformity. To such a relaxed law, no satisfaction is needed, and thus no mediator. Fuller analyzed this amended law with rigorous logic.

> If repentance and sincere obedience be all that ought to be required of men in their present state, then the law ought to be so framed, and allowance to be made by it for error and imperfection. But then it would follow, that where men *do* repent, and *are* sincere, there are no errors and imperfections to be allowed for. Errors and imperfections imply a law from which they are deviations; but if we be under no law, except one that allows for deviations, then we are as holy as we ought to be, and need no forgiveness.[52]

This doctrine is supposed to promote holiness of life and comes from those who brand the Calvinistic system with Antinomianism. But if the divine law is, as Scripture proclaims, holy, just, and good, its relaxation either in precept or penalty, 'without some expedient to secure its honor', certainly subverts good order and is an enemy to holiness, justice, and goodness.

Does Calvinism or Socinianism more consistently promote love for God, the foundation of all true piety? Priestley and other Socinians say

---

51 *Calvinistic and Socinian Systems Examined*, p. 130.
52 *Calvinistic and Socinian Systems Examined*, p. 140.

that the Calvinist doctrine of the atonement renders God as naturally implacable and thus unlovely. It represents him as a vindictive being and thus unlovely and not imitable as a Father. Calvinists represent God as a megalomaniac who desires that everything in creation redound to his glory rather than the happiness of the creatures. The Calvinist veneration of Christ detracts from the worship due to the Father alone.

Fuller concedes that the Calvinist view of God might indeed be one that incapacitates one of Mr. Priestley's disposition from loving him, but that does not render the view incorrect. The Calvinist doctrine of the atonement does not show God to be implacable. Rather, it stretches our vision of his placability to its highest possible pitch. God does not allow mercy to triumph over truth, righteousness, and equitable judgment? Thus, he does not forsake his intrinsic goodness for the sake of human sin. Moreover, his forgiveness of sinners comes because he gives his beloved Son as an atonement. 'Now judge, brethren', Fuller pleads, 'whether this view of things represent the Divine Being as *naturally implacable*,—whether the gift of Christ to die for us be not the strongest expression of the contrary.'[53]

Is God vindictive? Jonathan Edwards contended, and Fuller agreed, that the vindictive justice of God is a glorious attribute. Scripture represents God as one who takes vengeance, and the 'nature and fitness of things' shows that vindictive justice is necessary for order and benevolent government in society. As a Father God is imitable in that he teaches us to fear and obey for our own good and the good of the whole. This promotes love to God unless we can convince ourselves that one who allows disorder, thievery and homicide with impunity, general lawlessness, and shows partiality to the rebellious and seditious is a more lovely being than one who works for order, truth, and the good of the whole.

Is it right and lovely for God to determine that all things shall be done to his own glory? Again employing Edwards' *The Nature of True Virtue*, Fuller shows that this is exactly what should be expected toward one who has the most and the best of all existence. His glory is pre-eminent. In addition, Scripture unremittingly sets the true goal of all rational beings as lifting minds hearts and voices in praise to the worthiness and glory of God. Sin itself is falling short of the glory of God. This view of God assigns him the supreme place in being and thus, necessarily in our affections. To require less would be to require that we do not love God supremely. 'How such a view of things can tend to promote the love of God', Fuller wonders, 'unless a subordinate place in our affections be higher than the supreme, it is difficult to conceive.'[54]

---

53 *Calvinistic and Socinian Systems Examined*, p. 155.
54 *Calvinistic and Socinian Systems Examined*, p. 159.

Does an affirmation of the deity of Christ detract from love to God? Only if Christ is set up as a rival to the Father and as a separate deity from him. Christ is worshipped by the orthodox, however, precisely for those attributes and perfections that he has in common with the Father. The Scripture declarations of the love of the Father for the Son and the warnings to those who do not honor the Son as they honor the Father show that one cannot truly love the Father if he excepts the Son from that same love.[55]

On all counts which Socinians project as unfavorable to the love of God and proper reverence for him, Fuller shows that just the opposite tendency is true. It is, in fact, the tendency of the Socinian system to diminish love for God by diminishing one's awe, respect, and seriousness about his holiness. On the other hand, Calvinist doctrine promotes love to God for on these principles 'we have more to love him for than upon the other. On this system, we have much to be forgiven; and therefore, love much. The expense at which our salvation has been obtained, as we believe, furnishes us with a motive of love to which nothing can be compared.'[56]

Responses to Fuller

Socinian Responses

Priestley never saw fit to respond to Fuller's *Letters* of comparison. Perhaps the riots which destroyed his laboratory and his meeting house and the subsequent plans and preparations to move to America made such a response seem either impossible or unimportant.[57] Two others, however, did respond, Joshua Toulmin (1740–1815) and John Kentish (1768–1853).[58]

---

55   *Calvinistic and Socinian Systems Examined*, p. 161.
56   *Calvinistic and Socinian Systems Examined*, p. 161.
57   Fuller found the riots against Priestley outrageous but not worthy of such sympathy that he would refuse to engage his religious principles with all the severity that honesty and candor would allow. 'Detestable, however, as were the riots at Birmingham, no one can plead that they render the religious principles of Dr. Priestley less erroneous, or less pernicious; or an opposition to them, upon the fair ground of argument, less necessary.' So, Fuller, *Calvinistic and Socinian Systems Examined*, p. 111. For a brief discussion of the riots see Michael R. Watts, *The Dissenters:* Volume 1. *From the Reformation to the French Revolution* (Oxford: Clarendon Press, 1978), pp. 486-87.
58   Alan P.F. Sell, 'Andrew Fuller and the Socinians', *Enlightenment and Dissent* 19 (2000 [Festschrift issue for D.O. Thomas]), pp. 91-115, has documented the details of the responses of both these antagonists to Fuller. His discussion opens the details of their contra-Fuller expositions and Fuller's corresponding responses. Toulmin's work

The content of these responses falls into four categories. First, both seek to demonstrate the truth of Socinian doctrine (nomenclature which they disdain) by showing that great moral and spiritual changes accompanied the preaching of the apostles. This preaching did not contain any of the doctrinal distinctives in which Calvinists differ from Unitarians, as they preferred to be called.

Secondly, they mount a defense of the Socinian doctrine. They prefer, at least in some instances to express their doctrine in specifically scriptural language. They affirm the unity of God and his merciful forgiveness without the necessity of appeasing his anger. Conversely, the Calvinist, and 'orthodox', view of the Trinity cannot escape the just accusation of idolatry and thus intrude on the singular love Christians should have for the Father. Nor can their doctrine of an atonement fail to diminish the lovableness of the Father. That the Father's love must be won by such brutality cannot but leave the impression that he is a merciless tyrant.

Thirdly, Fuller's investigation of the morality of Socinians/Unitarians they felt was unfair and based on 'tales' told of private characters. They believed that the morality of leading Unitarian thinkers could well stand with the best of the orthodox and that seeking to secure an argument through judging the morality of one's opponents is not a fair and manly way of arguing.

Fourthly, they resented and disputed Fuller's argument that Socinianism tended toward Deism. The leading principles of Socinianism such as devotion to Christ distinguish them from the Deists.

Fuller engaged these rejoinders with vigor.[59] First, he pointed out that the defenses of the practical efficacy of Unitarian doctrine begged the question. They only prove what no one disputes, 'that the preaching of

---

was entitled *The practical efficacy of the Unitarian doctrine considered, in a series of letters to the Rev. Andrew Fuller* (London, 1801). Kentish wrote *The moral tendency of the genuine Christian doctrine*. Toulmin published a second edition of is work as did Kentish. Kentish also wrote a second response to Fuller entitled, *Strictures upon the reply of Mr. A. Fuller, to Mr. Kentish's discoures* (London, 1798). Fuller made no reply to this work of Kentish 'being well satisfied that the public should judge from the evidence that was before them' (see Fuller, *Calvinistic and Socinian Systems Examined*, p. 234), but did engage Toulmin and Thomas Belsham again.

59 Fuller, *Socinianism Indefensible on the Ground of its Moral Tendency* immediately follows the *Letters* in Fuller's *Works*, II, pp. 243-87. Fuller has covered so much ground in his initial work, that he has little of substance to add to his criticism, but much to say in regard to the method of interaction from Toulmin and Kentish. Fuller essentially restates the nature and ground of his argument, shows how he has addressed questions of doctrinal content within that framework, and demonstrates that Toulmin and Kentish severly beg the question of the controversy, shift the ground of discussion, and complain of Fuller's method, which he adopted to accommodate that which Socinians considered their chief advantage over Calvinism.

the apostles was productive of great moral effects'.[60] The task to which Fuller invites them is to demonstrate that apostolic doctrine in its full exposition is identical to Socinian doctrine. Merely assuming that New Testament language and the preaching of the apostles proves that Unitarian doctrine has powerful effects fails to engage the controversy. Fuller is quite amazed that so many pages are spent in this way. 'If Dr. Toulmin could fairly allege the same things in behalf of the body of modern Unitarians', Fuller chided, 'he need to "call upon the churches of Christ in Judea and Samaria" to bear witness to the holy efficacy of his doctrine.'[61]

The problem of begging the question continued, Fuller believed, in their defense of their doctrine. When Toulmin asserted that the truth of the 'great doctrines of the unity of God and the humanity of Christ remain' unaffected by Fuller's argument, Fuller pointed out that he should not be surprised that he would not attack doctrines with which he had full agreement. Nor would he attack the words of Scripture when they expressed their views in the plain unadorned text of the Bible. That approach, however, did nothing to defend the peculiarities of Socinianism. 'You ought not to expect that we should attack the words of Scripture; for it is not Scripture, but your glosses upon it, that we oppose', Fuller reminded his antagonist. 'It is mean in you to beg the question', Fuller continued, 'by taking it for granted that your sense of these passages is the true one.' Not through yet with his animated resistance to Toulmin's method, Fuller capped off his answer, 'It is no other than shrouding your obnoxious glosses under the sacred phraseology of Scripture, and it betrays an inclination in you to impose upon us the one under the form of the other.'[62]

The Socinians, however, were not short in full and clear affirmation of their body of doctrine as distinctive from that of the Calvinists. Though Priestley, Toulmin, Kentish, Belsham and others liked the unadorned language of Scripture as expressive of their belief, well-selected passages that is, none could remain unaware of their clear rejection of the deity of Christ, the personhood of the Holy Spirit, and the atonimg work of Christ. Kentish clearly felt that any temporizing on the differences was not right and admonished young ministers not to 'leave the world in ignorance concerning the object of worship, the rank of Christ, the terms of salvation, and the final destiny of man'. Any union with trinitarians was impossible for they pray 'avowedly to one God, but in effect to three: for they pray not only to God the Father, but to God the Son, and God the Holy Ghost. This worship is in our opinion, antichristian and

---

60 *Reply to Dr. Toulmin*, p. 246.
61 *Reply to Dr. Toulmin*, p. 54.
62 *Reply to Dr. Toulmin*, p. 249.

unscriptural.' Union on such a basis would make them guilty of idolatry.[63]

Fuller sought to have them engage the full range of Scripture. They have denied, Fuller believes, the principal ideas contained in the biblical confession 'Jesus is the Christ come in the flesh' and 'Jesus is the Son of God'. Christ is worshipped not for those attributes of the incarnation in which he differs essentially from the Father, but in those attributes in which he shares the essence of the Father, a worship and reverence which fills the pages of the New Testament and the hearts of the apostles. Not only do the Socinian principles of interpretation and their view of the origin of Scripture give them permission to criticize and reject portions which do not align with their rationalistic theism, their theology puts them outside the parameters of Christianity. 'Charity does not require us to acknowledge and treat that as Christianity, which, in our judgment, is not so', Fuller reasoned. 'We think it our duty, in love, and with a view to their conviction, both by our words and actions, to declare our decided disapprobation of their principles.'[64]

When he was criticized for taking an approach of examining moral tendencies, Fuller simply responded that he took up the challenge as it was issued. Pure and simple Christianity, according to the Socinian/ Unitarian idea, prior to the excrescences of orthodoxy, would be most advantageous to morality, just as simple apostolic doctrine was. Fuller assumed those same principles, then, would have like effect today. A simple examination of the *a priori* tendencies of both sets of doctrines along with an examination of available data should determine which was nearest apostolic doctrine. Fuller spent the majority of time on the tendencies and used factual discussion only where it was made available to him by the writings and admissions of Socinians themselves. A judgment rendered on Priestley's description of the kinds of person attracted to Socinianism led Fuller to remark: 'That doctrine, be it what it may, to which an indifference to religion is friendly, cannot be the gospel, or any thing pertaining to it, but something very near akin to infidelity.'[65]

---

63   John Kentish, *The Nature and Duties of the Christian Ministry*, and *The Co-operation of a Christian Society with the Labours of its Minister* (Birmingham: J. Belcher, 1803), pp. 13 and 26.

64   *Reply to Dr. Toulmin*, p. 258.

65   The argument pursued by Fuller, *Calvinistic and Socinian Systems Examined*, p. 134, employed the straightforward admission by Priestley that conversions to Socinianism happen when one has attained 'that cool unbiassed [sic] temper of mind *in consequence* of becoming more indifferent to religion in general, and to all the modes and doctrines of it'. People who are indifferent may certainly be converted, Fuller argued, but they are not converted in consequence of their indifference. Conversion assaults their indifference and implants a holy bias of mind in consequence of which they place faith in

To complain now of the method, seemed to Fuller like throwing down the gauntlet and then leaving the field of battle. He remarked that their complaint against his 'mode of arguing' had as much power as if the Philistines 'had complained of the unfairness of the weapon by which Goliath lost his head'.[66]

When accused of tending toward infidelity, Toulmin and Belsham asserted points in which Socinians differed from Deists. They also spoke of the great contributions made to a critical study of the Bible by Socinians. Fuller pointed out that the controversy was not on points in which they differed from Deism, but the points in which they agreed with them against Calvinism. Though they still profess to get their doctrine from the Bible, they so mutilate it, forsake its inspiration, and render its plain teachings obscurities that their advocacy of divine revelation rings hollow. Their similarity to Deism and other forms of infidelity has so many points of commonality, and in such vital areas, and founded on the same practice of the sufficiency of human reason.

Friendly Responses

Fuller noted in 1794 that his *Letters* had received 'an unusual tide of respect and applause'. This he considered a great trial of a different sort when he was reproached for his stance against false Calvinism. He felt that his 'heart might be too much elated'[67] and that God would visit a trial on him for this self-congratulating spirit.

John Pye Smith examined the controversy as a prelude to his engagement with Thomas Belsham on the same issues. Smith wrote: 'I should say, that the address and ability of the Unitarian advocates had succeeded in detecting several single instances in which Mr. Fuller was uninformed, or incautious, or otherwise culpable; but that they had left the vitals of his reasoning absolutely unimpaired. Were that acute and ingenious writer to avail himself of some of their remarks, especially several just and important biblical criticisms, he would render future editions of both his publications more impregnable and complete.'[68]

Christ and his righteousness. It seems that Socinianism is not friendly to deep affection in matters of religious importance and consequently is incapable of inculcating the deepest longings after holiness and piety.

66   *Reply to Dr. Toulmin*, p. 255.
67   *Work of Faith*, p. 214.
68   John Pye Smith, *Letters to the Rev. Thomas Belsham, on some important subjects of Theological Discussion referred to in his Discourse on Occasion of the Death the Rev. Joseph Priestley* (London, 1805), pp. 55-56.

Conclusion

Several challenges to contemporary Christian witness emerge from Fuller's defense of orthodoxy in general and Calvinism in particular. First, he sends a chastising message to those who are guardians of Baptist identity. Issues of civil freedom, while immensely important in the Baptist witness to the world, do not crowd out orthodox, evangelical theological concerns. Fuller's zeal for this cause emerged from a desire to show that the honor of Christ, the inspiration of Scripture, and the power of the gospel were more directly concerned in Baptist witness, especially Baptist Calvinists, than contention for the cause of civil liberty. The latter, certainly important and directly related to the Baptist view of the church, concerned a temporal right and good for all men in general; the former concerned the throne rights of the Tri-une God and the eternal welfare of sinners. Fuller, though an earnest advocate of the repeal of the Corporation and Test Acts and as fully committed to constitutional freedom as his friend Robert Hall, nevertheless coveted a clear presentation of the true nature of Christian doctrine and experience. He could be a Baptist without freedom, but he could not be a Baptist without Christ.

Second, Fuller has given a bold message about the necessary connection between true belief and true piety. Alan Sell has asserted that Fuller's 'chosen ground of argument is shaky indeed'.[69] One must recognize that the issue is precarious, can tend toward judgmentalism, can generate hurt feelings, and can get bogged down in name-calling and an effort to discover who has the most virtue. In this way the theological issues under investigation might be overwhelmed. Sell seems to agree with Fuller's opponents when he concedes that an effort to 'judge the moral tendency of an entire denomination is a hazardous epistemological undertaking'.[70] But it seems to me that that is just what Fuller avoided doing. His intent, and the execution of his intent, was to judge the moral tendency of the theological *principles*, not the 'entire denomination'. Fuller, in fact, showed a dogged tenacity in bringing each discussion into the arena of a closely reasoned argument. Each point overflowed with comparative theology and the relation of respective doctrinal points to the kind of spiritual perceptions and experiential outworking it would be the nature of each to generate. A person who believes that lying is permitted if it achieves one's goal for temporal advantage would hardly be brought to repentance for success in the enterprise. A person who believes we will not be judged for every violation of divine law, will not see the urgency of maintaining purity of heart, will see no cause for

---

69 Sell, 'Andrew Fuller', p. 111.
70 Sell, 'Andrew Fuller', p. 111.

consistent confession, and cannot be induced to rely on Christ alone for right standing before God.

Toulmin complained of Fuller's 'mode of arguing'. This moved Fuller to a lengthy and reasoned defense of the theological foundations of the mode. He did the same to a complaint from Mr. Kentish.[71] Even though the method generated such objections, Fuller defended it and seemed to think that he had hit exactly the right spot in the discussion.

Fuller should be commended for his approach and imitated in it. He had the boldness to hazard the wrath of his opponents in order to follow the views of Jesus and the instruction of Paul to Timothy. 'By their fruits ye shall know them', Jesus said, with the clear indication that belief affects conduct. Paul speaks of 'doctrine conforming to godliness' and gives lengthy discussion of the connection in both of his letters to Timothy. Not only did he remind Timothy that his teaching led to his 'conduct, purpose, faith, patience, love, perseverance, persecutions, and sufferings', but he warned that men like Jannes and Jambres (who opposed Moses) opposed the truth and, as a result, their folly eventually would be obvious to all. (2 Tim. 3.8-11). We must learn to see that, though true holiness comes from the internal operations of the Holy Spirit in his striving against the corrupting influence of the flesh, the cognitive aspect of the doctrine itself is the means congruent with the work of the Spirit by which former affections are expulsed and new affections introduced and nurtured all the way to glory.

The third observation flows from that one. Fuller reminds Christians how irreducibly connected is Christ to all distinctively Christian belief, worship, and piety. While Priestley labored to show that Christ was not an object of worship and should not be prayed to, Fuller gave full scope to the scriptural witness to the sinner's utter dependence on Christ for all blessings. His gratitude to God for forgiveness is impossible to conceive without Christ's deity and substitutionary death at the center. Michael Haykin has pointed out that Fuller took this issue so seriously that Fuller 'refused to recognize them [Socinians] as Christian brothers and sisters'.[72]

Since this is true, we must chasten our language in such a way as it reflects a truly biblical/Christian view of God. Christians should take a cue from Fuller and realize that Christ-centered trinitarianism constitutes the biblical revelation of God. Christian faith involves a congruity of mind with the great facts about the person and work of Christ. Neither forgiveness nor righteousness comes into human experience apart from the work of Christ. Knowledge of God is a chimera if not grounded in

---

71 *Reply to Dr. Toulmin*, pp. 256-58, and *Reply to Mr. Kentish*, in *Socinianism Indefensible*, pp. 265-81.
72 Haykin, 'A Socinian and Calvinist Compared', p. 195.

Christianity Pure and Simple 171

Christ as Son of God, eternally generated out of the essence of the Father and bound in the union of reciprocal knowledge, love, and communion by the eternal procession of the Holy Spirit from the Father and the Son. 'We find so much use for Christ, if I may so speak', Fuller affirmed, 'that he appears as the *soul* which animates the whole body of our divinity.' He continued, displaying Christ as

> the centre of the system, diffusing light and life to every part of it. Take away Christ; nay take away the Deity and atonement of Christ; and the whole ceremonial of the Old Testament appears to us little more than a dead mass of uninteresting matter: prophecy loses all that is interesting and endearing; the gospel in annihilated, or ceases to be that *good news* to lost sinners which it professes to be; practical religion is divested of its most powerful motives, the evangelical dispensation of its peculiar glory, and heaven itself of its most transporting joys.[73]

The fourth point of unusual relevance for contemporary Christians is Fuller's tenacity about fullness of biblical interpretation. When the Socinians boasted that their faith could be expressed in the bare words of Scripture, Fuller countered that the orthodox faith could assert the same. He demonstrated such on several occasions. The question, however, is not about a plausible meaning that can be imposed on isolated passages of Scripture, such as, assuming the Socinian doctrine to be true because Scripture says, 'There is one God', and also says that Jesus was 'a man approved of God'. Fuller not only rejected the Socinian's cavalier dismissal of texts which did not suit their rationally-contrived system, he called on them to develop a more responsible system of interpretation that took into account a synthesis of relevant texts from the entire corpus of Scripture.[74]

Near the end of his life, Fuller, at the request of John Ryland, Jr., commenced the writing of a *Body of Divinity*. He was unable to finish this, regrettably, but his first nine installments were produced. The initial emphasis points to the necessity of the systematic arrangement of divinity. Within this he shows the centrality of Christ for a proper systematic arrangement of biblical thought. 'Systematic divinity', Fuller reflects, has come to be viewed as 'the mark of a contracted mind, and the grand obstruction to free inquiry'. Fuller argues convincingly to the contrary that one 'whose belief consists of a number of positions arranged in such a connexion as to constitute a consistent whole...is in a

---

73 *Calvinistic and Socinian Systems Examined*, pp. 191-92.

74 While some justification for Sell's reference, 'Andrew Fuller', p. 112, to a '"fundamentalist" proof-texting approach to the words of the Bible' exists, the overall argument of Fuller depends much more on the development of an interpretation based on a wide range of texts. Fuller demonstrates throughout this work and virtually all his writings a great skill in theological reasoning as an element of his hermeneutics.

far more advantageous track for the attainment of truth, and a real enlargement of mind, than he who thinks without a system'. To have no system is virtually the same as to have no principles.[75]

In the seventh chapter (*Letter*), Fuller argues, 'Every Divine truth bears a relation to him [Christ]: hence the doctrine of the gospel is called "the truth as it is *in Jesus*." In the face of Jesus Christ we see the glory of the Divine character in such a manner as we see it not where else. The evil nature of sin is manifested in his cross, and the lost condition of sinners in the price at which our redemption was obtained. Grace mercy, and peace are in him. The resurrection to eternal life is through his death. In him every precept finds its most powerful motive, and every promise its most perfect fulfilment.'[76]

For this reason Fuller had no hesitance to introduce a confession of faith as the guideline by which he would preach and minister at Kettering[77] or for his advocacy of the use of subscription to creeds as a means of achieving consistent witness and discipline in a local congregation.[78] Both in matters of interpretation and confessional integrity, Fuller's polemic against Socinianism gives wise instruction.

Finally, this conflict should help renew the care churches take in admission of members. Fuller's interaction points to at least three issues that are important to consider. First, one's cognitive belief, as far as it goes, must be consistent with the biblical witness, and should not be reduced beyond the affirmation of the deity of Jesus and the necessity of his deity for the effectuality of the atonement. Secondly, true knowledge of these cognitive aspects results in a certain state of mind persons have about themselves. Do they, as a result of knowledge about Christ's deity and atoning work, lament their sin, cling to Christ as their only hope, and desire to honor and love him wholeheartedly? Thirdly, does such testimony of this belief and self-consciousness result in practical action?

---

75   Fuller, *The Nature and Importance of an Intimate Knowledge of Divine Truth*, in *Sermons and Sketches*, in *Works*, I, p. 165. Fuller used this sermon as the largest part of his first chapter entitled 'Importance of Systematic Divinity', see *The Importance of Systematic Divinity*, in *Letters on Systematic Divinity*, p. 684.

76   Fuller, *The Uniform Bearing of the Scriptures on the Person and Work of Christ*, in *Letters on Systematic Divinity*, p. 704.

77   *Work of Faith*, pp. 97-109.

78   Fuller, *Creeds and Subscriptions*, in *Essays, Letters, etc. on Ecclesiastical Polity*, in *Works*, III, pp. 449-451. In this article Fuller recognizes several points at which legitimate objection might be raised to the requirement of subscribing to a creed. Overall, however, they are necessary and no serious objection can be raised against their usefulness. 'If the articles of faith be opposed to the authority of Scripture, or substituted in the place of such authority, they become objectionable and injurious; but if they simply express the united judgment of those who voluntarily subscribe them, they are incapable of any such kind of imputation', p. 451.

Is their deportment observably consistent with the truth as it is in Jesus and subservient in principle to the Lordship of him who said, 'If ye love me, keep my commandments.'

CHAPTER 7

Andrew Fuller and Universalism

Barry Howson

Long before the eighteenth century the church had struggled with the teaching of universal salvation. When Andrew Fuller and William Vidler exchanged letters on the subject the controversy was not new, though it found new ground upon which to flourish during the Enlightenment. Fuller, not new to controversy, confronted one of his former Baptist colleagues, William Vidler, who had by 1792 espoused the doctrine of the universal salvation of humanity. Vidler was born at Battle, Sussex, in 1758. Raised in the Church of England he later became an Independent and then a Baptist under the ministry of Thomas Purdy of Rye. Baptized in January 1780, he was set apart for the Baptist ministry the following February and became pastor of a small Baptist church in Battle a month later. After eleven years he travelled among Baptist churches raising money for the building of a chapel. During his travels he came in contact with Arminian Baptists and a few universalists. By the end of 1792, under the influence of the universalist Elhanan Winchester, he publicly confessed his belief in universalism.[1] Consequently, his church split, and

---

1   Winchester was born in Massachusetts in 1751. In 1774, he was ministering to a Baptist congregation in South Carolina. About this time he began to have concerns regarding the restricted salvation of Calvinism. He became a universalist by 1781 after reading Georg Klien-Nikolai's *The Everlasting Gospel* and Sir George Stonehouse's *Restitution of All Things*. In 1787, Winchester went to England as a universalist missionary. He established a congregation in a former General Baptist chapel at Parliament Court, Artillery Lane, London. He described the congregation as 'Philadelphian'. He went on missionary journeys to the Midlands, East Anglia and Kent until 1794. That same year he left England returning to America. He died in 1797. During one of his missionary journeys, Winchester preached at Battle in 1792 winning Vidler to the universalist cause. As early as 1780, Vidler was troubled by some doubts on eternal punishment. Geoffrey Rowell writes: 'At his father's funeral that year he is said to have declared that "good men are finally saved, even though they might not apprehend saving faith"'. In his journal of 1784 he stated that he had some serious doubts about the divinity of Christ and the eternity of hell-torments, and was going to 'consider them

those who fell in with him were excommunicated from the Kent and Sussex Baptist Association in the summer of 1793.[2] A year later he was called to assist Winchester in London, splitting his time between the Battle and London churches. Vidler finished his Battle ministry in 1796 and served in the London church as sole pastor until 1815. By 1802, he had come to hold Unitarian views under the influence of Richard Wright.[3] Vidler died in August 1816 and was buried in the cemetery of the Hackney Unitarian chapel.[4]

It was in the years immediately following 1793 that Andrew Fuller and William Vidler exchanged letters defending their particular views of the scriptural teaching of the extent of salvation. Fuller began the salvo with a private letter to Vidler challenging his universalism, to which the latter made no reply. Two years later Fuller, by request, sent this letter to the *Evangelical Magazine* for publication under the signature 'Gaius'. In that same year, Vidler responded in the first two editions of his own magazine, *Universalist's Miscellany*. The publication of seven more letters came from Fuller with responses from Vidler.[5] The purpose of this chapter is to explore the history of this controversy, particularly showing how Fuller defended the traditional doctrine of non-universalism or, as we will call it, particularism. In addition, we will apply some of Fuller's teaching on the subject for our day. Universalism is most certainly not dead. Some evangelicals are espousing universalism today. Moreover, one has only to look under the subject of universalism on the world-

---

more minutely', see Geoffrey Rowell, 'The Origins and History of Universalist Societies in Britain, 1750–1850', *Journal of Ecclesiastical History* 22.1 (1971), pp. 38-42.

2   When the vote was taken on the question of universalism, 153 followed Vidler and 168 maintained the traditional view, Rowell, 'Origins and History of Universalist Societies', p. 41. See also Frank Buffard, *Kent and Sussex Baptist Associations* (Faversham: privately published, n.d. [1963], pp. 53-54 and *passim*.

3   Shortly after his conversion to Unitarianism, Hannah Lindsey wrote about Vidler, 'He has a grave, persuasive manner, with great good sense, and a ready elocution as an extempore preacher; his audience are all of the middling class, who will go on a rainy day as well as a fine day to attend Divine worship'. See Robert Millar MSS, 12:46:46, quoted in Rowell, 'Origins and History of Universalist Societies', p. 42.

4   A. Gordon, 'Vidler, William', in Sidney Lee (ed.), *Dictionary of National Biography* (London: Smith, Elder & Co., 1909), XX, pp. 303-304.

5   Andrew Fuller, *Letters to Mr. Vidler, on the Doctrine of Universal Salvation*, in *The Complete Works of the Rev. Andrew Fuller, With a memoir of his Life by the Rev. Andrew Gunton Fuller* (ed. and revised Joseph Belcher; 3 vols; Harrisonburg, Virginia: Sprinkle Publications, 1988 [3rd edn, 1845]), II, pp. 294-95. Fuller's eight letters were published together in *Letters to Mr. Vidler, on the Doctrine of Universal Salvation* (1802). This publication has been reprinted in his *Works*, II, pp. 292-327. Vidler countered with his *Letters to Mr. Fuller on the Universal Restoration* (1803). In addition, Vidler wrote in the midst of the controversy a short universalist treatise entitled, *God's Love to His Creatures asserted and vindicated* (1799).

wide-web to see that it is alive and well. Are their any lessons we can learn from Fuller that will help us address universalism in our generation?

In order to fulfil our objectives we will first give an outline of the history and theology of universalism from its earliest manifestation up to the present time. Then a general overview of Vidler's universalism will be presented, followed by a detailed analysis of Fuller's eight letters which challenged this teaching. Finally, some applications will be made for the church today.

History and Theology of Universalism[6]

This section of our study will not only give us a general understanding of universalism as well as the context in which Fuller and Vidler debated the issue, but it will also give us an understanding of present-day universalism so that we might see how Fuller's polemic against universalism might help twenty-first-century particularists address it.

The first Christian universalist of the early church was Origen of Alexandria.[7] Origen believed that God created all beings good, equal, and with absolute free will. Some of these beings misused their free will and became either devils or the souls of men. Consequently, God created the world as well as bodies for the souls of men in order that he might redeem and purify these souls through a process of discipline and chastisement. This process would not end at death but continue in hell until the soul repents and returns unto its pre-fall pristine state. Punishment for Origen was remedial not punitive with the hope that not only humans but also the devils would be restored and united to God in the end. Origen was heavily influenced by Platonism and the

---

6   For some historical surveys of universalism, see Richard Bauckham 'Universalism: A Historical Survey', *Themelios* 4.2 (January, 1979), pp. 48-54; J. McClintock and James Strong (eds), *Cyclopedia of Biblical, Theological and Ecclesiastical Literature* (10 vols; Grand Rapids, MI: Baker, 1981 [1867–87]), V, pp. 656-65; Samuel M. Jackson (ed.), *The New Schaff-Herzog Encyclopedia of Religious Knowledge* (12 vols; Grand Rapids, MI: Baker, 1977 [n.d.]), XII, pp. 95-97; James Hastings (ed.), *Encyclopædia of Religion and Ethics* (12 vols; Edinburgh: T&T Clark, reprint, 1980), XII, pp. 529-35; Hosea Ballou, *The Ancient History of Universalism* (Boston, 1829); and T. Whittemore, *The Modern History of Universalism* (Boston, 1860). The most recent study is Robin Parry and Chris Partridge (eds), *Universal Salvation? The Current Debate* (Carlisle: Paternoster Press, 2003).

7   Origen's predecessor, Clement of Alexandria, espoused aspects of universalism. It should be noted that the thesis concerning Origen's universalism has been challenged by Frederick W. Norris, 'Universal Salvation in Origen and Maximus', in Nigel M. de S. Cameron (ed.), *Universalism and the Doctrine of Hell* (Carlisle: Paternoster Press/Grand Rapids, MI: Baker, 1992), pp. 35-72.

transmigration of souls to purity; and, appealing to 1 Corinthians 15.28, he believed that through the purification process 'God shall be all in all'.

Richard Bauckham states that the final restoration of all souls was not uncommon in the eastern church after Origen. It was taught by Gregory of Nyssa as well as Didymus of Alexandria, Diodorus of Tarsus and Theodore of Mopsuestia. In AD 543, however, the eastern church condemned Origen's universalism at a council in Constantinople.

In the western church Augustine's stature kept the doctrine of universalism at bay throughout the Middle Ages into the Reformation. He argued for the truth of punishment of everlasting fire for the wicked on the basis of the plain teaching of Scripture. Likely with Origen in mind, Augustine wrote: 'Thus it is Scripture, infallible Scripture, which declares that God has not spared them [the devil and his angels]. This is the only reason why it is held as fixed and unchanging religious truth that the devil and his angels are never to return to the life and holiness of the saints.'[8]

Universalism did exist in the Middle Ages, notably in the philosophy of John Scotus Erigena (c.810–c.877), as well as during the Reformation years in some Anabaptists and Spiritualists, including John Denck.[9] Though there were few advocates of universalism throughout this period of time it was beginning to make inroads with the revival of the platonic tradition and the study of early Christian writings in the Renaissance, as well as with the seventeenth-century reaction to high Calvinism. Some of the Cambridge Platonists in seventeenth-century England, including Peter Sterry and Jeremiah White, held origenist universalism. They emphasized that God's love will overcome the sinner eventually bringing about purification. God's wrath is his love aimed at the sin in order to burn it up.[10] In the next century, universalism was espoused by the popular English writer William Law, along with the English bishop Thomas Newton of Bristol.

In nineteenth-century England universalism found a home in the teachings of some prominent scholars, including Dr Samuel Cox, Professor J.B. Mayor, F.W. Farrar, F.D. Maurice and Andrew Jukes.[11] For example, Cox found in the New Testament an 'undercurrent of deeper teaching...which points to the ultimate recovery of all souls'.[12] Few people, however, espoused a dogmatic universalism as did Cox, but a

---

8   Augustine, *City of God* (New York: Doubleday, Image Books, 1958), book 21, chapter 23, p. 505. He deals with this subject in book 21, chapters 17–27.

9   See George H. Williams, *The Radical Reformation* (London: Weidenfeld and Nicholson, 1962), pp. 155, 157, 202, 246, 252, 843.

10   Bauckham, 'Universalism', p. 50.

11   S.D.F. Salmond, *The Christian Doctrine of Immortality* (Edinburgh: T&T Clark, 1901), p. 504.

12   Quoted in Salmond, *Immortality*, p. 504.

growing number were simply uneasy with the traditional doctrine of hell. Bauckham writes: 'This led to arguments for conditional immortality; to undogmatic hopes for universal salvation; and to the idea that a man's fate is not sealed at death, but the intermediate state offers fresh opportunities for attaining salvation.'[13] A common belief in these musings, influenced by the theory of evolutionary progress, was that 'repentance, conversion, moral progress [were] still possible after death'.[14] In addition, they argued their point from the Scriptures. They believed that with the progress of doctrine in the later epistles of Paul, 'we get the more developed doctrine of a perfected kingdom of God upon earth and an ultimate restitution of all'.[15] Others reasoned that the Scriptures taught both universal salvation and eternal retribution. They believed them to be antimonies of Scripture similar to the sovereignty of God and human responsibility. We are simply unable to reconcile the two apparent contradictions because of 'our limited faculties to reach higher unity'.[16] These arguments were based on such verses as 1 Corinthians 15.22, 25-28 and Ephesians 1.10. The universalists also argued their position on the basis of the meaning of biblical words such as 'all' in John 12.32 where Jesus declares, 'And I, if I be lifted up from the earth, will draw all men unto Me.' They interpret the 'all' in a universal sense. The same can be said for Paul's words, 'The grace of God hath appeared, bringing salvation to all men' (Tit. 3:5). Moreover, they maintained that the word 'eternal' or 'everlasting' in Scripture does not necessarily convey the idea of permanence and changelessness. Furthermore, they argued that the love of God revealed in the gospel compels us to embrace universalism. It is inconceivable that the Father, who is essential and absolute love, 'should turn away finally from any of His children, that the strivings of the Divine Spirit should be defeated at last by any perverse soul'. It is not the will of our Father that any of his little ones should perish. 'Love is imperial in its claim.'[17]

The twentieth century marked a significant turning point for universalism. The universalists could no longer base their arguments on Scripture because most scholars recognized that the exegesis of putative universalist texts favoured the traditionalist interpretation. Consequently, one response was to see the texts that posited everlasting punishment to be threats and not predictions of the way things will be in eternity. Another response was simply to disregard these texts as Jewish, and to infer universalism from the gospel. For example, in 1917 C.W. Emmet writes, after surveying the New Testament,

---

13 Bauckham, 'Universalism', p. 51.
14 Bauckham, 'Universalism', p. 51.
15 Salmond, *Immortality*, p. 506.
16 Salmond, *Immortality*, p. 507.
17 Salmond, *Immortality*, p. 515.

It is best in fact to admit quite frankly that any view of the future destiny of [unbelievers] which is to be tolerable to us today must go beyond the explicit teaching of the New Testament... [This] does not really give us all we want, and it only leads to insincerity if we try to satisfy ourselves by artificial explanations of its language. And we are in the end on surer ground when as Christians we claim the right to go beyond the letter, since we do so under the irresistible leading of the moral principles of the New Testament and of Christ Himself.[18]

For the twentieth-century universalists the emphasis is no longer on interpretation of the New Testament but on broad theological ideas and philosophical arguments, in particular concerning the love of God. Two important modern universalists that follow this tack are J.A.T. Robinson and John Hick. According to Robinson, God wills universal salvation, but at the same time humans are given a choice between heaven and hell. The choice is real for humanity, but in the end God's will and God's omnipotent love will conquer all of humanity.[19] Hick's Christian universalism is similar to Robinson's. He believes the texts of universal salvation and eternal punishment are compatible because in the end everyone will repent. Humans will not reject God forever because they have a created bias towards God which will draw them to God's love. What is important for Hick is that universalism vindicates God as omnipotent and good; it works as a theodicy.[20] For both Hick and Robinson salvation and repentance are not restricted to this earthly life but extend after death.

At the beginning of the twenty-first century there are presently two kinds of universalism with which the Christian must contend. The first is pluralistic universalism, taught by such scholars as Ernst Troeltsch and John Hick, which teaches that religious traditions of the world are 'inextricably linked to the particular social and cultural patterns within which it developed over the centuries'.[21] Hick, in his most recent writings,

---

18   C.W. Emmet, 'The Bible and Hell', in B.H. Streeter (ed.), *Immortality* (London: Macmillan, 1917), ch. 5, cited by Bauckham, 'Universalism', p. 52.

19   See J.A.T. Robinson, *In the End God* (London: Collins, 2nd edn, 1968). For an analysis and critique of Robinson's universalism, see Trevor Hart, 'Universalism: Two Distinct Types', in de S. Cameron (ed.), *Universalism and the Doctrine of Hell*, pp. 17-33.

20   For Hick, see *Death and Eternal Life* (London: Collins, 1976). In his subsequent writings Hick has gone beyond Christian universalism to espouse a pluralist universalism that embraces all religions without any particularity for Christianity. For an extensive critique of Hick's pluralist universalism, see Ronald H. Nash, *Is Jesus the Only Savior?* (Grand Rapids, MI: Zondervan, 1994), pp. 29-100.

21   Hart, 'Universalism', p. 5. See Ernst Troeltsch, 'The Place of Christianity Among the World Religions', reprinted in J. Hick and B. Hebblethwaite (eds), *Christianity and Other Religions* (London: Collins, 1980).

maintains that Christianity is just one religious response to God.[22] Trevor Hart summarizes his discussion of pluralistic universalism, stating, 'The central contention of [the pluralist universalistic thesis] is that all will ultimately be saved regardless of their attitude to Jesus Christ and his death; regardless, indeed, of the person of Jesus at all, or any alleged significance of his actions.'[23]

The other form of universalism is specifically Christian. Hart again gives an excellent summary of this:

> The central Christian conviction that love is the very nature of God, and that the most fundamental relation of this God to all his creatures must therefore be one of love if he is to be true to himself; the concomitant conviction that this same God must ultimately have the final good of all his creatures in view, that 'he desireth not the death of (any) sinner, but rather that he may turn from his wickedness and live'; the gospel stress on the utter unconditionality of the salvation wrought by Christ, and the rejection of any notion that some might be more deserving than others of redemption; the clear affirmations in Scripture concerning the universality of the scope of Christ's saving passion and resurrection and the completeness of the salvation effected by the same (*i.e.* in some sense God *has* saved all in Christ); and lastly an insistence that God, as Lord of all, must prevail, that the universal saving will springing inevitably from his nature must be fulfilled in his creatures.[24]

Christian universalism maintains that all people will be saved through the work of Christ grounded in God's love. It is this form of universalism that Fuller encountered in the writings of William Vidler.

William Vidler's Universalism

A short time after the Fuller–Vidler letter exchange Vidler replied to a particularist tract entitled, *Free Strictures upon an Address to Candid and Serious Men, by some Friends of Revelation*, with his own tract, *God's*

---

22 E.g., J. Hick, *God and the Universe of Faiths* (London: Collins, 2nd edn, 1977), and 'The Non-Absoluteness of Christianity', in J. Hick and P.F. Knittner (eds), *The Myth of Christian Uniqueness* (Maryknoll, NY: Orbis Books, 1988).
23 Hart, 'Universalism', p. 15.
24 Hart, 'Universalism', pp. 15-16. Christian universalists defend their position on such New Testament Scriptures as Jn 6.37, 39; 12.32; 1 Cor. 15.22; 2 Cor. 5.19; Eph. 1.10; 1 Tim. 2.3-5; Tit. 2.11; 2 Pet. 3.9; 1 Jn 2.2; and Rev. 20.14. They believe that: 1) the purpose of God is the restoration of all things to what they were in the beginning (Acts 3.21); 2) the means and sanction of this recovery is by the office and work of Christ (Rom. 5.19 and Heb. 2.9); and 3) the nature of the ultimate salvation is the indwelling of God in every human soul (1 Cor. 15.24-28). See J.E. Odgers, 'Universalism', in Hastings (ed.), *Encyclopædia of Religion and Ethics*, XII, p. 530.

Love To His Creatures Asserted and Vindicated (1799).²⁵ In this reply we discover the main points of Vidler's universalism.

First, we will note his general arguments for universalism based on Scripture and reason. It was the Age of Reason, and for Vidler, as for many of his contemporaries, if an argument did not sound reasonable it was considered to be fallacious. Vidler believed that his universalism was based on both Scripture and reason. He wrote: 'The candid reader will see that we go on the ground of scripture: at the same time we do not hesitate to say that we believe *reason* to be the gift of God, and that to set reason and scripture at variance...is more worthy of the popish than the protestant character.'²⁶ One such general argument Vidler used had to do with the attributes of God. According to Vidler, since Scripture teaches that God is infinitely wise, powerful and good, it is reasonable to believe that his conduct for the welfare of all his rational creatures will be wise, powerful and good. Speaking to particularists he queries,

> Nor do we conceive how even you can dispute this without manifest absurdity; for you must either deny that God is infinitely wise, powerful, and good or that the final issue of his conduct will discover these perfections fully, or that though these perfections will be fully displayed, yet a great part of intelligent creation will not be benefitted [*sic*] by it.--- You will readily perceive the absurdity of admitting the full display of the Divine attributes, and yet no ultimate benefit arising from it to his creatures; because in this case it must follow, either that God made a part of his creatures with a *bad* design, and this impeaches his goodness; or that he made his creatures with a *good* design, which he cannot execute, and this impeaches his ability; or that he made them with *no* design, which is ascribing folly to our Maker.²⁷

Furthermore, Vidler reasons that if God is the First Cause of all things, 'so it is consistent with reason that he should seek the happiness of all his creatures'. Since all souls belong to him, and with him there is no respect of persons, and no creature has any claim upon his favour, it is logical to think that God would seek the welfare of every one of his creatures. Vidler states, 'The question is not what we are worthy to receive, but what

---

25   The full title is *God's Love to his Creatures Asserted and Vindicated being a reply to the 'Strictures Upon an Address to Candid and Serious Men'* (London: 1799). *Free Strictures upon an Address to Candid and Serious Men, by some Friends of Revelation* (1798) was itself a response to the universalist tract, *An Address to Candid and Serious Men, by some Friends of Mankind* (1798).

26   Vidler, *God's Love*, p. 35. Vidler, pp 7-9, held to the divinity of the Scriptures and the necessity of revelation.

27   Vidler, *God's Love*, p. 8. Later, p. 14, he says, 'We suppose that his power will accomplish what his wisdom planned and his goodness willed. We freely own that we cannot help making this inference, which seems so congenial to the divine perfections.'

is fit for him to give, for whatsoever he gives we are assured it is not for our sakes, but for his own name's sake that he doth it.'[28]

Vidler also believes that God seeks the happiness of *all* his creatures based on the Scripture that states he 'has no pleasure in the death of him that dieth'. The idea of endless damnation 'casts a dark and dismal shade over the character of Deity—lessens the glory of Christ—gives an acidity to the soul—disposes the man to shut out others from any participation of the divine favour—and, under pretence of glorifying God, it ascribes to him the disposition of Moloch'.[29]

In addition, Vidler maintains that as the First Cause of all things God should deal justly with humanity. Therefore, it is unjust of God to punish humans endlessly for a few years of transgressions committed in this life. Is not the punishment to be equal with the crime? 'Few stripes and many stripes, by weight and measure, for longer or shorter duration, is so consistent with reason.'[30] Does not punishment come to moral creatures from a loving God in order to make them holy and happy? 'God does not grieve willingly nor afflict the children of men; but he chastizes them for their profit, that they might be partakers of his holiness.'[31] God is moving all humanity to holiness and happiness; this present life is only the beginning of this process for all of humanity.[32] Sin in this world and God's judgement on sinners in this world will eventually be found to harmonize with the perfections of God.[33]

It must be understood that for Vidler the moral law is not a covenant of works. According to him there was no covenant of works. The covenant with Adam prior to the Fall was a covenant of grace and forgiveness. All men by nature are not under a covenant of works but are given into the hands of Christ (Jn 5.35) for salvation. Moreover, Christ has been given the mediatorial role of judge, and his judgement will be based on God's mercy; consequently, it will ultimately issue in the welfare of every rational creature. For Vidler the immensity of the Divine goodness—mercy, grace, and love—is the first principle of revelation. Vidler concludes, 'We confess that we cannot see this goodness of the Deity "extending to all his creatures—in full harmony with all his perfections," without inferring the Restoration of all Things as its consequence.'[34]

---

28   Vidler, *God's Love*, p. 9.
29   Vidler, *God's Love*, p. 10.
30   Vidler, *God's Love*, p. 10.
31   Vidler, *God's Love*, p. 12.
32   Vidler, *God's Love*, p. 13.
33   Vidler, *God's Love*, p. 15.
34   Vidler, *God's Love*, p. 16.

Vidler also gives numerous specific arguments for universalism from Scripture of which we will take note in turn. He begins by stating his rule for interpreting Scripture:

> The only safe and certain way of explaining any passage in the Old Testament, which is quoted and explained in the New, is to consult, first of all, what the New Testament writers have said concerning it, and them to abide by their interpretation as the only just and proper one; remembering that they had the Divine spirit to lead them into all truth; consequently, that every explanation which is in substance and meaning different from that which they have given, is to be rejected as false.[35]

Vidler begins with the promise to Abraham and the patriarchs that in Abraham all the families of the earth will be blessed. This applies to more than just the church, that is, to Christ and to those who believe. This is the proper interpretation of Galatians 3.8-26, but it is not the full import of the promise made to Abraham, as can be seen from Acts 3.19-26 where the restitution of all things is connected with this promise.[36]

Similarly, Paul interprets Isaiah 25.7-8 as the first resurrection in 1 Corinthians 15.54. However, Vidler writes, 'We are persuaded that it reaches much further than the first resurrection, or even than the general resurrection, if we are to go by the application of it which we find in the New Testament.' Vidler sees the resurrection in these verses to be a threefold progression—'Christ as the firstfruits, afterwards they that are Christ's at his coming, but *every man...in his proper rank*.' Moreover, as each human has borne the image of the first Adam so will each one bear the image of the second Adam (1Cor. 15.49).[37] This conformity to Christ, the second Adam, however, will not take place at the same time for everyone. Those who do not believe the gospel in this life will have to pass through the second death 'before they can receive their measure of conformity to Christ in his resurrection state'. Death is swallowed up in victory when the tabernacle of God will be with men, and God makes all things new (Rev. 21.3-5).[38]

Again similarly, Vidler sees the judgement of God as gradual and progressive as was the resurrection. Interpreting Isaiah 45.23, Philippians 2.10 and Romans 14.11 he maintains that every person will bow the knee to Christ willingly. The final result of judgement and punishment 'will be universal subjection and universal swearing allegiance to Christ'. There is no forced submission here. Is not a willing submission much more

---

35   Vidler, *God's Love*, p. 16.
36   Vidler, *God's Love*, p. 17.
37   Vidler, *God's Love*, p. 18.
38   Vidler, *God's Love*, p. 19.

honourable to God than a forced one? Does it not bring greater glory to God?[39]

Vidler moves on to discuss the salvation of devils or fallen angels. On the basis of Psalm 145.9 ('The Lord is good to all, and that his tender mercies are over all his works') he is persuaded 'that his mercy will finally prevail over their guilt, and his goodness will make them holy and happy'.[40] When Christ took upon himself the nature of Abraham's seed it included the angels:

> For if he lays hold of that order of beings who were originally made lower than the angels, then we many suppose he has not totally passed by the higher order. Our Lord himself has taught us, that a man is more worth than many sparrows, because he is of an higher order of beings than a sparrow; surely, then an angel is, for the same reason, more worth than a man, and a fallen angel than a fallen man.[41]

According to Vidler, certain texts of Scripture, like Colossians 1.19-20 and Ephesians 1.10, include the angels in salvation. The 'things' that Christ reconciles to God are 'all things...whether they be things in earth or things in heaven', and he will 'gather together in one all things in Christ, both which are in heaven and which are on earth'. The 'all things' include all rational creatures as the interpretation of 'all things' in Colossians 1.15 undoubtedly teaches.[42] The Scripture indicates that every creature, even those in hell, will bow the knee to Jesus (Phil. 2.10-11, where 'under the earth' must mean hell).[43]

Vidler next addresses the issue of sufferings in this world and the next. For him, the punishment of hell is intended to humble and subdue sinners just as sufferings/punishment in this life are to accomplish the same.[44]

Another verse that teaches universalism according to Vidler is 1 Timothy 2.4: '[God] will have all men to be saved, and to come unto a knowledge of the truth.' This verse expresses God's *purpose* or *decree* for humans not his *command* to them. In v. 5 God is designated 'one' because he is our common Father, and Christ is called our 'mediator' because he mediates between this Father and all his creatures—he is a ransom for *all* humans.[45]

---

39   Vidler, *God's Love*, p. 19.
40   Vidler, *God's Love*, p. 5.
41   Vidler, *God's Love*, pp. 20-21.
42   Vidler, *God's Love*, p. 21.
43   Vidler, *God's Love*, p. 22.
44   Vidler, *God's Love*, p. 23.
45   Vidler, *God's Love*, p. 24. Vidler also discusses 1 Tim. 6.10, and 1 Cor. 15.24-28.

As expected Vidler addresses the meaning of the Greek words translated in the New Testament as 'everlasting' or 'for ever'. Vidler believes that the word itself will not prove the proper eternity of any thing, but 'the subject only can determine in what sense to understand it'.[46] Concerning the Greek word αἰών Vidler maintains that as a substantive it means 'age' not 'eternity' in the New Testament. Consequently, its adjectival derivative αἰώνιος describes 'the duration of something relating to that particular αἰών or *age* spoken of', and should be rendered 'agelasting'.[47] For Vidler the punishment of which the New Testament speaks is not *endless* but *limited* in duration; it is *age-long*.[48] Moreover, the longest age or αἰών in the New Testament is the mediation of Christ and is of limited duration. It is rendered in English as 'forever and ever'. It includes the past ages (Rom. 16.25), the present age (1 Tim. 6.17) and the ages to come (Eph. 2.7). However, this mediatorial αἰών will have its end when Christ hands over the kingdom to his Father (1 Cor. 15.24-28). Consequently, Vidler concludes, 'We may, without blame, therefore, say the *age-lasting* gospel, *age-lasting* consolation, *age-lasting* punishment, &c. &c.'[49]

Vidler was a typical premillennialist until it came to his interpretation of events after the millennium. He believed that after the general resurrection and general judgement (which were not final for God's creatures), 'Christ will create the *new heavens and the new earth*, and will go on to destroy death, (*even the second death*, for no other death can then remain to be destroyed) and will wipe away tears from the eyes of men without restriction.' In other words, after the creation of the new heavens and earth Christ will continue to win his rational creatures from their place of punishment until all are retrieved, and the second death is destroyed. Then the New Jerusalem will descend from God, and he shall dwell with men—this is the 'grand closing scene of all that revelation at large exhibits of all God's dealings with his rational creatures'.[50]

In conclusion, he writes to particularist adversaries: 'You may, we hope, see the unhappiness of your own cause, which appears so contradictory to

---

46 Vidler, *God's Love*, p. 28.
47 Vidler, *God's Love*, p. 31.
48 Vidler, *God's Love*, p. 35, also maintains that the meaning of 'unquenchable fire' in the New Testament has the Old Testament meaning of 'fire that should perform the purpose intended. See 2 Kings xxii. 17. 2 Chron. xxxiv.25. Jer. vii. 20. Isai. I. 28. 31. xxxiv. 10. Ezek. xx. 47-49. In these texts we read of unquenchable fire, which however has long been extinguished. In like manner the worm that dieth not, is an expression that is taken from the animal body in putridity, Isai. lxvi. 24. It requires a strong imagination indeed, and a great departure from common sense to raise the idea of *endless* misery from such expressions as these.'
49 Vidler, *God's Love*, pp. 32-33.
50 Vidler, *God's Love*, p. 34.

the scriptures of truth, so dishonourable to the character of that God who is love, so inglorious to the mediation of Jesus, and so inimical to the final welfare of millions of the intelligent offspring of Deity.'[51]

Fuller's Letters to Vidler against Universalism

In this section we will examine in turn each of Fuller's eight letters to Vidler in detail, making reference to the latter's letters where necessary.

Letter I

This first letter was a private one sent to Vidler in 1793 when Fuller understood that the former 'had imbibed the doctrine of universal salvation'.[52] Sometime later when the *Evangelical Magazine* asked for some thoughts on the subject Fuller sent the letter to the editor, and it was published in September 1795. The letter was of a personal nature requesting that Vidler consider three things concerning his acceptance of universalism. But before Fuller lays out his concerns he makes some introductory comments concerning Vidler's coming to universalism, and the effect of his teaching on the eternal welfare of those who fall under it. Then briefly, he lays out his three concerns. The first has to do with the nature of endless punishment. He asks Vidler, 'Whether [his] change of sentiment has not arisen from an idea of endless punishment being, in itself, *unjust*.'[53] He challenges Vidler to consider whether his judgement on this issue is not clouded by the effects of sin. That he is not taking into account the way sin affects our reasoning. Fuller uses the analogy of criminals as judges of the equity and goodness of a law that condemns them. They would obviously be improper judges because their judgement is clouded by their nature as criminals. The same applies for us as sinners on this issue. Fuller further reasons that if endless punishment is unjust, then 'exemption from it must be the sinner's *right*, and can never be attributed to *mercy*; neither could a mediator be needed to induce a righteous God to liberate the sinner, when he had suffered his full desert'. He concludes his point reflecting on Vidler's own conversion experience when he went through great distress of soul because of his awareness of 'deserving to be cast out of God's favour, and banished for ever from his presence'. Fuller asks, 'Can you *now* say

---

51 Vidler, *God's Love*, p. 35.
52 Fuller, *Letter I. Expostulations with Mr. Vidler, on his having Embraced the Doctrine of Universal Salvation*, in *Letters to Mr. Vidler*, p. 294
53 *Letter I*, p. 293.

that you did not deserve this? Do you not deserve it still? If you do, why not others?'[54]

Secondly, Fuller asks Vidler to consider 'whether the genius of the sentiment in question be not opposite to that of every other sentiment in the Bible'. Does not all of Scripture teach that it will be well with the righteous, and it will be ill with the wicked? But universal salvation says it will be well at last with both. Where does Scripture teach this? Fuller questions whether Vidler is not preaching 'another gospel' that is not only good tidings to the meek, the mourners and broken-hearted, but also to the proud and impenitent. 'The gospel of Christ', Fuller maintains, 'is a system of holiness; a system entirely opposite to every vicious bias of the human heart; a system, therefore, which no unrenewed heart embraces.'[55] But Vidler's gospel demands no change of heart that it may be embraced.

Thirdly, Fuller asks Vidler to consider whether his teaching on this subject be not similar to the words of the devil to our first parents, 'Ye shall not surely die.' Vidler teaches to the ungodly part of his audience that even if they die in their filthiness though they shall 'encounter devouring fire, yet they shall not dwell in *everlasting* burnings'.[56] If what he says proves to be false how will he be able to look at these people in the face on the day of judgement; and more importantly how will he be able to look in God's face who charged him to be free from the blood of all men.

In conclusion, Fuller challenges Vidler to beware of the 'whirlpool of Socinianism' which appears to be present in the 'nature and tendency' of his principles. Fuller recognizes that not all universalists are Socinians, but most Socinians hold this teaching.[57]

Letter II

Fuller's second letter begins by giving his reasons for not answering Vidler's response to his first letter. After the first letter in the *Evangelical Magazine*, Vidler wrote an answer in his own magazine, *Universalist Miscellany*, in its first two issues. Fuller gives three reasons for not writing at the time, assuring Vidler that it was not because the latter's letters were unanswerable. First, he did not know if Vidler would publish his response in the *Miscellany* and he did not want to give it in the *Evangelical Magazine* without both sides being represented. Secondly, he did not want Vidler's universalist teaching to receive unnecessary

---

54 *Letter I*, p. 293.
55 *Letter I*, pp. 293-94.
56 *Letter I*, p. 294.
57 *Letter I*, p. 294.

publicity knowing that certain folk upon reading it would undoubtedly imbibe it. Therefore, it was better to leave it unanswered. Thirdly, Vidler's two letters appeared to Fuller 'to contain so many misapprehensions, and such a quantity of perversion of the plain meaning of Scripture' that he 'felt it a kind of hopeless undertaking to go about to correct them'.[58] Fuller then elaborates on this latter reason accusing Vidler of not understanding the plain meaning of the former's words in his first letter. Fuller goes on to explicitly give the meaning of some of his sentences and words that Vidler has misunderstood.

For the rest of the letter Fuller addresses Vidler's response to the three questions of concern from the former's first letter. Vidler considered these questions irrelevant but still offered answers to parts of them. Fuller then puts aside for the moment the parts that were answered and highlights for his readers the parts that were not addressed by Vidler in order for them to judge whether they are truly irrelevant.

First, Fuller points out that Vidler has not made clear the ground of a person's exemption from eternal punishment; is it a 'right' or is it grounded on the death of Christ? Fuller's conclusion is that 'notwithstanding all you say of grace and love, it is not on the footing of grace, but debt, that you hold with universal salvation'.[59] God does not give it to us but owes it to us. Secondly, Fuller questions the irrelevance of his second concern (in his first letter). He asks, 'What doctrine...you would find in the Bible which affords encouragement to a sinner going on still in his trespasses...?' There is none besides that of universal salvation. The Scripture, however, teaches that there must be a change of heart and repentance in order to have hope and joy. Vidler did not address this question which appears to be quite relevant. Thirdly, he did not answer Fuller's concern in his third question regarding the hopes of the ungodly, that though they live and die in sin they will not be eternally punished. Vidler's main argument on this question was to deny the doctrine of endless punishment. Fuller responds to this in the rest of the letter.

He first addresses Vidler's appeal to the meaning of the words *aion* and *aionos*. He realizes that words like these are sometimes used in an improper or figurative sense due to 'the poverty of language' or the 'inequality of the number of words to the number of ideas'.[60] Fuller recognizes that the word 'infinite' in Nahum 3.9 is used figuratively when speaking of Ethiopia and Egypt's strength, but is used plainly to express God's 'unlimited' understanding in Psalm 147.5. But does Vidler recognize this? He goes on to ask Vidler, 'Could stronger terms

---

58   Fuller, *Letter II. Reasons for not Continuing the Controversy, and Replies to Mr. Vidler's Objections to the Foregoing*, in *Letters to Mr. Vidler*, p. 295.
59   *Letter II*, p. 296.
60   *Letter II*, p. 296.

have been used, concerning the duration of future punishment, than are used?... What expressions could have been used that would have placed the subject beyond dispute?'[61] Fuller's point is that words may have a literal or a figurative sense depending on the context. Therefore, it is not in 'the power of language to stand before such methods of criticising and reasoning as those on which [Vidler] builds' his system. Even though *aion* may have a limited sense, 'the nature of the subject, the connexion and scope of the passages, together with the use of various other forms of expression, which convey the same thing, are sufficient to prove that, when applied to the doctrine of future punishment, they are to be understood without any limitation'.[62] Fuller then strengthens his argument concluding with some illustrations of contextual interpretation of words like *forever, everlasting, day and night* from Scripture in general, and from the Book of Revelation and Matthew 25.46 in particular.

Letter III

This letter addresses the difficulties and inconsistencies in Vidler's system as Fuller understands it. The first inconsistency he mentions is that Vidler affirms both everlasting life for all as well as the notion of annihilation. This, however, was not the case. Vidler did not hold the latter notion and Fuller acknowledges so in his seventh letter.[63] A second inconsistency has to do with Vidler's belief that at some time sinners 'will *not have mercy upon them*, on the supposition that *all punishment, of all degrees and duration, is itself an exercise of mercy.*' However, Fuller's greatest concern of inconsistency lies in Vidler's reconciliation of his system with Scripture. For example, when God says in Isaiah 57.16, 'I will *not* contend forever', Vidler interprets this to mean duration without end. But if it simply said, 'I *will* contend forever', Vidler would have interpreted this to mean only a limited duration. But the context shows that 'forever' refers only to the present life. Other verses interpreted by Vidler are challenged by Fuller, including Daniel 9.24, Matthew 8.29, James 2.13 and Psalm 62.12. Moreover, he challenges Vidler's argument that the judgement of God on Sodom by fire and on Pharaoh by water was for their good, and so by analogy the punishment of those sinners in the afterlife is God's mercy working for their salvation.[64] According to Fuller, God's judgement on Sodom and Pharaoh were not remedial but

---

61   *Letter II*, p. 297.
62   *Letter II*, p. 297.
63   See the discussion of *Letter VII* below.
64   Fuller, *Letter III. Difficutlies Attending Mr. Vidler's Scheme, and its Inconsistency with Scripture*, in *Letters to Mr. Vidler*, p. 299.

final, not for their good but for their destruction. In addition, Fuller cannot agree that 'the gathering together in one all things in Christ which are in heaven, and which are on earth', and that 'he shall have put down all rule, and all authority, and power, and shall have subdued all things unto himself', will occur ages beyond the last judgement. For Fuller, the restitution of all things (Acts 3.21) includes the final resurrection and judgement. Consequently, Vidler's restitution and that of the Scriptures are not the same. Fuller, addressing Vidler, concludes,

> Except in the productions of a certain maniac in our own country, I never recollect to have seen so much violence done to the word of God in so small a compass.
>
> According to your scheme, all things work together for good to them that love not God, as well as to them that love him. Thus you confound what the Scriptures discriminate.
>
> Our Lord told the Jews, that if they believed not that he was the Messiah, they should *die in their sins*, and whither he went they *could not come* (John vii. 21); but, according to your scheme, they might die in their sins, and yet be able to go whither he went, and inherit eternal life.[65]

Letter IV

After some preliminary remarks Fuller again focuses on universal salvation 'as a right' and not grounded in mercy. In his previous letter Vidler has called this issue a 'quibble'. Fuller believes that this is a fundamental principle in Vidler's system 'and which proves it to be fundamentally wrong'.[66] Vidler teaches that 'God will deal with his creatures according to his character' and that 'sinners will be punished according to their works'; in other words for Fuller this means that *'justice* will have its course on the ungodly; and that whatever punishment they endure, whether it be vindictive or corrective, endless or temporary, it is all that their sins *deserve*'.[67] According to Fuller, if sinners endure the full desert of their sin Vidler's universalism leaves no room for the grace of God to the sinner as 'undeserved favour'. Fuller writes: 'Your universal salvation, therefore, is no part of that which arises

---

65 *Letter III*, p. 301. After these words Fuller takes several paragraphs to show up the inconsistencies of Vidler's system with his belief in annihilation for the impenitent. As we mentioned earlier, Vidler did not hold to annihilationism. Consequently, we will pass over them.

66 Fuller, *Letters IV. Replies, and Defences of Former Reasonings*, in *Letters to Mr. Vidler*, p. 303.

67 Vidler, *Miscellany*, II, p. 42, quoted in Fuller, *Letters IV*, p. 304.

from the grace of God, or the death of Christ; nor is it, properly speaking, salvation at all, but a legal discharge, in consequence of a full satisfaction to Divine justice being made by the sufferings of the sinner.'[68]

In the rest of the letter Fuller addresses Vidler's claim that the former deals in 'suppositions, instead of arguments', and rests his 'conclusions on unfounded assumptions'. One of those unfounded assumptions that Fuller made against universalism, and in this letter defends, is that universal salvation '*does* afford encouragement to a sinner going on still in his trespasses, and *does* furnish ground for hope and joy, even supposing him to persevere in sin till death'. For Fuller this assumption from Vidler's universalism is self-evident. Vidler would respond that as long as the sinner does not repent, punishment will continue. Fuller considers this response trifling, because it does not negate the fact that the sinner will have joy and hope of eternal life though he remains in sin till death.

Vidler would then counter that the doctrine of election also affords encouragement to the sinner who remains in his sins. Fuller agrees that it could, but he also states that 'no sinner, while going on in his trespasses, is warranted to consider himself as elected to salvation; therefore that doctrine affords no ground of hope and joy to persons of this description'.[69] Consequently, there is no other doctrine 'which gives encouragement to a sinner, while in his sins, to believe that in the end it shall be well with him', only universal salvation.[70]

A second assumption of which Vidler accuses Fuller is that the former's 'views invalidate the Divine threatenings towards sinners'. Fuller made this assumption on the basis of the deceiver's lie to our first parents, that if they eat of the tree they 'shall not surely die'. According to Fuller Vidler's universal salvation declares the same to humankind after the Fall. Both universalism's and the devil's words persuade their hearers that though they sin they will not die eternally. Therefore, both encourage sinners to be less fearful of transgression. Fuller concludes his letter: 'Notwithstanding all your challenges, and calling out for more to be written, you have not yet answered [my] first Letter.'[71]

---

68 *Letters IV*, p. 304. Vidler could argue that the liberation of the sinner (shortening his punishment) is due to the grace of God and the death of Christ. If this were Vidler's argument then Fuller believed Vidler would have to give up his belief that sinners are punished according to their works and that God's threatenings will be fully discharged on them.

69 *Letters IV*, p. 305.

70 *Letters IV*, p. 305.

71 *Letters IV*, p. 306.

Letter V

This letter is taken up with the principal grounds on which Fuller bases his doctrine of endless punishment. He makes four points of which all are scriptural. First, Fuller bases his doctrine on 'all the passages of Scripture which describe the future states of men in contrast', and he does so by stringing together twenty-four passages.[72] For example, he quotes from Matthew 7.13-14: 'Wide is the gate, and broad is the way, that leadeth to destruction, and many there be who go in thereat; because strait is the gate, and narrow is the way, that leadeth unto life, and few there be that find it.' Fuller maintains that this and the other passages speak of the final state of men and no other. He gives three reasons why this is so. First, since these passages provide a contrast between the state of the righteous and the wicked, and the state of the righteous is considered to be final in these passages, therefore, the state of the wicked in these passages must be final. Secondly, all of these passages are silent concerning purgation or temporary correction, in fact there is no account of this state anywhere in Scripture. Finally, the phraseology of most of these passages is 'inconsistent with any other state following that which they describe'. For example, in the Matthew passage cited above, the universalist interpretation would be, 'The broad way doth not lead to destruction, but merely to a temporary correction, the end of which is everlasting life.'[73]

Secondly, Fuller bases his doctrine of endless punishment on all those passages which speak of the duration of future punishment by the terms *everlasting*, *eternal*, *for ever*, and *for ever and ever*.[74] He illustrates his point with twelve passages including, 'Some shall awake to everlasting life, and some to shame and *everlasting* contempt' (Dan. 12.2); 'It is better for thee to enter into life halt, or maimed, than having two hands, or two feet, to be cast into *everlasting* fire' (Mt. 18.8); 'Depart, ye cursed, into *everlasting* fire' (Mt. 25.41); and 'They shall be punished with *everlasting* destruction, from the presence of the Lord, and from the glory of his power' (2 Thess. 1.9). Fuller recognizes that the word 'everlasting' has both a literal and figurative meaning in Scripture, in which case he follows the generally accepted rule of interpretation, '*That every term be taken in its* PROPER *sense, except there be something in the subject or connexion which requires it to be taken otherwise.*' Lexicographers maintain that the literal meaning of αἰών is 'always being', and the term αἰώνιος is 'endless, everlasting or eternal'. On the

---

72 Fuller, *Letter V. Evidences of Endless Punishment*, in *Letters to Mr. Vidler*, p. 306.
73 *Letter V*, p. 308.
74 *Letter V*, p. 308.

basis of the above rule of interpretation Fuller maintains that these words in connection with punishment are best interpreted with the normal literal meaning. For example, 'Everlasting punishment is, in some of them, opposed to everlasting life; which, so far as an antithesis can go to fix the meaning of the term, determines it to be of the same force and extent.'[75] The case is even stronger regarding αἰών and αἰώνιος in the New Testament.

Thirdly, Fuller holds to eternal punishment on the basis of 'all those passages which express the duration of future punishment by implication, or by forms of speech which imply the doctrine in question'.[76] To make his point he gives thirteen examples including, 'The blasphemy against the Holy Spirit *shall not be forgiven unto men*, neither in this world, neither in the world to come' (Mt. 12.32); 'If we sin willfully, after we have received the knowledge of the truth, there remaineth no more sacrifice for sins, but a fearful looking for of judgment which shall devour the adversaries' (Heb. 10.26-27); and 'Their worm dieth not, and fire is not quenched' (Mk 9.48). Fuller briefly expounds each of the passages he quotes. For example, concerning Mattew 12.32, he reasons, 'If there be some that never will be forgiven, there are some that never will be saved; for forgiveness is an essential branch of salvation. Let there be what uncertainty there may be in the word *eternal* in this instance, still the meaning is fixed by the other branch of the sentence,—*they shall never be forgiven.*'[77]

Fourthly, he maintains endless punishment on the basis of 'all those passages which intimate that a change of heart, and a preparedness for heaven, are confined to the present life'.[78] He proves his point quoting nine passages. For example, he quotes from Luke 13.23-25, 27-28,

> '...Then said one unto him, Lord, are there few that shall be saved? And he said unto them, Strive to enter in at the strait gate: for many, I say unto you, shall seek to enter in, and shall not be able. When *once* the master of the house is risen up, and hath shut to the door, and ye begin to stand without, and to knock at the door, saying, Lord, Lord, open unto us; he shall answer and say unto you, I know you not whence you are—Depart from me, all ye workers of iniquity—there shall be weeping and gnashing of teeth...'

In this passage the Lord does not answer the disciple's question but 'he assures us that there are many who will not be saved; or, which is the same

---

75 *Letter V*, p. 309.
76 *Letter V*, p. 310.
77 *Letter V*, p. 310.
78 *Letter V*, p. 311.

thing, who will not be able to enter in at the strait gate. None, it is plainly intimated, will be able to enter there who have not agonized here'.[79]

Letter VI

This letter is a response to Vidler's objections to Fuller's fifth letter. Vidler sought to discredit Fuller's scriptural evidence for endless punishment. His argument was that the word 'everlasting' is only used five times in the Bible with regard to the future punishment of humans but is used at least ninety times 'in relation to things that either have ended or must end'.[80] The same can be said for the word 'eternal'— forty times in the Bible, two of which can be related to future punishment.

Fuller's first objection to Vidler's argument is that this word's designation as future punishment five or six times in Scripture 'may be as large a proportion as the subject requires', 'being applied to more than twenty different subjects'.[81]

Fuller's second argument is that if the meaning of 'everlasting' as future punishment can be discredited upon its use only five of six times then the same can be said for the existence of God which is 'applied not much more frequently'.[82] Thirdly, conclusions concerning the meanings of words should be drawn not from translations but from the original languages which would increase the total number of words that refer to future punishment.[83] Fourthly, Fuller challenges Vidler's interpretation of the word 'everlasting' in the Old Testament. He finds that the Hebrew word '*lm* is more frequently applied to 'an unlimited duration' than 'limited'.[84] Moreover, he believes that one would expect the reverse in the Old Testament where so little is revealed on the future state. In addition, Fuller notes that where the word is used in its limited sense, this limitation 'arises necessarily from the kind of duration, or state of being, which is spoken of'. For example, 'When Hannah gave Samuel to the Lord *for ever*, there was no limitation in her mind; she did not intend that

---

79 *Letter V*, p. 311.
80 Vidler, *Universalist's Miscellany*, XXXV, p. 328, quoted in Fuller, *Letter VI. Replies to Objections*, in *Letters to Mr. Vidler*, p. 312.
81 *Letter VI*, p. 312.
82 *Letter VI*, p. 313.
83 It could be added that Vidler did not examine the words 'for ever' and 'for ever and ever' in his computations which would have increased the number of words referring to future punishment. Earlier in this letter Fuller, *Letter VI*, p. 312, questioned Vidler on this score.
84 *Letter VI*, p. 313.

he should *ever* return to a private life.'⁸⁵ Moreover, Fuller challenges Vidler's contention that though the word 'everlasting' is to be taken in an endless sense when applied to a future state, it is not to be taken so in those passages that relate to future punishment. Fuller charges him with pleading for a meaning to the term 'which has nothing parallel in the Scriptures to support it'.⁸⁶ Furthermore, the New Testament use of the words 'everlasting, eternal, for ever, &c. are generally applied in the endless sense' of which Vidler is aware. Fuller concludes that surely the assertion 'that the Scriptures *appear*, at least, to teach the doctrine of everlasting punishment' is justified.⁸⁷

Fuller goes on to object to Vidler's rule of interpretation that 'where a word is used in relation to different things, the subject itself must determine the meaning of the word'.⁸⁸ Fuller believes that this would imply that no words have a 'proper meaning of their own' because almost all words are used in relation to different things. The word's proper meaning has to play a part in the interpretation. He concludes, 'To allow no meaning to a term, except what shall be imparted to it by the subject, is to reduce it to a cipher.'⁸⁹ Fuller again restates his own rule of interpretation from his last letter which 'allows a proper meaning to every Scripture term, and does not attempt to set it aside in favour of one that is improper, or figurative, unless the scope of the passage, or the nature of the subject require it'. He maintains that 'this is a very different thing from not admitting it, unless the subject, from its own nature, render it absolutely necessary', as Vidler does.⁹⁰

Fuller answers Vidler's claim that in Scripture the same word can be used in the same text in a different sense. As an example Vidler cites Habakkuk 3.6 where the text says 'the everlasting mountains were scattered' and '[God's] ways are everlasting'.⁹¹ The latter is to be interpreted in an endless sense but the former in a limited sense. From this he interprets Matthew 25.46 in the same way, 'everlasting punishment' is limited and 'everlasting life' is endless. Fuller strongly disagrees; even if the antithesis in Habakkuk holds, the opposition in Matthew is not between God and hills but 'between *life* and *punishment*, and the adjective *everlasting* is applied in common to both; which, instead

---

85 *Letter VI*, p. 313.
86 *Letter VI*, p. 313.
87 *Letter VI*, p. 314. It should be noted that after this Fuller responded to Vidler's discussion of the Greek words αἰών and αἰώνιος. He concluded, p. 315, that these words 'are no less expressive of endless duration than the English words *everlasting* and *eternal*'.
88 Vidler, *Miscellany*, XXXV, p. 333, quoted in Fuller, *Letter VI*, p. 315.
89 *Letter VI*, p. 315.
90 *Letter VI*, p. 316.
91 Vidler, *Miscellany*, XXXV, p. 331, quoted inFuller, *Letter VI*, p. 316.

of requiring a different sense to be given it, requires the contrary'.[92] The Matthew verse is more akin to John 5.29 than to Habakkuk. Furthermore, the Hebrew words in Habakkuk are different and the Greek words in Matthew are the same which makes Vidler's interpretation even more strained.[93]

Letter VII

In his seventh letter Fuller addresses Vidler's whole universalist system.[94] Vidler's first maxim for his system is since God created humans, and those humans have fallen into sin, in order that God not be charged with injustice, He has willed that all should be saved. Fuller answers that God is not chargeable with injustice because he permits humans to fall into sin and die eternally. God does not will evil as evil 'but permits its existence for wise ends'.[95] God did place humans in circumstances which he foreknew would issue in their fall, and he did warn them of the consequences. Does this take away, therefore, the 'accountableness of his creatures, and to charge him with the evil of their sin?' Fuller charges Vidler with making God responsible and accountable for human sin, and not the sinner. 'Thus...you undermine the justice of all punishment, present and future, and every principle of moral government.'[96] Fuller further charges Vidler saying, 'If what you have suggested be true, it must follow that there is no need of a mediator, or forgiving mercy... All that is necessary to recover man is justice. If the Creator only be accountable for evil, it belongs to him to remedy it. Thus, instead of supporting the doctrine of universal salvation, you undermine all salvation at the very foundation.'[97]

Fuller concurs with Vidler's second maxim: 'That whatever God does, is intended by his goodness, conducted by his wisdom, and accomplished

---

92 *Letter VI*, p. 317.

93 Fuller ends the letter answering Vidler's argument that if the Holy Spirit wanted to teach endless punishment He would have used stronger language. For example, he could have used ἀκατάλυτος found in Hebrews 7:16 translated 'endless.' Or he could have used 'world without end' from Isa. 45.17. Fuller responds by showing the real meaning of the Greek and Hebrew words, and concludes 'that all your [Vidler's] arguments have, hitherto, been merely founded upon *English phraseology*'. See Vidler, *Miscellany*, XXXV, pp. 334, 364, cited by Fuller, *Letter VI*, pp. 317-18.

94 Fuller, *Letter VII. An Examination of Mr. Vidler's System, and of his Argument in Support of It*, in *Letters to Mr. Vidler*, p. 318, begins by acknowledging that Vidler does not adhere to annihilationism.

95 *Letter VII*, p. 319.

96 *Letter VII*, p. 319.

97 *Letter VII*, p. 319.

by his power.' However, he does not agree with Vidler's application of it. First, Fuller maintains that the greater part of it is trifling. No one believes, as Vidler supposes, that eternal punishment is a benefit to God or a pleasure to him for its own sake. Or that it 'is inflicted for the *honour, pleasure,* or *benefit* of the sinner'.[98] Secondly, Fuller believes that some parts of Vidler's application which object to endless punishment on the grounds that it cannot be for the honour of God and benefit of creatures 'proceed altogether upon *unfounded assumptions*'.[99] Vidler provides no proof but merely asserts that 'every unsophisticated heart would so determine' that endless punishment cannot be for the honour of God. Concerning the benefit of creatures Vidler believes that no possible good can arise to society from the punishment of sinners except that of *'safety'*. Fuller does not believe that 'safety' is the only end of punishment. The punishment of death also provides society with examples expressing the displeasure of God against sin, for example, Sodom and Gomorrah destroyed, and Pharaoh and his army drowned in Red Sea.

Thirdly, Fuller maintains that Vidler's application of this maxim 'would overturn *all* future punishment'. Under Vidler's system there is no honour, pleasure or benefit to God to have any of his creatures miserable for a period of future punishment. The same can be said for the punished themselves; and 'if their salvation could be accomplished without it, it cannot be any benefit to them. If they may not be saved without it, it must be either because there was not efficacy enough in the blood of Christ for the purpose, or else that "the full efficacy of the atonement was withheld by the Divine determination."'[100] As to the benefit, pleasure or honour of humanity, temporary future punishment provides none, except the benefit of safety. Fuller concludes: 'As, then, future torments can answer no possible good end to any one in the universe, I conclude them to be neither the work nor will of God; and, consequently, not the doctrine of Scripture!'[101]

For the rest of the letter Fuller answers some of Vidler's arguments which are based on human reasoning. For example, Vidler thinks 'there is a vast difference, indeed, in the nature of future blessedness and future punishment; such as fully to justify us in giving a very different sense to the word eternal, when applied to these subjects'.[102] Fuller agrees that this may be so but that these thoughts 'prove nothing'. Vidler accuses Fuller of 'ascribing a proper eternity to sin and misery'. But Fuller does not do so; he maintains that both the existence of intelligent creatures and their

---

98   *Letter VII*, p. 320.
99   *Letter VII*, p. 320.
100 *Letter VII*, p. 321.
101 *Letter VII*, p. 321.
102 Vidler, *Miscellany*, XXXV, p. 331, quoted in Fuller, *Letter VII*, p. 321.

moral qualities are not eternal but that God may perpetuate both to an endless duration. Fuller goes on to argue, 'Holiness and happiness, in respect to creatures, are not necessarily eternal, any more than sin and misery.' Consequently, 'It would be as improper to ascribe eternity to the purity and blessedness of the saved as to the sin and misery of the lost, seeing that the endless duration of both depends upon the will of God.' This is contrary to Vidler's contention that the 'life and blessedness of holy beings' have 'their root and foundation in God; and that, being thus grounded in him, they will be, like him, eternal in duration'. For Fuller this is simply not true; the unsinning angels and Adam and Eve in their innocence derived their life and blessedness from God. They are not, like their Author, 'eternal in duration'.[103]

Another of Vidler's arguments is that 'sin and misery being contrary to the holiness and benevolence of God...must come to an end'. Fuller charges him with assertion but no proof. Further, Fuller believes that one might as well say that the holiness and benevolence of God should not exist in the present and future. But this is contrary to fact and only leads to atheism. He concludes: 'I cannot but tremble for the man who begins to travel in this unwary path, by measuring the Divine administration by his own unhallowed notions of moral fitness.'[104]

Letter VIII

This final letter continues Fuller's examination of Vidler's universalist system. Fuller begins by discussing the ideas of 'proper eternity' and 'successive duration'. The former belongs to God alone, but the latter belongs to creatures. He is unsure whether successive duration is the proper way to speak of the future state; however, when he has used the term it has been used with reference to the present state of things. For Fuller 'successive duration' will end, just as for Vidler 'day and night' will cease when Christ shall deliver up the kingdom to his Father. Both Vidler and Fuller agree that the states of creatures will be forever fixed at some future time. Fuller sees this taking place at the last judgment and includes the fixed state of endless punishment. But Vidler extends this fixed state to ages beyond the last judgment. He contends that 'the day of judgment is not the finishing period of Christ's kingdom'. Having already answered the greater part of Vidler's reasons for this contention, Fuller proceeds to consider the rest. Vidler's first reason is that, 'This earth (which is to be the hell of wicked men 2 Pet. iii. 7-13) is to be

---

103 *Letter VII*, p. 322.
104 *Letter VII*, p. 323.

renewed, whereby hell itself will be no more.'[105] Fuller answers that hell already exists, being the place of torment and darkness for sinning angels and wicked humans. Therefore, it is not presently on earth, and consequently, need not be present at the conflagration of the earth. Hell is able to exist beyond the conflagration. In addition, Fuller argues, if the earth is the hell of ungodly men, 'their punishment must *precede* the day of judgment, instead of following it'. However, according to Vidler's system it takes place a thousand years after Christ's second coming. Furthermore, does not the 'perdition of ungodly men' (2 Pet. 3.7) mean the destruction of their *lives* and not their *souls*? This text is used in connection with the flood in Noah's time in which the wicked lost their lives and not their souls.

Vidler argues that the statement 'every knee shall bow to Christ' means voluntary submission, and is inconsistent 'with a stubborn knee, even in hell'. Fuller disagrees and, using Romans 3.19 and 14.10-12, he maintains that these verses refer to the ungodly as well as the saints.[106]

Fuller also challenges Vidler's interpretation of Colossians 1.20 and 1 Corinthians 15.25-28 that all things must eventually be reconciled to God, and that all death, including eternal death, will be destroyed. Concerning the latter passage Fuller argues that its language refers to the resurrection of the bodies of those who sleep in Jesus which precedes the last judgment, not follows it, and so includes the second death (eternal death).

Finally, Fuller challenges Vidler's argument that 'the character of God is LOVE; which is expressly against the horrible idea of the endless misery of any of his rational creatures'.[107] Fuller argues that if this be so one might infer that the punishment of any of God's creatures in hell until they repent is 'horrible and incredible'. To further prove his point, Fuller makes an analogy from monarchical government. He asks, is it inconsistent with the king's benevolence that he doom certain characters to death? Is it not an exercise of his benevolence? Yes it is. The malefactor is only fooling himself and his companions if he thinks that the king 'cannot possibly consent to their execution, without ceasing to be that lovely and good character for which he is famed'. Fuller concludes, 'Would not this reasoning be as false in itself as it was injurious to the king? Nay, would it not be inimical to his own interest and that of his fellow criminals; as, by raising a delusive hope, they are

---

105 Vidler, *Miscellany*, XXXV, p. 365, quoted in Fuller, *Letter VIII. A Further Examination of Mr. Vidler's Scheme, with Replies to his Animadversions*, in *Letter's to Mr. Vidler*, p. 324.

106 *Letter VIII*, p. 324.

107 Vidler, *Miscellany*, XXXV, p. 365, quoted in Fuller, *Letter VIII*, p. 325.

prevented from making a proper and timely application to the throne for mercy?'[108]

Fuller concludes this letter with replies to some of Vidler's animadversions. Vidler's arguments are based on his presuppositions of the nature and purposes of God. For example, he writes, 'If any [humans] be finally incorrigible, it must be in consequence of the Divine purpose, or else the purpose of God has been frustrated.' Or, 'That God cannot or will not make an end of sin; that there is not efficacy enough in the blood of Christ to destroy the works of the devil; or else that the full efficacy of the atonement is withheld by the Divine determination.' Fuller answers these criticisms as well as several others with arguments based on his general and specific understanding of Scripture, as has been his habit.

Summary of Fuller's Particularism

It is quite evident from Fuller's letters that he uses both reason and Scripture to argue for particularism, with the latter being his foundational and primary authority. Foundationally, he believes that Scripture teaches that it will be well for the righteous and ill for the wicked, and that this is a fixed and final state. This is contrary to universalism's contention that eventually it will be well for both. For Fuller this fixed state is determined on the basis of the person's life here on earth. If a person remains in their sin, the plain meaning of texts like Hebrews 10.26-27 is that punishment is the sinner's lot for eternity. On the other hand, if a person is born again—their heart has been changed by the Holy Spirit—then eternal life is their lot. In addition, Fuller believed that the meaning of Greek words like αἰών in certain contexts must be translated in its literal unlimited sense with the meaning of 'endless', as in Matthew 25.41, 46.

Fuller also maintained that no place in Scripture explicitly teaches that there will be a purgation or temporary correction after death. Ephesians 1.10 and 1 Corinthians 15.24-28 should be understood to take place at the time of the final resurrection and judgement. In addition, there is no indication in Scripture that hell ceases to exist at some future time or that all of God's judgement is remedial and disciplinary. Neither Egypt and Pharaoh's nor Sodom and Gomorrah's punishment was used to bring either to repentance but to end their earthly existence.

Moreover, universalism dupes humanity into thinking all is well; it continues to spread the serpent's lie in Genesis 3 that though a person disobey God he will surely not die. Universalism does not encourage

---

108 *Letter VIII*, p. 325.

repentance from and humility for sin, but encourages the sinner to remain in his sin.

Furthermore, Fuller believes that God can be both merciful towards sinners and just in eternal judgement. The justice of endless punishment is based on the accountableness of humans for their sin before a holy God. Vidler's universalism, as Fuller understood it, destroys grace and mercy, and makes salvation a right and deserved because humanity's failure in sin is God's fault. Since God made humanity with the capability to sin, it is his responsibility for justice's sake to save humanity—it is the creatures' right to have eternal life. Fuller rightly reasons that this leaves no place for the mercy of God and the death of Christ, if this be Vidler's argument.

Conclusion

If human sentiment and reason were our authority on this matter of the universal salvation of all rational creatures, then I wholeheartedly endorse it. I concur with J.I. Packer when he stated ten years ago, 'No evangelical, I think, need hesitate to admit that in his heart of hearts he would like Universalism to be true. Who can take pleasure in the thought of people being eternally lost? If you want to see folk damned, there is something wrong with you! Universalism is thus a comfortable doctrine in a way that alternatives are not.'[109] The fact is, however, human sentiment and reason are not our authority as evangelical Christians—the word of God, the Scriptures are our final authority on this matter of salvation. It is evident from Fuller's letters that Scripture stands over reason—he was quite willing to use reason in his arguments against universalism but his final authority was certainly God's word. Vidler, on the other hand, appears to have placed Scripture and reason on a par, at least in practice if not in theory.

From our study of Fuller's response to Vidler the most important thing we can learn from him in our stand against universalism is to keep Scripture before us as our authority, bringing every thought captive to the obedience of Christ. With Fuller we should question the propriety of following our fallen reason when it counters Scripture. As he maintained the noetic effects of sin can easily lead to faulty thinking that leads away from truth. It is so easy for fallen humans to reason that God is unjust to *eternally* condemn people for their sin. But are we then seeing things through God's holy eyes or through our own fallen ones? Sin has a

---

109 J.I. Packer, 'Evangelicals and the Way of Salvation. New Challenges to the Gospel: Universalism, and Justification by Faith', in Kenneth Kantzer and Carl Henry (eds), *Evangelical Affirmations* (Grand Rapids, MI: Zondervan, 1990), p. 117.

powerful ability to distort the thinking of even the most sagacious people, even God's people. Evangelicals are always in danger of falling prey to the god of reason. May we follow in Fuller's footsteps standing firmly on the Word of God.

CHAPTER 8

Andrew Fuller and Abraham Booth

Robert W. Oliver

Andrew Fuller's theology did not remain static after the publication of *The Gospel Worthy of All Acceptation* in 1785. Controversy, extensive reading and reflection continued to hone his thinking. The influence of Jonathan Edwards, Sr., on Fuller's early theological development is well known. In the years after 1785 he read with growing interest the works of Edwards's New England disciples, Joseph Bellamy, Samuel Hopkins, Jonathan Edwards, Jr., and Stephen West. These men made a number of adjustments to the theology of the elder Edwards and aspects of their teaching were embraced by Fuller and some of his close associates.[1] Not all Particular Baptists, however, were happy about these developments and Fuller found himself at odds with Abraham Booth, perhaps the most respected theologian of his denomination.

Booth, the doyen of the London ministers, had been pastor of the Little Prescot Street church since 1769. Originally a General Baptist, he became a Calvinist, publishing in 1768 *The Reign of Grace*, an exposition of his new creed. This work immediately secured his reputation as an exponent of historic Calvinism. A steady stream of writings on current theological issues enhanced his reputation. *The Reign of Grace*, a warmly evangelical volume, made it clear that in his rejection of Arminianism, Booth had not reacted to the extreme of High Calvinism.[2] Until the mid-1790s, Fuller's relations with Booth were generally cordial and Booth gave warm support to the Missionary Society.[3] By the end of the eighteenth century

---

1   Joseph Bellamy (1719–90) had been a pupil of the elder Edwards, as had Samuel Hopkins (1721–1803), Stephen West (1735–1819) and Jonathan Edwards, Jr., (1745–1801). These men all ministered in New England and were prolific writers. For biographical and theological details, see F.H. Foster, *A Genetic History of the New England Theology* (Chicago: University of Chicago Press, 1907).

2   A. Booth, *The Reign of Grace*, in *The Works of Abraham Booth* (3 vols; London: Button and Sons, 1813), I, pp. 59, 78, 96-98, 103-107.

3   It was Booth who recommended John Thomas as a colleague for Carey, see Fuller's Letters: 'A. Fuller to Thomas Steevens' (n.d. c.1793); cf. 'A. Fuller to John

Abraham Booth and Andrew Fuller were the leading Particular Baptist theologians in England. Both men were self-taught and had reached their mature theological convictions after a severe struggle. Both owed much to giants of the past, Booth especially to John Owen and Fuller to Jonathan Edwards. Theologically they had come from widely differing starting points. In addition they ministered to churches many miles apart and seldom met. It is perhaps not surprising that there were differences between them. These surfaced in discussions about the warrant of faith and the nature of the atonement. In both of these debates there is some evidence of misunderstanding.

The Warrant of Faith

Tensions emerged in 1796 after the publication of Booth's *Glad Tidings to Perishing Sinners or the Genuine Gospel a Complete Warrant for the Ungodly to Believe in Jesus*.[4] As the full title indicates, Booth was concerned to establish that the gospel warranted any sinner to believe in Christ. No subjective qualifications were required for the exercise of faith. He propounded this thesis over against the High Calvinist insistence that the inward work of the Holy Spirit constituted a warrant for believing in Christ.[5]

Booth's book, warmly recommended by an anonymous reviewer in the *Evangelical Magazine*,[6] was well received by evangelical Calvinists. Generally it was seen to argue the case for which Fuller had pleaded eleven years earlier in his *Gospel Worthy of all Acceptation*.[7]

Saffery, 30th May 1793'; 'A. Fuller to W. Carey, 9th Aug. 1769'. Booth also encouraged Fuller to write *The Calvinistic and Socinian Systems Examined*, see 'A. Fuller to T. Steevens, n.d. c. 1791'. See The Letters of Andrew Fuller, Angus Library, Regents Park College, Oxford.

4   A. Booth, *Glad Tidings to Perishing Sinners or the Genuine Gospel a Complete Warrant for the Ungodly to believe in Jesus* (London, 1796). Quotations are from the edition published in Booth's *Works*, II.

5   In this chapter the term 'High Calvinist' is employed to describe the non-offer position that in the nineteenth century was described as 'Hyper-Calvinist'. This terminology follows the usage of Fuller and his contemporaries.

6   *The Evangelical Magazine* 4 (1796), pp. 348-49. Fuller, however, complained, 'Some of our monthly editions have bestowed indiscriminate praise without at all understanding the ground of the controversy.' See Fuller's Letters, 'A. Fuller to S. Hopkins, 17 March 1798'.

7   Fuller's Letters: 'A. Fuller to W. Carey, 6 Sept. 1797': 'People reckon, and so let them reckon, that his book is on the same side as my Gospel of Xt etc.' See also, Fullers Letters, 'A. Fuller to S. Hopkins, 17 March 1798': 'They think his first part savours of an agreement with me; and reckon therefore that the whole book was written in order to favour my sentiments on the duty of sinners to believe in Christ.'

Fuller, of course, had taught that all men have a duty to believe the gospel and so to be saved. Nevertheless, he was extremely uneasy about Booth's work. To Carey he confided, in September 1797,

> Mr B's book is controversial, but very difficult to know who or what it opposes. What he aims to establish in the former part is denied by nobody that I know of, except the High Calvinists—yet he did not mean, I am persuaded to oppose them.[8]

Booth had made no reference to Fuller in the book, but Fuller wrote,

> I believe it was his intent to oppose our sentiments, and that he chose to attack us under Hopkins's name. The latter part I think is erroneous.[9]

He later concluded, 'in fact it was written with a view to opposing me or of going between our views and those of High Calvinism'.[10] Fuller was in correspondence with Hopkins over Booth's *Glad Tidings* and the American theologian wrote a reply. Out of respect for Booth, this was never published.[11] Booth, however, saw the manuscript and, according to Fuller, 'he is since rigidly set against everything from America'.[12]

In the meantime, the Anglican theologian Thomas Scott attempted to mediate between the positions of Hopkins and Booth in his *The Warrant and Nature of Faith in Christ*.[13] Fuller claimed Scott as a supporter. Scott did not refer to Booth by name but, in a review in the *Evangelical Magazine*, Fuller wrote, 'the design of the treatise if we rightly comprehend it, is to discuss various important points advanced in Mr Booth's "Glad Tidings to Perishing Sinners".'[14] Fuller returned to the discussion in a review of the second edition of Booth's *Glad Tidings*.[15]

---

8 See Fuller's Letters: 'A. Fuller to W. Carey, 6 Sept. 1797'.
9 Fuller's Letters: 'A. Fuller to W. Carey, 6 Sept. 1797'.
10 Fuller's Letters: 'A. Fuller to W. Carey, 22 Aug. 1798'.
11 Fuller's Letters: 'A. Fuller to W. Carey, 22 Aug. 1798'.
12 Fuller's Letters: 'A. Fuller to W. Carey, 22 Aug. 1798'.
13 Thomas Scott, *The Warrant and Nature of Faith in Christ* (1797). Quotations are given from the 2nd edition (Buckingham, 1801). In December 1796, Scott wrote: 'I am about to write a pamphlet on the sinner's *warrant* to believe in Christ, and the *nature* of justifying faith, by the desire of several of my brethren; as the American divines especially Hopkins, with those who hold the negative of the modern question have run into one extreme and many others into the contrary, particularly Mr Abraham Booth in a late pamphlet entitled, "Glad Tidings".' See J. Scott, *The Life of the Rev. Thomas Scott* (London, 1823), p. 313.
14 *Evangelical Magazine* 7 (1799), p. 199. The review is anonymous, but is included in A. Fuller, *The Complete Works of Andrew Fuller* (London: Henry G. Bohun, 1862), p. 964.
15 *Evangelical Magazine* 8 (1800), pp. 548-50. This, too, is anonymous and included in Fuller's *Works*, p. 965.

He also attacked Booth's position in an appendix to the second edition of the *Gospel Worthy of all Acceptation*. Here he linked his treatment of Booth's ideas with a discussion of the teaching of the Scottish Baptist, Archibald McLean, whose teaching was in some ways similar to that of Booth.

The Area of Debate

As already indicated, both Booth and Fuller insisted as against the High Calvinists that the gospel itself provided sufficient warrant for sinners to believe in Christ. Fuller, however, had maintained that regeneration takes place in a man with a view to faith although it is an act of God of which he is not immediately conscious.[16] Booth considered that such a belief compromised the fact that faith was the immediate duty of the ungodly. He opposed what he saw as a tendency to suggest that regeneration is temporally prior to faith and justification. They were simultaneous. He developed an analogy from the birth of a child.

> For the human nature, derived from his parents, and the relation of a son, being of completely the same date, there is no such thing as priority, or posteriority, respecting them, either as to the order of time, or the order of nature. They are inseparable; nor can the one exist without the other. —Thus it is I conceive, with regard to regeneration, faith in Christ, and justification before God.[17]

Booth's theology led him to reject any attempt to prescribe any particular pathway to faith.

Scott also criticized some American theologians for the way in which they expected men to acquiesce in the justice of their own condemnation before they could believe.[18] For Booth, particularly obnoxious was the statement of Samuel Hopkins that,

> A hearty submission to, and acquiescence and delight in, the law of God, rightly understood, and so a true hatred of sin, must take place IN ORDER to any degree of true approbation of the Gospel, and FAITH AND TRUST in Christ.[19]

---

16 Fuller developed this argument particularly in controversy with the General Baptist Dan Taylor, see Fuller, 'Reply to Philanthropos', in *Complete Works*, pp. 211-16.

17 A. Booth, *Glad Tidings*, in *Works*, II, p. 123.

18 Scott, *Warrant of Faith*, p. 3: 'Perhaps they insist unduly on the necessity of a man's seeing the justice of God in his condemnation as a transgressor of the holy law, before he can believe in Christ to salvation.'

19 Quoted by Booth, *Glad Tidings*, p. 77.

Booth rounded on this and similar statements,[20] using them to accuse Hopkins of incipient legalism,[21] Arminianism[22] and even Romanism.[23] He argued that Hopkins's statements gave the impression that men had to be good before they could be saved and so were directly opposed to the preaching of the Apostles, who

> were commissioned to proclaim glad tidings to the profligate, impious and wicked world. Those, however, who are truly penitent and possessed of real holiness, are not *of the world*, but *of God*.[24]

Thomas Scott sought to show that two distinct controversies had become confused. In New England, Edwards and his successors had tried to guard against some careless evangelistic preaching. They had, therefore, analysed the psychological preparation for conversion, but they had never made such preparation a qualification for saving faith.[25] In England the controversy had been whether unbelievers had a duty to believe in Christ.[26] That had not been an issue in New England. Scott agreed with Booth and Fuller that the Bible provided the sinner with all the warrant he needed to believe in Christ.[27] He went on to argue that there was a difference between an objective warrant to believe and a subjective disposition to do so.[28] The sinner should never look in himself for a warrant to believe, but

> It can never discourage a trembling sinner, who honestly inquires, 'What he must do to be saved,' to describe the nature of faith and explain the way of salvation; and then to invite, exhort and persuade him to believe in the Lord Jesus Christ, not doubting but in so doing he will certainly be saved.[29]

Over against Booth, Scott had no doubt that saving faith was the result of regeneration and therefore faith was a holy exercise of the soul. At this

---

20 Booth, *Glad Tidings*, p. 162, where he quotes Hopkins: 'The necessity of the sinner's exercising virtue, antecedent to his justification, and in order to it, is not because he needs any worthiness of his own, or can have any; but because by this ALONE can his heart be so united to the Mediator, as to be the proper ground of his being looked upon and treated so far one with him, as that his merit and righteousness may be properly imputed to him, or reckoned in his favour, so as to avail for his pardon and justification.'
21 Booth, *Glad Tidings*, p. 162.
22 Booth, *Glad Tidings*, p. 169.
23 Booth, *Glad Tidings*, p. 171.
24 Booth, *Glad Tidings*, p. 79.
25 Scott, *Warrant of Faith*, p. 3.
26 Scott, *Warrant of Faith*, p. 3.
27 Scott, *Warrant of Faith*, p. 12.
28 Scott, *Warrant of Faith*, pp. 24-28.
29 Scott, *Warrant of Faith*, p. 27.

point Scott and Fuller were agreed. Scott saw no danger of legalism in this position because no man really understood the complex events of conversion until after he believed. The unbeliever had an immediate duty to believe and to do so in the consciousness that he was a sinner needing salvation. As soon as he believed, he would look back and realize that prior to faith, God had been working in him to bring him to salvation. Scott concluded his discussion of the issues by urging his readers to distinguish between such matters as

> A warrant to believe and a disposition to believe; between a man's being spiritually alive and in part sanctified, and his knowing himself to be so; between the holy nature of faith, and the sinner's perception of that holiness and taking courage from it in coming to Christ.[30]

The Significance of the Debate

Fuller felt himself under powerful attack from Booth. Particularly he resented the criticism of Hopkins, with whose views he felt considerable sympathy. More seriously, he was being attacked at a very sensitive point. In *The Gospel Worthy of All Acceptation* Fuller had challenged the concept of a subjective warrant of faith as taught by the High Calvinists. In his own spiritual experience he had struggled painfully until he could see that Scripture itself provided an objective warrant of faith. The insinuation, therefore, that his system implied a subjective warrant was galling.

As already indicated, Fuller seems to have suspected that Booth's motive was to mediate between his own position and that of the High Calvinists. Whatever Booth's aim, Fuller soon came to see that some High Calvinists were being drawn towards his position. Writing of his own and Booth's books in 1798, he declared,

> The High Calvinists, who will not read mine, read that, and some of them by that means are coming over to us.[31]

It is not surprising that such an effect should have been noticed, once men were prepared to consider Booth's views whose statement of man's duty was clear as was his insistence on the free offer of the gospel.[32]

---

30 Scott, *Warrant of Faith*, p. 122.
31 Fuller's Letters: 'A. Fuller to W. Carey, 22 Aug. 1798'.
32 Booth, *Glad Tidings*, p. 190: 'For some, at least of the thirsting ones to whom the offer is there made, are spending money for that which is not bread, and their labour for that which satisfieth not.'

Greater anxiety began to express itself when Fuller's Calvinism seemed to be changing. These changes became apparent after 1800 and were the subject of further concern to Booth. Significantly, it was against the second edition of *The Gospel Worthy of All Acceptation* (1801) and Fuller's subsequent writings that early Strict Baptist polemic was directed.

Controversy on the Atonement

The Course of the Controversy

When Andrew Fuller published the second edition of *The Gospel Worthy of All Acceptation* in 1801, he admitted that his views had changed somewhat in the fifteen years since the publication of the first edition.[33] Some of these changes alarmed Booth. Fuller was anxious for a better understanding and, when in London in May 1802, had several meetings with Booth. Although the two men enjoyed a measure of agreement, Booth charged Fuller with having changed his views on imputation and substitution.[34] The disagreement was soon common knowledge and Fuller told Ryland,

> About the middle of July, reports were circulated, both in town and country, that I had acknowledged myself to Mr Booth to be an Arminian.[35]

Fuller was prepared to ascribe Booth's criticisms in part to old age. In November 1802 he wrote to Carey,

> Mr Booth gets old, and I think jealous and peevish. His memory also fails him. He has set strange reports of me this summer as if I had owned it to him that I did not believe in the substitution of Xt. and the imputation of sin to him when it was merely a misunderstanding. But I am resolved to have no open dispute with him. He is jealous of our having written to you agst him: but I think I have never sd so much before as now. He is a good man and upright, tho' I think his views of imputation are too much like those of Dr Crisp, as tho' in the imputation of sin something

---

33 A. Fuller, *The Gospel Worthy of All Acceptation: or the Duty of Sinners to believe in Jesus Christ* (Clipstone, 2nd edn, 1801), p. i: 'It would have been inexcusable for him to have lived all this time without gaining any additional light, by what he has seen and heard upon this subject.'

34 Fuller's account of the controversy is published in his *Six Letters to Dr Ryland respecting The Controversy with The Rev. A. Booth*, in *Works*, pp. 317-19. These letters, written between 3 and 22 January 1803, were first published in the first collected edition of Fuller's *Works* in 1831.

35 *Six Letters to Dr Ryland*, pp. 317-18.

more was transferred than the penal effect of it; and as tho' Xt was something more than treated as tho' he had been a sinner.[36]

Booth apparently wrote to John Ryland about Fuller's views and so in January 1803 Fuller wrote his *Six Letters to Dr Ryland* to defend himself. Booth was clearly not satisfied with Fuller's explanations and decided to deal with the question publicly without mentioning Fuller by name. In September 1803 he preached a sermon at the monthly meeting of London Baptist ministers. This he entitled *Divine Justice Essential to the Divine Character*.[37] He expanded and published this with a lengthy *Appendix, Relative to the Doctrine of Atonement by Jesus Christ*. In the *Appendix* he went on to discuss Fuller's teaching on the doctrine of particular redemption. Fuller considered that he had been misrepresented and replied with a series of dialogues entitled *Three Conversations on Imputation, Substitution and Particular Redemption*.[38] These were not published until 1806,[39] the year of Booth's death. The death of Booth removed Fuller's most able critic, but the issues which had not been resolved were to prove significant in the development of Particular Baptist theology.

The Issues

IMPUTATION

The concept of imputation is linked with the classic Protestant doctrine of justification by faith. This passed into Particular Baptist teaching. *The 1689 Confession of Faith* states that God justifies sinners 'by imputing Christs active obedience unto the whole Law, and passive obedience in his death, for their whole and sole Righteousness'.[40] Although the term 'impute' is not used to describe the reckoning of sin to Christ, the *Confession* does refer to him 'undergoing in their stead, the penalty due unto them: make a proper, real, and full satisfaction to *Gods* justice in their behalf'.[41]

---

36   Fuller's Letters: 'A. Fuller to W. Carey, 26 Nov. 1802'.
37   A. Booth, *Divine Justice Essential to the Divine Character* (1803), in *Works*, III, pp. 3-95.
38   Fuller presented his case in the form of a dialogue between Peter (Booth), James (Fuller) and John (Ryland). This was probably written in manuscript soon after the appearance of Booth's *Divine Justice*.
39   A. Fuller, *Dialogues, Letters and Essays on Various Subjects* (London, 1806).
40   *1689 Confession*, XI.1, in W.L. Lumpkin, *Baptist Confessions of Faith* (Valley Forge, PA: Judson Press, 2nd edn, 1969), p. 266,
41   *1689 Confession*, XI.3, p. 266.

The debate between Booth and Fuller was over the way in which man's sin was imputed to Christ and in which Christ's righteousness is imputed to man. Fuller described this imputation as figurative rather than proper. To grasp Fuller's meaning it is important to note the way in which he defined his terms. Proper imputation he considered to be the reckoning of a person according to his true moral character. Thus a wicked man's sin is properly imputed to him. Figurative imputation on the other hand takes place when guilt or righteousness is imputed to a person whose personal character does not accord with the imputed gift.[42] Thus he wrote,

> [Christ] was accounted in the Divine Administration AS IF HE WERE, OR HAD BEEN, the sinner; that those who believe on him might be accounted AS IF THEY WERE, OR HAD BEEN, righteous.[43]

As Fuller's letter to Carey of November 1802 indicates, he considered that Booth's teaching was too close to that of Tobias Crisp, who in the seventeenth century had written, 'God reckons Christ the very sinner'.[44] Fuller, however, complicated the issue by using the term guilt in a way which differed from Booth's usage. Thus he opposed any suggestion that actual guilt is imputed to Christ. He explained,

> Some have defined guilt as an obligation to punishment; but a voluntary obligation to endure the punishment of another is not guilt, any more than a consequent exemption of obligation in the offender is innocence. Both guilt and innocence, though transferable in their effects, are themselves untransferable.[45]

Since he could not accept the idea of a real imputation of sin to Christ or of righteousness to man, Fuller was cautious in his treatment of Christ's sufferings as punishment.

> As to Christ's being punished I have no doubt, and I never had, of his sufferings being penal any more than I have of our salvation being a reward; but as the latter is not a reward to us, so I question whether the former can properly said to be a punishment to Him.[46]

---

42   *Six Letters to Dr Ryland*, p. 319.
43   *Six Letters to Dr Ryland*, p. 319.
44   Tobias Crisp, *Christ Alone Exalted* (ed. J. Gill; 2 vols; London, 1791 [1690]), I, p.11. John Gill, Crisp's eighteenth-century editor, considered Crisp's statement sufficiently unguarded to insert the footnote, 'that is by imputation; not as the author and committer of sin'.
45   *Six Letters to Dr Ryland*, p. 320.
46   *Six Letters to Dr Ryland*, p. 320.

In opposition to the views of Fuller, Booth insisted that imputation should be described as real. He wrote,

> If, therefore Jesus was made a curse, he was punished in a real and proper sense PUNISHED: for scarcely any words can convey the idea of punishment more forcibly than those which are here used by the Apostle.[47]

To make the position absolutely clear, he went on to develop the idea of punishment.

> What is punishment but the infliction of natural evil, for the commission of moral evil? Punishment, necessarily supposes criminality, either personal or imputed; and here it must be understood of the latter.[48]

Booth also insisted that the imputation of Christ's righteousness to the believer must be real.

> It is not merely for the sake of Christ, or of what he has done, that believers are accepted of God, and treated as completely righteous; but it is IN him as their Head, Representative and Substitute: and by the imputation of that very obedience, which as such, he performed to the divine law, that they are justified. Hence they are said to be made, not barely righteous but righteousness; not even that only, but the righteousness of GOD.[49]

Booth and Fuller clearly were not using the terms 'real' and 'figurative' in the same sense. Booth had earlier written, 'that justification, therefore, about which the Scriptures principally treat...is not by a *personal*, but by an *imputed* righteousness'.[50] What Fuller described as 'real', Booth called 'personal' and what Fuller labelled 'figurative', Booth called 'imputed'. It is perhaps not surprising that confusion ensued.

However, Booth was not without grounds for supposing that Fuller may have opened the door to dangerous ideas from New England. In his sermon on *Divine Justice*, Booth again criticized Hopkins, thereby suggesting that he recognized the source of Fuller's ideas.[51] Certainly an appreciation of the New England theologian recurs through Fuller's correspondence[52] and his views on imputation in particular seem very

---

47 Booth, *Divine Justice*, p. 52.
48 Booth, *Divine Justice*, p. 52.
49 Booth, *Divine Justice*, pp. 47-48.
50 Booth, *Reign of Grace*, p. 141, my italics.
51 Booth, *Divine Justice*, p. 50.
52 Declining a doctorate from the College of New Jersey, Fuller wrote, 'I should esteem it as coming from that quarter which beyond any other in the world, I most

similar to those developed by Hopkins. Frank Hugh Foster, the historian of the New England theology, wrote of Hopkins's theology, 'the definition of justification contains no real imputation'.[53] The related question of the imputation of Adam's sin to his posterity was not discussed by Booth and Fuller, but here Fuller seems to follow Hopkins, who taught that such imputation must rest on consent. Fuller wrote,

> Does it not belong to the nature of imputation that the party to whom the imputation is made, approves of the good or evil of what is imputed, ere it can benefit or injure him? And if so, is there anything to fear from Adam's sin with regard to dying infants?[54]

On this subject Hopkins wrote,

> It is not to be supposed that the offence of Adam is imputed to them [his posterity] to their condemnation while they are considered as in themselves, in their own persons innocent; or that they are guilty of the sin of their first father, antecedent to their own sinfulness. But all that is asserted as what the Scripture teaches on this head is, that, by a divine constitution, there is a certain connection between the first sin of Adam and the sinfulness of his posterity.[55]

Hopkins went on to explain that the 'certain connection' was consent.

> It was made certain, and known, and declared to be so, that all mankind should sin as Adam had done, and fully consent to his transgression, and join in the rebellion he began; and by this bring upon themselves the guilt of their father's sin, by consenting to it, joining with him in it, and making it their own sin.[56]

As already indicated, Fuller accused Booth of views similar to those of Tobias Crisp, whose teaching had provoked a controversy at the end of the seventeenth century.[57] Booth does not respond to this charge perhaps because he realized that his writings were free from the ambiguities of Crisp. To defend himself he appealed to such accepted standards of orthodoxy as the Church of England homilies and the writings of John Owen and Herman Witsius, indicating that he considered himself to be in

---

approve.' See, Fuller's Letters: A. Fuller to S. Hopkins, 17 March 1789'; cf. 'A Fuller to J. Ryland, 21 April 1794'; 'A. Fuller to J. Sutcliff, 7 Jan. 1801.'

53   Foster, *Genetic History of New England Theology*, p. 185
54   Fuller's Letters: 'A. Fuller to J. Ryland, 24 Dec, 1795'.
55   Samuel Hopkins, *System of Doctrines* (1793), in *The Works of Samuel Hopkins with a Memoir of his Life and Character by E.A. Park* (3vols; Boston, 1852), I, p. 218.
56   Hopkins, *System of Doctrines*, p. 218.
57   See p. 211 above, and also Fuller, *Six Letters to Dr Ryland*, p. 320. For an account of the Crispian controversy, see P. Toon, *The Emergence of Hyper-Calvinism in English Nonconformity, 1689–1765* (London: Olive Tree, 1967), pp. 49-50.

the mainstream of Calvinistic thinking.[58] Confusion about the nature of imputation lies at the heart of the controversy between Booth and Fuller. From it arose their differences on substitution and particular redemption.

SUBSTITUTION

Particular Baptist theology expressed in the *1689 Confession* states that the sufferings of Christ were a penal substitute for men's sins.[59] As already indicated, Andrew Fuller accepted the penal character of Christ's substitutionary work. He was, however, wary of any way of stating this doctrine which made it seem like a commercial transaction. He was concerned to guard against teaching which measured the degree of the sufferings of Christ by the number of the elect or the extent of their sins.

> The sufferings of Christ in our stead, therefore, are not a punishment inflicted in the ordinary course of distributive justice, but an extraordinary interposition of infinite wisdom and love; not contrary to, but rather above the law, deviating from the letter, but more than preserving the spirit of it.[60]

Once again Fuller's inspiration appears to have come from New England, where Joseph Bellamy and Jonathan Edwards, Jr., had resurrected the governmental theory of the atonement. This view had been originally developed by the Dutch jurist Hugo Grotius in the early seventeenth century. It presented God not as an offended judge to whom satisfaction must be made, but as the moral governor of the universe, who must do something to show his abhorrence of sin. The cross demonstrates this divine resentment, but must not be regarded as a strictly substitutionary penalty.[61] The governmental theory was expounded by Stephen West in his *The Scripture Doctrine of the Atonement Proposed to Careful Examination* (1785).[62] In 1795 Fuller described this to Sutcliff as a book 'for wh I wd not take 1/1 [one guinea].'[63]

---

58   Booth, *Divine Justice*, pp. 46-49.
59   *1689 Confession*, VIII.4.
60   Fuller, *Three Conversations*, in *Works*, p. 313.
61   Foster, *Genetic History of New England Theology*, pp. 115-16, 199-206. E.F. Clipsham, 'Andrew Fuller's Doctrine of Salvation' (BD thesis, University of Oxford, 1971), p. 68: 'Another point at which Edwards's influence was felt was with regard to Christ's atoning death, though here the influence was indirect, being mediated through the writings of his followers. With Edwards's theological system as a foundation his disciples, notably his son, Jonathan Edwards the younger, came to work out a "governmental" theory of the atonement.'
62   Foster, *Genetic History of New England Theology*, p. 204.
63   Fuller's Letters: 'A. Fuller to J. Sutcliffe, 22 Jan. 1795.' Cf. J. Ryland, *The Work of Faith, the Labour of Love and the Patience of Hope in the Life and Death of the Rev. Andrew Fuller* (London: Button and Sons, 1818), p. 226: 'I have read Dr Edwards on Free Grace and Atonement with great pleasure. I suppose I read it some time ago; but I

It has been alleged that by the time of the publication of the second edition of *The Gospel Worthy of All Acceptation* in 1801, Fuller had adopted the governmental theory of the atonement.[64] Certainly he admired the New England theologians who were propounding this theory and was influenced in measure by them. Like them he had been profoundly influenced by the elder Edwards. At times he was using governmental language. At the same time there is no evidence that he rejected the substitutionary position. At the time of his controversy with Booth, he assured Ryland,

> Whether Christ laid down his life as a *substitute* for sinners, was never a question with me. All my hope rests upon it; and the sum of my preaching the gospel consists in it. If I know anything of myself I can say of Christ crucified for us, as was said of Jerusalem, 'If I forget thee, let my right hand forget; if I do not remember thee, let my tongue cleave to the roof of my mouth. I have always considered the denial of this truth as being of the essence of Socinianism.[65]

Fuller insisted on the absolute necessity of satisfaction to divine justice:

> If God required less than the real demerit of sin for an atonement, then there could be no *satisfaction* made to Divine justice by such an atonement. And though it would be improper to represent the great work of redemption as a kind of commercial transaction between a creditor and his debtor, yet the satisfaction of justice in all cases of offence requires *that there be an expression of the displeasure of the offended against the conduct of the offender, equal to what the nature of the offence is in reality.*[66]

In his survey of Particular Baptist theology Tom Nettles admits that Fuller used 'governmental language', but insists that use of governmental concepts 'did not involve him in the errors of the governmentalists'.[67] In this respect Fuller's position appears to be similar to that of Jonathan Edwards the elder who has also been unjustly charged with governmentalism.[68]

---

never relished it so well before'. Later, p. 227: 'I very much longed for West *on the Atonement.*'

64 See, e.g., R. Philip Roberts, *Continuity and Change: London Calvinistic Baptists and the Evangelical Revival, 1760–1820* (Wheaton, IL: Richard Owen Roberts, 1989), p. 198.

65 Fuller, *On Substitution*, in *Works*, p.320.

66 Fuller, *On the Deity of Christ, The Deity of Christ Essential to Atonement*, in *Works*, p. 938.

67 T.J. Nettles, *By His Grace and for His Glory: A Historical, Theological, and Practical Study of the Doctrines of Grace in Baptist Life* (Grand Rapids, MI: Baker Book House, 1986), p. 128.

68 J.H. Gerstner, *The Rational Biblical Theology of Jonathan Edwards* (3 vols; Orlando, FL: Ligonier Ministries, 1991–93), II, p. 436, defends Edwards against the

On the other hand it has to be remembered that Booth was aware of moves towards governmentalism in New England by the end of the eighteenth century. There Edwards's successors had moved beyond their teacher's position. Booth knew this and was alarmed by what he considered to be indications that this view was being promoted in the writings of Fuller.[69]

It was in the light of his understanding of Fuller's teaching that Booth declared,

> No one can be pardoned and accepted of God, except on the ground of its [the Law's] righteous precepts being perfectly performed, and its equitable sanction completely satisfied by the vicarious obedience, and the substitutionary sufferings of our all sufficient sponsor.[70]

In 1798, Fuller had informed Hopkins that Booth was 'a great admirer of Owen, Vitringa, Verema etc; and seems to suppose that these have gone to the *ne plus ultra* of discovery'.[71] Later that year Hopkins replied to Fuller:

> I am far from wishing to say or do anything to alter your opinion of the honesty and holiness of Mr Booth; but from what I have seen of his writings,—which are only his Reign of Grace and Glad Tidings,—I cannot consider him a divine of a clear or orthodox head; and I think I have a divine warrant to say, that the religion which has its foundation on the principles he has asserted in both his Glad Tidings and Reign of Grace (see pp. 248, 270 of the latter edition of 1795) is altogether a selfish religion, and therefore abominable to God.[72]

These were strong words indeed, but it is significant that Fuller himself continued to speak of Booth in the highest terms even though the two men found themselves in disagreement.

---

charge of governmentalism. He writes of statements which it is alleged indicate this view in Edwards's writings: 'these are never at the expense of the satisfaction theory. Rather they are founded on it. True the manifestation of God's abhorrence of sin is as essential for Edwards as it is for Grotius. The difference is that for Grotius the manifestation is enough. For Edwards it is not only not enough, it is nothing apart from the satisfaction for sin on which the reality as a manifestation of divine abhorrence depends.'

69   In *Divine Justice*, Booth argued powerfully for substitution, e.g., p. 38: 'What adequate cause can be assigned for this amazing anguish; except that of his vicarious character—of his bearing imputed sin and of his undergoing the curse of the law, for those that were justly condemned?'

70   Booth, *Divine Justice*, pp. 17-18. Cf. pp. 24-26.
71   Fuller's Letters: 'A. Fuller to S. Hopkins, 17 March 1789'.
72   Samuel Hopkins, *Memoir* (Boston, 1852), in *Works*, I, p. 224.

PARTICULAR REDEMPTION

This doctrine states that the saving purpose of Christ's sacrifice on the cross was the salvation of the elect alone. Since the Particular Baptists identified themselves by belief in this doctrine, it was not surprisingly regarded as a test of orthodoxy, and discussion of it was a delicate issue. By the last quarter of the eighteenth century, Andrew Fuller's American friends had abandoned belief in particular redemption, substituting for it the doctrine of general redemption, which in England, of course, was the distinguishing tenet of the General or Arminian Baptists. In New England, Joseph Bellamy had pioneered this change. He retained a belief in the doctrine of election but rejected particular redemption on the ground that it choked the free offer of the gospel.[73] The doctrine of general redemption was popularized by Jonathan Edwards, Jr., in his *Three Sermons on the Atonement* and expounded in greater detail by Stephen West in his *The Scripture Doctrine of the Atonement*, both published in 1785. The strictly substitutionary view of the atonement required either that the sins of the elect were imputed to Christ and he atoned for these alone or that he died for all and saved all, which was universalism, long opposed by orthodox Christians. It was in controversy with the universalists that the New England men restated their governmental theory of the atonement and linked it to the doctrine of general redemption, thus jettisoning strict substitution.[74]

As has already been demonstrated, Fuller was influenced by the North American men in his thinking on imputation and substitution. He also admitted to Ryland in 1803 that since his controversy with Dan Taylor, he had modified his views on particular redemption.[75] The change can be seen by comparing Fuller's answers to the objection that it is futile to exhort to faith those who do not as yet know whether Christ has died for them. His replies, as given in the 1785 and 1801 editions of the *Gospel Worthy of All Acceptation*, are not the same. In 1785 he wrote,

> Surely it cannot but be right for a man, whether he have a spiritual interest in Christ's death or not, to receive what God says in the love of it—to approve things that are excellent—to allow from his very heart of the Lord Jesus Christ in all his

---

73 J. Bellamy quoted by Foster, *Genetic History of New England Theology*, pp. 116-17: 'If Christ did not design by his death, to open a door for all to be saved conditionally, that is upon condition of faith, then there is no such door opened; the door is not opened wider than Christ designed it should be; there is nothing more purchased by his death than he intended; if this benefit was not intended, then it is not procured; if it be not procured, then the non-elect can not any of them be saved, consistently with divine justice.'

74 Foster, *Genetic History of New England Theology*, pp. 199-206. Fuller's appreciation of West's *Atonement* is noted above p. 203.

75 *Six Letters to Dr Ryland*, p. 322.

offices and excellencies—to desire an interest in him—and to resolve to no longer trust in his own sufficiency, which is but trusting in a lie, but to cast his soul upon Christ for mercy, determined either to be saved by him or perish at his feet.[76]

He went on to say, 'there is no fear of Christ ever destroying any that venture upon him'.[77]

In the 1801 edition Fuller abandoned this method of answer entirely. Instead, he rejected the idea of atonement as 'the literal payment of a debt' and proceeded on the assumption that,

> Its [the atonement's] grand object was to express the Divine displeasure against sin, and so to render the exercise of mercy in all the ways wherein sovereign wisdom should determine to apply it, consistent with righteousness.[78]

The language at this point may appear to be governmental, but as has already been shown, Fuller had not abandoned substitution. However, he went on to argue for a redemption which depended for its particularity upon God's decree and the execution of that decree by the Holy Spirit. From these effects he reasoned back to the purpose of the atonement.

> The application of redemption is solely directed by sovereign wisdom, so like every other event, it is the result of previous design. That which is actually done was intended to be done.[79]

The problem with this enunciation of the doctrine is that while making a statement about redemption an important aspect of that redemption is distanced from the cross. The limitation of Christ's sacrifice does not seem to relate to what actually happened at the cross. Fuller appears not to face up to the question of whether the sins of the elect were specifically imputed to Christ. To Ryland, he wrote,

> If I speak of it irrespective of the purpose of the Father and the Son, as to the objects who should be saved by it, merely referring to what it is in itself sufficient for, and declared in the gospel to be adapted to, I should think that I answered the question in a Scriptural way by saying, It was for sinners as sinners; but if I have respect to the purpose of the Father in giving his Son to die and to the design of Christ in laying down his life, I should answer, It was for the elect only.[80]

Fuller was clearly stating a position long held by many Calvinists that 'the death of Christ was sufficient for all, but efficient for the elect'. He

---

76 A. Fuller, *The Gospel Worthy of All Acceptation* (Northampton, 1st edn, 1785), p. 132.
77 *Gospel Worthy* (1st edn), p. 133.
78 *Gospel Worthy* (2nd edn), p. 109.
79 *Gospel Worthy* (2nd edn), p. 110.
80 *Six Letters to Dr Ryland*, p. 321.

was concerned to safeguard an unfettered presentation of Christ to all, but at the same time to teach that the atoning sacrifice of Christ fulfilled the purpose of God in election.

Booth was unhappy with Fuller's arguments at this point. He admitted 'the sufficiency of Immanuel's death to have redeemed all mankind, had all the sins of the whole human species been equally imputed to him'.[81] This was however a hypothetical point.

> We cannot perceive any solid reason to conclude that his propitiatory sufferings are sufficient for the expiation of the sins he did not bear or for the redemption of sinners whom he did not represent as a sponsor, when he expired on the cross.[82]

In the *Appendix* to *Divine Justice* Booth discussed Fuller's views on the atonement, although without naming him. He considered that Fuller was conflating the doctrine of particular redemption with related doctrines and in so doing isolating it from the doctrine of the atonement. Fuller wrote, 'I do not consider particular redemption as being so much a doctrine of itself as a branch of the great doctrine of election.'[83] Booth was concerned to sustain the particularity of Christ's atoning sacrifice.

> From the doctrine of Divine Justice, as it respects the atonement of Christ, we are led to infer, that redemption by his blood is not general but particular, and peculiar to the chosen of God. Redemption by Jesus Christ cannot, I conceive, be justly considered as either more or less extensive than his voluntary substitution; or than the number of persons for whom he performed that vicarious work which was finished on the cross. If, in his perfect obedience and penal death, he acted and suffered as the substitute of *all mankind*, they are all redeemed: but if, as the representative of *the elect only*, redemption must be considered as exclusively theirs. For, to imagine that the death of Christ, as the price of deliverance from the curse of the law, redeemed any for whom as a substitute, he did not suffer; and to suppose, that any of those for whom as a surety, he sustained the penalty of death are *not redeemed*, seem equally indefensible and absurd.[84]

For Booth Fuller's explanation could only weaken the scriptural testimony that 'Christ died for our sins'. The concepts of sacrifice and propitiation were weakened by an emphasis that made election and effectual calling to the exclusion of the historic event of Calvary the

---

81   Booth, *Divine Justice*, p. 61.
82   Booth, *Divine Justice*, p. 61. R.A. Coppenger, 'Abraham Booth, 1734–1806: A Study of his Thought and Work' (PhD thesis, University of Edinburgh, 1953), p. 108 misinterprets Booth at this point when he says that 'Booth was in complete accord with Fuller on the limited atonement, which they both interpreted as limited in its application, but not in its sufficiency'.
83   Fuller, *Three Conversations on Imputation, Substitution and Particular Redemption*, in *Works*, p. 315.
84   Booth, *Divine Justice*, pp. 59 -61.

means of making salvation as a personal reality. He claimed that in the view taught by Fuller,

> there is nothing in the atonement of Christ that infallibly ascertains its application to all those for whom it was made.[85]

He also rejected Fuller's suggestion that 'the principal design of our Lord's atonement was the manifestation of God's hatred to sin'. He accepted that God's hatred of sin was demonstrated in the atonement but,

> the grand idea suggested to the enlightened mind in the atonement of Christ, and to which the New Testament abundantly directs our attention, is, not God's hatred to sin, but to love sinners...not his inclination to punish, but his determination to pardon.[86]

Fuller was passionately loyal to historic Calvinism as he understood it but felt that Booth had misrepresented him.[87]

It was in the second edition of *The Gospel Worthy of All Acceptation* that Fuller's revised views became widely known. Fuller was concerned to extricate the free offer of the gospel from the objection that a man could not flee to Christ who was not sure that Christ had died for him. Booth did not see the resolution of the problem in 'universal sufficiency'. He insisted that Fuller's teaching represented 'a reconciling expedient or compromise'.[88] Fuller was aware that the New England men to whom he owed so much had abandoned the doctrine of particular redemption. Booth knew this too and his alarm at the direction of events in England is understandable.

It is clear, however, that there was a difference over particular redemption between the two men. It was a difference which went back to their divergence of understanding about imputation. Booth's greater emphasis on imputation and substitution led him to stress the particularity of the atonement in the events of Calvary itself.[89] He believed that Fuller had weakened in his adherence to particular redemption. Fuller refused to concede this and felt that Booth was old and stubborn. He believed that rather than weakening the doctrine of particular redemption by conceding that the atonement was sufficient for all mankind he had rescued it from neglect and confusion.[90] Perhaps Booth did underestimate Fuller's commitment to the doctrine under discussion. Fuller did, however, admit a change of emphasis. However, to suggest that

---

85   Booth, *Divine Justice*, p. 84.
86   Booth, *Divine Justice*, pp. 89-90.
87   *Three Conversations*, pp. 314-15.
88   Booth, *Divine Justice*, p. 78.
89   Booth, *Divine Justice*, pp. 87-88.
90   *Six Letters to Dr Ryland*, p. 322.

Fuller had become an Arminian is wrong. The 'sufficient for all, but efficient for some' formula had long been accepted in Reformed circles. Calvin appeared to allow the possibility and it was explicitly stated in the Canons of Dort.[91] Booth dismissed this as a hypothetical position, which was not germane to the issue on the grounds that it was what God intended that was accomplished at Calvary. William Newman commented later,

> Some appear to have imbibed a vague notion of atonement while redemption properly so-called is overlooked... Mr. Booth thought Mr. Fuller was verging to this extreme, in this however, I believe he misunderstood Mr. Fuller.[92]

There was certainly misunderstanding, but it was not simply on one side.

The death of Abraham Booth in 1806 removed Fuller's most able critic among the Particular Baptists. Fuller stood out as a theologian and a leader. Years before he had dared to challenge the prevalent non-offer teaching and although at first resisted by many he saw a large number of his fellow Particular Baptists accepting his views, while a growing number of High Calvinists were ready to co-operate with him in the missionary society. The presidents of the three Baptist colleges, John Ryland, William Newman and William Steadman,[93] were sympathetic to his teaching and so it was likely that a growing number of the younger ministers from these institutions would also be. His victory was not, however, quite complete. There were churches and individuals who remained loyal to the old High Calvinism and yet others who felt that belief in particular redemption was in danger of being lost. No one seemed able to give the theological lead that was needed. However, in John Stevens and William Gadsby there appeared two preachers with considerable powers of leadership who were to rally the High Calvinists and to present their teaching in a new and popular way. Unlike Button and Martin, they were able to build up a growing body of support beyond their own churches. They also revealed a readiness to go their own way outside the local

---

91 J. Calvin, *Commentary on The Gospel according to St John, 11–21 and I John* (trans. T.H.L. Parker; Edinburgh: T&T Clark, 1972), p. 244. See also *The Three Forms of Unity ..., The Canons of the Synod of Dort*, Second Head, Article 3, regarding the extent of the atonement.

92 Newman's Diary quoted in G. Pritchard, *Memoir of the Rev. William Newman, D.D.* (London, 1837), p. 336.

93 John Ryland at Bristol was of course Fuller's correspondent and biographer. William Newman of Stepney expressed his admiration in a memorial sermon, *A Sermon occasioned by the death of the Rev. Andrew Fuller* (London, 1815). Of William Steadman, Principal of the Northern Academy (1805–35), his son, T. Steadman, *Memoir of the Rev. William Steadman, D.D.* (London, 1838), p. 459, wrote, 'in digesting the system of religious truth, he was guided by the counsels and strictures of Fuller's herculean understanding'.

associations and the Baptist Union. Both Gadsby and Stevens attacked Fuller's developed views which became known in the years after 1800, although neither would have been happy with the first edition of the *Gospel Worthy of All Acceptation* or even with Booth's *Glad Tidings*. It is regrettable that there was no theologian of the calibre of Abraham Booth to continue to challenge Fuller's thinking and to guide men who were exercised by these issues. In the years to come much of the criticism of Andrew Fuller was unthinking and hostile to a degree that his positive contribution to the life of the churches was dismissed without proper consideration.

CHAPTER 9

Andrew Fuller and the Sandemanian Controversy[1]

Michael A.G. Haykin

Ecclesial reformation and renewal are rarely the work of one individual, contrary to the impression given by some popular church histories. Collegiality is central to such times of spiritual blessing. Thus, for example, after the theological and spiritual devastation wrought by Arianism in the eastern Mediterranean, it was the writing and preaching of the fourth-century Cappadocian Fathers—Basil of Caesarea (c.330–79), his younger brother, Gregory of Nyssa (d. c.394), and his close friends Gregory of Nazianzus (c.329–89) and Amphilochius of Iconium (c.340–95)—that was central in re-fructifying the churches of the East. Again, during the time of the French Reformation, the friendship and theological collaboration of John Calvin (1509–64), Guillaume Farel (1489–1565), and Pierre Viret (1511–71) played such a vital role in the advance of evangelical truth that by 1572 there were some two million individuals in evangelical congregations in France.

Yet a third example can be found in the revival of the Calvinistic Baptist community in England during the last quarter of the eighteenth century. For most of that century far too many Baptist churches were moribund and without vision for the future or passion for the salvation of the lost at home or abroad. Definite tendencies towards 'hyper-Calvinism', an introspective piety, and an inability to discern God's hand at work in the Calvinistic Methodist revivals of their day, as well as various social and political factors, were central in their decline.[2] By the first decade of the next century, however, the low-burning embers in their churches had been fanned into white-hot flame as this Baptist community became a world leader in the foreign missionary enterprise.[3] The man whose writings, above all others, provided the theological underpinnings

---

1   For help with various aspects of this paper, I would like to thank Dr Brian Talbot of Cumbernauld, Scotland, and Mr Nigel Pibworth of Biggleswade, Bedfordshire.

2   See Michael A. G. Haykin, *One Heart and One Soul: John Sutcliff of Olney, His Friends and his Times* (Darlington: Evangelical Press, 1995), pp. 15-33 and *passim*.

3   For some details, see chs 1 and 10.

for this revival was Andrew Fuller (1754–1815), who, because of the weightiness of his theological influence and acumen, has been rightly called 'the elephant of Kettering'.[4] But, and this is vital to recognize, he did not accomplish this alone.

There is little doubt in the mind of this author that Fuller's friendship with a number of like-minded Baptist pastors from the Midlands—in particular the elder Robert Hall of Arnesby (1728–91), John Sutcliff (1752–1814) of Olney, John Ryland, Jr. (1753–1825) of Northampton, William Carey (1761–1834), and Samuel Pearce (1766–99) of Birmingham—was indispensable to the transformative impact of his theology.[5] These men took the time to think and reflect together, as well as to encourage one another and pray together. They shared a love for the Scriptures that they regarded as inerrant and sufficient for all of the needs of God's people. A personal covenant written by Fuller in 1780 well expresses this common conviction when it speaks of Fuller's 'determination to take up no principles at second-hand, but to search for every thing at the pure fountain of [God's] word'.[6]

They also shared a common admiration of the writings of the leading eighteenth-century theologian of revival, Jonathan Edwards (1703–58). It was during his time as a pastor in Soham that Fuller, for example, began a life-long study of Edwards' works. For Fuller, Edwards was his major theological tutor after the Word of God. 'No man', he once said of Edwards, 'possessed a clearer insight into these difficult subjects' of the various roles played by the understanding, the will, and the affections in the matter of conversion and the Christian life.[7]

These rich theological perspectives of Edwardsean Calvinism, along with Fuller's humble submission to the absolute authority of the infallible Scriptures, the theological help of his friends, and the fearless exercise of

---

4   David Phillips, *Memoir of the Life, Labors, and Extensive Usefulness of the Rev. Christmas Evans* (New York: M.W. Dodd, 1843), p. 74.

5   For the story of this friendship and the revival of the eighteenth-century English Baptists, see Haykin, *One Heart and One Soul, passim.* Also see above, ch. 1.

6   Cited John Ryland, Jr., *The Work of Faith, the Labour of Love, and the Patience of Hope Illustrated; in the Life and Death of the Reverend Andrew Fuller* (London: Button & Son, 2nd edn, 1818), p. 129.

7   *The Gospel Worthy of All Acceptation*, in A. Fuller, *The Complete Works of the Rev. Andrew Fuller* (ed. J. Belcher; 3 vols; Harrisonburg, VA: Sprinkle Publications, reprint, 1988), II, p. 411 n. †.

8   For example, he could state: 'If any man venerate the authority of Scripture, he must receive it as being what it professes to be, and for all the purposes for which it professes to be written. If the Scriptures profess to be Divinely inspired, and assume to be the infallible standard of faith and practice, we must either receive them as such, or, if

his mind,[8] enabled him to decisively respond to a number of theological errors of his day, including Sandemanianism.[9]

Sandemanianism and the Nature of Saving Faith

The roots of Sandemanianism lie in the 1720s when John Glas (1695–1773), minister of the Church of Scotland work in Tealing, Scotland, and a man of considerable erudition, gradually came to the conviction that Christ's kingdom is one that is completely spiritual and as such independent of both state control and support.[10] A church of some seventy believers was formed in the parish of Tealing, and over the next couple of decades Glasite congregations could be found in Dundee, Perth, Edinburgh, and booming textile centres such as Paisley and Dunkeld. Although the Glasites were never numerous, Glas' views exercised a wide sphere of influence, especially through the travels of his son-in-law, Robert Sandeman (1718–71), throughout the British Isles and America and the latter's writings, whom D. Martyn Lloyd-Jones rightly describes as 'a born controversialist'.[11] They adopted such practices as

---

we would be consistent, disown the writers as imposters'. See A. Fuller, *The Calvinistic and Socinian Systems Examined and Compared, as to their Moral Tendency*, in *Works*, II, p. 196. See also James D. Knowles, 'Character of Andrew Fuller', *The American Quarterly Observer* 2 (1834), p. 120.

9   D. Martyn Lloyd-Jones, in an address entitled 'Sandemanianism', felt that the key theologian who was raised up to refute the errors of this movement was 'the famous Andrew Fuller' who 'more or less demolished Sandemanianism' in his *Strictures on Sandemanianism*. See his D. Martyn Lloyd-Jones, *The Puritans: Their Origins and Successors. Addresses Delivered at the Puritan and Westminster Conferences 1959–1978* (Edinburgh: Banner of Truth Trust, 1987), p. 173.

10   For Glas, see Derek B. Murray, 'The Influence of John Glas', *Records of the Scottish Church History Society* 22 (1984), pp. 45-56, and 'An Eighteenth-Century Baptismal Controversy in Scotland', in Stanely E. Porter and Anthony R. Cross (eds.), *Baptism, the New Testament and the Church: Historical and Contemporary Studies in Honour of R.E.O. White* (Journal for the Study of the New Testament Supplement Series, 171; Sheffield: Sheffield Academic Press, 1999), pp. 419-29; Thomas J. South, 'The Response of Andrew Fuller to the Sandemanian View of Saving Faith' (ThD thesis, Mid-America Baptist Theological Seminary, 1993), pp. 47-57.

11   Lloyd-Jones, 'Sandemanianism', 172. On Sandeman, see D. MacFayden, 'Glasites (Samdemanians)', in James Hastings (ed.), *Encyclopaedia of Religion and Ethics* (13 vols; New York: Charles Scribner's Sons, reprint, 1961), VI, pp. 230-31; South, 'Response of Andrew Fuller', pp. 57-77; Derek B. Murray, 'Sandeman, Robert', in Donald M. Lewis (ed.), *The Blackwell Dictionary of Evangelical Biography* (2 vols; Oxford/Cambridge, MA: Blackwell Publishers, 1995), II, pp. 970-71. For treatments of later Sandemanianism, see Geoffrey Cantor, *Michael Faraday: Sandemanian and Scientist. A Study of Science and Religion in the Nineteenth Century* (New York: St

foot-washing, the love feast (which they celebrated with Scotch broth!), and holy kissing (from which, in New England at least, the Sandemanians were derisively called 'Kissites'[12]). They insisted on the use of lots to determine God's will, and on unanimity in all church decisions ('Nothing', they would say, 'is decided by the vote of the majority'[13]). The insistence of Glas and Sandeman on such 'trivia of church order' set them apart from the mainstream of eighteenth-century Evangelicalism.[14] Most significantly, Glas' and Sandeman's followers also distinguished themselves from other eighteenth-century Evangelicals by a predominantly intellectualist view of faith. They became known for their cardinal theological tenet that saving faith is 'bare belief of the bare truth'.[15]

Sandeman, who assumed the leadership of the movement in the 1750s, was insistent that faith becomes a work of human merit if it includes anything beyond simple assent to the truth of what God has done through Christ's death and resurrection.[16] In Sandeman's reading of New Testament passages like Romans 4:5 ('to him who does not work but believes on him who justifies the ungodly, his faith is accounted for righteousness', NKJV), justification by faith has everything to do with God instilling into the minds of impenitent men and women the belief that God gave his dear Son for sinners. Essentially it has nothing to do with the exercise of the will in repentance or the engagement of the heart's affections towards God. 'Faith is given apart from any "willing or doing" on the part of the unbeliever.'[17] Sandeman also turned to 1 John 5:1, which states that 'whoever believes that Jesus is the Christ is born of God' (NKJV), to argue that regeneration accompanies intellectual assent to the central truth of the Christian faith, namely, that Jesus of Nazareth is the Christ and that he died and rose again for sinners. Thus, Sandeman could talk of 'bare faith', 'bare persuasion of the truth', and 'bare belief in the bare gospel'. This centre-piece of Sandeman's doctrine is well seen in the inscription on Sandeman's tombstone in Danbury, Connecticut. There Sandeman is described as one who 'long

---

Martin's Press, 1991), *passim*; Jean F. Hankins, 'A Different Kind of Loyalist: The Sandemanians of New England during the Revolutionary War', *The New England Quarterly* 60.2 (June, 1987), pp. 223-49.

12   Hankins, 'Different Kind of Loyalist', p. 226.

13   Fuller, *Strictures on Sandemanianism*, in *Works*, II, p. 636; H.M. Pickles, *Benjamin Ingham: Preacher Amongst the Dales of Yorkshire, the Forests of Lancashire, and the Fells of Cumbria* (Coventry: privately published, 1995), p. 111.

14   Murray, 'Sandeman, Robert', p. 971.

15   *Strictures on Sandemanianism*, p. 566; South, 'Response of Andrew Fuller', 63.

16   South, 'Response of Andrew Fuller', pp. 63-77 and J.I. Packer, 'History Repeats Itself', *Christianity Today* 33.13 (22 September 1989), p. 22.

17   South, 'Response of Andrew Fuller', p. 68.

and boldly contended for the ancient faith; that the bare work of Jesus Christ, without a deed, or thought on the part of man, is sufficient to present the chief [of] sinners spotless before God'.[18]

In a genuine desire to exalt the utter freeness of God's salvation, Sandeman sought to remove any vestige of human reasoning, willing or desiring in the matter of saving faith. Sandeman was convinced that if the actions of the will or the affections are included in saving faith, then the Reformation assertion of 'faith alone' is compromised.[19] Thus, in the Sandemanian system, saving faith is reduced to intellectual assent to the gospel proclamation about Christ. To be fair to Sandeman, it should be noted that he was quite prepared to admit that affections come into play once a person believes. But at the time of conversion, they play no role in saving faith.[20]

Moreover, in rejecting the affections of the heart as having any part in saving faith, Sandeman does appear to have been responding to the unduly introspective temper of some circles of eighteenth-century Evangelicalism. Andrew Fuller well summed up Sandeman's concern in this regard. Fuller agreed with Sandeman that the attention of far too many Christians of their day 'appears to have been too much drawn towards what may be called *subjective* religion, to the neglect of that which is *objective*'. They place 'the essence of faith...not in a belief of the gospel, but in a persuasion of our being interested in its benefits'.[21] But, as we shall see, Fuller rightly stressed that the solution is not to reject the subjective aspect of Christianity in favour of the objective, as Sandemanianism proposes. Rather, both are needed.

It should occasion no surprise that many of those who embraced Sandeman's intellectualist view of faith became stunted in their Christian lives. James Haldane (1768–1851), the Scottish Baptist evangelist and pastor, was prepared to admit that there was genuine spiritual life in the Sandemanian communitites, but, he went on to remark, their 'expansive powers are contracted and dwarfed'.[22] Likewise, Andrew Fuller can admit that there were 'things worthy of imitation' among the Sandemanians, such as their diligence to study the Bible and live under its authority. Yet,

---

18   South, 'Response of Andrew Fuller', p. 61.
19   See *Gospel Worthy of All Acceptation*, p. 406, where he summarizes Sandeman's argument in this regard: 'It is supposed that the including of holy affection in the nature of faith, and rendering it necessary to acceptance with God, (no matter under what consideration,) must, of necessity, lead the sinner from Christ, to rely on something good in himself.'
20   *Gospel Worthy of All Acceptation*, p. 329, note *. See also the remarks of Michael A. Eaton, *Baptism with the Spirit: The Teaching of Martyn Lloyd-Jones* (Leicester: Inter-Varsity Press, 1989), pp. 214-15.
21   *Strictures on Sandemanianism*, p. 564.
22   Cited by Pickles, *Benjamin Ingham*, p. 116.

he said, their spirituality 'resembles a rickety child, whose growth is confined to certain parts: it wants that lovely uniformity or proportion which constitutes the beauty of holiness'.[23] Christmas Evans (1766–1838), an influential Welsh Baptist leader, adopted Sandemanian views for a number of years in the late 1790s, but eventually found himself in the grip of 'a cold heart towards Christ, and his sacrifice, and the work of his Spirit' and dwelling in 'the cold and sterile regions of spiritual frost'.[24]

Sandemanianism, however, did not go not unopposed. A number of key eighteenth-century Evangelical leaders wrote replies and rebuttals of this system, including the Methodist preacher John Wesley (1703–91), the Welsh Calvinistic Methodist preacher and hymn writer William Williams of Pantycelyn (1717–91), the American Baptist champion of religious liberty Isaac Backus (1724–1806), and the Anglican biblical commentator Thomas Scott (1747–1821). It was Andrew Fuller, though, who drew up what many regard as the definitive response to Sandeman and his views.[25]

An Initial Response by Fuller

Fuller came into contact with Sandemanianism when he traveled throughout Scotland in the late 1790s and early 1800s seeking to raise financial support for the Baptist Missionary Society and their mission at Serampore, India. In the Scottish lowlands he encountered the Scotch Baptists, also known as the McLeanite Baptists after their chief theologian and apologist, Archibald McLean (1733–1812), who essentially adhered to the Sandemanian view of saving faith.[26] Due to McLean's financial support of the Baptist Missionary Society, Fuller met with him in the autumn of 1799, when the English Baptist leader first visited Scotland. The two men subsequently met at Kettering for two or three days' conversation as well as corresponding regularly regarding a variety of issues including their differences over the nature of saving faith. McLean

---

23 *Strictures on Sandemanianism*, pp. 623-24. See also p. 562.

24 Cited by Phillips, *Christmas Evans*, pp. 75-76. For the date, see Alan P.F. Sell, 'John Chater: From Independent Minister to Sandemanian Author', in *Dissenting Thought and the Life of the Churches: Studies in an English Tradition* (San Francisco: Mellen Research University Press, 1990), p. 415.

25 Lloyd-Jones, 'Sandemanianism', p. 173; South, 'Response of Andrew Fuller', p. 106.

26 On McLean, see W. Jones, 'Memoir of the Author', in *The Miscellaneous Works of Archibald McLean* (6 vols; Elgin: Peter MacDonald, 1847), I, pp. xv-lxviii; South, 'Response of Andrew Fuller', pp. 77-82; Derek B. Murray, 'McLean, Archibald', in Lewis (ed.), *Blackwell Dictionary*, II, p. 728.

used these letters to attack Fuller's position on saving faith in *The Commission Given by Jesus Christ to His Apostles Illustrated*, first published in 1785. In this work he attacked Fuller's position—though he did not mention him by name in the book—as subverting justification by faith alone. When 'men include in the very nature of justifying faith such good dispositions, holy affections and pious exercises of heart as the moral law requires, and so make them necessary...to a sinner's acceptance with God', McLean argued, 'it perverts the Apostle's doctrine' and 'makes justification to be at least "as it were by the works of the law"'.[27]

Fuller had enormous respect for McLean: 'An acute reasoner, and mighty in the Scriptures', was the way that he described him on one occasion.[28] But he was never one to allow what he considered vital error to go unchecked. 'Truth ought to be dearer to us', he was convinced, 'than the greatest or best of men'.[29] Fuller's initial response was thus to draw up a reply that was published as an appendix to the second edition of *The Gospel Worthy of All Acceptation* (1801).

In this work Fuller had sought to show from Scripture that faith, though a sheer gift from God, is also a duty.[30] Fuller noted that McLean was in hearty agreement with him on this central matter.[31] What then was the difference between the two Baptists? Fuller understood their disagreement to be 'confined to the question, What the belief of the gospel includes'. McLean wanted to so define faith that it was 'a passive reception of the truth' with 'nothing in it of a holy nature'.[32] In McLean's words: 'To deny that faith is the exercise of a virtuous temper of heart is to refuse some praise to the creature.'[33] McLean's great fear was that the heart disposition of the sinner as God leads him or her to faith would be regarded as a 'ground of acceptance with God'.[34]

Fuller could appreciate McLean's concern, though he strongly believed the Scottish Baptist's position to be both illogical and unscriptural. 'It is impossible', he argued, 'to maintain that faith is a duty, if it contain no holy exercises of the heart', for 'God requires nothing of intelligent creatures but what is holy'.[35] Moreover, genuine faith must have holiness in its nature, otherwise it is dead. True faith

---

27 McLean, *The Commission Given by Jesus Christ to His Apostles*, in *Miscellaneous Works*, I, p. 66.
28 Jones, 'Memoir of the Author', p. xxxv.
29 *Gospel Worthy of All Acceptation*, p. 397.
30 See above, ch. 2.
31 *Gospel Worthy of All Acceptation*, pp. 393-94.
32 *Gospel Worthy of All Acceptation*, p. 393.
33 *Gospel Worthy of All Acceptation*, p. 395.
34 *Gospel Worthy of All Acceptation*, p. 394.
35 *Gospel Worthy of All Acceptation*, p. 395.

produces a holy life—which McLean was prepared to admit—only if it is holy, for 'the nature of the fruit corresponds with that of the root'.[36] Looking at this same point from the perspective of the Spirit as the giver of faith, Fuller argued that 'whatever the Holy Spirit as a Sanctifier produces, must resemble his own nature'.[37]

Strictures on Sandemanianism (1810)

A published book-length response to McLean's Sandemanianism came nearly a decade later in a series of letters that Fuller penned to a friend and which he published in 1810 as *Strictures on Sandemanianism*.[38]

Fuller was quite willing to admit that there was much in Sandemanianism that he considers 'worthy of serious attention'.[39] Sandeman's critique of the undue subjectivism that reigned in certain quarters of eighteenth-century Evangelicalism, for instance, was not without merit. As Fuller noted:

> If the attention of the awakened sinner, instead of being directed to Christ, be turned inward, and his mind be employed in searching for evidences of his conversion, the effect must, to say the least, be uncomfortable, and may be fatal; as it may lead him to make a righteousness of his religious feelings, instead of looking out of himself to the Saviour.

> Nor is this all: If the attention of Christians be turned to their own feelings, instead of the things which should make them feel, it will reduce their religion to something vastly different from that of the primitive Christians. Such truths as the following were the life of their spirits: 'Jesus Christ came into the world to save sinners' [1 Timothy 1:15]—'Christ died for our sins according to the Scriptures, and was buried, and rose again the third day, according to the Scriptures' [1 Corinthians 15:3-4]—'Remember that Jesus Christ, of the seed of David, was raised from the dead according to my gospel' [2 Timothy 2:8]—'We have a great High Priest that is passed into the heavens, Jesus, the Son of God' [Hebrews 4:14], etc. But by the turn of thought and strain of conversation in many religious connexions of the present day, it would seem as if these things had lost their influence. They are become 'dry doctrines,' and the parties must have something else. The elevation

---

36 *Gospel Worthy of All Acceptation*, pp. 395-96.
37 *Gospel Worthy of All Acceptation*, p. 398.
38 George Smeaton, *The Doctrine of the Holy Spirit* (London: Banner of Truth Trust, 1958), p. 347, noted that Fuller 'wrote admirably against Sandemanianism', but he was convinced that the English Baptist's *Strictures on Sandemanianism* would have been 'more conclusive had he followed Sandeman step by step instead of turning aside to less able men'. However, Fuller had to deal with lesser men like McLean since he had directly attacked Fuller and it was McLean's writings that were being read by the English Baptists.
39 *Strictures on Sandemanianism*, p. 562.

and depression of their hopes and fears, joys and sorrows, is with them the favourite theme. The consequence is, as might be expected, a living to themselves rather than to him that died and rose again...[40]

Fuller shared Sandeman's concern that some professing believers of their day are more taken with their experiences of Christ than with Christ himself. For them, faith was all but reduced to religious feeling. Yet, he went on to argue, the solution to such an unbalanced focus on the subjective elements of Christianity is not to be found by rejecting them out of hand: 'Subjective religion is as necessary in its place as objective.'[41] While faith, as Fuller rightly argued in the above quote, can never be identified simply with feeling, nor can it be ever divorced from the affections of the heart. Fuller was greatly exercised that the Sandemanian perspective designs to 'exclude all holy affections from faith, as being favourable to self-reighteousness'.[42] Genuine faith 'does not pertain to the understanding only', Fuller stressed.[43] In elaborating this position, Fuller made a number of telling points against the Sandemanian system.

The Sandemanian concern that allowance of any subjective, human element in the matter of salvation will compromise the sufficiency of Christ's objective work can also be applied to the act of faith itself. As Fuller rightly insisted, people 'may also make a righteousness of their faith'.[44]

Second, if faith does concern only the mind, then there would be no way to distinguish genuine Christianity from nominal Christianity. A nominal Christian mentally assents to the truths of Christianity, but those truths do not grip the heart and re-orient his or her affections. The so-called faith of a nominal Christian, Fuller pointed out, is really little different from that of the fallen angels, whom we are told in James 2:19 'believe' in the existence of one God and 'tremble'.[45]

Third, the opposite of saving faith in Scripture, Fuller noted, is not 'simple ignorance', which it would be if the Sandemanian view of faith were correct. Its opposite is an ignorance that has its roots in a deep-seated hatred of the true God. Christ can therefore state that unbelief rejects him because, in the words of John 3:19, 'darkness is loved rather than light'. Or when Ephesians 4:18 talks about the understanding of unbelievers being darkened 'because of the ignorance that is in them,

---

40   *Strictures on Sandemanianism*, p. 564.
41   *Strictures on Sandemanianism*, p. 565.
42   *Strictures on Sandemanianism*, p. 574.
43   *Strictures on Sandemanianism*, p. 580.
44   *Strictures on Sandemanianism*, p. 574.
45   *Strictures on Sandemanianism*, pp. 583-89. See also the remarks of South, 'Response of Andrew Fuller', pp. 127-28.

because of the blindness of their heart', surely, Fuller reasoned, the ignorance in view here is much more than mere lack of knowledge. Does it not entail, he asked, a deep-seated aversion to God and holy things?[46]

By way of support, Fuller could turn to the *magnum opus* of the Puritan theologian John Owen (1616–83), his monumental *A Discourse Concerning the Holy Spirit*. Commenting upon the same text from Ephesians 4, Owen observed that the 'blindness' mentioned in the verse is not 'mere ignorance..., but a stubborn resistance of light and conviction'.[47] In Fuller's words again, this time from his earlier response to Sandemanianism: 'Spiritual blindness is ascribed' by this passage in Ephesians 'to aversion of heart... The obstinacy and aversion of the heart is the film to the mental eye, preventing all spiritual glory entering into it.'[48] But if unbelief comprises much more than ignorance, then faith must entail more than knowledge. If unbelief involves an aversion to the truth and a forthright rejection of the gospel, then faith in it must include a love and receptive approbation of the truth.[49]

Fourth, knowledge of Christ and the things of God is a distinct type of knowledge. Knowing Christ, for instance, involves far more than knowing certain things about him, such as the fact of his virgin birth or the details of his crucifixion. It involves a desire for fellowship with him, a delight in his presence, a recognition that among all the beings of this universe he is truly the most beautiful. 'The very essence of Scriptural knowledge', Fuller wrote, 'consists in the discernment of Divine beauties, or the *glory of God in the face of Jesus Christ.*'[50]

To substantiate this critical point, Fuller reproduced an extremely lengthy passage from Jonathan Edwards' *Treatise Concerning Religious Affections*, which was first published in 1746.[51] For Fuller, as we have noted, Edwards was his major theological tutor after the Word of God. The passage that Fuller cited is from Part III, Section 4 of the *Religious Affections*, in which Edwards was detailing the fourth of twelve ways or

---

46 *Strictures on Sandemanianism*, pp. 598-600. See also *Strictures on Sandemanianism*, pp. 613-14.

47 *Strictures on Sandemanianism*, p. 600 n. †. For the actual statement, see *A Discourse Concerning the Holy Spirit*, in *The Works of John Owen* (ed. William H. Goold; 16 vols; 1850–53 edn; Edinburgh: Banner of Truth Trust, reprint, 1965), III, p. 252.

48 *Gospel Worthy of All Acceptation*, pp. 410-11.

49 *Strictures on Sandemanianism*, p. 602. See also his *Gospel Worthy of All Acceptation*, pp. 399-400.

50 *Strictures on Sandemanianism*, p. 602.

51 The passage that Fuller cites, *Strictures on Sandemanianism*, pp. 602-606, runs for six pages in the most recent critical edition of the *Religious Affections*. For the passage, see *Religious Affections*, in *The Works of Jonathan Edwards*. Volume 2 (ed. John E. Smith; New Haven, CT: Yale University Press, 1959), pp. 270-75.

signs in which genuine Christian spirituality reveals itself. Edwards was arguing that biblical Christianity has at its core a spiritual way of knowing or understanding that encompasses both the will's inclinations and the heart's affections. The dichotomy that many have posited between heart and head is here transcended by Edwards. In Edwards' own words: 'spiritual understanding...consists in a sense of the heart, of the supreme beauty and sweetness of the holiness or moral perfection of divine things, together with all that discerning and knowledge of things of religion, that depends upon, and flows from such a sense.'[52]

Edwards went on to make a marked contrast between this understanding that the Spirit imparts to all true believers and that which is purely intellectual.

> There is a distinction to be made between a mere notional understanding, wherein the mind only beholds things in the exercise of a speculative faculty; and the sense of the heart, wherein the mind don't only speculate and behold, but relishes and feels. That sort of knowledge, by which a man has a sensible perception of amiableness and loathsomeness, or of sweetness and nauseousness, is not just the same sort of knowledge with that, by which he knows what a triangle is, and what a square is. The one is mere speculative knowledge; the other sensible knowledge, in which more than the mere intellect is concerned; the heart is the proper subject of it, or the soul as a being that not only beholds, but has inclination, and is pleased or displeased. And yet there is the nature of instruction in it; as he that has perceived the sweet taste of honey, knows much more about it, than he who has only looked upon and felt of it.
>
> Spiritual understanding primarily consists in this sense, or taste of the moral beauty of divine things; so that no knowledge can be called spiritual, any further than it arises from this, and has this in it. But secondarily it includes all that discerning and knowledge of things of religion, which depends upon, and flows from such a sense.[53]

Merely intellectual knowledge, which the Sandemanians maintained was the essence of saving faith, feels no attraction towards or aversion away from the object known. Knowledge of such geometrical shapes as a triangle or a square, for example, is unaccompanied by either a relish for them or a hatred of them. Genuine knowledge of God in true Christian experience, though, is inseparable from a delight in him and a relish of his person. Such a knowledge differs as much from a merely speculative

---

52 Edwards, *Religious Affections*, p. 272.
53 Edwards, *Religious Affections*, p. 272.

knowledge as the taste of honey differs from the simple understanding that honey is sweet.[54]

Edwards then proceeded to give some illustrations of this spiritual understanding that accompanies all genuine faith.

> When the true beauty and amiableness of the holiness or true moral good that is in divine things, is discovered to the soul, it as it were opens a new world to its views... By this sense of the moral beauty of divine things, is understood the sufficiency of Christ as a mediator: for 'tis only by the discovery of the beauty of the moral perfection of Christ, that the believer is let into the knowledge of the excellency of his person, so as to know anything more of it than the devils do: and 'tis only by the knowledge of the excellency of Christ's person, that any know his sufficiency as a mediator; for the latter depends upon, and arises from the former. 'Tis by seeing the excellency of Christ's person, that the saints are made sensible of the preciousness of his blood, and its sufficiency to atone for sin; for therein consists the preciousness of Christ's blood, that 'tis the blood of so excellent and amiable a person. And on this depends the meritoriousness of his obedience, and sufficiency and prevalence of his intercession. By this sight of the moral beauty of divine things, is seen the beauty of the way of salvation by Christ; for that consists in the beauty of the moral perfections of God, which wonderfully shines forth in every step of this method of salvation, from beginning to end... By this is seen the excellency of the Word of God: take away all the moral beauty and sweetness in the Word, and the Bible is left wholly a dead letter, a dry, lifeless, tasteless thing. By this is seen the true foundation of our duty, the worthiness of God to be so esteemed, honored, loved, submitted to, and served, as he requires of us, and the amiableness of the duties themselves that are required of us. And by this is seen the true evil of sin: for he who sees the beauty of holiness, must necessarily see the hatefulness of sin, its contrary. By this men understand the true glory of heaven, which consists in the beauty and happiness that is in holiness. By this is seen the amiableness and happiness of both saints and angels. He that sees the beauty of holiness, or true moral good, sees the greatest and most important thing in the world, which is the fullness of all things, without which all the world is empty, no better than nothing, yea, worse than nothing. Unless this is seen, nothing is seen that is worth the seeing: for there is no other true excellency or beauty. Unless this be understood, nothing is understood that is worthy of the exercise of the noble faculty of understanding. This is the beauty of the Godhead, and the divinity of Divinity (if I may so speak), the good of the infinite Fountain of Good; without which, God himself (if that were possible) would be an infinite evil: without which we ourselves had better never have been; and without which there had better have been no being. He therefore in effect knows nothing, that knows not this: his knowledge is but the shadow of knowledge, or the form of knowledge, as the Apostle calls it.[55] Well therefore may the Scriptures represent those who are destitute of that spiritual sense by which is perceived the beauty of holiness, as

---

54 George M. Marsden, 'Jonathan Edwards Speaks to our Technological Age', *Christian History* 4.4 (1985), p. 28. See also the comments of John E. Smith, 'Editor's Introduction', *Religious Affections*, pp. 30-33.

55 An allusion by Edwards to Romans 2:20.

totally blind, deaf, and senseless, yea, dead. And well may regeneration, in which this divine sense is given to the soul by its Creator, be represented as opening the blind eyes, and raising the dead, and bringing a person into a new world.[56]

Little wonder that Fuller felt, as he drew his *Strictures on Sandemanianism* to a close, that this spiritual classic from Edwards' pen 'proved beyond all reasonable contradiction that the essence of true religion' lies in genuine spiritual affections in which mind and heart, affections and understanding, are as intimately united as heat and light in a fire.[57]

Conclusion

There were other areas with which Fuller took issue with Sandemanianism, especially its 'punctilious adherence to the letter of Scripture'.[58] But central to Fuller's response to the teaching of Sandeman and followers like McLean was the issue of the nature of saving faith. Fuller rightly believed from Scripture and from his own experience that true conversion is rooted in a radical change of the affections of the heart and manifest in a lifestyle that seeks to honour God.[59]

Twenty years before the publication of the *Strictures on Sandemanianism*, during the winter of 1790–91, Fuller and his close friend John Sutcliff paid a visit to John Berridge (1716–93), the gifted though unconventional Evangelical vicar of Everton, Bedfordshire. After conversing for a while, the three men prayed together. What deeply impressed Fuller about Berridge's prayers was what he later described as 'such sweet solemnity, such holy familiarity with God and such ardent love to Christ'.[60] The affective element that is prominent in this description of Berridge's prayers epitomizes Fuller's understanding of the necessary concomitants of saving faith. Measured by this standard, Sandemanianism's view of faith was a paltry thing. And it is not surprising that Fuller reckoned that 'it would lead the Christian world, if

---

56   I have taken this quotation from Edwards, *Religious Affections*, pp. 273-75 and *passim*.
57   *Strictures on Sandemanianism*, p. 641.
58   *Strictures on Sandemanianism*, p. 624.
59   E.F. Clipsham, 'Andrew Fuller and Fullerism: A Study in Evangelical Calvinism. 1: The Development of a Doctrine', *BQ* 20.3 (July, 1963), pp. 106-107.
60   John Sutcliff, 'An Interview with the Late Mr Berridge', *The Evangelical Magazine* 2 (1794), p. 76.

not to downright infidelity, yet to something that comes but very little short of it'.[61]

---

61 *Strictures on Sandemanianism*, p. 646.

CHAPTER 10

Andrew Fuller as an Apologist for Missions

Peter Morden

Introduction

Late in 1792, Andrew Fuller called at the London home of the evangelical clergyman Thomas Scott (1747–1821). Fuller spoke of the impression that had been made by his fellow Particular Baptist, William Carey (1761–1834), when he had preached at the Northamptonshire Association meeting on 30 May earlier that year. Carey had taken as his text Isaiah 54.2-3: 'Enlarge the place of thy tent...for thou shalt break forth on the right hand and on the left; and thy seed shall inherit the Gentiles, and make the desolate cities to be inhabited.' Carey's two points, as Fuller related them, were that they should '*expect* great things' and then '*attempt* great things'. This was presented to Scott by Fuller as being one of the key events leading to the formation of the Baptist Missionary Society.[1]

The 'Particular Baptist Society for Propagating the Gospel among the Heathen' (hereafter BMS), was founded on 2 October 1792. William Carey was not only the central figure in its formation but also its first missionary, eventually arriving in India, with his family and his co-worker John Thomas (1757–1800) on 10 November 1793. Fuller had called on Scott in his capacity as secretary of the new society, not just to share information but also to seek a donation, and his 'collecting book' shows that Scott did indeed become a contributor.[2] In his account of Fuller's visit, Scott's son and biographer hinted at the huge significance of what was happening. Where the BMS was leading, other societies, like the

---

1 John Scott, *The Life of Rev. Thomas Scott D.D.* (London: Seeley, 1836), p. 115. This meeting between Scott and Fuller is also mentioned in I.H. Murray, *The Puritan Hope* (Edinburgh: Banner of Truth, 1971), p. 130. For the origins of the BMS, including comments on the title of Carey's Leicester sermon, see ch. 1.

2 B. Stanley, *The History of the Baptist Missionary Society, 1792–1992* (Edinburgh: T&T Clark, 1992), p. 21. Stanley is citing J. Wilson, *Memoir of...Thomas Wilson, Esq.* (London: John Snow, 2nd edn, 1849), pp. 126-27 n..

Congregational London Missionary Society and the Anglican Church Missionary Society, would soon follow.³ Doubtless Baptist historians, and others, have sometimes claimed too much for the BMS, and the description of Carey as the 'father of modern missions' is in many ways misleading.⁴ Carey and Thomas were not the first Protestant missionaries to be sent out by European churches, and Carey himself was particularly conscious that he was standing in a long line of earlier pioneers.⁵ Both he and Fuller had in fact been influenced by the efforts of North American missionaries such as David Brainerd (1718–47), whose life and work was mediated to them through Jonathan Edwards' (1703–58) biography of his friend.⁶

Yet despite all this, there is no doubt that something of huge importance *was* happening. As Brian Stanley states in the society's official history, '[The] early missionaries of the BMS were among the first impressions of a renewed endeavour by Western Christians to refashion the rest of the globe in a Christian image—a movement which was to have profound implications for the history of the non-European world over the next two centuries.'⁷ There were precedents, but nevertheless the forming of the BMS marks a 'turning point'.⁸ Fuller certainly made his own personal response to Carey's famous sermon and 'motto', both expecting and attempting great things for God on behalf of the society. His importance as one of the founders of the BMS, and his subsequent work as secretary, has already been outlined in the biographical sketch of his life (chapter 1). In this chapter I will attempt a brief survey of Fuller's contribution to the BMS as a missionary theologian, before focusing more narrowly on his work as an apologist.

---

3   Scott, *Life of Thomas Scott*, p. 115. For Thomas Scott and a brief note on his son, who also became a clergyman, see D.M. Lewis (ed.), *Dictionary of Evangelical Biography, 1730–1860* (2 vols; Oxford: Blackwells, 1995), II, pp. 989-91. The LMS was formed in 1795, the CMS in 1799.

4   Some of the Baptist historiography on this subject is summarized by W.H. Brackney, 'The Baptist Missionary Society in Proper Context: Some Reflections on the Larger Voluntary Religious Tradition', *BQ* 34.8 (October, 1992), p. 364.

5   For a brief summary of some of the most significant Protestant missionary work before 1792, see T. George, *Faithful Witness: The Life and Mission of William Carey* (Leicester: InterVarsity Press, 1991), pp. 40-45. Carey himself was particularly influenced by the missionary activity of the Moravians.

6   For Fuller's reading Edwards' biography of Brainerd, see *The Complete Works of the Rev Andrew Fuller, With a memoir of his Life by the Rev. Andrew Gunton Fuller* (ed. A.G. Fuller; rev. edn J. Belcher; 3 vols; Harrisonburg, VA: Sprinkle Publications, 1988 [3rd edn, 1845]), II, p. 329.

7   Stanley, *History of the BMS*, p. 1.

8   S. Neill, *A History of Christian Missions* (Pelican History of the Church, 6; Harmondsworth, Middlesex: Penguin, 1964), p. 261.

Fuller as Missionary Theologian

In his article 'Andrew Fuller and the Baptist Mission', E.F. Clipsham argues that Fuller played a vital theological role for the BMS, quoting B.G. Griffith: '[Fuller] was pre-eminently the thinker, and no movement can go far without a thinker.'[9] As secretary, Fuller was in a unique position to influence the theological direction of the young society, and this was something he did in a number of ways, for example, through his involvement in the selection and preparation of new recruits, and his continued contact with them once they were on the field. Clipsham highlights four areas where Fuller made an key contribution.

Firstly, Clipsham states that Fuller emphasized that 'God has uniquely and finally revealed himself in Jesus Christ'. Secondly, Fuller was clear that 'In the gospel, God is freely offering Christ to the world' (with the corollary that the missionaries too must 'offer' Christ).[10] If the first point was hardly a matter of debate among Particular Baptists, the second certainly had been and continued to be so for a significant minority. On the importance of the 'free offer of the gospel' Fuller was, of course, absolutely clear. A third emphasis was that 'only those means...consistent with the nature of the gospel [were] worthy of a Christian Missionary'. In other words the character and conduct of the missionaries was important. 'Beware that you do not misrepresent your blessed Lord and his glorious gospel', he advised Carey and Thomas before they set out.[11] Clipsham could have developed this point further by highlighting the way that Fuller habitually urged missionaries and their families to nurture a deep spirituality. For example, in a letter of 1806 to two missionaries and their wives about to set sail he wrote: 'there is the greatest necessity for us all to keep near to God... Beware of drawing a veil between him and you... Be very conversant with your Bibles.'[12] The fourth emphasis was an

---

9   E.F. Clipsham, 'Andrew Fuller and the Baptist Mission', *Foundations* 10.1 (January, 1967), p. 8. The quotation from Griffith is from his Presidential address to the Baptist Union Assembly, 27 April 1942. See also the use Hayden makes of Clipsham's work, R. Hayden, 'The Life and Influence of Andrew Fuller', in R.L. Greenall (ed.), *The Kettering Connection, Northamptonshire Baptists and Overseas Missions* (Leicester: Department of Adult Education, University of Leicester, 1993), pp. 7-8.

10   See P.J. Morden, *Offering Christ to the World: Andrew Fuller (1754–1815) and the Revival of Eighteenth Century Particular Baptist Life* (Studies in Baptist History and Thought, 8; Carlisle: Paternoster Press, 2003).

11   In 1793. Cited by Clipsham, 'Andrew Fuller and the Baptist Mission', p. 7.

12   Fuller to 'Mr and Mrs Chater and Mr and Mrs Robinson', 5 April 1806, in J. Ryland, Jr., *The Work of Faith, the Labour of Love, and the Patience of Hope Illustrated in the Life and Death of the Rev. Andrew Fuller* (London: Button and Son, 2nd edn, 1818), p. 161. For William Robinson's and James Chater's missionary careers, see Stanley, *History of the BMS*, pp. 54-55, 140, 168.

eschatological one, that 'the final triumph of Christ and his cause is assured'. Fuller applied his Edwardsean postmillennialism to his thinking about world mission. One of Fuller's earliest letters to Carey, not cited by Clipsham, illustrates the point: 'For my part, I believe in God, and have little doubt that a matter, begun as this was, will meet His approbation... I confess I feel sanguine, but my hopes are fixed in God. Instead of failing in the E. Indian enterprise, I look to see not only that but many others accomplished.'[13] Fuller, to quote Carey's dictum again, was *attempting* great things, precisely because he *expected* great things. This spirit pervaded the whole society.

Clipsham's instinct for what was important is sound, and we will see that a number of these themes reoccur when we look at more closely at Fuller's apologetic work. But Clipsham's analysis is open to question in at least one respect. He at least infers that some of these points were Fuller's particular contribution. But the extent to which Fuller was, for example, responsible for the society's belief that 'The final triumph of Christ and his cause is assured' is doubtful. Certainly such a view was all pervasive in the early days of the mission, but it was held by all the leading figures of the Northamptonshire Association, as of course was the belief that 'God has uniquely and finally revealed himself in Jesus Christ'.[14] The point that 'In the gospel, God is freely offering Christ to the world' had more of a claim to be Fuller's distinctive, through his work in *The Gospel Worthy of All Acceptation*. But this belief was also held by all the key Northamptonshire men, who had come to this conclusion by various routes. The BMS was in fact full of theological 'thinkers', both at home and abroad.

Yet there is no doubt that Fuller made a real contribution to the theological shaping of the mission, and it was *The Gospel Worthy* and the 'open offer of the gospel' that was most important. Granted that there were a number of others who had held the same views as Fuller. But it was in *The Gospel Worthy* that the Northamptonshire Association's warm evangelical Calvinism was given its fullest and most significant expression. This was the theology which underpinned the work of the BMS and to which all its early missionaries were committed. If it was the 'duty of man' to believe, and therefore the duty of ministers to 'offer Christ' to the unconverted, it was a logical extension of this that the gospel should be taken overseas. And as well as being a key foundation of the mission itself, Fuller's work was also crucial in creating a favourable ecclesiastical climate at home in which a venture such as the BMS would be accepted, supported and could prosper. It is certainly

---

13 S.P. Carey, *William Carey D.D.* (London: Hodder and Stoughton, 1923), p. 112.
14 This particular point is acknowledged by Clipsham, 'Andrew Fuller and the Baptist Mission', p. 6, who recognizes that belief in the uniqueness and finality of Christ was not 'peculiar to Fuller or his associates'.

worthy of note that regions that were most resistant to *The Gospel Worthy*, such as London and East Anglia, were the least fertile in terms of support for the new society.¹⁵ Where the theology which became known as 'Fullerism' was accepted, support was forthcoming. It is Fuller's decisive contribution to the spread of evangelical theology, a theology which by the 1790s was dominant among English Particular Baptist churches and which so characterized the BMS, which means that he can indeed be called the 'leading theologian of the missionary movement'.¹⁶

Fuller as Missionary Apologist

Fuller was also the mission's leading apologist. The two texts which we will consider are both included in Fuller's *Collected Works*. The first of these is the sermon preached at a ministers' meeting at Clipstone on 27 April 1791, already referred to in chapter 1. This was printed as *The Pernicious Consequences of Delay in Religious Concerns* later that year.¹⁷ The original title of the message was 'The Instances, Evil, and Tendency of Delay, in the Concerns of Religion', and the verse Fuller preached on was Haggai 1.2: 'Thus speaketh the Lord of Hosts, saying, This people say, the time is not come, the time that the Lord's house should be built.' In this message Fuller advocated the cause of overseas mission to an audience of Particular Baptists at a time when many of them doubted that engagement in such work was either necessary or practical. The second text was published in 1808 after the mission had become established. Here Fuller defended the missionaries in India from those who described them as 'fools, madmen, tinkers, Calvinists and schismatics', accusing Carey and his colleagues of endangering the rule of law by 'interfering' with the religious views of the indigenous Indian

---

15   For the lack of support for the BMS in these areas, see Stanley, *History of the BMS*, pp. 17-18. For parallel opposition to *The Gospel Worthy*, see, e.g., Fuller to Thomas Stevens of Colchester, 'I know the opposition made to "Andrew Fuller" in S_____ and N_____' (4/5/2), Fuller Letters, Angus Library (n.d.). S. and N. are certainly Suffolk and Norfolk. This letter is also cited by R.W. Oliver, 'The Emergence of a Strict and Particular Baptist Community Among the English Calvinistic Baptists, 1770-1850' (PhD thesis, CNAA [London Bible College], 1986), p. 86 n..
16   George, *Faithful Witness*, p. viii.
17   A. Fuller, *The Pernicious Consequences of Delay in Religious Concerns* (Clipstone: J.W. Morris, 1791), in *Works*, I, pp. 145-51. All subsequent quotations are taken from these pages. Fuller's message was originally published with Sutcliff's *Jealousy of the Lord of Hosts Revisited* in the same volume. For another short summary of Fuller's sermon see M.A.G. Haykin, *One Heart and Soul: John Sutcliff of Olney, His Friends and His Times* (Durham: Evangelical Press, 1994), pp. 210-12.

population.[18] Although some of those who attacked the BMS described themselves as Christians, they were certainly no friends of evangelicals or Dissenters. These opponents of the mission wanted the missionaries recalled, or at least silenced. This chapter therefore examines Fuller's work as a missionary apologist on two quite different fronts.

'The Instances, Evil, and Tendency of Delay'

This was a message that was important in the genesis of the BMS, both in its spoken and printed form (see chapter 1). In a wide ranging address, the most significant challenge Fuller gave his hearers was one concerning involvement in world mission. Fuller began by carefully setting the verse in its historical context. The Israelites had returned from exile in Babylon but had failed to rebuild the temple, concentrating not on 'the Lord's house' but on 'the building and ornamenting of houses for themselves'. This failing was because of what Fuller termed a 'procrastinating spirit', a spirit which also afflicted many of his hearers, both unbelievers and believers. The former put off commitment to Christ to some future time. The latter were 'prevented from undertaking any great or good work for the cause of Christ, or the good of mankind'. Some undertakings were indeed 'impractical', but often this was used as a cover by people to hide the real reasons for not attempting something difficult for God, namely the effort and expense involved, and the fact that significant opposition might be faced.

Fuller then cited the sixteenth century German Reformer Martin Luther and the first century apostles as positive examples for his hearers. If Luther had been deterred by opposition, Fuller argued, 'the glorious work of the Reformation' would never have happened, and if the apostles had been put off by difficulties they would never have responded to the 'Great Commission' of Matthew 28.19-20. As Michael Haykin points out, both the Reformation and 'the rise of what has been termed the modern missionary movement' are watersheds in the history of the church, and 'from our standpoint...it is fascinating to see these two events linked together'.[19] Luther himself famously believed that the Great Commission was for the original apostles and that it did not apply to the church in succeeding generations, and so he was not, in common with the other magisterial reformers, committed to world mission.[20] This was a fact

---

18   A. Gunton Fuller, *Men Worth Remembering: Andrew Fuller* (London: Hodder and Stoughton, 1882), p. 118.
19   Haykin, *One Heart and Soul*, pp. 210-11
20   R.E. Davis, 'The Great Commission from Christ to Carey', *Evangel* 14.2 (Summer, 1996), pp. 44-49. The Anabaptists were notable exceptions to this trend in the sixteenth century.

of which Fuller was almost certainly aware, making his use of Luther at this point even more intriguing. Fuller went on to state that rather than putting off action until difficulties eased, in many cases obstacles should be considered 'as purposely laid in our way, in order to try the sincerity of our religion'. It was at this point that he had some important things to say to those who believed 'the time had not yet come' for world mission.

Arguments in Favour of World Mission

Fuller suggested that it was because of the prevailing 'procrastinating spirit' that so 'so few and so feeble efforts [had] been made for the propagation of the gospel in the world'. The argument which followed was powerful and obviously had a profound effect on many of those who heard him. Returning to the 'Great Commission' he stated that:

> When the Lord Jesus commissioned his apostles, he commanded them to go and teach 'all nations' and preach the gospel to 'every creature;' and that notwithstanding the difficulties and oppositions that would lie in their way. The apostles executed their commission with assiduity and fidelity; but, since their days, we seem to sit down half contented that the greater part of the world should still remain in ignorance and idolatry. Some noble efforts have indeed been made; but they are small in number, when compared with the magnitude of the object.

Fuller had stopped just short of saying that Matthew 28.19-20 was binding on all believers in every age, although it could be argued that such a view was implicit in the point he was making. In addition to David Brainerd's work amongst the indigenous Indian population in North America, the 'noble efforts' which Fuller had in mind probably included the similar pioneering work among native Americans of John Eliot in the seventeenth century.[21] Fuller was increasingly convinced of the need for similar and more concerted action. He continued:

> Are the souls of men of less value than heretofore? No. Is Christianity less true or less important than in former ages? This will not be pretended. Are there no opportunities for societies, or individuals, in Christian nations, to convey the gospel to the heathen? This cannot be pleaded so long as opportunities are found to trade with them, yea, and (what is a disgrace to the name of Christians) to buy them, and sell them, and treat them with worse than savage barbarity? We have opportunities in abundance; the improvement of navigation, and the maritime and commercial turn of this country furnish us with these; and it deserves to be considered whether this is not a circumstance that renders it a duty peculiarly binding on us.

---

21 See *Works*, II, p. 329. For Eliot and Brainerd, see Davis, 'The Great Commission', pp. 45-47; George, *Faithful Witness*, pp. 42-45.

Fuller's appeal was predicated on the eternal truth, relevance and power of the gospel. But it was also tied to the challenge of the times in which he and his hearers lived. Rather than being 'impracticable', real opportunities had opened up for taking the gospel to unreached peoples, opportunities which Christians in late eighteenth century Britain were particularly well placed to exploit. Also worth noting are Carey's words, that it was the accounts of Captain Cook's voyages to Australia and the South Seas that were 'the first thing that engaged my mind to think of missions'.[22] The establishment of the BMS was a considered response to the particular opportunities and challenges of the age.

Fuller then alluded to the 'Prayer Call' of 1784, which had established regular prayer meetings focused on the need for world revival, stating:

> We *pray* for the conversion and salvation of the world, and yet neglect the ordinary *means* by which those ends have been used to be accomplished. It pleased God, heretofore, by the foolishness of preaching, to save them that believed; and there is reason to think it will still please God to work by that distinguished means. Ought we not then at least to try by some means to convey more of the good news of salvation to the world around us than has hitherto been conveyed? The encouragement to the heathen is still in force, '*Whoever shall call upon the name of the Lord shall be saved:* but how shall they call on him in whom they have not believed? and how shall they believe in him whom they have not heard? and how shall they hear without a preacher? And how shall they preach except they be sent?'

The twin emphases, on divine sovereignty and human responsibility, were by now absolutely typical of Fuller. Prayer was vital, but it had to be accompanied by action, for although it was God who did the work, he worked through 'ordinary means', in particular the 'foolishness of preaching'.[23] As he was later to say, 'The Hindoos (sic) can never be converted by mere *human means*, though we are equally persuaded they will never be converted without them.'[24] Fuller was applying the thoroughgoing evangelical Calvinism of *The Gospel Worthy* to the subject of overseas mission. His central message to his Particular Baptist audience was clear: the time to make a real effort to convey 'more of the good news of salvation to the world around us had come'. As he bluntly put it here: 'we wait for we know not what'.

---

22   E. Carey, *Memoir of William Carey* (London, 1836), p. 18, quoted by Stanley, *History of the BMS*, p. 8. Probably these were the accounts of Cook's second and third voyages, published in 1784.

23   As he was to put it in a letter to John Fawcett of Hebden Bridge, 'we now think we ought to do something more than pray', Fuller to J. Fawcett, 28 January, 1792, in J. Fawcett, Jr., *The Life, Ministry and Writings of John Fawcett D.D.* (London: Baldwin, Craddock and Joy, 1818), p. 294. Fuller's comments reveal a 'high' view of preaching, as Haykin points out, *One Heart and Soul*, p. 212.

24   *Works*, II, p. 821.

Fuller and Carey

A year later, Carey himself published on the subject of world mission. His famous pamphlet entitled *An Enquiry into the Obligations of Christians to use Means for the Conversion of the Heathens*[25] was to become the 'charter' of the emerging missionary movement.[26] Stanley notes that some of Carey's language in the *Enquiry* 'corresponded closely' to that already used in Fuller's 1791 sermon.[27] Carey referred to the Great Commission and then stated 'that multitudes sit at ease, and give themselves no concern about the greater part of their fellow sinners, who, to this day, are lost in ignorance and idolatry'. Later he commented that 'it has been said that some learned divines have proved from Scripture that the time is not yet come that the heathen should be converted'.[28] Other examples could have been cited, and similarities between Carey and Fuller, both in argument and in the actual language used, are obvious to a careful reader of both works.

That Carey was drawing from Fuller's Clipstone sermon seems the natural conclusion, but in fact this is by no means certain. Fuller had seen and critiqued an early manuscript of the *Enquiry* before he preached at Clipstone[29] and it is possible that he had borrowed from Carey, rather than vice versa.[30] Moreover, Carey daringly argued that the Great Commission was still binding on present day disciples and did so at length. This was more than Fuller had done at this point, as by now will be clear. Carey certainly influenced Fuller, but it is probable that the younger man also drew on the Clipstone sermon to some extent, and, if this is true, Fuller's influence is further highlighted. But what is certain is that on the central issue the two men were agreed—it was time to act. This is exactly what they did, Carey, in Fuller's terms, going 'down the mine',

---

25   William Carey, *An Enquiry into the Obligations of Christians, to use Means for the Conversion of the Heathens...* (Ann Ireland: Leicester, 1792). A facsimile edition was printed in 1892, again in 1934 and then with an introduction in 1961 (London: Kingsgate Press, 1961). The *Enquiry* was also reissued and published by the Baptist Union of Great Britain (Didcot, 1991), with a Preface by B. Stanley, the only difference to the 1961 edition being that the spelling was modernized. It is also reproduced in George, *Faithful Witness*, pp. E.1-57. Subsequent references are from the London facsimile edition of 1961. Despite its enduring significance, the *Enquiry* was far from a best seller in its own day.

26   J.A. De Jong, *'As the Waters Cover the Sea:' Millennial Expectations in the Rise of Anglo–American Missions, 1640–1810* (Kampen: J.H.Kok NV, 1970), p. 178.

27   Stanley, *History of the BMS*, p. 12.

28   This and the following quotations are from Carey, *Enquiry*, pp. 8 and 12.

29   Ryland, *Andrew Fuller*, 2nd edn, p. 148; Haykin, *One Heart and Soul*, p. 187.

30   As Stanley notes, *History of the BMS*, p. 12.

while he 'held the ropes'.[31] Fuller had argued that Particular Baptists should now actively engage in the cause of world mission. The subsequent success of the missionary enterprise would produce more apologetic challenges for Fuller.

Growth and Opposition

The BMS, as well as stimulating the growth of other evangelical societies, also made significant advances in the years following 1792.[32] For example, in 1799 Joshua Marshman (1768–1837), William Ward (1764–1823), Daniel Brunsdon (1777–1801) and William Grant (d.1799), came to India to augment the work of the mission. Of these Marshman and Ward were the most significant (Grant died from cholera and dysentery less than a month after their arrival in India). Together with Carey, Marshman and Ward became known as the 'Serampore Trio', deriving their name from the missionaries base of operations from 1800 onwards. Carey engaged in extensive Bible translation work and Ward, a printer, was instrumental in establishing a press at Serampore so that the Scriptures and other literature could be printed and distributed. The first Hindu convert under Carey's ministry was Krishna Pal (d. 1822), a carpenter converted and baptized in 1800. Fuller continued to be an enthusiastic advocate for the society at home, both in his own denomination and in the wider evangelical constituency, especially through his regular preaching engagements away from Kettering, which included his longer preaching tours.

But as the society's secretary, Fuller now had to defend the cause of the mission on a second front as well. From the moment Carey and Thomas stepped ashore in India, without an official permit from the British East India Company, Fuller was aware that the mission there 'hung by the slenderest of political threads', and was extremely careful not to do anything that would jeopardize the future of the work.[33] In this he was helped by some of the Anglicans who made up the evangelical 'Clapham Sect', particularly Charles Grant, whom Fuller described as a 'faithful friend'. It was Grant, once the East India Company's senior merchant in India and from 1805 deputy chair of its Court of Directors, who advised him to be careful when sending goods which could be turned into money, a move which could have laid the missionaries open

---

31   This famous image probably originated with Fuller himself (see ch. 2).
32   For information in this paragraph, see Neill, *Christian Missions*, pp. 262-64; E. Daniel Potts, *British Baptist Missionaries in India 1793–1837: The History of Serampore and its Missions* (Cambridge: Cambridge University Press, 1967), p. 172; George, *Faithful Witness*, pp. 122; 129-32.
33   Stanley, *History of the BMS*, p. 24.

Andrew Fuller as an Apologist for Missions   247

to an accusation that they were in fact acting as traders.[34] Fuller was grateful for this sort of inside information, but needed no encouragement to be scrupulously thorough in his efforts to avoid offending the authorities. But despite this, the BMS activity in India was regularly under threat. This was especially true in 1807–08 and again in 1813. The situation that arose in 1807 can be taken as an example, as it forms the background to the second text we will consider.

The Vellore Mutiny and its Aftermath

A mutiny among the East India Company's sepoy troops stationed at Vellore in June 1806 was attributed by some to interference with the religious views of native Indians,[35] and for a time the missionaries had to operate under severe restrictions. Carey wrote to Fuller, urging the home committee to 'try to engage men such as Mr Grant, Mr Wilberforce and others to use their influence to procure for us the liberty we want, viz. Liberty to preach the gospel throughout India'. 'Do your utmost', Carey urged, 'to clear our way'.[36] At home the missionaries were attacked with violent language, and plans were made to introduce a motion in the Company's Court of Proprietors which would lead to the expulsion of Carey and his colleagues.[37]

Fuller's response was both restrained and thorough. He worked privately, together with his Clapham friends visiting a number of the directors, while at the same time preparing a statement defending the Indian mission. This was to be distributed at a meeting on 7 June 1807 where the possible recall of the missionaries was to be discussed. Grant, however, persuaded Fuller it would be better to leave the matter in the hands of himself and some others on the committee who were sympathetic. This low key approach paid off and the motion was defeated.[38] According to Gunton Fuller, some involved with the LMS had been critical of Fuller's careful approach while he had been in London,

---

34   Clipsham, 'Andrew Fuller and the Baptist Mission', pp. 12, 17 n..
35   See John Clark Marshman, *The Story of Carey, Marshman and Ward, The Serampore Missionaries* (London: Alexander Strahan, 1864), pp. 117-18. The European garrison at Vellore, in the Madras presidency, was attacked with considerable loss of life.
36   W. Carey and others to BMS, Serampore, 2 September 1806, BMS MSS, Angus Library, Oxford, quoted in Potts, *Baptist Missionaries in India*, p. 178. 'Mr Wilberforce' is William Wilberforce, the evangelical social reformer and parliamentarian, another member of the 'Clapham Sect'.
37   See Gunton Fuller, *Men Worth Remembering*, p. 118. *The Edinburgh Review* was one journal that had attacked the BMS in this vein.
38   Stanley, *History of the BMS*, pp. 24-26; Clipsham, 'Andrew Fuller and the Baptist Mission', p. 13; Ryland, *Andrew Fuller*, 2nd edn, pp. 156-57.

describing Grant as 'timid and irresolute' and urging Fuller to disregard the advice of his friend and 'act on the offensive'.[39] But Fuller's tactics were almost certainly correct, and showed him to be a safe pair of hands as far as looking after the society's interests was concerned.

By the end of the year, however, the attacks against the missionaries had intensified. A tract was produced from the Serampore Press, known as 'The Persian Pamphlet', which was unwisely negative about Islam, using intemperate language to accuse Muslims of perverting God's commands, thereby incurring the 'wrath of God'.[40] An appendix, a biographical sketch of Mohammed's life, opened with the words 'An Account of a certain Tyrant from his birth to his death...'. Carey knew nothing of the tract and was alarmed when parts of it were read to him. It had actually been written by a Muslim convert to Christianity and it appears that Ward, who by now was supervising the press day to day, had not properly read it before it was printed. The circulation of the tract was stopped, but the damage had been done, and it appeared for a while that the missionaries' presses might be closed.

In addition to this development, there were a series of pamphlets produced in Britain which attacked Carey and his colleagues. The first of these was Thomas Twining's *A Letter to the Chairman of the East India Company, on the danger of Interfering in the Religious Observances of the Natives of India* in 1807.[41] Twining, a member of the famous tea trading family, believed that the activities of the missionaries could result in no less than the expulsion of the British from India, and repeated the charge that they were responsible for the Vellore massacre. More works followed in the same vain. The most important of these for our purposes were those written by two army officers, Major John Scott-Waring and an anonymous 'Bengal Officer', who was Major Charles Stewart. Scott-Waring had been forty years in India in the Company's service, and for a time was on the personal staff of the Governor General, Warren Hastings. He published his *Observations on the Present State of the East India Company* also in 1807.[42] Stewart had served as an officer in the East

---

39 Gunton Fuller, *Men Worth Remembering*, p. 119; cf. Marshman, *Carey, Marshman and Ward*, p. 124.

40 See Potts, *British Baptist Missionaries in India*, pp. 177-89, for the details in this paragraph.

41 The tract is wrongly attributed to Richard Twining, a director of the East India Company, by Clipsham, 'Andrew Fuller and the Baptist Mission', p. 13. Thomas Twining, who actually wrote four 'Letters' on the 'danger of interfering in the religious opinions of the natives in India', the last in 1808, was one of Richard Twining's sons. See Sir Leslie Stephens and Sir Sydney Lee (eds), *Dictionary of National Biography, from the Earliest Times to 1900* (21 vols; Oxford: Oxford University Press, 1921–22), XIX, pp. 1314-316.

42 J.C. Marshman, *Carey, Marshman and Ward*, p. 149

India Company's Bengal Army from 1781 to 1808. The latter added to the arguments of the others by speaking in highly favourable terms of Hinduism as a system. According to J. Clark Marshman, Stewart had 'abjured Christianity and embraced Hinduism', much to the 'ridicule' of the local population.[43] The waters were further muddied by a sermon by Dr William Barrow, which advocated restricting missionary activity to those in the Church of England. This time Fuller believed he had to make a public defence, and produced his *Apology for the Late Christian Missions to India* in 1808.[44]

Fuller's *Apology for the Late Christian Missions to India*

Fuller's *Apology* was divided into three parts, and the edition published in his *Collected Works* also contains an appendix, which was originally published separately. Clipsham's assessment of the work as a whole is that it was 'not a polished literary production', in some respects 'tedious' and 'repetitive'. Fuller, now working under intense pressure, had to produce the work in a short space of time and was answering specific and detailed allegations.[45] Much of his opponents' work was riddled with inaccuracies and what Fuller described as 'low abuse', which he clearly found tedious.[46] Of Scott-Waring in particular he said, 'I am weary of contending with this foul opponent'.[47] But the *Apology* was a more or less effective rebuttal of the charges laid against the mission and Clipsham's judgement is a little harsh.[48] Nevertheless, Fuller certainly returns repeatedly to the same themes as he answers the charges made against the missionaries. Consequently the best way to approach the *Apology* is to consider each of these main themes in turn, rather than working systematically through the text. A number of Fuller's points, important at the time but less relevant today, can be dealt with quickly.

---

43   *Dictionary of National Biography*, XVIII, pp. 1163-64; Marshman, *Carey, Marshman and Ward*, p. 153.

44   *Works*, II, pp. 763-836. Fuller's *Apology* was originally published by Button and Son, London, in 1808, the three parts initially appearing separately at intervals during the year, see J.C. Marshman, *Carey, Marshman and Ward*, p. 155. The majority of the short appendix to the *Apology*, in *Works*, II, pp. 831-36, was not part of the 1808 publication. The letter that begins on p. 835 is actually earlier than the *Apology*, having appeared originally in the *Theological and Biblical Magazine* (1802).

45   As Clipsham also points out, 'Andrew Fuller and the Baptist Mission', p. 13.

46   *Works*, II, p. 786.

47   *Works*, II, p. 815.

48   Although Marshman, *Carey, Marshman and Ward*, p. 155, was certainly guilty of overstatement when he wrote, 'On no occasion did his controversial acumen appear to greater advantage'.

Fuller rejected the charge that Baptists were at all to blame for Vellore, pointing out that no evidence had been produced to substantiate what had become a repeated accusation.[49] Dealing with the 'Persian Pamphlet' was more difficult. Fuller privately agreed that its publication had been an error, and pointed out in the *Apology* that it had not been written by one of the missionaries. But he was also able to show that an anonymous English 'translation' of the pamphlet that was circulating, at one point describing the Hindus as 'barbarians', was inaccurate. Fuller believed that this translation was done expressly 'to inflame the minds of the directors and the government against the missionaries'. He obtained a second translation from a student at the Baptist Academy in Bristol, where Ryland was now Principal, which he printed alongside extracts of the first. It was about the best Fuller could have done in the circumstances, but by 1808 Carey's prompt reaction in withdrawing the pamphlet had already mollified the authorities—on the ground in India at least.

Elsewhere in the *Apology* Fuller defended the missionaries themselves, chiefly by reproducing written testimonies as to their character.[50] He also sought to show that accounts of contemporary Hindu practices from Twining and particularly Stewart were one sided, to say the least. Some of Fuller's strictures on the majority religion in India, based on information received from the missionaries, can seem harsh when read today. But the 'Serampore Trio' could write sympathetically on aspects of the culture, and a book by Ward on the manners and customs of Hindus is described by Stephen Neill as 'as one of the best and most sympathetic delineations of Hindu thought ever produced by a foreigner'.[51] What they could not accept were some of the practices such as ritual infanticide, *ghat* murders, where the sick and dying were exposed on the banks of the Ganges, and *sati*, where widows threw themselves on the funeral pyres of their dead husbands.[52] These and other such practices were rigorously opposed. The social concern that Fuller had earlier shown in his Clipstone sermon, where he attacked slavery, was also evident here. In addition, Fuller and the missionaries were not prepared to compromise on their belief in the uniqueness of Christ and the Christian faith. This was non-negotiable, and, as will become increasingly clear, the *raison d'être* of their missionary activity.

The suggestion by Barrow that missionary activity should be confined to the established church, was dealt with graciously by Fuller, who was

---

49   *Works*, II, eg. pp. 768-69.
50   In the Appendix, *Works*, II, pp. 829-31.
51   Neill, *A History of Christian Missions*, pp. 264-65. Ward's book was published in 1806.
52   See George, *Faithful Witness*, pp. 149-52. *Ghats* were the steps leading down to the river. Fuller, *Works*, II, e.g. pp. 765-66, 796-800, describes some of these customs and rituals.

keen not to offend his Clapham friends. The Baptists were not looking to make converts to a sect or 'party', but to turn 'sinners to God through Jesus Christ'.[53] Further, he declined to give his views on the propriety of setting up a religious establishment in India. Similar issues would come to the fore again in 1813, where the insertion of a 'pious clause' in the East India Company's charter gave missionaries an assured legal status on the Company's territories. But the new charter also set up an Anglican establishment in India, financed from Company funds, and Nonconformists would still have to apply to the Company for a licence. Toleration for missionary activity in India had finally been secured, but, as Stanley states, 'on terms few Baptists could applaud'.[54] These were some of the arguments Fuller deployed to refute the particular attacks on his friends, but there are three themes that recur in Fuller's work that are worth looking at in more detail, the first of these being his plea for the 'toleration' of the missionaries by company's board and the government.

Fuller on Toleration

Twining had argued that the activities of the missionaries was against 'the mild and tolerant spirit of Christianity'.[55] He clearly believed that Carey and his colleagues should not be allowed to make converts, and hoped that 'our religious subjects in India' would be 'permitted quietly to follow their own religious opinions'. Fuller's answer to these points was carefully nuanced. Any attempt to coerce Indian Hindus or Muslims to follow Christ would be quite wrong, and indeed impossible. If any so-called 'missionary' tried to do this, or deliberately sought to disturb the 'peace of society', they could have no complaints if they were dealt with severely by the government. Overthrowing another religion by force was anathema to Fuller, as were any 'measures subversive of free choice'. In his reply to Barrow he wrote approvingly of the government, 'distinguished by its tolerant principles', which guarded the 'rights of conscience' of those of all religions in India.[56] As an English Nonconformist, grateful for the 1689 Act of Toleration, but still experiencing significant social and legal discrimination at home, Fuller was committed to freedom of conscience in religion.

But when Fuller came to define toleration positively, it was clear that his views were very different from Twining's. In a statement crucial to his

---

53 *Works*, II, pp. 828-29.
54 Stanley, *History of the BMS*, p. 26.
55 For these and other quotations in this paragraph, unless otherwise stated, see *Works*, II, pp. 763-64, 768.
56 *Works*, II, p. 825.

argument, Fuller wrote that 'Toleration was a legal permission not only to enjoy your own principles unmolested, but to make use of all the fair means of persuasion to recommend them to others'. In other words, people should be free not only to hold to certain principles, but also to *propagate those principles* through all reasonable means. Only this view of toleration squared with the Scriptures. In fact Twining's views were actually corrosive of religious freedom. Turning the tables on his opponent, Fuller argued that Twining was himself being 'intolerant' by saying that Christians in India 'must not be allowed to make proselytes', or indeed circulate the Scriptures in the Indian languages. This was not 'toleration' but 'persecution'. Later on in the tract he appealed directly to Parry:

> May I not take it for granted, sir, that a British government cannot refuse to tolerate protestant missionaries; that a protestant government cannot forbid the free circulation of the Scriptures; that a Christian government cannot exclude Christianity from any part of its territories?... I trust I may.

Fuller had argued for a distinctively Christian view of toleration, with a commitment to a free and truly tolerant society which was not incompatible with evangelistic activity or indeed claims to absolute truth.

A Missionary's Attitude to the Authorities

This was an important theme for Fuller. His views of a missionary's proper attitude to the government were hinted at in the previous extracts. In fact on this matter Fuller was quite explicit.

> We solemnly aver before God and our country that we are most sincerely attached to its constitution and government; that we regard its authority with sentiments of the highest respect, and hold ourselves bound to be obedient to its lawful commands. Obedience to the ruling powers we conceive to be enjoined in Scripture, where, however, an exception is expressly made in favour of those cases in which the commands of man are directly opposed to the revealed commands of God.[57]

This statement needs to be understood against the background of the government's fear of radical politics following the 1789 French Revolution, and the suspicion, not always without cause, that some Dissenters were sympathetic to the French. The accusation that the missionaries were French spies was never far away.[58] Fuller's concern, of course, was to defend the missionaries from these accusations. Also, his own political leanings were decidedly conservative. In 1799, Fuller had

---

57 *Works*, II, p. 816.
58 Potts, *British Baptist Missionaries in India*, p. 180

written to Carey saying that 'those ministers who have been the most violent partizans (sic) for democratic liberty...are commonly not only cold hearted in religion but the most imperious in their own churches'. Moreover, the leaders of the French Revolution were 'unprincipled infidels' bent on destroying true Christianity.[59] But the precarious situation of the missionaries and Fuller's own political views cannot fully explain his approach. Fuller was clear, as the extract quoted shows, that obedience to the government of the day was 'enjoined in the Scriptures', unless such obedience clearly conflicted with a believer's prior allegiance to God. As far as Carey, Marshman and Ward were concerned, it was relatively straightforward for Fuller to defend them. As Potts writes: 'The patriotic British Serampore Trio...always emphasised the virtue of Indians being loyal to the established government'.[60] Some of the younger missionaries, however, gave Fuller grave concern. Those who were reproved included Jacob Grigg (1769–1835), sent to begin a mission in Sierra Leone in 1795, and John Fountain (1767–1800), who had arrived in India before Marshman and Ward in 1797.[61]

Fountain in particular alarmed and angered Fuller by freely making his republican views known. In September 1797, just a few months after Fountain's arrival in India, Fuller warned him concerning his 'too great edge for politicks'.[62] Later, in 1800, he would write to William Ward deploring Fountain's 'rage for politics', lamenting that he 'seemed incapable of refraining from talking about them in any company'.[63] Fountain died in India in 1800, but not before he had almost been recalled by the Home Committee. Grigg had in fact been expelled from Sierra Leone in 1797, an action by the governor Zachary Macaulay (another member of the Clapham Sect), that had Fuller's full support.[64]

Fuller believed, quite correctly, that this sort of behaviour endangered the whole mission. His strong treatment of these men, with the full backing of the Committee, is unsurprising in the circumstances. But Fuller's strong biblical convictions are again clear. As he wrote to Carey,

---

59   Fuller to W. Carey, 18 April 1799, Angus Library, Oxford (H/1/3), quoted by Stanley, *History of the BMS*, p. 23.
60   Potts, *British Baptist Missionaries in India*, p. 169.
61   For these men, see B. Amey, 'Baptist Missionary Society Radicals', *BQ* 26.8 (October, 1976), pp. 363-76; Haykin, *One Heart and Soul*, pp. 245-48.
62   Fuller to J. Fountain, 7 September 1797, in Gunton Fuller, *Men Worth Remembering*, p. 143; cf., Stanley, *History of the BMS*, p. 24. As early as 25 March 1796, before Fountain had even sailed from London, Fuller had warned him that 'all political concerns are only affairs of this life', Fuller to J. Fountain, bound volume of Fuller's Letters, Angus Library (III/170), p. 23.
63   Fuller to W. Ward, 21 September 1800, bound volume of Fuller's Letters, Angus Library (III/170), p. 136.
64   Stanley, *History of the BMS*, p. 24.

'Jesus spent His [time] in accomplishing a moral revolution in the hearts of men.' Missionaries, indeed 'good men in general', should do likewise.[65] Consequently his advice to Fountain contained the following: 'Well does the apostle charge us who have engaged to be soldiers of Christ, not to entangle ourselves in the affairs of this life.'[66] Fuller's social concern has already been noted, but his attitude to the activities of men such as Grigg and Fountain reflected his overriding emphasis on evangelism, or 'accomplishing a moral revolution in the hearts of men'. For Fuller, it was this that was the major work of Christian mission, and nothing could stand in its way.

The Great Commission

A third key theme of the *Apology* is the affirmation of the Christian mandate to go into all the world and preach the gospel. Fuller stated that 'The principle ground on which we act is confined to a narrow compass: it is the commission of our Saviour to his disciples, "Go—teach all nations."' This commission, Fuller was now clear, was not 'confined to the apostles', the reason being that 'his promised presence to them who should execute it extends "to the end of the world".'[67] The church was 'obliged to do its utmost' in the 'use of those means which Christ has appointed for the discipling of all nations'. If Carey had been drawing from Fuller's Clipstone sermon in one or two passages in the *Enquiry*, Fuller was most certainly drawing from Carey now. Fuller continued:

> If we believe the Scriptures (and if we do not we are not Christians), we must believe that all nations are promised to the Messiah *for his inheritance*, no less than the land of Canaan was promised to the seed of Abraham; and we, as well as they, ought, in the use of those means which he has appointed, to go up and endeavour to posses them. It is not for us, having obtained a comfortable footing in Europe, like the Israelites in Canaan, to make leagues with other parts of the world, and, provided we may but live at ease, to consent for them to remain as they are. Such a spirit, though complimented by some as liberal, is mean, and inconsistent with the love of either God or man.

Fuller was careful about how he deployed such arguments in a work in which he was contending with those he could not regard as Christians, and which he hoped would have a wide and diverse readership. Consequently passages such as this do not dominate the *Apology*. But

---

65 Fuller to W. Carey, 18 January 1797, Fuller Letters, Angus Library (4/5/1), also cited in E.A. Payne, 'Andrew Fuller as Letter Writer', *BQ* 15.7 (July, 1954), p. 295.

66 Fuller to J. Fountain, 7 September 1797, in Gunton Fuller, *Men Worth Remembering*, p. 144.

67 See *Works*, II, pp. 817-18, for the quotations in this paragraph.

Fuller's commitment to the Great Commission, and to the uniqueness of Christ and his gospel are clear. Other familiar themes are present: belief in the Scriptures (note how the whole paragraph is steeped in Old Testament analogy), and the need to use God's appointed means to reach the nations (Fuller would have been thinking particularly of preaching). Familiar, too, is the note of urgency that had been so central to his Clipstone sermon. His commitment to the missionary cause was undimmed. To sit still and do nothing would be 'inconsistent with the love of either God or man'.

Conclusion

When Fuller shut himself away to write the *Apology* there was a real possibility the Serampore missionaries would be recalled, but the fears of Carey and the BMS Home Committee were not, after all, to be realized. Although the influence of Grant and others on the board of the East India Company was crucial in safeguarding the interests of the mission, what Stanley describes as Fuller's 'political discretion' was important as well.[68] His apologetic writing played only a small part in this, although J. Clark Marshman commented that Fuller's *Apology* 'produced a powerful and favourable effect on the public mind'.[69] But his work remains as a testimony to his commitment to the missionary cause, and to his friend for whom he had promised to 'hold the rope'.

What Fuller said as an apologist for world mission is worthy of reflection today, when the universal claims of the gospel are rejected, and where a form of 'toleration' abounds which is not dissimilar to that propounded by Fuller's opponents. For the church the urgency of Fuller's appeal for prayerful action, present in both the texts we have considered, speaks loudly too. Over 200 years on from the formation of the BMS, the call remains for the church to both expect great things and continue to attempt great things for God.

---

68 Stanley, *History of the BMS*, p. 25.
69 J.C. Marshman, *Carey, Marshman and Ward*, p. 156.

A Select Bibliography of Primary and Secondary Sources

Greg Meadows

Amey, Basil 'Baptist Missionary Society Radicals', *BQ* 26.8 (October, 1976), pp. 363-76.

_____. 'Hold not Back: Serampore Thanksgiving Sermon.' *BQ* 35.3 (July 1993), pp. 134-38.

Anon. *Carmen Flebile, or, An ode to the Memory of the Late Rev. Andrew Fuller of Kettering, who Departed this Life, Much and justly Lamented May 7, 1815* (London: Gale & Fenner, Button & Son, etc., 1815).

Anon. *Christian Biography: Containing the Lives of Rev. Andrew Fuller, Mrs. Harriet Newell, etc.* (n.p., n.d. [c.1810]).

Anon. *Life of Andrew Fuller in Bengali. By a Native Convert* (Calcutta: B.M. Press, 1892).

Anon. *Sketches of the lives of three children of the Rev. Andrew Fuller* (Philadelphia: American Sunday School Union, 1839).

Anon. *The Last Remains of the Rev. Andrew Fuller. Sermons, Essays, Letters and Other Miscellaneous Papers, Not Included in His Published Works. By the Editor of his 'Complete Works'* (Philadelphia: American Baptist Publication Society, 1856).

Armitage, Thomas. *The History of the Baptists; traced by their Vital Principles and Practices, from the Time of Our Lord and Saviour Jesus Christ to the Year 1886* (2 vols; New York: Bryan, Taylor, and Chicago: Morningside, 1887. Repr. Minneapolis: James and Klock Christian Publishing, 1977).

Ascol, Thomas Kennedy, 'The Doctrine of Grace: A Critical Analysis of Federalism in the Theologies of John Gill and Andrew Fuller' (PhD thesis, Southwestern Baptist Theological Seminary, 1989).

Baldwin, F.J. 'Association Life in Yorkshire and Lancashire', *BQ* 23.5 (January, 1970), pp. 208-14.

Binfield, J.C.G. 'Congregationalism's Two Sides of the Baptistry', *BQ* 26.3 (July, 1975), pp. 119-33.

Boreham, F.W. *A Bunch of Everlastings* (London: Epworth Press, 1955).

Brackney, William H. s.v. 'Fuller, Andrew (1754–1815)', in William H. Brackney, *Historical Dictionary of the Baptists* (Lanham, MD: Scarecrow Press, 1999), p. 171.

———. 'The Baptist Missionary Society in Proper Context: Some Reflections on the Larger Voluntary Religious Tradition', *BQ* 34.8 (October, 1992), pp. 364-77.

———. *The Baptists* (Denominations in America, 2; ed. Henry Warner Bowden; New York: Greenwood Press, 1988).

———, ed. *Baptist Life and Thought: 1600–1980. A Source Book* (Valley Forge, PA: Judson Press, 1983).

Briggs, J.H.Y. 'Evangelical Ecumenism: The Amalgamation of General and Particular Baptists in 1891', Part I *BQ* 34.3 (July, 1991), pp. 99-115; Part II *BQ* 34.4 (October, 1991), pp. 160-79.

———. 'F.A. Cox of Hackney: Nineteenth-Century Baptist Theologian, Historian, Controversialist, and Apologist', *BQ* 38.8 (October, 2000), pp. 392-411.

———. *The English Baptists of the Nineteenth Century* (A History of the English Baptists, 3; Didcot: Baptist Historical Society, 1994).

Brown, Raymond. *The English Baptists of the Eighteenth Century* (A History of the English Baptists, 2; London: Baptist Historical Society, 1986).

Button, William. *Remarks on a treatise entitled, The gospel of Christ worthy of all acceptation. Wherein the nature of special faith in Christ in* [sic] *considered, and several of Mr. F's mistakes are pointed out* (London: J. Buckland, 1785).

Carlile, John C. *The Story of the English Baptists* (London: James Clarke, 1905).

Cathcart, William (ed.). *The Baptist Encyclopædia: A Dictionary of the Doctrines, Ordinances, Usages, Confessions of Faith, Sufferings, Labors, and Successes, and of the General History of the Baptist Denomination in All Lands. With Numerous Biographical Sketches of Distinguished American and Foreign Baptists, and a Supplement* (Philadelphia: Louis H. Everts, 1881). *s.v.* 'Fuller, Rev. Andrew', pp. 420-422.

Catherall, Gordon A. 'Bristol College and the Jamaican Mission: A Caribbean Contribution.' *BQ* 35.6 (April, 1994), pp. 294-302.

———. 'The Native Baptist Church', *BQ* 24.2 (April, 1971), pp. 65-73.

Champion, L.G. 'Evangelical Calvinism and the Structures of Baptist Church Life', *BQ* 28.5 (January, 1980), pp. 196-208.

———. 'The Letters of John Newton to John Ryland', *BQ* 27.4 (October, 1977), pp. 157-63.

———. 'The Theology of John Ryland: Its Sources and Influences', *BQ* 28.1 (January, 1979), pp. 17-29.

Champion, L.G. (ed.) *The Communication of the Christian Faith: Presented to The Rev. Dr. A. Dakin Principal Emeritus of Bristol*

Baptist College on the occasion of his 80th birthday 21st November, 1964 (Bristol: Bristol Baptist College, 1964).

Clipsham, E.F. *Andrew Fuller and the Baptist Mission Foundations* 10.1 (January, 1967), pp. 4-18.

———. 'Andrew Fuller and Fullerism: A Study in Evangelical Calvinism': '1: The Development of a Doctrine', *BQ* 20.3 (July, 1963), pp. 99-114; '2: Fuller and John Calvin', *BQ* 20.4 (October, 1963), pp. 146-54; '3: The Gospel Worthy of All Acceptation', *BQ* 20.5 (January, 1964), pp. 214-25; '4: Fuller as a Theologian', *BQ* 20.6 (April, 1964), pp. 268-76.

———. 'Andrew Fuller's Doctrine of Salvation' (BD thesis, University of Oxford, 1961).

———. 'Fuller, Andrew', in Donald M. Lewis (ed.), *The Blackwell Dictionary of Evangelical Biography 1730–1860*. Volume I: *A–J* (Oxford: Blackwell, 1995), pp. 414-15.

Coleridge, Samuel Taylor. *Notes on English Divines* (ed. Derwent Coleridge; London: E. Moxon, 1853).

Conant, William C. *Narratives of remarkable conversions and revival incidents... An Account of the rise and progress of the Great Awakening of 1857-8* (New York: Derby & Jackson, 1858).

Cook, Richard B. *The Story of the Baptists in all Ages and Countries* (Greenwood, SC: Attic Press, 1976 [1884]).

Cox, F.A. *History of the Baptist Missionary Society, from 1792 to 1842, to which is Added a Sketch of the General Baptist Mission* (2 vols; London: T. Ward, and G. & J. Dyer, 1842).

Cox, Norman Wade (ed.). *Encyclopedia of Southern Baptists*. Volume I: *Ab–Ken* (Nashville, TN: Broadman Press, 1958), s.v. 'Fuller, Andrew,' pp. 513-14.

Crist, T. 'Isaac Mann's Collection of Letters', *BQ* 26.3 (July, 1975), pp. 134-39.

Cross, Anthony R. 'Dispelling the Myth of English Baptist Baptismal Sacramentalism', *BQ* 38.8 (October, 2000), pp. 367-91.

Crunden, P.H. 'Records Stored at Clipston Baptist Church', *BQ* 25.7 (July, 1974), pp. 305-308.

Dix, Kenneth. *Strict and Particular: English Strict and Particular Baptists in the Nineteenth Century* (Didcot: Baptist Historical Society, 2001).

———. 'Varieties of High Calvinism Among Nineteenth-Century Particular Baptists', *BQ* 38.2 (April, 1999), pp. 56-69.

Duncan, Pope Alexander, Sr.. 'The Influence of Andrew Fuller on Calvinism' (ThD thesis, Southern Baptist Theological Seminary, 1917).

Eddins, John William, Jr.. 'Andrew Fuller's Theology of Grace' (ThD thesis, Southern Baptist Theological Seminary, 1957).

Ella, George M. 'John Gill and the Charge of Hyper-Calvinism', *BQ* 36.4 (October, 1995), pp. 160-77.

_____. *Law and Gospel in the Theology of Andrew Fuller* (Eggleston: Go Publications, 1996).

Elwyn, T.S.H. 'Particular Baptists of the Northamptonshire Baptist Association as Reflected in the Circular Letters 1765-1820', *BQ* 36.8 (October, 1996), pp. 368-81.

_____. 'Particular Baptists of the Northamptonshire Baptist Association as Reflected in the Circular Letters 1765-1820 (*continued*)', *BQ* 37.1 (January, 1997), pp. 3-19.

_____. *The Northamptonshire Baptist Association* (London: Carey Kingsgate Press, 1964).

Fuller, Andrew. *A Sermon on the Importance of a Deep and Intimate Knowledge of Divine Truth; Delivered at an Association of Baptist Ministers and Churches at St. Albans, Hertfordshire, June 1, 1796* (Elizabeth-Town: Shepard Kollock for Cornelius Davis, New York, [c.1797]).

_____. *Dialogues, letters, and Essays on Various Subjects. To Which is Annexed an Essay on Truth: Containing an Inquiry into its Nature and Importance with the Causes of Error, and The Reasons of Its Being Permitted* (Middlebury, VT: Samuel Swift, 1811).

_____. *Memoirs of Rev. Samuel Pearce, A.M., Who was United with Carey and Others in Establishing Missions in India, 1793...with additions from his correspondence with Dr. Carey &c. by his son, Rev. W.H. Pearce, missionary at Calcutta* (New York: American Tract Society, [c.1830]).

_____. *The Backslider: or, an Enquiry Into The Nature, Symptoms, and Effects of Religious Declension, with the means of Recovery* (New York: American Tract Society, 1840).

_____. *The Calvinistic and Socinian Systems Examined and Compared; As To Their Moral Tendency; in a Series of Letters Addressed to the Friends of a Vital and Practical Religion* (Philadelphia: Lang & Ustick, 1796).

_____. *The Complete Works of the Rev. Andrew Fuller, With a Memoir of his Life by the Rev. Andrew Gunton Fuller* (ed. A.G. Fuller; rev. ed. J. Belcher; 3 vols; Harrisonburg, VA: Sprinkle Publications, 1988 [1845]).

_____. *'Pure Religion and Undefiled': Spiritual Letters of Andrew Fuller* (compiled by Michael A.G. Haykin; Toronto: Canadian Christian Publications, 1994).

Fuller, Andrew Gunton. *Andrew Fuller* (London: Hodder & Stoughton, 1882).

_____. *The Principal Works and Remains of the Rev. Andrew Fuller with a Memoir of His Life by His Son* (London: Henry G. Bohn, 1852).

Fuller, Thomas Ekins. *A Memoir of the Life and Writings of Andrew Fuller. By his grandson, Thomas Ekins Fuller* (London: J. Heaton & Son, 1863).
Gooding, William J. *A Discharge of Royal Artillery from the Citadel of Truth, upon Fuller's Fleet in Arminian Bay, under the Command of Sigma* (Woodbridge: n.p., 1812).
Gordon, Grant. 'The Call of Dr John Ryland, Jr.', *BQ* 34.5 (January, 1992), pp. 214-28.
Greenall, R.L. (ed.). *The Kettering Connection: Northamptonshire Baptists and Overseas Mission* (Leicester: Department of Adult Education, University of Leciester, 1993).
Griffith, Gwilym Oswald. *A Pocket History of the Baptist Movement* (London: Kingsgate Press, n.d.).
Haldane, Robert. *Letter to Dr. Ryland* (Edinburgh: n.p., 1816).
Hancock, N.P. 'Healing the Breach: Benjamin Godwin and the Serampore "Schism"', *BQ* 35.3 (July, 1993), pp. 121-33.
Harrison, F.M.W. 'Nottinghamshire Baptists: Rise and Expansion', *BQ* 25.2 (April, 1973), pp. 59-73.
_____. 'The Nottinghamshire Baptists: Church Relations, Social Composition, Finance, Theology', *BQ* 26.4 (October, 1975), pp. 169-91.
Hayden, Eric W. 'Joshua Thomas: Welsh Baptist Historian', *BQ* 23.3 (July, 1969), pp. 126-37.
Haykin, Michael A.G.. '"A Habitation of God, Through the Spirit": John Sutcliff (1752–1814) and the Revitalization of the Calvinistic Baptists in the Late Eighteenth Century', *BQ* 34.7 (July, 1992), pp. 304-19.
_____. 'Andrew Fuller (1754–1815) and the Free Offer of the Gospel', *Reformation Today* 183 (September–October, 2001), pp. 29-32.
_____. 'A Socinian and Calvinist Compared: Joseph Priestley and Andrew Fuller on the Propriety of Prayer to Christ', *Nederlands Archief voor Kerkgeschiedenis/Dutch Review of Church History* 73 (1993), pp. 178-98.
_____. 'On Friendship: John Ryland and Andrew Fuller', *Reformation Today* 140 (July–August, 1994), pp. 26-30.
_____. 'Fuller, Andrew', in Timothy Larsen (ed.), *Biographical Dictionary of Evangelicals* (Leicester: InterVarsity Press, 2003), , pp. 241-44.
_____. '"Hazarding All for God at a Clap": The Spirituality of Baptism among British Calvinistic Baptists', *BQ* 38.4 (October, 1999), pp. 185-95.
_____. 'Particular Redemption in the Writings of Andrew Fuller (1754–1815', in D.W. Bebbington (ed.), *The Gospel in the World*

(Studies in Baptist History and Thought, 1; Carlisle: Paternoster Press, 2002), pp. 107-28.

_____. '"Resisting Evil": Civil Retaliation, Non-resistance, and the Interpretation of Matthew 5:39a among Eighteenth-Century Calvinistic Baptists', *BQ* 36.5 (January, 1996), pp. 212-27.

_____. *The Armies of the Lamb: The Spirituality of Andrew Fuller* (Classics of Reformed Spirituality, 3; Dundas, ON: Joshua Press, 2001).

_____. '"The Oracles of God": Andrew Fuller and the Scriptures', *Churchman* 103 (1989), pp. 60-76.

Hervey, G. Winfred. *The Story of Baptist Missions in Foreign Lands, from the Time of Carey to the Present Date* (St. Louis: C.R. Barns Publishing, rev. edn, 1892).

Ivimey, Joseph. *The Perpetual Intercession of Christ for His Church; a source of consolation under the loss of useful ministers. A sermon preached at Eagle-Street meeting, London, May the 21st, 1815, as a tribute of respect to the memory of the late Rev. Andrew Fuller, of Kettering, secretary to the Baptist missionary society* (London: T. Gardiner & Son, 1815).

James, Sharon. 'Revival and Renewal in Baptist Life: The Contribution of William Steadman (1764–1837)', *BQ* 37.6 (April, 1998), pp. 263-82.

Keown, Harlice Edmond. 'The Preaching of Andrew Fuller' (ThM thesis, Southern Baptist Theological Seminary, 1957).

Kirkby, Arthur H. *Andrew Fuller* (London: Independent Press, 1961).

_____. 'The Theology of Andrew Fuller and its Relation to Calvinism' (PhD thesis, University of Edinburgh, 1956).

Landels, William. *Baptist Worthies: A Series of Biographical Sketches of Distinguished Men who have held and advocated the Principles of the Baptist Denomination* (London: Baptist Tract and Book Society, 1883).

Laws, Gilbert. *Andrew Fuller, Pastor, Theologian, Ropeholder* (London: Carey Press, 1942).

Lord, F. Townley. *Achievement: A Short History of the Baptist Missionary Society, 1792–1942* (London: Carey Press, n.d.).

Manley, Kenneth R. 'John Rippon and Baptist Historiography', *BQ* 28.3 (July, 1979), 109-25.

_____. 'Ordination Among Australian Baptists', *BQ* 28.4 (October, 1979), pp. 159-83.

_____. 'Robert Bowyer: Artist, Publisher and Preacher', *BQ* 23.1 (January, 1969),pp. 32-46.

_____. 'The Making of an Evangelical Baptist Leader', *BQ* 26.6 (April, 1976), pp. 254-74.

Martin, John. *Thoughts on the Duty of Man Relative to Faith in Jesus Christ; in which Mr Andrew Fuller's Leading Propositions on that Subject are Considered* (3 vols; London, 1788–89).

McBeth, H. Leon. *A Sourcebook for Baptist Heritage* (Nashville, TN: Broadman Press, 1990).

_____. *The Baptist Heritage: Four Centuries of Baptist Witness* (Nashville, TN: Broadman Press, 1987).

McLean, Archibald. *A reply to Mr. Fuller's Appendix to his book on The gospel worthy of all acceptation* (New York: Scatcherd and Adams, 1839).

Milner, J. 'Andrew Fuller', *Reformation Today* 17 (January–February, 1974), pp. 18-29.

Moon, Norman S. 'Caleb Evans, Founder of the Bristol Education Society', *BQ* 24.4 (October, 1971), pp. 175-89.

Morden, Peter. *Offering Christ to the World: Andrew Fuller (1754–1815) and the Revival of Eighteenth Century Particular Baptist Life* (Studies in Baptist History and Thought, 8; Carlisle: Paternoster Press, 2003).

Morris, J.W. *Memoirs of the Life and Writings of the Rev. Andrew Fuller, late Pastor of the Baptist Church in Kettering, and Secretary to the Baptist Missionary Society* (High Wycombe, 1816; London: Wightman and Cramp, 2nd edn, 1826; Boston: Lincoln & Edmands, 1830 [1st American edn from the last London edn]).

_____. *Periodical Accounts Relative to the Baptist Missionary Society* [*Periodical Accounts Relative to a Society, formed among The Particular Baptists, for Propagating the Gospel among the heathen*] (3 vols; London: J.W. Morris, 1800).

Murray, D.B. 'Baptists in Scotland Before 1869', *BQ* 23.6 (April, 1970), pp. 251-65.

_____. 'The Scotch Baptist Tradition in Great Britain', *BQ* 33.4 (October, 1989), pp. 186-98.

Myers, John Brown (ed.). *The Centenary Volume of the Baptist Missionary Society 1792–1892* (2 vols; Holborn: Baptist Missionary Society, 1892).

Naylor, Peter. *Calvinism, Communion and the Baptists: A Study of English Calvinistic Baptists from the Late 1600s to the Early 1800s* (Studies in Baptist History and Thought, 7; Carlisle: Paternoster Press, 2003).

_____. *Picking up a Pin for the Lord: English Particular Baptists from 1688 to the Early Nineteenth Century* (Durham: Grace Publications Trust, 1992).

Nettles, Thomas J. 'Andrew Fuller (1754–1815)', in Michael A.G. Haykin (ed.), *The British Particular Baptists 1638–1910*. Volume II (Springfield, MO: Particular Baptist Press, 2000), pp. 97-141.

_____. *By His Grace and for His Glory: A Historical, Theological and Practical Study of the Doctrines of Grace in Baptist Life* (Grand Rapids, MI: Baker, 1986).

Newman, William. *Reflections on the Fall of a Great Man. A sermon...death of Rev. Andrew Fuller, of Kettering* (London: n.p., 1815).

Nuttall, Geoffrey F. 'Letters from Robert Hall to John Ryland 1791–1824', *BQ* 34.3 (July, 1991), 127-31.

———. 'The State of Religion in Northamptonshire (1793) by Andrew Fuller', *BQ* 29.4 (October, 1981), pp. 177-79.

Nutter, Bernard. *The Story of the Cambridge Baptists and the Struggle for Religious Liberty* (Cambridge: W. Heffer & Sons, 1912).

Oliver, R.W. 'The Emergence of a Strict and Particular Baptist Community Among the English Calvinistic Baptists, 1770–1850', (PhD thesis, CNAA [London Bible College], 1986)

Payne, E.A. 'Abraham Booth 1734–1806', *BQ* 26.1 (January, 1975), pp. 28-43.

———. 'Andrew Fuller and James Deakin, 1803', *BQ* 7 (1934–35), pp. 326-33.

———. 'Andrew Fuler as a Letter Writer', *BQ* 15.7 (July, 1954), pp. 290-96.

———. 'An 1820 Letter on Election', *BQ* 24.4 (October, 1971), pp. 170-74.

———. 'Baptists and the Ministry', *BQ* 25.2 (April, 1973), pp. 51-58.

———. *The Baptist Union: A Short History* (London: Baptist Union of Great Britain and Ireland, 1959).

———. *The First Generation: Early Leaders of the Baptist Missionary Society in England and India* (London: Carey Press, [1936]).

———. 'The Venerable John Stanger of Bessels Green', *BQ* 27.7 (July, 1978), pp. 300-20.

Potts, E. Daniel. *British Baptist Missionaries in India 1793–1837: The History of Serampore and Its Missions* (Cambridge: Cambridge University Press, 1967).

———. 'William Ward's Missionary Journal', *BQ* 25.3 (July, 1973), pp. 111-14.

Ramsbottom, Paul. 'A Chiliasm of Despair?: The Community Worshipping at St. George's Road Baptist Chapel, Manchester', *BQ* 37.5 (January, 1998), pp. 227-37.

Rimmington, Gerald T. 'The Baptist Churches and Society in Leicester in 1881–1914', *BQ* 38.7 (July, 2000), pp. 332-49.

Roberts, Phil. 'Andrew Fuller', in Timothy George and David S. Dockery (eds), *Baptist Theologians* (Nashville, TN: Broadman Press, 1990), pp. 121-39.

Robison, O.C. 'The Particular Baptists in England: 1760–1820' (DPhil thesis, University of Oxford, 1963).

Rushton, William, Jr. *A defence of particular redemption; wherein the doctrine of the late Mr. Fuller, relative to the atonement of Christ, is tried by the word of God*. In four letters to a Baptist minister (New York: Joseph Spencer, 1834).

Ryland, John. *The work of faith, the labour of love, and the patience of hope illustrated; in the life and death of the Rev. Andrew Fuller, late Pastor of the Baptist Church at Kettering, and Secretary to the Baptist Missionary Society, from it's Commencement, in 1792* (London: Button and Son, 1816;2nd edn, 1818).

_____ (ed.). *The life and death of the Rev. Andrew Fuller, late pastor of the Baptist church at Kettering, and secretary to the Baptist Missionary Society...chiefly extracted from his own papers by John Ryland, D.D.* (Philadelphia: American Baptist Publication Society, 1818).

Scrutator [Jerram, Charles]. *Letters to an universalist; containing a review of the controversy between Mr. Vidler and Mr. Fuller* (Clipstone: J.W. Morris, 1802).

Sell, Alan P.F. '*The Gospel its own Witness*: Deism, Thomas Paine and Andrew Fuller', in Alan P.F. Sell, *Enlightenment, Ecumenism, Evangel: Theological Themes and Thinkers 1550–2000* (Studies in Evangelical History and Thought; Carlisle: Paternoster Press, 2005), ch. 4.

_____. *The Great Debate: Calvinism, Arminianism and Salvation* (Eugene, OR: Wipf & Stock, 1998 [1982]).

Sellers, Ian. 'John Howard Hinton, Theologian', *BQ* 33.3 (July, 1989), pp. 119-32.

_____. 'Other Times, Other Ministries: John Fawcett and Alexander McLaren', *BQ* 32.4 (October, 1987), pp. 181-99.

_____. 'W.T. Whitley: A Commemorative Essay', *BQ* 37.4 (October, 1997), pp. 159-73.

Sharpe, Eric. 'Bristol Baptist College and the Church's Hymnody', *BQ* 28.1 (January, 1979), pp. 7-16.

Shelley, Bruce L. 'Where Would We Be Without Staupitz?', *Christianity Today* 35.15 (16 December 1991), pp. 29-31.

Short, K.R.M. 'A Note on the Sierra Leone Mission and Religious Freedom', *BQ* 28.8 (October, 1980), pp. 355-60.

Smith, A. Christopher. 'The Spirit and Letter of Carey's Catalytic Watchword: A Study in the Transmission of Baptist Tradition', *BQ* 33.5 (January, 1990), pp. 226-37.

South, Thomas Jacob. 'The Response of Andrew Fuller to the Sandemanian View of Saving Faith' (ThD thesis, Mid-America Baptist Theological Seminary, 1994).

Stanley, Brian. 'Planting Self-Governing Churches: British Baptist Ecclesiology in the Missionary Context', *BQ* 34.8 (October, 1992), pp. 378-89.

———. 'Spurgeon and the Baptist Missionary Society', *BQ* 29.7 (July, 1982), pp. 319-28.

———. *The History of the Baptist Missionary Society 1792–1992* (Edinburgh: T&T Clark, 1992).

Stewart, W.J. *The Pioneer Secretary of Modern Missions* (Saint John, NB: n.p., 1890).

Stillwell, J.R. *A Hundred Years of Baptist Work in Heathen Lands, 1792–1892* (Toronto: Dudley & Burns, 1892).

Stuart, Charles. *A Short Memoir of the Late Mr. Andrew Fuller* (London: Britten & Son, 1815).

Taylor, Dan. *The Friendly conclusion occasioned by the letters of Agnostos to Andrew Fuller* (London, 1790).

Agnostos [Dan Taylor]. *The reality and efficacy of divine grace...Considered in a series of letters to the Rev. Mr. Andrew Fuller; containing remarks upon the observations of the Rev. Dan Taylor, on Mr. Fuller's reply to Philanthropos By Agnostos* (London: Lepard, [1788]).

Taylor, Rosemary. 'English Baptist Periodicals', *BQ* 27.2 (April, 1977), pp. 50-82.

Thomson, Ronald W. *Heroes of the Baptist Church* (London: Carey Kingsgate Press, 1937), pp. 111-16.

Torbet, Robert George. *A History of the Baptists* (Valley Forge, PA: Judson Press, 1963).

Tull, James E. *Shapers of Baptist Thought* (Valley Forge, PA: Judson Press, 1972; Macon, GA: Mercer University Press, 1984).

Underhill, Edward Bean. *Christian Missions in the East and West, in Connection with the Baptist Missionary Society: 1792–1873* (London: Yates & Alexander, 2nd edn, 1873).

Underwood, A.C. *A History of the English Baptists* (London: Kingsgate Press, 1947).

Vedder, Henry C. *A Short History of the Baptists* (Philadelphia: American Baptist Publication Society, 1907).

Walker, Michael. 'The Presidency of the Lord's Table among Nineteenth Century English Baptists', *BQ* 32.5 (January, 1988), pp. 208-23.

Ward, W.R. 'The Baptists and the Transformation of the Church, 1780–1830', *BQ* 25.4 (October, 1973), pp. 167-184.

Ward, William R.. *A sketch of the character of the late Rev. Andrew Fuller...Lal Bazar Chapel, Calcutta* (Bristol: J.G. Fuller, 1817).

Watts, Michael R. *The Dissenters.* Volume I: *From the Reformation to the French Revolution* (Oxford: Clarendon Press, 1978).

_____. *The Dissenters*. Volume II: *The Expansion of Evangelical Nonconformity 1791–1859* (Oxford: Clarendon Press, 1995).

Weller, Paul. 'Freedom and Witness in a Multi-Religious Society: A Baptist Perspective': Part I, *BQ* 33.6 (April, 1990), pp. 252-64; Part II, *BQ* 33.7 (July, 1990), pp. 302-15.

Wheeler, Heather. 'Pole Moor Baptist Chapel, Scammonden, Huddersfield: Reflections on the Early History; also the 1790 Covenant', *BQ* 37.3 (July, 1997), 108-30.

Whelan, Timothy. 'Robert Hall and the Bristol Slave-Trade Debate of 1787–1788', *BQ* 38.5 (January, 2000), pp. 212-24.

Whitley, W.T. *A History of the British Baptists* (London: Charles Griffin, 1923; London: Kingsgate Press, 2nd rev. edn, 1932).

White, B.R. 'Open and Closed Membership among English and Welsh Baptists', *BQ* 24.7 (July, 1972), pp. 330-34.

Williams, Glanmor. 'Welsh Baptists in an Age of Revolution 1776–1832', *BQ* 33.5 (January, 1990), pp. 204-14.

Young, Doyle L. 'The Place of Andrew Fuller in the Developing Modern Missions Movement' (PhD thesis, Southwestern Baptist Theological Seminary, 1981).

Websites

http://docsouth.unc.edu/imls/fuller/fuller.html [The Great Question Answered, No. 42, By Rev. Andrew Fuller]

http://www.mun.ca/rels/restmov/texts/believers/weishampelthw/THW036.HTM ['Conversion of Rev. Andrew Fuller', compiled by J.F. Weishampel, Sr., *The Testimony of a Hundred Witnesses* (1858)]

http://www.evangelica.de/The_Evangelical_Liberalism_of_Andrew_Fuller.htm

http://www.evangelica.de ['Why I am Not a Follower of Andrew Fuller']

http://www2.tnweb.com/pbc/Baptists/afuller.htm ['Election Consistent']

Subject Index

Act of Toleration (1689) 4, 251, 252, 255
Age of Reason 181
Anabaptists 177
Anglicans 137, 205, 228, 246
annihilationism 190
antinomianism/antinomians 7, 24, 45, 47, 48, 74-82, 142, 162
Arianism/Arians 44, 77, 88, 139
Arminian Methodists 25
Arminianism/Arminians 4, 21, 22, 44, 45, 47, 49, 58, 59, 63, 64, 83-121, 139, 142, 203, 207, 217, 221
Arnesby Baptist Church 8
assurance 18, 19
Athanasian Creed 143
atonement 24, 49, 52, 66, 72, 87, 91, 108, 109, 110, 112, 114, 115, 116, 119, 120, 139, 145, 146, 148, 153, 156, 163, 172, 200, 214-17, 218, 219, 220

baptism 6, 16, 80, 144
Baptist colleges 221
Baptist historiography 3, 4
Baptist Missionary Society 1, 12, 14, 17, 27, 31-39, 41, 203, 228, 237-55
Baptist Union 222
Baptists 128, 137, 144, 169, 251
Baxterianism 80
Bengal 36
Bible translation 37, 246
biblical prophecy 28, 29
Bristol Baptist Academy 3, 250
British and Foreign Bible Society 137

Call to Prayer (1784) 12, 21, 27-31, 244
Calvinism/Calvinists 74, 76, 80, 82, 86, 87, 88, 89, 91, 93, 95, 96, 101, 105, 106, 115, 117, 118, 119, 120, 121, 139, 143, 144, 147, 148, 149, 150, 151, 152, 154, 157, 161, 162, 163, 164, 165, 166, 168, 169, 177, 203, 209, 218, 220, 241, 244
Calvinistic Methodists 25, 37, 223, 228
calvinistic antinomianism 74
Cambridge Platonists 177
Cannon Street Baptist Church, Birmingham 14
Christology 141, 145, 153, 164
Church Missionary Society 238
Church of England 4, 17, 144, 213
Church of Scotland 225
Clapham Sect 246, 247, 251
Clipstone Baptist Church 32
Congregationalists 9, 17, 43, 45, 137
conversion 5, 6, 11, 12, 57, 151-54, 161, 162, 207, 227
Corporation Act (1661) 143
covenant 2, 25, 79, 112, 182

Deism/Deists 23, 44, 74, 75, 76, 122-38, 165, 168
Dissent/Dissenters 2, 4, 141, 143, 144, 242, 252
doctrinal antinomianism 76
Dutch Remonstrance (1610) 44
duty faith 43, 52, 53, 54, 56-58, 78, 81

Earthen Vessel Baptists 81
East India Company 246, 247, 248, 249, 251
election/elect 48, 49, 51, 52, 53, 87, 101, 102, 105, 106, 107, 108, 116, 118, 120, 217, 218, 219
Enlightenment, the 174
eschatology 15, 28
evangelical Anglicans 235
evangelical Arminianism/Arminians 90, 91, 93
Evangelical Awakening 153
evangelical Baptists 47-66
evangelical Calvinism/Calvinists 11, 12, 22, 26, 43, 46, 47-66, 145, 204, 209, 244

Subject Index

Evangelicalism/Evangelicals 36, 46, 202, 226, 227, 228, 230, 242
Evangelical Revival 4, 8, 11

faith 102, 115, 120, 156, 206, 208, 227
federal theology 79
foreknowledge 107, 113, 117
Founders movement 48
free agency 94, 95
French Revolution (1789) 23, 252, 253
Fullerism/Fullerites 22, 23, 41, 44, 48, 72, 76, 77, 81, 241

General Baptists 40, 44, 90, 174, 203, 217
George Street Baptist Church, Hull 23
Gillism 49, 72
Glasites 225
God's Word (see Scripture)
Gospel Standard Baptists 80
grace 53, 54, 86, 87, 88, 98, 99, 100, 101, 105, 107, 118, 120

Hebden Bridge Baptist Church 35
High Calvinism/Calvinists 2, 3, 4, 5, 6, 7, 8, 9, 11, 12, 19, 21, 22, 24, 36, 40, 43-73, 75, 76, 77, 78, 79, 80, 81, 82, 85, 86, 203, 204, 205, 206, 208, 221, 222
Holy Spirit 2, 5, 12, 28, 45, 46, 54, 55, 68, 71, 78, 87, 93, 100, 103, 104, 105, 117, 120, 128, 130, 136, 153, 166, 204, 218, 230
Huntingdonian antinomianism 76, 77, 78, 79
hyper Calvinism/Calvinists (see High Calvinism)
hyperism 75, 78

imputation 58, 210-14, 217, 220
Independents 174
infant baptism 90
inspiration 128, 135, 136
irresistable grace 91

justification/justification by faith 2, 43, 47, 48, 49, 51, 80, 145, 153, 206, 210, 213, 226, 227, 229

Kent and Sussex Baptist Association 175
Kettering Baptist Church (the 'Little Meeting') 10, 12, 13, 14, 15, 16-18, 22, 31, 38, 40, 141

latitudinarianism 44
Little Prescot Street Baptist Church, London 203
London Confession (1644) 143
London Missionary Society 238, 247
Lord's Supper 80

McLeanite Baptists 228, 229, 230
Methodism/Methodists 89, 90, 137, 153, 154
millennium, the 15, 29, 185
miracles 123
missionary movement 74, 75
moderate Calvinism, see evangelical Calvinism
Modern Question, the 9, 40, 43-73, 80
moral ability/inability 58-66
moral law 80, 82

Neonomianism 78, 80
New Connexion of General Baptists 22, 64, 90
New Divinity School/Movement 24, 25, 62
New England Theology 64, 85, 203, 212, 213, 214, 215, 220
New Jersey College 26
Newtonian science 123
Nicene Creed 143
Nonconformists 251
Northamptonshire Baptist Association 8, 10, 11, 13, 14, 22, 27, 28, 29, 30, 32, 33, 47, 125, 127, 128, 237, 240

Olney Baptist Church 8, 32, 127, 128
original sin 44, 62, 63, 66, 67

Particular Baptist Fund 10
Particular Baptists 1, 2, 3, 4, 5, 8, 12, 21, 22, 23, 24, 26, 30, 31, 40-42, 44, 76, 125, 131, 143, 145, 203, 204, 210, 214, 215, 217, 221, 223, 237, 239, 241, 244

particular redemption 87, 110, 111, 118, 119, 217-22
particularism 200
passive faith 43
Pelagianism/Pelagians 44, 46, 59, 67, 70, 93
perseverence of the saints 48, 118, 119, 120
Platonism 176
postmillennialism 15, 28, 29, 240
practical antinomianism 75
Prayer Call (1784), see Call to Prayer (1784)
preaching 13-15
predestination 87, 115, 148
premillennialism 185
propitiation 115
pseudo-Calvinism/pseudo-Calvinists 86, 87, 90, 108, 109, 115, 116
Puritanism/Puritans 19, 77, 85, 232

reason 123, 181
regeneration 55, 60, 91, 94, 104, 105, 118, 206, 207
Renaissance, the 177
repentance 57
reprobation 43, 47, 48
revelation 123, 129, 134, 135
righteousness 45, 50, 211, 212
Roman Catholics/Romanism 29, 207
Rothwell Congregational Church 45

sanctification 101, 102
Sandemanianism 23, 50, 54, 223-36
Scotch Baptists 37
Scottish Baptists 23, 54, 206, 227, 228, 229, 230
Scripture(s)/God's Word 55, 85, 86, 90, 92, 102, 103, 107, 111, 112, 113, 114, 116, 123, 124, 126, 127, 128, 129, 130, 131, 133, 134, 135, 136, 137, 138, 146, 147, 148, 159-61, 162, 163, 166, 167, 168, 171, 177, 178, 179, 181, 182, 183, 187, 188, 190, 192, 200, 202, 208, 224
Second London Confession (1677/1689) 69, 210, 211
Serampore Press 248
Serampore Trio 246, 250, 253
Six Articles (1770, General Baptist) 90, 93

Socinianism/Socinians 23, 44, 49, 74, 75, 76, 77, 139-73, 185
Soham Baptist Church 2, 3, 4, 5, 6, 7-8, 10-11, 16, 24, 141, 224
soteriology 58, 59, 63, 86, 87, 88, 90, 136, 142
Southern Baptist Convention 48
Spiritualists 177
St Mary's Baptist Church, Norwich 23
statement of faith 12
Strict and Particular Baptists 47, 80
Strict Baptist Historical Society 48
Strict Baptists 209
subjectivism 230, 231
substitution 112, 214-17, 219, 220
supralapsarianism 43, 47
Synod/Canons of Dort (1619) 44, 70, 86, 117, 221

Taylorism 66
Test Act (1673) 143
toleration 251-52
total depravity 2, 91, 92, 93, 94, 95, 96, 97, 104, 105, 107, 110, 118
Trinity 126, 148, 161, 165, 169, 170, 171

Unitarianism/Unitarians 23, 44, 139, 165, 166, 167, 175
universalism 44, 45, 113, 174-202, 217

Vellore Mutiny 247-49, 250

warrant of faith 6
Warwickshire Baptists 30
Welsh Baptists 228
Wesleyan Methodists 17
Western [Baptist] Association 3, 5, 30
Westminster Confession (1647) 70
Wisbech Baptist Church 8
Word of God, see Scripture(s)

Yale College 27

Person Index

Ames, W. 64
Amphilochius of Iconium 223
Arminius, J. 44
Ascol, T. 48
Augustine 141, 177

Backus, I. 228
Barrow, Dr W. 249, 250
Basil of Caesarea 223
Bauckham, R.J. 177, 178
Baxter, R. 80
Belcher, J. 41
Bellamy, J. 9, 24, 64, 203, 214, 217
Belsham, T. 142, 145, 152, 154, 157, 159, 161, 166, 168
Berridge, J. 235
Booth, A. 24, 25, 54, 80, 203-22
Brackney, W.H. 34
Brainerd, D. 9, 50, 238, 243
Briggs, J.H.Y. 8
Brine, J. 3, 40, 46, 47, 51, 57, 64, 75, 76, 78, 79
Brunsdon, D. 246
Bunyan, J. 85
Button, Mr 90
Button, W. 22, 80, 221

Calvin, J. 86, 116, 136, 141, 221, 223
Carey, S.P. 33
Carey, W. 31, 32, 33, 34, 35, 47, 50, 73, 137, 205, 211, 224, 237, 238, 239, 240, 241, 244, 245, 246, 247, 248, 250, 251, 253, 254, 255
Clayton, Mr 144
Clipsham, E.F. 21, 48, 129, 239, 240, 249
Collins, A. 123
Cox, S. 177, 178
Crisp, T. 74, 75, 211, 213

Denck, J. 177
Didymus of Alexandria 177
Diodorus of Tarsus 177
Diver, J. 7, 8

Doddridge, P. 9
Dwight, T. 27

Edwards, Dr. John 11
Edwards, J. 9, 11-12, 15, 19, 24, 25, 27, 28, 29, 30, 41, 42, 50, 58, 59, 60, 61, 62, 63, 64, 67, 85, 86, 154, 155, 163, 203, 204, 207, 215, 216, 224, 232, 233, 234, 235, 238
Edwards, Jr, J. 24, 203, 214, 217
Eliot, J. 50, 243
Ella, G.M. 48
Emmet, C.W. 179
Erasmus, D. 141
Erigena, J.S. 177
Erskine, J. 27, 36
Evans, C. 3, 228
Evans, H. 3
Eve, J. 2, 3, 4, 5, 7, 8

Farel, G. 223
Farrar, F.W. 177
Fawcett, J. 34, 244
Fawkner, R. 131
Finney, C. 70
Foreman, J. 81
Foskett, B. 3
Foster, F.H. 213
Fountain, J. 253, 254
Fuller, A.G. 1, 6, 7, 13, 14, 16, 247
Fuller, Ann (née Coles) 20, 37
Fuller, Bathoni 19
Fuller, R. (father) 1, 2
Fuller, R. (son) 20
Fuller, Sarah (née Gardiner) 9, 19

Gadsby, W. 80, 81, 221, 222
George, T. 48, 52
Gerstner, J.H. 63
Gill, J. 3, 40, 43, 46, 47, 48, 49, 51, 52, 57, 64, 74, 75, 76, 78, 80, 81, 85, 211
Glas, J. 225, 226
Grant, C. 246, 247, 248, 255
Grant, W. 246

Gregory of Nazianzus 223
Gregory of Nyssa 177, 223
Griffith, B.G. 239
Grigg, J. 253, 254
Grotius, H. 214
Gunton, Philippa (grandmother) 2
Gunton, Philippa (mother) 1, 2

Haldane, J. 36, 37, 227
Haldane, R. 36, 37
Hall, J.K. 18
Hall, Jr, R. 39, 41, 143, 144, 148, 169
Hall, Sr, R. 8, 11, 18, 32, 47, 48, 224
Hann, I. 5
Harris, H. 4
Hart, T. 180
Hastings, W. 248
Hayden, R. 3, 14
Haykin, M.A.G. 1, 170, 242
Hick, J. 179, 180
Hindmarsh, B. 19
Hopkins, S. 24, 26, 203, 205, 206, 207, 208, 212, 213
Huntingdon, W. 76, 77, 81, 82
Hussey, J. 3, 43, 44, 45

Ivimey, J. 26, 46

Jukes, A. 177

Kentish, J. 164, 165, 166, 170
Kinghorn, J. 22, 23
Kirby, A.H. 22
Klien-Nikolai, G. 174

Law, W. 177
Lindsey, Hannah 175
Lindsey, T. 142, 159, 161
Lloyd-Jones, D.M. 225
Luther, M. 141, 242

Macauley, Z. 253
Machen, J.G. 69
Marshman, J. 246, 253, 137
Marshman, J.C. 249, 255
Martin, J. 22, 80, 222
Maurice, F.D. 177
Maurice, M. 45
Mayor, J.B. 177
McLaurin, J. 65

McLean, A. 23, 24, 54, 205, 228, 229, 230, 235
McPherson, D. 20
More, Hannah 41, 42
Morris, J.W. 1, 17, 35, 40, 83, 85
Murray, J. 71

Naylor, P. 57
Neill, S. 31, 250
Nettles, T. 48, 51, 215
Nettleton, A. 70, 71
Newman, W. 221
Newton, J. 19, 45
Newton, T. 177
Nuttall, G.F. 41

Oliver, R.W. 48
Origen 176, 177
Owen, J. 85, 204, 213, 216, 232

Packer, J.I. 201
Paine, T. 23, 122, 123, 124, 125, 126, 127, 128, 129, 130, 131, 132, 135, 136, 137
Pal, K. 246
Payne, E.A. 41
Pearce, S. 14, 20, 224
Pelagius 141
Pighius, A. 141
Potts, E.D. 253
Priestley, J. 139, 140, 142, 143, 146, 147, 148, 149, 150, 151, 153, 154, 155, 156, 157, 158, 159, 160, 162, 163, 164, 166, 167, 170
Prochaska, F.K. 125
Purdy, T. 174

Reymond, R. 72
Rippon, J. 34, 40, 41, 75
Robinson, J.A.T. 179
Robinson, R. 131, 145
Rowell, G. 174
Ryland, Jr, J. 8, 10, 14, 15, 16, 17, 18, 22, 25, 26, 29, 30, 32, 33, 34, 36, 37, 39, 45, 47, 76, 84, 85, 86, 125, 131, 134, 171, 210, 215, 217, 218, 221, 224, 250
Ryland, Sr, J. 52

Sandeman, R. 225, 226, 227, 228, 230, 231

Person Index

Scott, T. 205, 206, 207, 208, 228, 237
Scott-Waring, Major J. 248, 249
Sell, A.P.F. 46, 169
Shedd, W.G.T. 61, 62
Silliman, Mr 27
Skepp, J. 46
Smith, J.P. 168
Stanley, B. 17, 33, 35, 238, 245, 251, 255
Steadman, W. 217
Sterry, P. 177
Stevens, J. 81, 221, 222
Stewart, Major C. 248, 249
Sutcliff, J. 8, 27, 28, 29, 32, 33, 85, 86, 127, 128, 135, 214, 224, 235

Taylor, Abraham 9, 47, 85
Taylor, Azor 89
Taylor, D. 22, 64, 67, 83, 88, 89, 90, 91, 93, 94, 95, 96, 98, 99, 100, 108, 109, 110, 112, 120, 206, 217
Taylor, John (brother of Dan) 89
Taylor, John (of Norwich, Arminian) 58
Taylor, John (Unitarian) 44
Taylor, Mary 89
Taylor, N. 62
Theodore of Mopsuestia 177
Thomas, John 18, 237, 238, 239
Thomas, Joshua 22

Timms, J. 31
Tindal, M. 123
Toland, J. 122, 123
Toller, T. 17
Toon, Mrs 20
Toulmin, J. 164, 165, 166, 168, 170
Troeltsch, E. 179
Twining, T. 248, 250, 251

Ursinus, Z. 67

Vidler, W. 24, 174, 175, 176, 180, 181-86, 187, 188, 189, 190, 191, 194, 195, 196, 197, 198, 199, 200, 201
Viret, P. 223

Wallis, B. 31
Wallis, Martha 31
Walpole, Sir R. 37
Ward, W. 39, 137, 246, 253
Wesley, C. 4
Wesley, J. 4, 48, 89, 228
West, S. 203, 214, 217
White, J. 177
Whitefield, G. 4
Whitley, W.T. 41
Wilberforce, W. 128, 247
Williams, S. 58, 59
Williams, W. 228
Witsius, H. 213
Wright, R. 175

Studies in Baptist History and Thought

(All titles uniform with this volume)
Dates in bold are of projected publication
Volumes in this series are not always published in sequence

David Bebbington and Anthony R. Cross (eds)
Global Baptist History
(SBHT vol. 14)

This book brings together studies from the Second International Conference on Baptist Studies which explore different facets of Baptist life and work especially during the twentieth century.

2005 / 1-84227-214-4

David Bebbington (ed.)
The Gospel in the World
International Baptist Studies
(SBHT vol. 1)

This volume of essays from the First International Conference on Baptist Studies deals with a range of subjects spanning Britain, North America, Europe, Asia and the Antipodes. Topics include studies on religious tolerance, the communion controversy and the development of the international Baptist community, and concludes with two important essays on the future of Baptist life that pay special attention to the United States.

2002 / 1-84227-118-0 / xiv + 362pp

Damian Brot
Church of the Baptized or Church of Believers?
A Contribution to the Dialogue between the Catholic Church and the Free Churches with Special Reference to Baptists
(SBHT vol. 26)

The dialogue between the Catholic Church and the Free Churches in Europe has hardly taken place. This book pleads for a commencement of such a conversation. It offers, among other things, an introduction to the American and the international dialogues between Baptists and the Catholic Church and strives to allow these conversations to become fruitful in the European context as well.

2006 / 1-84227-334-5 / *approx. 364pp*

November 2004

Dennis Bustin
Paradox and Perseverence
Hanserd Knollys, Particular Baptist Pioneer in Seventeenth-Century England
(SBHT vol. 23)

The seventeenth century was a significant period in English history during which the people of England experienced unprecedented change and tumult in all spheres of life. At the same time, the importance of order and the traditional institutions of society were being reinforced. Hanserd Knollys, born during this pivotal period, personified in his life the ambiguity, tension and paradox of it, openly seeking change while at the same time cautiously embracing order. As a founder and leader of the Particular Baptists in London and despite persecution and personal hardship, he played a pivotal role in helping shape their identity externally in society and, internally, as they moved toward becoming more formalised by the end of the century.

2006 / 1-84227-259-4 / approx. 324pp

Anthony R. Cross
Baptism and the Baptists
Theology and Practice in Twentieth-Century Britain
(SBHT vol. 3)

At a time of renewed interest in baptism, *Baptism and the Baptists* is a detailed study of twentieth-century baptismal theology and practice and the factors which have influenced its development.

2000 / 0 85364-959-6 / xx + 530pp

Anthony R. Cross and Philip E. Thompson (eds)
Recycling the Past or Researching History?
Studies in Baptist Historiography and Myths
(SBHT vol. 11)

This collection of essays examines the issues of historiography and myths in Baptist history and theology: these include the idea of development in Baptist thought, studies in the church, baptismal sacramentalism, community, spirituality, soul competency, women, Baptist bishops, creeds and the Bible, and overseas missions.

2005 / 1-84227-122-9

Anthony R. Cross and Philip E. Thompson (eds)
Baptist Sacramentalism
(SBHT vol. 5)

This collection of essays includes biblical, historical and theological studies in the theology of the sacraments from a Baptist perspective. Subjects explored include the physical side of being spiritual, baptism, the Lord's supper, the church, ordination, preaching, worship, religious liberty and the issue of disestablishment.

2003 / 1-84227-119-9 / xvi + 278pp

Anthony R. Cross and Philip E. Thompson (eds)
Baptist Sacramentalism 2
(SBHT vol. 25)

This second collection of essays exploring various dimensions of sacramental theology from a Baptist perspective includes biblical, historical and theological studies from scholars from around the world.

2006 / 1-84227-325-6

Paul S. Fiddes
Tracks and Traces
Baptist Identity in Church and Theology
(SBHT vol. 13)

This is a comprehensive, yet unusual, book on the faith and life of Baptist Christians. It explores the understanding of the church, ministry, sacraments and mission from a thoroughly theological perspective. In a series of interlinked essays, the author relates Baptist identity consistently to a theology of covenant and to participation in the triune communion of God.

2003 / 1-84227-120-2 / xvi + 304pp

Stanley K. Fowler
More Than a Symbol
The British Baptist Recovery of Baptismal Sacramentalism
(SBHT vol. 2)

Fowler surveys the entire scope of British Baptist literature from the seventeenth-century pioneers onwards. He shows that in the twentieth century leading British Baptist pastors and theologians recovered an understanding of baptism that connected experience with soteriology and that in doing so they were recovering what many of their forebears had taught.

2002 / 1-84227-052-4 / xvi + 276pp

Michael A.G. Haykin (ed.)
'At the Pure Fountain of Thy Word'
Andrew Fuller as an Apologist
(SBHT vol. 6)

One of the greatest Baptist theologians of the eighteenth and early nineteenth centuries, Andrew Fuller has not had justice done to him. There is little doubt that Fuller's theology lay behind the revitalization of the Baptists in the late eighteenth century and the first few decades of the nineteenth. This collection of essays fills a much needed gap by examining a major area of Fuller's thought, his work as an apologist.

2004 / 1-84227-171-7 / xxii + 276pp

Michael A.G. Haykin
Studies in Calvinistic Baptist Spirituality
(SBHT vol. 15)

In a day when spirituality is in vogue and Christian communities are looking for guidance in this whole area, there is wisdom in looking to the past to find untapped wells. The Calvinistic Baptists, heirs of the rich ecclesial experience in the Puritan era of the seventeenth century, but, by the end of the eighteenth century, also passionately engaged in the catholicity of the Evangelical Revivals, are such a well. This collection of essays, covering such things as the Lord's Supper, friendship and hymnody, seeks to draw out the spiritual riches of this community for reflection and imitation in the present day.

2005 / 1-84227-149-0

Brian Haymes, Anthony R. Cross and Ruth Gouldbourne
On Being the Church
Revisioning Baptist Identity
(SBHT vol. 21)

The aim of the book is to re-examine Baptist theology and practice in the light of the contemporary biblical, theological, ecumenical and missiological context drawing on historical and contemporary writings and issues. It is not a study in denominationalism but rather seeks to revision historical insights from the believers' church tradition for the sake of Baptists and other Christians in the context of the modern–postmodern context.

2005 / 1-84227-121-0

Ken R. Manley
From Woolloomooloo to 'Eternity'
A History of Baptists in Australia
(SBHT vol. 16)

From their beginnings in Australia in 1831 with the first baptisms in Woolloomoolloo Bay in 1832, this pioneering study describes the quest of Baptists in the different colonies (states) to discover their identity as Australians and Baptists. Although institutional developments are analyzed and the roles of significant individuals traced, the major focus is on the social and theological dimensions of the Baptist movement.

2005 / 1-84227-194-6

Ken R. Manley
'Redeeming Love Proclaim'
John Rippon and the Baptists
(SBHT vol. 12)

A leading exponent of the new moderate Calvinism which brought new life to many Baptists, John Rippon (1751–1836) helped unite the Baptists at this significant time. His many writings expressed the denomination's growing maturity and mutual awareness of Baptists in Britain and America, and exerted a long-lasting influence on Baptist worship and devotion. In his various activities, Rippon helped conserve the heritage of Old Dissent and promoted the evangelicalism of the New Dissent

2004 / 1-84227-193-8 / xviii + 340pp

Peter J. Morden
Offering Christ to the World
Andrew Fuller and the Revival of English Particular Baptist Life
(SBHT vol. 8)

Andrew Fuller (1754–1815) was one of the foremost English Baptist ministers of his day. His career as an Evangelical Baptist pastor, theologian, apologist and missionary statesman coincided with the profound revitalization of the Particular Baptist denomination to which he belonged. This study examines the key aspects of the life and thought of this hugely significant figure, and gives insights into the revival in which he played such a central part.

2003 / 1-84227-141-5 / xx + 202pp

Peter Naylor
Calvinism, Communion and the Baptists
A Study of English Calvinistic Baptists from the Late 1600s to the Early 1800s
(SBHT vol. 7)
Dr Naylor argues that the traditional link between 'high-Calvinism' and 'restricted communion' is in need of revision. He examines Baptist communion controversies from the late 1600s to the early 1800s and also the theologies of John Gill and Andrew Fuller.
2003 / 1-84227-142-3 / xx + 266pp

Ian M. Randall, Toivo Pilli and Anthony R. Cross (eds)
Baptist Identities
International Studies from the Seventeenth to the Twentieth Centuries
(SBHT vol. 19)
These papers represent the contributions of scholars from various parts of the world as they consider the factors that have contributed to Baptist distinctiveness in different countries and at different times. The volume includes specific case studies as well as broader examinations of Baptist life in a particular country or region. Together they represent an outstanding resource for understanding Baptist identities.
2005 / 1-84227-215-2

James M. Renihan
Edification and Beauty
The Practical Ecclesiology of the English Particular Baptists, 1675–1705
(SBHT vol. 17)
Edification and Beauty describes the practices of the Particular Baptist churches at the end of the seventeenth century in terms of three concentric circles: at the centre is the ecclesiological material in the Second London Confession, which is then fleshed out in the various published writings of the men associated with these churches, and, finally, expressed in the church books of the era.
2005 / 1-84227-251-9 / approx. 230pp

Frank Rinaldi
'The Tribe of Dan'
A Study of the New Connexion of General Baptists 1770–1891
(SBHT vol. 10)
'The Tribe of Dan' is a thematic study which explores the theology, organizational structure, evangelistic strategy, ministry and leadership of the New Connexion of General Baptists as it experienced the process of institutionalization in the transition from a revival movement to an established denomination.
2006 / 1-84227-143-1 / approx. 330pp

Peter Shepherd
The Making of a Modern Denomination
John Howard Shakespeare and the English Baptists 1898–1924
(SBHT vol. 4)

John Howard Shakespeare introduced revolutionary change to the Baptist denomination. The Baptist Union was transformed into a strong central institution and Baptist ministers were brought under its control. Further, Shakespeare's pursuit of church unity reveals him as one of the pioneering ecumenists of the twentieth century.

2001 / 1-84227-046-X / xviii + 220pp

Karen Smith
The Community and the Believers
A Study of Calvinistic Baptist Spirituality in Some Towns and Villages of Hampshire and the Borders of Wiltshire, c.1730–1830
(SBHT vol. 22)

The period from 1730 to 1830 was one of transition for Calvinistic Baptists. Confronted by the enthusiasm of the Evangelical Revival, congregations within the denomination as a whole were challenged to find a way to take account of the revival experience. This study examines the life and devotion of Calvinistic Baptists in Hampshire and Wiltshire during this period. Among this group of Baptists was the hymn writer, Anne Steele.

***2005** / 1-84227-326-4 / approx. 280pp*

Martin Sutherland
Dissenters in a 'Free Land'
Baptist Thought in New Zealand 1850–2000
(SBHT vol. 24)

Baptists in New Zealand were forced to recast their identity. Conventions of communication and association, state and ecumenical relations, even historical divisions and controversies had to be revised in the face of new topographies and constraints. As Baptists formed themselves in a fluid society they drew heavily on both international movements and local dynamics. This book traces the development of ideas which shaped institutions and styles in sometimes surprising ways.

***2006** / 1-84227-327-2 / approx. 230pp*

Brian Talbot
The Search for a Common Identity
The Origins of the Baptist Union of Scotland 1800–1870
(SBHT vol. 9)

In the period 1800 to 1827 there were three streams of Baptists in Scotland: Scotch, Haldaneite and 'English' Baptist. A strong commitment to home evangelization brought these three bodies closer together, leading to a merger of their home missionary societies in 1827. However, the first three attempts to form a union of churches failed, but by the 1860s a common understanding of their corporate identity was attained leading to the establishment of the Baptist Union of Scotland.

2003 / 1-84227-123-7 / xviii + 402pp

Philip E. Thompson
The Freedom of God
Towards Baptist Theology in Pneumatological Perspective
(SBHT vol. 20)

This study contends that the range of theological commitments of the early Baptists are best understood in relation to their distinctive emphasis on the freedom of God. Thompson traces how this was recast anthropocentrically, leading to an emphasis upon human freedom from the nineteenth century onwards. He seeks to recover the dynamism of the early vision via a pneumatologically-oriented ecclesiology defining the church in terms of the memory of God.

2005 / 1-84227-125-3

Linda Wilson
Marianne Farningham
A Plain Working Woman
(SBHT vol. 18)

Marianne Farningham, of College Street Baptist Chapel, Northampton, was a household name in evangelical circles in the later nineteenth century. For over fifty years she produced comment, poetry, biography and fiction for the popular Christian press. This investigation uses her writings to explore the beliefs and behaviour of evangelical Nonconformists, including Baptists, during these years.

2006 / 1-84227-124-5

Other Paternoster titles relating to Baptist history and thought

George R. Beasley-Murray
Baptism in the New Testament
(Paternoster Digital Library)

This is a welcome reprint of a classic text on baptism originally published in 1962 by one of the leading Baptist New Testament scholars of the twentieth century. Dr Beasley-Murray's comprehensive study begins by investigating the antecedents of Christian baptism. It then surveys the foundation of Christian baptism in the Gospels, its emergence in the Acts of the Apostles and development in the apostolic writings. Following a section relating baptism to New Testament doctrine, a substantial discussion of the origin and significance of infant baptism leads to a briefer consideration of baptismal reform and ecumenism.

2005 / 1-84227-300-0 / x + 422pp

Paul Beasley-Murray
Fearless for Truth
A Personal Portrait of the Life of George Beasley-Murray

Without a doubt George Beasley-Murray was one of the greatest Baptists of the twentieth century. A long-standing Principal of Spurgeon's College, he wrote more than twenty books and made significant contributions in the study of areas as diverse as baptism and eschatology, as well as writing highly respected commentaries on the Book of Revelation and John's Gospel.

2002 / 1-84227-134-2 / xii + 244pp

David Bebbington
Holiness in Nineteenth-Century England
(Studies in Christian History and Thought)

David Bebbington stresses the relationship of movements of spirituality to changes in their cultural setting, especially the legacies of the Enlightenment and Romanticism. He shows that these broad shifts in ideological mood had a profound effect on the ways in which piety was conceptualized and practised. Holiness was intimately bound up with the spirit of the age.

2000 / 0-85364-981-2 / viii + 98pp

November 2004

Clyde Binfield
The Country a Little Thickened and Congested?
Nonconformity in Eastern England 1840–1885
(Studies in Evangelical History and Thought)
Studies of Victorian religion and society often concentrate on cities, suburbs, and industrialisation. This study provides a contrast. Victorian Eastern England—Essex, Suffolk, Norfolk, Cambridgeshire, and Huntingdonshire—was rural, traditional, relatively unchanging. That is nonetheless a caricature which discounts the industry in Norwich and Ipswich (as well as in Haverhill, Stowmarket, and Leiston) and ignores the impact of London on Essex, of railways throughout the region, and of an ancient but changing university (Cambridge) on the county town which housed it. It also entirely ignores the political implications of such changes in a region noted for the variety of its religious Dissent since the seventeenth century. This book explores Victorian Eastern England and its Nonconformity. It brings to a wider readership a pioneering thesis which has made a major contribution to a fresh evolution of English religion and society.
2005 / 1-84227-216-0 / approx. 274pp

Christopher J. Clement
Religious Radicalism in England 1535–1565
(Rutherford Studies in Historical Theology)
In this valuable study Christopher Clement draws our attention to a varied assemblage of people who sought Christian faithfulness in the underworld of mid-Tudor England. Sympathetically and yet critically he assess their place in the history of English Protestantism, and by attentive listening he gives them a voice.
1997 / 0-946068-44-5 / xxii + 426pp

Anthony R. Cross (ed.)
Ecumenism and History
Studies in Honour of John H.Y. Briggs
(Studies in Christian History and Thought)
This collection of essays examines the inter-relationships between the two fields in which Professor Briggs has contributed so much: history—particularly Baptist and Nonconformist—and the ecumenical movement. With contributions from colleagues and former research students from Britain, Europe and North America, *Ecumenism and History* provides wide-ranging studies in important aspects of Christian history, theology and ecumenical studies.
2002 / 1-84227-135-0 / xx + 362pp

Keith E. Eitel
Paradigm Wars
The Southern Baptist International Mission Board
Faces the Third Millennium
(Regnum Studies in Mission)

The International Mission Board of the Southern Baptist Convention is the largest denominational mission agency in North America. This volume chronicles the historic and contemporary forces that led to the IMB's recent extensive reorganization, providing the most comprehensive case study to date of a historic mission agency restructuring to continue its mission purpose into the twenty-first century more effectively.

2000 / 1-870345-12-6 / x + 140pp

Ruth Gouldbourne
The Flesh and the Feminine
Gender and Theology in the Writings of Caspar Schwenckfeld
(Studies in Christian History and Thought)

Caspar Schwenckfeld and his movement exemplify one of the radical communities of the sixteenth century. Challenging theological and liturgical norms, they also found themselves challenging social and particularly gender assumptions. In this book, the issues of the relationship between radical theology and the understanding of gender are considered.

2005 / 1-84227-048-6 / approx. 304pp

David Hilborn
The Words of our Lips
Language-Use in Free Church Worship
(Paternoster Theological Monographs)

Studies of liturgical language have tended to focus on the written canons of Roman Catholic and Anglican communities. By contrast, David Hilborn analyses the more extemporary approach of English Nonconformity. Drawing on recent developments in linguistic pragmatics, he explores similarities and differences between 'fixed' and 'free' worship, and argues for the interdependence of each.

2005 / 0-85364-977-4

Mark Hopkins
Nonconformity's Romantic Generation
Evangelical and Liberal Theologies in Victorian England
(Studies in Evangelical History and Thought)
A study of the theological development of key leaders of the Baptist and Congregational denominations at their period of greatest influence, including C.H. Spurgeon and R.W. Dale, and of the controversies in which those among them who embraced and rejected the liberal transformation of their evangelical heritage opposed each other.
2004 / 1-84227-150-4 / xvi + 284pp

Galen K. Johnson
Prisoner of Conscience
John Bunyan on Self, Community and Christian Faith
(Studies in Christian History and Thought)
This is an interdisciplinary study of John Bunyan's understanding of conscience across his autobiographical, theological and fictional writings, investigating whether conscience always deserves fidelity, and how Bunyan's view of conscience affects his relationship both to modern Western individualism and historic Christianity.
2003 / 1-84227- 151-2 / xvi + 236pp

R.T. Kendall
Calvin and English Calvinism to 1649
(Studies in Christian History and Thought)
The author's thesis is that those who formed the Westminster Confession of Faith, which is regarded as Calvinism, in fact departed from John Calvin on two points: (1) the extent of the atonement and (2) the ground of assurance of salvation.
1997 / 0-85364-827-1 / xii + 264pp

Donald M. Lewis
Lighten Their Darkness
The Evangelical Mission to Working-Class London, 1828–1860
(Studies in Evangelical History and Thought)
This is a comprehensive and compelling study of the Church and the complexities of nineteenth-century London. Challenging our understanding of the culture in working London at this time, Lewis presents a well-structured and illustrated work that contributes substantially to the study of evangelicalism and mission in nineteenth-century Britain.
2001 / 1-84227-074-5 / xviii + 372pp

November 2004

Stanley E. Porter and Anthony R. Cross (eds)
Semper Reformandum
Studies in Honour of Clark H. Pinnock

Clark Pinnock has clearly been one of the most important evangelical theologians of the last forty years in North America. Always provocative, especially in the wide range of opinions he has held and considered, Pinnock, himself a Baptist, has recently retired after twenty-five years of teaching at McMaster Divinity College. His colleagues and associates honour him in this volume by responding to his important theological work which has dealt with the essential topics of evangelical theology. These include Christian apologetics, biblical inspiration, the Holy Spirit and, perhaps most importantly in recent years, openness theology.

2003 / 1-84227-206-3 / xiv + 414pp

Meic Pearse
The Great Restoration
The Religious Radicals of the 16th and 17th Centuries

Pearse charts the rise and progress of continental Anabaptism – both evangelical and heretical – through the sixteenth century. He then follows the story of those English people who became impatient with Puritanism and separated – first from the Church of England and then from one another – to form the antecedents of later Congregationalists, Baptists and Quakers.

1998 / 0-85364-800-X / xii + 320pp

Charles Price and Ian M. Randall
Transforming Keswick

Transforming Keswick is a thorough, readable and detailed history of the convention. It will be of interest to those who know and love Keswick, those who are only just discovering it, and serious scholars eager to learn more about the history of God's dealings with his people.

2000 / 1-85078-350-0 / 288pp

Jim Purves
The Triune God and the Charismatic Movement
A Critical Appraisal from a Scottish Perspective
(Paternoster Theological Monographs)

All emotion and no theology? Or a fundamental challenge to reappraise and realign our trinitarian theology in the light of Christian experience? This study of charismatic renewal as it found expression within Scotland at the end of the twentieth century evaluates the use of Patristic, Reformed and contemporary models (including those of the Baptist Union of Scotland) of the Trinity in explaining the workings of the Holy Spirit.

2004 / 1-84227-321-3 / xxiv + 246pp

Ian M. Randall
Evangelical Experiences
A Study in the Spirituality of English Evangelicalism 1918–1939
(Studies in Evangelical History and Thought)
This book makes a detailed historical examination of evangelical spirituality between the First and Second World Wars. It shows how patterns of devotion led to tensions and divisions. In a wide-ranging study, Anglican, Wesleyan, Reformed and Pentecostal-charismatic spiritualities are analysed.
1999 / 0-85364-919-7 / xii + 310pp

Ian M. Randall
One Body in Christ
The History and Significance of the Evangelical Alliance
In 1846 the Evangelical Alliance was founded with the aim of bringing together evangelicals for common action. This book uses material not previously utilized to examine the history and significance of the Evangelical Alliance, a movement which has remained a powerful force for unity. At a time when evangelicals are growing world-wide, this book offers insights into the past which are relevant to contemporary issues.
2001 / 1-84227-089-3 / xii + 394pp

Ian M. Randall
Spirituality and Social Change
The Contribution of F.B. Meyer (1847–1929)
(Studies in Evangelical History and Thought)
This is a fresh appraisal of F.B. Meyer (1847–1929), a leading Free Church minister. Having been deeply affected by holiness spirituality, Meyer became the Keswick Convention's foremost international speaker. He combined spirituality with effective evangelism and socio-political activity. This study shows Meyer's significant contribution to spiritual renewal and social change.
2003 / 1-84227-195-4 / xx + 184pp

Geoffrey Robson
Dark Satanic Mills?
Religion and Irreligion in Birmingham and the Black Country
(Studies in Evangelical History and Thought)
This book analyses and interprets the nature and extent of popular Christian belief and practice in Birmingham and the Black Country during the first half of the nineteenth century, with particular reference to the impact of cholera epidemics and evangelism on church extension programmes.
2002 / 1-84227-102-4 / xiv + 294pp

Alan P.F. Sell
Enlightenment, Ecumenism, Evangel
Theological Themes and Thinkers 1550–2000
(Studies in Christian History and Thought)

This book consists of papers in which such interlocking topics as the Enlightenment, the problem of authority, the development of doctrine, spirituality, ecumenism, theological method and the heart of the gospel are discussed. Issues of significance to the church at large are explored with special reference to writers from the Reformed and Dissenting traditions.

2005 / 1-84227330-2 / xviii + 422pp

Alan P.F. Sell
Hinterland Theology
Some Reformed and Dissenting Adjustments
(Studies in Christian History and Thought)

Many books have been written on theology's 'giants' and significant trends, but what of those lesser-known writers who adjusted to them? In this book some hinterland theologians of the British Reformed and Dissenting traditions, who followed in the wake of toleration, the Evangelical Revival, the rise of modern biblical criticism and Karl Barth, are allowed to have their say. They include Thomas Ridgley, Ralph Wardlaw, T.V. Tymms and N.H.G. Robinson.

2006 / 1-84227-331-0

Alan P.F. Sell and Anthony R. Cross (eds)
Protestant Nonconformity in the Twentieth Century
(Studies in Christian History and Thought)

In this collection of essays scholars representative of a number of Nonconformist traditions reflect thematically on Nonconformists' life and witness during the twentieth century. Among the subjects reviewed are biblical studies, theology, worship, evangelism and spirituality, and ecumenism. Over and above its immediate interest, this collection provides a marker to future scholars and others wishing to know how some of their forebears assessed Nonconformity's contribution to a variety of fields during the century leading up to Christianity's third millennium.

2003 / 1-84227-221-7 / x + 398pp

Mark Smith
Religion in Industrial Society
Oldham and Saddleworth 1740–1865
(Studies in Christian History and Thought)

This book analyses the way British churches sought to meet the challenge of industrialization and urbanization during the period 1740–1865. Working from a case-study of Oldham and Saddleworth, Mark Smith challenges the received view that the Anglican Church in the eighteenth century was characterized by complacency and inertia, and reveals Anglicanism's vigorous and creative response to the new conditions. He reassesses the significance of the centrally directed church reforms of the mid-nineteenth century, and emphasizes the importance of local energy and enthusiasm. Charting the growth of denominational pluralism in Oldham and Saddleworth, Dr Smith compares the strengths and weaknesses of the various Anglican and Nonconformist approaches to promoting church growth. He also demonstrates the extent to which all the churches participated in a common culture shaped by the influence of evangelicalism, and shows that active co-operation between the churches rather than denominational conflict dominated. This revised and updated edition of Dr Smith's challenging and original study makes an important contribution both to the social history of religion and to urban studies.

2005 / 1-84227-335-3 / approx. 300pp

Martin Sutherland
Peace, Toleration and Decay
The Ecclesiology of Later Stuart Dissent
(Studies in Christian History and Thought)

This fresh analysis brings to light the complexity and fragility of the later Stuart Nonconformist consensus. Recent findings on wider seventeenth-century thought are incorporated into a new picture of the dynamics of Dissent and the roots of evangelicalism.

2003 / 1-84227-152-0 / xxii + 216pp

Haddon Willmer
Evangelicalism 1785–1835: An Essay (1962) and Reflections (2004)
(Studies in Evangelical History and Thought)

Awarded the Hulsean Prize in the University of Cambridge in 1962, this interpretation of a classic period of English Evangelicalism, by a young church historian, is now supplemented by reflections on Evangelicalism from the vantage point of a retired Professor of Theology.

2005 / 1-84227-219-5

Linda Wilson
Constrained by Zeal
Female Spirituality amongst Nonconformists 1825–1875
(Studies in Evangelical History and Thought)
Constrained by Zeal investigates the neglected area of Nonconformist female spirituality. Against the background of separate spheres, it analyses the experience of women from four denominations, and argues that the churches provided a 'third sphere' in which they could find opportunities for participation.
2000 / 0-85364-972-3 / xvi + 294pp

Nigel G. Wright
Disavowing Constantine
Mission, Church and the Social Order in the Theologies of John Howard Yoder and Jürgen Moltmann
(Paternoster Theological Monographs)
This book is a timely restatement of a radical theology of church and state in the Anabaptist and Baptist tradition. Dr Wright constructs his argument in dialogue and debate with Yoder and Moltmann, major contributors to a free church perspective.
2000 / 0-85364-978-2 / xvi + 252pp

Nigel G. Wright
New Baptists, New Agenda
New Baptists, New Agenda is a timely contribution to the growing debate about the health, shape and future of the Baptists. It considers the steady changes that have taken place among Baptists in the last decade – changes of mood, style, practice and structure – and encourages us to align these current movements and questions with God's upward and future call. He contends that the true church has yet to come: the church that currently exists is an anticipation of the joyful gathering of all who have been called by the Spirit through Christ to the Father.
2002 / 1-84227-157-1 / x + 162pp

Paternoster
9 Holdom Avenue
Bletchley
Milton Keynes MK1 1QR
United Kingdom
Web: www.authenticmedia.co.uk/paternoster

November 2004

www.ingramcontent.com/pod-product-compliance
Lightning Source LLC
Chambersburg PA
CBHW071232230426
43668CB00011B/1406